D0141363

Cinema of Flames

Balkan Film, Culture and the Media

Dina Iordanova

 Publishing

For my parents

First published in 2001 by the
British Film Institute
21 Stephen Street, London W1T 1LN

The British Film Institute promotes greater understanding of,
and access to, film and moving image culture in the UK.

Cover design: Kelly Maguire/Default
Cover illustrations: (front) *Pretty Village, Pretty Flame/Lepa sela, lepo gore*
(Srdjan Dragojević, 1995); (back) *Eternity and a Day/Mia aiwniothta kai
mia mera* (Theo Angelopoulos, 1998).

Set in Minion by Wyvern 21 Ltd, Bristol
Printed in Malta by Interprint Limited

British Library Cataloguing–in–Publication Data
A catalogue record for this book is available from the British Library
ISBN 0–85170–847–1 pbk
ISBN 0–85170–848–x hbk

Contents

Acknowledgments

I owe an intellectual debt to many. First and foremost, I would like to thank Nevena Daković, Victor Friedman and Marko Živković for their consistent support, for their responsiveness and insights, and for helping me to learn and understand.

I am indebted to the colleagues working in Eastern European film – Paul Coates, Herbert Eagle, Janina Falkowska, Peter Hames, Ronald Holloway, Andy Horton, Dan Goulding, Vida Johnson, Louis Menashe, Vlada Petric, Graham Petrie, Cathy Portuges – whose work set the path for my own.

Many other people helped me with their knowledge and expertise. I am particularly grateful for the advice I received from Arjun Appadurai, Milica Bakić, Jacqui Bhabha, Jasmina Bojić, Keith Brown, Maria Bucur, Ludmila Cvikova, Nancy Condee, Alma Dzubur, Geoff Eley, Deniz Göktürk, James Gow, Tom Gunning, Bob Hayden, Elissa Helms, Aida Hozic, J. Paul Hunter, Valya Izmirlieva, Pavlina Jeleva, Kostas Kazazis, Dona Kolar-Panov, John Kolsti, Tvrtko Kulenović, Blagoja Kunovski, Dušan Makavejev, Milcho Manchevski, Bojidar Manov, Vesna Maslovarik, Milena Mihalski, Suzana Milevska, Misha Nedeljkovic, David Norris, Boyan Papazov, Chris Paterson, Bojana Pejic, Dušan Puvacić, Sabrina Ramet, Robert Rosenstone, Svetlana Slapšak, Ivo Slavnić, Annabelle Sreberny, Milos Stehlik, Lazar Stojanović, Maria Todorova, Katie Trumpener, Ivana Tutman, Danilo Udovicki, Ginette Vincendeau, Bill van Wert, Stevan Weine and Susand Woodward. I am also grateful for the consistent friendly support of John Downing and Francesca Talenti in Texas, and Ivan Mazukov in Tasmania.

I would like to thank all those who sustained my work in the capacity of editors: John D. Bell, Fred Casmir, Daniel Cordle, David Culbert, Nick Cull, Don Dyer, Oliver Gaycken, Andrew James Horton, Yahia Kamalipour, Philip Lee, Peter Lev, John Neubauer, Gust Olson, Dan Pinkerton, Georg Schölhammer, Jim Schwoch, Slavko Splichal, Denise Youngblood, Nancy Wood, the readers of my manuscript, as well as Andrew Lockett for his insightful and constructive comments.

My work was made possible through grants from the Rockefeller Foundation and the Chicago Humanities Institute, the Arts and Humanities Research Board (UK) and from the University of Leicester.

One of the challenges of my research was getting access to the films which I discuss, as many of them were not available via traditional channels. Several institutions were particularly helpful in my effort: the International Film Festivals in Thessaloniki, Rotterdam and Berlin, the Festival of Young East European Cinema in Cottbus, Germany, the Alpe-Adria Film Meetings in Trieste, Italy, and the 'Brothers Manaki' Film Festival in Bitola, Macedonia, the Toronto International Film Festival Library, as well as the Cinematheque of Macedonia. In my research, I enjoyed the consistent support of librarians like Gary Lay in Texas, Janet Crayne in Michigan, Brian Marshall and the colleagues from the inter-library loans section at the University of Leicester. Many film-makers, like Leslie Asako Gladsjo, Bill Carter, François Lunel, Sarita Matijević and Zoran Solomun, as well as distributors like Ikarus/First Run or Women Make Movies, were so kind to send me their work.

For the past five years, since the birth of my son, I have had to move home three times. Leaving friends and family behind and changing places became an intricate part of my migratory existence. It would not have been possible to complete my work on this book if it had not been for the enormous help of my mother. My deepest gratitude is to her, for being there, and to George, who, throughout all this time, was the best son I could wish for.

Note to the Reader

The majority of films which I discuss here were originally made in different languages, and then translated into English. In the text, I have used the original title alongside the English language only at the first time a given film is mentioned. From there on, I have used the English title. In the filmography, both the English and the original title are listed.

The film *Bure baruta* (Goran Paskaljević, 1998) was distributed as *Powder Keg* in Europe, but as *Cabaret Balkan* in the USA. I have used the original translation of the title, *Powder Keg*.

Earlier versions of Chapters 3 and 6 of this book appeared as articles in the *Historical Journal of Film, Radio and TV*, in 1998 and 1999 respectively. An earlier version of Chapter 2 was published in the journal *Balkanistica*, Vol. 13 (2000). Parts of Chapters 1 and 9 were published in *Media Development* in 1999 and 2000.

Introduction

- Continuous footage taken through the window of a moving car: the houses on both sides of the road are either completely burned out or half destroyed. It goes on like this mile after mile.
- Footage taken with a hand-held camera: men and women sitting in puddles of their own blood on the pavement where they were lining up for bread moments ago, stretching out hands to the man behind the camcorder, and thus to the spectator.
- A medium-close shot of a scruffy young peasant holding a packet wrapped in a glittery green material – he is a father bending over the dead body of his infant son. There is not even a casket for the baby, just this piece of bright synthetic fabric, leaving an intensely coloured imprint of grief on one's visual memory.

Bosnia. Sarajevo. Further on, the image inventory contains pictures of elderly villagers lying in the mud of their backyards with bullet holes in the backs of their hand-knitted jackets, checkpoints controlled by paramilitary thugs with ponytails and cockades on fur caps, pedestrians on city streets half-running to escape the sniper fire, and large peasant women in black kerchiefs and aprons shouting, distraught, at the camera, fed up with being filmed again, and asking again about their missing husbands.

So much death and destruction has been filmed, and the footage of crippled children and desolate people is so abundant that it is easy to forget that behind each image there is the enormity of real suffering. Contrary to the commonly held opinion, I do not think that these images left audiences indifferent. There is plenty of evidence suggesting that print and broadcast media, journalists and film-makers did a lot to show the ugly face of ethnic war. The diminished receptiveness and responsiveness of people living in a media environment saturated with images of conflict is a whole different matter. Still, the efforts of those who did not stay passive but did their best to register the moving image of war and disseminate it through the modern medium of film were impressive and must be recognised.

During the past five years I spent hours every day watching images of death and destruction for my work on this project. The birth and the infancy of my own son and the early joys of motherhood coincided with my daily exposure to photographs and footage of dead and crippled children. Yet I was living in the safety and comfort of the West. The Bosnian suffering was just a moving image caught on a videocassette or a .jpeg file on my desktop. I could choose whether – or not – to be exposed to it. At any moment, I could get instant relief from the feelings of guilt and helplessness, which all this videographic evidence was pressing on me, simply by turning off the screen.

I, however, continued watching and then writing about what I saw. The mountainous landscape of Bosnia looked so painfully familiar – the red roofs, the hamlets scattered between hills, the old villages deserted by the young who had migrated to the grey apartment complexes in the city – that it reminded me of my native Bulgaria, almost next door to Bosnia. Though Bulgaria did not suffer like Bosnia, this nightmarish projection of destruction onto my native land led to a realisation of just how fragile and vulnerable to violence it was. Not that Bulgaria was much different from the other Balkan countries – if I was from Macedonia, Romania or even Greece, I could have easily projected the devastation of the Bosnian countryside onto these places, and the images would have triggered the same visceral reaction of pain and desolation.

But I was raised in communist Bulgaria and had lived there long enough to get the foretaste of the burgeoning nationalism: the first street demonstration I saw in Sofia in 1989 was not a pro-democracy one, incited by clandestine dissidents against the communist government, but a nationalist one, sanctioned by the communist government against the ethnic Turk minority. In April 1990, while attending a conference in Dubrovnik, I stumbled upon another nationalist gathering. This one was calling for the secession of Croatia, a cause which at least seemed legitimate. Nevertheless, it looked and sounded equally frightening and forbidding. What was going on?

Before I knew the exact answer, I had become an émigré, and so had most of my friends.

A decade later, the region that I left behind looks like a place full of disorderly people overtaken by the petty concerns of the poor and resentful of expatriates like myself for deserting the misery which they face on a daily basis. For a while, I used to blame it mostly on them: the political and economic mess they had allowed to take hold, their inability to manage their own affairs, and the pointless effort to evade rules rather than live by them. All of this, I believed, was keeping them from leaping forward to an era in which the neat and pretty dreams of democracy and affluence, put on hold indefinitely by communism, could be fulfilled. Everything that people in the Balkans were doing was inviting their fall from grace: they were voting the communists back into office, only this time freely, with no pressure or fraud; they were neglecting human rights concerns, allowing their countries to be blacklisted internationally; they were splitting up on all levels (parties, unions, churches, associations and friend-ships); and instead of voluntarily adopting the transitional template drafted for them by benevolent democracies, they were paranoidly proclaiming it to be a product of geopolitical conspiracies.

But my distaste for their wrongdoings, though it persisted, was soon to be re-examined. Was it only – and entirely – their fault? Wasn't I, now happily inte-grated in the West, frequently stumbling on poorly concealed double standards in politics and economics, in speech and action? How come in the mid-1990s, when the most important task for educators and academics seemed to be to defeat the stereotypes of East and West, celebrity experts would recite so many of the cold war clichés and come up with even more hateful ones? How come some in the West were choosing to shield themselves behind intricate rhetoric and were only concerned to contain the deepening conflict rather than inter-vene effectively? It was a sobering process which left me standing at a midway point, looking on at a series of mediated misinterpretations – the wrong expectations that the Balkans had of the West, and the stiff and unsympathetic notions that the West had of the Balkans. I was somewhere in between, dis-placed, neither comfortable with where I had come from, nor enthusiastic about where I had ended up, gradually turning into someone whose scholar-ship could not be other than polemical and political. The mediated exchange between cultures became my focal point of interest. And this is how this text came into being.

I first became interested in the films made in response to the Balkan crisis in 1994. Only in the autumn of 1996, however, did I have the chance to start sys-tematically researching and exploring this body of cinematic works. It was at that time when a well-wishing academic friend told me I was probably wasting my time. The formal end of the hostilities, he claimed, also meant fading interest in the topic. Only if the bloodshed continued, he said, could I expect to get publishers interested in my study.

Well, it is difficult to say now if he was right or wrong – there was more bloodshed, thus granting a sustained interest in my work. I wish the other sce-nario had materialised – I would easily give away the interest in my writing for a lasting peace. As I write this in 2000, however, in the post-Kosovo and even post-Milosević era, I am still not sure this is the end of the road. At moments there are glimpses of hope, while at others the tensions look nowhere near settled. Former Yugoslavia was the focus of news once again in 1998, 1999 and 2000, when the well-known visuals of the Bosnian war were recycled once more. TV stations scanned their archives for documentary footage of the notorious visit of Slobodan Milosević to Kosovo in 1987 – this very footage that was discovered by accident in the archive of Belgrade TV by researchers for *Yugoslavia: The Death of a Nation* (1995). This same documentary was itself edited and rebroadcast in the UK during the Kosovo war, and made a well-suited background introduction to the continuation of hostilities. Names of Bosnian places which had appeared and then disappeared from the public mind – Goražde, Prijedor, Jajce, Zvornik – were replaced by another set of names – Kosovo's Priština, Decani, Račak, Mitrovica. Authors who began their careers as freelancers in Bosnia, and who in the meantime became established experts on all things Balkan, now returned to their files looking for research notes dealing with ethnic Albanians or Montenegrins – notes that had never been used, because up until recently there had been no need to use them. Even I was told that I should think of becoming more actual and devote more attention to the films that appeared in the aftermath of Kosovo – the Serbian feature *Nebeska udica/Sky Hook* (1999), or documentaries like the Austrian *The Punishment* (1999), or the British *The Valley* (1999) and *Moral Combat* (2000).

I do not see much point in making my scholarship as directly dependable on political developments. My commentary is, indeed, mostly based on examples from the Bosnian war. The Balkan context seems to be changing incessantly, and the story continues to unravel. The role of film and other visual mediation in the cross-cultural representation of the Balkans, however, remains invariably important and controversial. And it is this subtle role that I hope to have captured and problematised in my work.

Chapter 1
War in the Balkans – Moving Images

This book surveys the wide range and variety of films that were made in response to the 1990s crisis in the Balkans, and in particular the Bosnian war. It tries to compensate for the insufficient attention paid to the ambiguous roles the mediated moving images of conflict in the Balkans play.

Why film?

First, because the visual has a crucial role in discourse formation at any level and because the informative power of transmitted images is at least as influential as the exchange that takes place in spoken and written language. Unlike the written word, however, the role of mediated images is so subtle that it often remains unaccounted for. Looking at cinematic texts helps bring to light the underlying dynamics of cross-cultural image-making as it unravels within the wider context of communicated concepts and interpretations. Second, because in today's world of electronic media, images reach out wider than writings, a fact which is still rarely recognised or explored in a persistent manner. Nowadays it is the moving image rather than the printed word that carries more persuasive weight.

By analysing film and visual representation, I remain confined to explanations that do not offer solutions. I cannot explain how to put an end to the violence or settle the competing claims. I do not know how to shelter hungry and desolate refugees, how to provide therapy for raped and traumatised women, or how to give children with amputated limbs the self-esteem they will need when growing up. All I can do is critically examine the politics of representation and its impact on the developments in the troubled Balkans.

This is, however, more significant than it may at first seem.

I analyse the transformations in Balkan narrative discourse and visual representation that take place in the context of the global exposure the region received through the medium of film. My study is not just an account of the film-making effort that came into being as a response to the Balkan crisis. Rather, it is an attempt to show how film registered the dynamic interplay of perceptions and self-perceptions, and to show why the continuity and the direction of cinematic mediation is of crucial importance.

In my study I persistently point out that cross-cultural causality is a crucial area on which to focus, because it has more to do with the construction of marginality via selectively mediated images than nationalist discourse does (this last one I see as a derivative of the 'Balkans as a socio-cultural periphery' motif).

Key Concepts
Specific features of my approach throughout the text involve the way I look at the concept of 'Balkans' and at the issues of transition and context.

Balkans
In my approach I retain 'the Balkans' as a common denominator when referring to this diverse and complex region, which allows me to name and critique important transnational issues that often remain neglected when the exploration is limited to individual countries. Abandoning the one-county approach and taking the issues on a cross-cultural level, even within the boundaries of a region, is a necessary precondition of this research. What we see when looking at one country, we see even more clearly when we transpose it onto the region at large.

'Any serious consideration of the Balkan peninsula', writes Misha Glenny, 'runs up against the unanswerable question of borders' (Glenny, 1999, p. xxii). He points out that every definition of the Balkans is compelled to use 'a mixture of the geographical, historical, and political'. When brought together, these elements often do not coincide with concrete countries and leave the conceptual contours of the region fuzzy and flexible.

My concept of the Balkans is not identical with the former Yugoslavia, but relates to a wider region in South-East Europe bordering on Asia Minor, the islands of the east Mediterranean and the Black Sea shores of the Caucasus – the lands travelled by such a quintessential Balkan author as Romanian Panait Istrati.[1]

In my usage, the Balkans is not a geographical concept but one that denotes a cultural entity, widely defined by shared Byzantine, Ottoman and Austro-Hungarian legacies and by the specific marginal positioning of the region in relation to the western part of the European continent. Nominally, the Balkans include Bulgaria, Macedonia, Serbia and Montenegro, Bosnia and Herzegovina, and Albania. Countries such as Croatia, Slovenia, Greece, Romania, Moldova and Turkey are also 'Balkan' in a number of elements of their history, heritage and self-conceptualisation, even though some of them may be, for a variety of reasons, positioned differently in the modern Western imaginary.

More importantly, however, my concept of 'the Balkans' is especially concerned with this unique positioning, defined by some as marginality, but by others as a crossroads or a bridge across cultures. (In the same way, my concept of Europe relates not only to West European countries but also to the Western hierarchies of values and lifestyles. Only occasionally is Europe referred to in this book in its geographical sense, mostly to point out the trivial fact that the Balkans happen to be located there.)

There were some who criticised my description of countries like Turkey or Greece as 'Balkan'. Turkey, I was told, did not belong, as it stood with the Islamic/Middle Eastern world. Greece could not fit into the Balkan mould either, because in many contexts it 'stands' for civilisation, and moreover is an EU and NATO member. I have had no comments on why Romania, Slovenia or Croatia may not be suitable for inclusion, but I have no doubt that other critics could pick on these as well.

While I agree that there are contexts in which these countries do not appear 'Balkan', there is a range of contexts in which they do, and in the concrete discussion of the first part of this book I will show in what precise contexts they fall under the 'Balkan' concept. Where do the Balkans end, as Žižek (1994) has shown, is a question which cannot be answered in a precise definition, as this would require measuring the imaginary.[2]

I have several reasons for insisting on an inclusive understanding of the Balkans. First, all countries here share a common socio-cultural legacy and modern-day trends. Although the concept of the 'Ottoman legacy' is far too often abused by journalists to explain every manifestation of lesser political culture, the very fact that the Balkans were part of the Ottoman empire should not be ignored, as it is in the roots of shared trends such as the orientalist isolation of the region, the hostility to Islam and the numerous territorial claims which most often can be traced back to political decisions taken in response to the dissolution of the Ottoman monolith. The legacies of communism, shared by many of the countries in the region, should also be considered when one explores their present-day economic volatility, the state-sanctioned nationalism and the lack of stable political structures.

Furthermore, as 'the Balkans' have been labelled and treated by the West as an indivisible semantic space characterised by common traits, the critical examination of this labelling and treatment should not be carried out piecemeal, but as a whole. Take all the media speculation of contagious Balkan violence, of the Balkans as a 'powder keg', or even of the Balkans as *balkanised* – in most of these not much difference is recognised between the Balkan countries.

The war in former Yugoslavia has, no doubt, had serious repercussions on all the other Balkan countries. Many of the phenomena we witness in the former Yugoslavia – such as the malicious nationalist propaganda, the large-scale emigration or the profaned public space – can be considered as an extrapolation of trends present in other Balkan countries. This is why, while my

discussion often focuses solely on Yugoslav examples, it can often be expanded
to apply to the Balkan sphere at large.

One more reason why we should look at these together is that according to
the image offered to Westerners by the media, the Balkan countries all look alike
on a visual level. The similarity in landscape, architecture and dress styles
justifies their blurring into one shared inventory of images – the Kosovo
Albanian villager is easily mistaken for a Bosnian Muslim, Bulgarian Pomak or
a Romanian Vlach, and as far as demeanour and appearance is concerned, there
is not much difference between politicians like Albanian Sali Berisha and
Bosnian Serb Radovan Karadžic. The Balkan iconic repertoire of Western
media remained unchanged with the eruption of the new crisis in Kosovo, as
the same visual tropes were repeated all over again. The media face of the
Balkans is one of destroyed churches and mosques, refugee women in camps,
stray sheep on the dusty streets of villages and alien UN forces.

While it would be relatively easy for me to persuade a Western audience that
I have good reasons to insist on an inclusive Balkan concept, such an endeavour is likely to face fierce resistance within the Balkan context itself. If one looks
from the West, the Balkans are often perceived as culturally coherent and
homogeneous. If one looks from within, however, they are more often perceived as diverse and heterogeneous. People in the Balkan countries generally
do not relate very favourably to each other and prefer to think of themselves as
unique rather than similar to their Balkan neighbours.[3] In spite of the shared
heritage, they prefer to stress the difference rather than the closeness. Take the
variety of alphabets – Greek, Cyrillic, Latin (and even this most common one
is modified with a variety of phonetical diacritics for each of the languages in
the region). Or the readily articulated differences in language, religion, history
and foreign orientation. The failure to acknowledge shared traits and the lack
of interaction results in unproductive isolation from each other. It is a specific
feature of the Balkan situation that each one of the countries in the region
prefers to look at some West European country for cultural identification rather
than to any of its Balkan neighbours. Greeks look traditionally to the UK,
Romanians to France, Bulgarians to Germany and the Slovenes to Austria and
Italy.[4]

The Balkans do not conceptualise themselves together, and this resistance to
togetherness has become an essential part of the concept of *balkanisation*,
which connotes them as consistent only in their persistence to stay divided. The
unwillingness to recognise that cultural closeness to the neighbours is logical
and may even be beneficial is a profound characteristic of the national philosophy of most Balkan countries, lying much deeper than the economic
cooperation or formal political interaction that are occasionally observed on
the surface.

Having said all this, I must underline that there are examples of a movement toward mutual recognition and assertion of a shared Balkan cultural space. In cinema in the 1990s there have been a series of co-productions involving various Balkan countries.[5] The film festival at Thessaloniki specialises in showcasing Balkan cinema, Balkan film programmes are a regular feature at the other film festivals in the region, *Balkan Media* magazine regularly reviews and compares the cinematic output of all Balkan countries and the Greek Helsinki Monitor works systematically on studies of hate speech and media in the region.

Repositioning

In the 1990s, the cold-war line dividing Europe into two was abolished. The changing international balance meant that all countries in the region had to reposition themselves within the wider context of the new Europe.

Did the new times mean a deletion of the mental division of Europe along the lines of 'the West and the Rest', however? Was there public consensus on the ideas of mutual understanding and harmony in a pan-European shared home? The international roles of all countries in the East were dynamically changing. Unlike Central Eastern Europe, which seemed to gravitate toward Europe 'proper', the shift in the Balkans seemed to move in the opposite direction. The Yugoslav breakup enhanced the isolation of the region. The Balkans gravitated from a dreary unpredictable outpost of the old Soviet Empire toward a gloomy orientalist fringe of the new Europe. Within a short time, they became more 'other' than they used to be.

In discussing this repositioning, opinion-makers readily applied a cultural approach. The journalistic and diplomatic discourse on the Balkans more and more often referred to the juxtaposition of Ottoman and Austro-Hungarian legacies, and was largely built up on concepts such as the 'clash of civilisations', 'ethno-linguistic tapestry' and 'dormant ethnic tensions'. The continuing reconceptualisation of the Balkan space set the context for a perception of the Balkans as 'Third World', and defined the terms of their quest for admission to Europe. I believe the cultural aspects of this process to be of utmost importance and will be analysing them in my text.

Textual Versus Contextual Analysis

In my approach I am more preoccupied with contextual rather than textual analysis. Where world cinema is concerned, textual analysis only makes sense if grounded in a good contextual study, which takes into account a whole range of socio-political and cultural specifics, one that gives as much weight to the background and implicit politics of a film as it does to its aesthetics and cinematic language. This is why I often choose to survey a large body of works and see how they coexist in the dynamic context of film production, distribution, exhibition and reception, rather than concentrate on analysing one particular text. I feel I can offer more insights into a given film by continually contextualising rather than by textually analysing.

For such an analysis to be meaningful, I widely employ the concept of Balkan cinema. As there has been little regional unity or even cultural interaction between the Balkan countries in the past decades, such a concept may seem somewhat artificial. My knowledge of the cinematic traditions of the countries in the region, however, reveals a number of consistent aesthetic, stylistic and thematic features that allow me to be confident when speaking of Balkan cinema as an entity. Film has a long and rich tradition in countries such as Greece and Yugoslavia, and the cinemas of Turkey, Bulgaria, Romania and Albania have yielded sensitive and beautiful works, many of which will be discussed in this text. I do not doubt that in the years to come we will see the concept of Balkan cinema recognised in film scholarship, and studies on Balkan film will appear to fill in the current gap.

The Films

The cinematic image of the deconstruction of the Berlin Wall became synonymous with the new era for East Europeans and was used in documentaries and features. It was not the demolition of the Berlin Wall, however, but the crisis in the Balkans that became the subject of most extensive cinematic interest. The Bosnian war was explored in nearly forty features and over two hundred documentaries made worldwide, thus becoming the event that occupied the minds of the largest number of film-makers since 1989.

I think it is significant here that I first and foremost highlight the films that I consider most important. While the US–UK co-production *Welcome to Sarajevo* (1997) undoubtedly received the best distribution and became the most widely seen film on the topic of the Bosnian war, it ranks far below other films in artistic merit. In my view, the most significant films made in response to Yugoslavia's breakup are: *Pred dozhdot/Before the Rain* (1994), *To vlemma tou Odyssea/Ulysses' Gaze* (1995), *Underground* (1995), *Lepa sela, lepo gore/Pretty Village, Pretty Flame* (1996) and *Bure baruta/Powder Keg/Cabaret Balkan* (1998). Looking back over the cinema of the Balkans, I feel I should also mention several works which, were they better known, would greatly assist the understanding of today's aesthetic quests of Balkan film-makers and the way history and politics are treated in the cinema of the region: Theo Angelopoulos' *O Thiassos/The Traveling Players* (1975), Lordan Zafranović's *Okupacija u 26 slika/Occupation in 26 Scenes* (1978), Emir Kusturica's *Otac na sluzbenom putu/When Father Was Away on Business* (1985) and the early works of Dušan Makavejev, Želimir Žilnik and Živojn Pavlović.

After several years of working on this project, I still cannot say for sure exactly how many films – features and documentaries – were made as a reaction to the breakup of Yugoslavia and the overall crisis in the Balkans during the 1990s. Even after completing an annotated filmography listing over two hundred titles, I have reasons to believe that at least another hundred remain unaccounted for. Every week I come across reports about new films being shown at festivals or that are currently in production.

Sometime in 1998 I decided that it was now futile to try to keep up. I am still doing my best to see as many of the new films as possible, but none of those that I have seen since the end of 1997 has challenged or changed the essence of the claims that I make in this book. Therefore, in 1999, I could draw the line and go public with what I had to say on the issues that had concerned me during this period.

The body of film productions about the Balkan conflict is, in its nature, a truly international project. From the point of view of its international perception, the Bosnian war was often compared to the civil war in Spain. Hundreds of intellectuals engaged in public support for the cause of ending the war in ex-Yugoslavia. The most visible expression of solidarity came from the international community of film-makers. Gathering in the Balkans from many different countries around the world – the UK, USA, Canada, France, Belgium, the Netherlands, Switzerland, Austria, Norway, Spain, Italy, the Czech Republic, Greece, Australia, New Zealand and Russia – they engaged in a truly transnational cinematic project. Unlike Spain, in Bosnia the cameras had firmly taken over from arms, giving a clear indication that, with time, media had acquired an equal combat power.

References to the Balkan war are scattered throughout a number of films from the 1990s: from *Blue* (1993) by the late British director Derek Jarman who, while chronicling his own death from AIDS, talked about the plight of Bosnian refugees, to Hungarian Ibolya Fekete's *Bolshe Vita* (1996), which featured documentary footage from the Bosnian war in the epilogue; from *Viageim ao Princípio do Mundo/Journey to the Beginning of the World* (1997) by Portuguese veteran Manuel de Oliveira, which featured Marcello Mastroianni, in his last role, talking about Sarajevo, to Elia Suleiman's *Chronicle of a Disappearance* (1996), where radio commentary on the Bosnian war provides the background to the daily concerns of the Palestinian protagonists.

The global trend that turns all feature film-making into a multinational enterprise is clearly visible in the case of the features (at least thirty) that looked at aspects of the Yugoslav breakup. *Territorio comanche/Comanche Territory* (1997), for example, told a story about Sarajevo but was a co-production of Spain, Germany, France and Argentina. *Tudja Amerika/Someone Else's America* (1995) was written and directed by Serbs, and told the story of exiles from

Montenegro and Spain who lived in New York but who also travelled to the Texan–Mexican border at Rio Grande. The film was produced by France, the UK, Germany and Greece, though none of these countries was referred to in the film in any way. *Before the Rain* was financed by France, the UK and Macedonia. *Welcome to Sarajevo* was an UK–USA co-production.

Some of the films, indeed, were produced with financing from only one country, but nevertheless featured a diverse crew and cast. The New Zealand production, *Broken English* (1996), the story of an inter-ethnic couple oppressed by a violent Croatian father, brought Maoris, Croatians and Chinese together on the set. The Italian *Il carniere/Gamebag* (1997) used a Bulgarian actress in the leading role and told the story of two Italian hunters caught in the middle of the Sarajevan siege. The Greek film *Ulysses' Gaze* featured American Harvey Keitel, Swede Erland Josephson and Romanian Maia Morgenstern.

Major European directors turned their attention to the Balkans: some to enjoy acclaim, like Goran Paskaljević with his *Powder Keg*, some to stir controversy, like Emir Kusturica with his *Underground*, some to face criticism, like Jean-Luc Godard with his *Forever Mozart* (1996).

Still, most features came from the countries of the former Yugoslavia – Bosnia and Herzegovina (*Savrseni krug/Perfect Circle*, 1997), Serbia (*Pretty Village, Pretty Flame*), Croatia (*Kako je poeeo rat na mom otoku/How the War Started on My Little Island*, 1996) and Macedonia (*Before the Rain*).

The films were telling different stories. The most ambitious ones were tackling the complex history of the Balkans, like *Underground* or *Ulysses' Gaze*. Some chose to focus on the fate of displaced children in Sarajevo (*Perfect Circle*), others on the stagnation in Belgrade (*Ubistvo s predumišljajem/ Premeditated Murder*, 1995; *Dupe od mramora/Marble Ass*, 1995), on committed journalists (*Welcome to Sarajevo*; *Comanche Territory*), on the difficult choices in taking sides (*Before the Rain*; *Pretty Village, Pretty Flame*; *Shot through the Heart*, 1998; *Savior*, 1998), or on the experiences of displacement (*Broken English*; *Müde Weggefährten: Funf Geschichten aus dem Krieg/Tired Companions*, 1997).

The mushrooming of new countries after the breakup of Yugoslavia was felt as far as the entertainment field: as early as 1994 critics in trade journals could not help noticing the proliferation of East European entries for the Oscar competition. Whereas before, Yugoslavia would submit only a single entry, now there were five countries in competition. Rump Yugoslavia's entry for 1994, for example, was Boro Drašković's *Vukovar – jedna priča/Vukovar: Poste Restante*, a co-production between the USA, Cyprus, Italy and Yugoslavia, and for 1995, Emir Kusturica's *Underground*, a co-production between France, Germany and Hungary, with the participation of Radio-TV Serbia. The international involvement clearly indicated that one-country financing for film was no longer a possibility for smaller countries in the 1990s.

The Balkan crisis attracted the attention of internationally renowned documentarians, such as French veterans Chris Marker, Marcel Ophuls and German Helga Reidemeister, along with many more, bringing the number of documentaries to well over 200. Documentaries were made not only by professional film-makers but also by well-known public intellectuals whose usual domain is the written word, like Frenchman Bernard-Henri Lévy and Canadian Michael Ignatieff. A number of displaced Yugoslav directors returned from exile to make their films, while others had to go into exile to continue their work.[6]

Documentaries scrutinised and critically investigated a wide variety of topics – Western mercenaries,[7] the UNPROFOR and the UN involvement,[8] the perpetrators,[9] the workings of media[10] and the refugee camps.[11] There was a range of documentaries on issues as far apart as the Serbian point of view,[12] cultural criticism of Neue Slovenische Kunst (NSK),[13] life in Bosnia after the war[14] and, most recently, Kosovo-themed documentaries.[15] The best-known documentary probably remains the international TV co-production *Yugoslavia: Death of a Nation* (1995), which used a large variety of documentary sources and featured interviews with most of the main political figures involved in the conflict.[16]

Critical voices from within Yugoslavia came up with a specific genre of short films, which can be placed somewhere between documentary and fiction for their use of re-enactment and autobiographical elements. The hilarious Studio B92 Želimir Žilnik's *Tito po drugi put medju srbima/Tito among the Serbs for a Second Time* (1993), which featured a Tito impersonator taking a stroll around downtown Belgrade, revealed a great deal about the state of mind of ordinary Serbs and provided more social insights than any other piece of investigative journalism. Films like *Ghetto* (1995), another production of the dissident Studio B92, depicting a rock musician cruising around his native Belgrade and witnessing the profanation of public life, or *Rupa u dusu/Hole in the Soul* (1994) by cosmopolitan exile Dušan Makavejev, testifying to the isolation of Yugoslavia, are the deeply personal and painful works of concerned intellectuals.

Sarajevo was the subject for several dozen films. Parallel with its destruction, the city was perpetually revived in the films that chronicled its proud survival. There were films telling about the inhumanity of everyday life in Sarajevo, about the children of Sarajevo, about the women, about the villains, about the artists, about the horrors of war and the insanity of it all. There were also features set in Sarajevo, and seen by larger audiences. Of these, only the stories of *Perfect Circle*, about the bonding of a lonely writer and two orphaned boys, and of *Heroje/Heroes* (1998), concerning a tense evening spent awaiting the return of a missing friend, were told from the point of view of locals; all the rest followed the formula of the transplanted Western narrator. There were films that told the story from a very personal point of view, like the documentary made by the Australian who, while filming the movie, fell in love with his Bosnian sound engineer. There were films that proved that the humour of Sarajevans, though black, is still intact, like *Mizaldo* (1994), which was made as an extended infomercial about the city. And there were the testimonies shot by Sarajevans themselves – the works of the Sarajevo Group of Authors (SaGA), who chronicled day by day the agony and the strength of their city.

Besides feature and documentaries, there were various productions that remain unknown and difficult to track down. There were indie movies by film-makers who, inspired purely by humanitarian urges, travelled to Yugoslavia and filmed whatever they came across, but then did not know how to distribute the product of their work. Besides the television documentaries produced and aired by BBC 1 and BBC 2, CNN, PBS, Channel 4 and others, there were many lesser-known television programmes. While most of the British documentaries were made for television and thus received better exposure, the bulk of American documentaries were made independently and received little exposure, mostly seen at festivals or at occasional screenings. There was also the genre of the so-called home-videos, shot on the spot in former Yugoslavia and then distributed via clandestine channels to the relevant diasporas across the world. In addition to film, there has been intensive activity in the field of multimedia, and new technologies were widely used for projects such as the French-supported Sarajevo on-line journalism site, the on-line exhibits of the Sarajevo pop group Trio or the web-site of the Zagreb-based feminist group Nona, featuring the creative work of refugee women.[17]

Reputed international film festivals, with their attentive and committed audiences, proved to be the ideal venue for the films about Bosnia. And, indeed, programmers across the world did a lot to bring the films about the conflict in former Yugoslavia to their festivals. The first major venue to schedule a special series related to Bosnia was Berlinale. In February 1993, it held a programme called 'No More War'. Ironically, this scheduling was a bit rushed – only a few films had appeared by that time, and the end of the war was nowhere near in sight. The programme included a few documentaries by German and French film-makers. As no feature had yet been made, a film by Bosnian-born Emir Kusturica was screened – *Arizona Dream* (1993), which dealt with America and barely touched on the Bosnian crisis.[18]

After 1993, films related to the war in former Yugoslavia started appearing regularly at all major feature and documentary festivals. In 1994 Milcho Manchevski's *Before the Rain* won the Golden Lion at the Venice Film Festival. The 1995 Cannes season brought awards to Kusturica's *Underground* and Theo Angelopoulos' *Ulysses' Gaze*. Michael Winterbottom's *Welcome to Sarajevo* was one of the contestants at Cannes in 1997. Srdjan Dragojević's *Pretty Village, Pretty Flame* enjoyed acclaim at festivals all over the world, and an award at Sao Paulo. Kenović's *Perfect Circle* won the main award at the 1997 Tokyo Film Festival. Films from and about the Balkans played at special panoramas at the International Documentary Filmfest in Amsterdam in 1993, at the International Feminist Filmfest in Créteil in 1997 and at the Toronto International Film Festival in 1997. Films about Bosnia are regularly featured at Sundance, at the Human Rights Watch Film Festival and in Montreal, Vancouver, San Francisco, Chicago, Mannheim, Karlovy Vary and London.

Two festivals that regularly showcase the production of films from and about the region should be mentioned in particular: the Thessaloniki Film Festival and the Alpe-Adria cinema meetings in Trieste. Local festivals that take place in the countries of former Yugoslavia are also important as it is here that most of the domestic productions are shown – Pula, Belgrade, Subotica and Bitolja. In 1995, a special series called 'Sarajevo Film Days' was organised in Zagreb. Sarajevans themselves were quite active in scheduling film events and there were several organised during the siege by courageous groups and individuals. The Sarajevo International Film Festival was first held in the autumn of 1997 and has since become a regular event. It is at this venue that Sarajevans themselves get to see many of the films made about Bosnia.[19]

Depending on the background of the film-maker, the specific approach or the target audiences of the distributor, various films received visibility through various channels. *Miss Sarajevo* (1995), for example, made by a U2 fan, Bill Carter, became well known to *Billboard* and *MTV* fans, whereas turbo-folk fans in Serbia watched the populist show of *Arkan and Ceca's Wedding* (1995). *Calling the Ghosts* (1996) became best known to feminist audiences, as it tells of the difficult path taken by two rape survivors from the Bosnian camps who decide to talk publicly about their experiences. Polish *Demony wojny/Demons of War* (1998), a sequel in the popular series *Pigs* starring Bogusław Linda, attracted fans of the action-adventure genre. Other films reached out to religious audiences: the Croat story of the Virgin Mary's appearance, *Gospa* (1993), was exhibited by a California-based Catholic film distribution network. The gay community expressed interest in *Marble Ass*, featuring a transvestite prostitute from Belgrade who fights violence in his own special way. Anthropologists showed their students films made by other anthropologists, featuring communal rituals at the intersection of tradition and modernity.[20] As a result of this segmented audience, some films achieved popularity within a limited reception framework while remaining virtually unknown beyond it. Only a few enjoyed a wider exposure. Many of the acclaimed films about the Balkans were classified as low entertainment value by distributors. Seen only at festivals, they were never picked up for theatrical distribution. The situation is only partially

corrected by some distributors of arthouse type feature films, such as the Amer-
ican New Yorker (they currently carry *Forever Mozart*, *Underground* and
Vukovar: Poste Restante) or October Films (they distribute *Someone Else's
America*).

There were also some paradoxes: with a few exceptions, films made by film-
makers associated with Serbia (Srdjan Dragojević, Boro Drašković, Predrag
Antonijević, Goran Paskaljević) enjoyed theatrical and video exposure in
the West, while those made by Croats (Vinko Brešan) or Bosnians (Ademir
Kenović) were only seen at festivals. The bottom line is, however, that films
made about the Balkan conflict by Westerners enjoyed much better international exposure than most films made by Balkan film-makers. A good
example is provided by the contrasting fates of the widely publicised *Predictions
of Fire* (1996) by American Michael Benson and the largely unknown *Laibach:
A Film from Slovenia* (1988) by Yugoslav Goran Gajić, both of which dealt with
the phenomenon of the Neue Slovenische Kunst and the rock group Laibach.
Another example is Frenchman Bernard-Henri Lévy's *Bosna!* (1994), which
makes extensive use of footage shot under fire by the members of SaGA, and
which was distributed in various formats, and the films produced by SaGA that
have screened only at a handful of festivals.

Whereas the feature films at least have the chance for exposure in the system
of non-theatrical distribution or within the festival circuit, the outlook for documentaries is deplorable. Only a few have found distributors, and even those
are quite often poorly advertised or are listed at prices that even institutions can
rarely afford. Electronic Arts Intermix, for example, which carries the remarkable Chris Marker's *Le 20 heures dans les camps/Prime Time in the Camps* (1993)
only advertises to programmers; the Cinema Guild routinely charges $300 for
a video: *Truth under Siege* (1994), an excellent documentary tackling the workings of independent media across the former Yugoslavia, has ended up on their
list, severely limiting its distribution chances. There is a huge unrealised potential in documentary distribution. The documentary body of work about Bosnia
remains, and will remain, largely unseen and un(der)exposed.

There have been some archival efforts, like those of the International
Monitor Institute in Los Angeles and the Documentation Centre of Social
Movements in Amsterdam. The Audiovisual Department at the Central European University, Budapest, has a collection of videotapes related to the conflict
in former Yugoslavia. The branches of the Soros Foundation in Bosnia, Croatia
and other countries of former Yugoslavia and Eastern Europe have been
involved with a number of projects to promote the work of local film-makers
about the conflict. The researchers at the video department of the US Holocaust
Museum in Washington, DC, organised the exhibit 'Faces of Sorrow' in 1994,
and are collecting videotapes related to the conflict in former Yugoslavia. But

even if they manage to compile a comprehensive collection of tapes, these will be available only to researchers.

The Scholarship

While I believe that the films about the Balkan crisis were at least as instrumental in the formation of the public discourse as the written texts, my writing evolved in a context largely informed by scholarship and popular writing. (I give a detailed account on the various works that informed my writing in the Bibliography.)

My material were the films about the troubled Balkans, but my topic was the dynamics of marginality and self-perception. It was interesting to realise, however, that the books which most influenced me were not necessarily ones that dealt directly with South-East Europe.

Critical studies

The two studies that had most influence on my initial understanding of Balkan issues were by women, who, like myself, were born and raised in the Balkans, but had then continued their academic careers in the West – Maria Todorova (1994, 1997) and Milica Bakić-Hayden (1995). They were ready to abandon the one-country approach, to reach out and bring into the discussion of the Balkan realm the orientalist and the post-colonial theories that were first created for the discursive needs of other marginalised but non-Slavic and non-European cultures, and to show Balkan marginalisation as a result of the workings of a culturist discursive construction. My work follows in their footsteps.

Milica Bakić-Hayden's 1995 article was a direct continuation of an earlier one, written by herself and Robert M. Hayden and published in *Slavic Review* in 1992. It was the first text to point to the dangers of the orientalist treatment of the 'Balkans' that came into being during the early stages of the Yugoslav dissolution. It is a seminal piece in Balkan studies, and needs to be acknowledged as such.

Then, there was Larry Wolff's (1994) exploration of the Enlightenment's construction of the notions of Russia and Eastern Europe. Wolff was probably the only author who dealt with Russia but whose conclusions I was able to transplant to the territory I was studying. In spite of my familiarity with the cultural studies work that focused on the former Soviet Union and Eastern Europe, very little of the findings in that field were relevant to my work, as they remain locked in the self-centred universe of most studies that deal with Russia. The studies that examine what is now called Central Eastern Europe were equally self-absorbed. Most of the influential scholarly work on Eastern Europe was preoccupied with the formation of the concept of Central Europe, a notion the very development of which was based on the conceptual exclusion of the Balkan space (Garton Ash, 1989; Rupnik, 1990; Graubard, 1992). The important works of Central Eastern Europe's critical intellectuals always looked to the West and never to the lands of the South-East (Michnik, 1985; Vaculik, 1987; Haraszty, 1987; Brinton and Rinzler, 1990; Baranczak, 1990; Havel, 1985, 1987, 1990, 1992; Konrád, 1995).

At first I was surprised to realise that the theories that had materialised out of the ideological needs of Third World cultures, and that therefore barely seemed relevant to the Balkans as part of the Eastern bloc, turned out to be the most insightful and informative. Besides Benedict Anderson's (1983) conceptualisation of the nation as an imagined community, Edward Said's (1978) and Homi Bhabha's (1990, 1994) views were crucial, as was the entire post-colonial discourse, raising issues such as the nation's need for metaphors and the functioning of the subaltern and the hybrid. Stuart Hall's discussion on 'the West and the Rest', though not directly related to this discursive lineage, was another strong shaping influence on my work (Hall and Gieben, 1992). In the context of my research, Arjun Appadurai's (1996) work was one of extreme importance – maybe because he was the only cultural theorist whose work moved from a preoccupation with a particular region (post-colonial India), through a study of global issues, to a discussion, in *Modernity at Large*, of the Balkan conflict and its cross-cultural perception as a manifestation of universal trends. Appadurai's text contains many insights. More than anything, however, he confirmed my belief that one can legitimately extrapolate from the regional to the global, and that to work in regional issues does not mean shutting oneself out of the world's dynamics, however safe such a self-contented immersion in the local microcosm that one is familiar with may seem.

Other studies that looked at things globally were also important, such as Benjamin Barber's (1995) tireless highlighting of the dynamic dichotomy between the cosmopolitan and the regionalist and Samuel Huntington's (1993, 1996) theories of the clash of civilisations, which, though retrograde and hateful, must be taken into account precisely because of their potential harmfulness. Paul Gilroy's (1993) discussion of the dynamics of culture and politics in the context of the African diaspora greatly influenced my views when I came to look at the migrations that resulted from the Balkan crisis. The numerous Holocaust references that the Balkan crisis triggered brought back to mind Hannah Arendt and Bruno Bettelheim's texts, but also inspired me to look at a diverse range of more recent interpretations of the Holocaust legacy (Bauman, 1989; Felman and Laub, 1992; Todorov, 1996).

Balkan cultural studies

Most attractive to me, unsurprisingly, were the books conceptually discussing Balkan culture, in particular the works by Todorova and Bakić-Hayden I have already mentioned. The literary explorations by Vesna Goldsworthy (1998),

Andrew Wachtel (1998), Branimir Anzulović (1999) and David Norris (1999), all important studies containing a wealth of material and interesting observations and insights, were published too late in the course of my own work to call them major influences, but they nonetheless developed views that I have taken into account throughout my study. Further, there were the works of anthropologists, abounding with important observations on national character and complexes. I most valued the works of Michael Herzfeld (1987) on the self-perception of modern Greece, of Ivan Čolović (1994a) on the idiosyncrasies of Serbian popular discourse and of Marko Živković on the stories that Serbs tell about themselves. In spite of the fact that Slavoj Žižek's (1994, 1995) comments on Balkan issues are scattered amid an avalanche of critical commentary on a range of Western cultural concerns, he has spelled out some most important preconceptions about – and within – the Balkans that are missed by many other critics.

Film Studies

The disintegration of what used to be called the Eastern bloc into the new geopolitical spheres of Central Eastern Europe and the Balkans rendered further research on East European cinema as an entity meaningless, and 'the cinema of Eastern Europe', explored by authors such as Mira and Antonín Liehm (1977), David Paul (1983), Daniel Goulding (1989) and Thomas Slater (1992), is gradually becoming a concept of the past.[21] Although a forthcoming scholarly collaborative effort, edited by Daniel Goulding and Catherine Portuges, discusses the cinemas of the former Eastern bloc countries, it is my feeling that this will be the last edited volume to approach the cinema of 'Eastern Europe' as an entity.

The next logical step is to regroup the cinemas of the region to reflect newer geopolitical realities. As more and more thematic and stylistic affinities will be rediscovered, supporting the change of conceptual focus, there is bound to be more and more talk of 'Balkan cinema', a concept which will include the cinemas of the former Yugoslav lands, Albania, Greece, Bulgaria, Romania and Turkey. With a few exceptions in Germany (Grbić et al., 1995) and Italy (Germani, 2000), no comprehensive studies exist on the cinema of the Balkans as a whole, and scholarship on Balkan cinema is mostly represented by monographs focusing on single countries or directors. The amount of English-language writing on Balkan cinema is really scarce. There are only two American studies that claim to deal with Balkan cinema as an entity, both of which are by Michael J. Stoil (1974, 1982). However, they do not systematically concentrate on the subject matter, widely use cold war rhetoric and speculate on issues of 'Zhdanovist' cinema without giving an idea of what the cinema of the Balkans is like.

The cinemas of the various countries of the region have been studied separately. Berlin-based film critic Ron Holloway has carried out extensive filmographic and critical work, which has seen little exposure due to the fact it is mostly published by organisations that do not have a distribution arm. The most comprehensive study on Yugoslav cinema to date is by Daniel Goulding (1985), while Bulgarian film is discussed by Ronald Holloway (1986) and Greek cinema is covered by Mel Schuster (1979) and a reference work by Dimitris Koliodimos (1999). Andrew Horton's persistent and enthusiastic involvement with the cinemas of the Balkan countries, and particularly his long-standing interest in Greece, resulted in a number of articles, chapters and screenwriting projects. His most important contribution is the monograph on Greek director Theo Angelopoulos (1997a), a remarkable study not only of Angelopoulos' work but also of the spirit of Balkan film-making. Horton also edited a collection of articles on Angelopoulos (1997b) and has written widely on Yugoslav cinema and on humour in Balkan film.

Overall, very little has been published on Balkan cinema, one of the most interesting film cultures in Europe. But while other lesser-known cinemas are coming out of obscurity to take the spotlight, the treasures of Balkan cinema remain unknown even to cineastes. The masterpieces of Živojin Pavlović, Želimir Žilnik, Branko Gapo, Karpo Godina, Pantelis Vulgaris, Nikos Kunduros, Ali Ozgentürk, Zeki Ökten, Dimither Anagnosti, Kujtim Çashku, Liviu Ciulei, Mircea Veroiu, Rangel Vulchanov, George Dyulgerov, Binka Zhelyazkova and many others remain virtually unknown beyond the borders of their respective countries, and even the work of internationally celebrated veterans such as Theo Angelopoulos, Michalis Cacoyannis, Yilmaz Güney, Dušan Makavejev and Lordan Zafranović is considered exotic and rarely seen.

Balkan cinema is still to develop as an area of study – not because of a shortage of cinematic traditions, but because there is a shortage of scholarship that recognises the affinities within the region. I hope that this book will help to precipitate a move away from the prevalent one-country approach.

I also became increasingly interested in the issues of film and history, particularly as explored in the work of theorist Robert Rosenstone, whose *Visions of the Past* (1995) made me think of the choices that film-makers face when representing historical material.

Studies looking at general issues of cross-cultural representation were, once again, of great importance in my work. Ella Shohat and Robert Stam's *Unthinking Eurocentrism* (1994) was a major influence, mostly because it outlined the controversial effects of the Eurocentric construct, and systematically challenged it on the ground of Hollywood film-making. An earlier discussion of recent trends in European cinema organised by the British Film Institute, and including contributions by Ien Ang, Stuart Hall and Fredrick Jameson, was also very useful (Petrie, 1992). Further, a series of books that explored issues of inter-national cinema and cross-cultural Western representation turned out to be directly relevant to my research in Balkan cinema (Armes, 1987; Downing, 1989; Naficy and Gabriel, 1993; Scherzer, 1996; Bernstein and Studlar, 1997; Naficy, 1999). My work was also greatly informed by studies of diasporic media consumption (Naficy, 1993; Gillespie, 1995; Cunningham and Jacka, 1996; Clifford, 1997; Ong, 1999), by accounts of the national cinemas of southern countries, such as Israel and Spain (Shohat, 1989; Kinder, 1993), and to some extent by studies that dealt with Holocaust film (Insdorf, 1983; Avisar, 1988), war and film (Virilio, 1984) and film and history (Rosenstone, 1995b). My judgment was often influenced by a preference for certain film critics: Jonathan Rosenbaum (*Chicago Reader*), Emanuel Levy (*Variety*), Derek Malcolm (The *Guardian*) and Kenneth Turan (*LA Times*).

Structure

The chapters in the first part of the book, 'Europe: Location or Destination?', explore different aspects of the continuing repositioning of the Balkans within post-cold war Europe. I maintain that the representation and conceptualisation of ethnic conflict should be considered and understood in this wider context. In Chapter 2 I outline some basic discrepancies in the conceptualisation of *Balkans* and *Europe* and explore a series of mediated misperceptions in the Balkan's quest for admission to the European semantic space. Chapter 3 explores traditional narrative structures that enable the positioning of the Balkans as a cultural space beyond the boundaries of what is considered legitimately European. Here I show how the dominant travelogue narrative of the large number of 'Balkan' plots is internalised in Balkan cinema, thus reiter-ating existing stereotypes and furthering the conceptual exclusion of the Balkans by perpetuating a trend of self-exoticism. In Chapter 4 I focus on some problematic aspects of the teleological construction of the Balkans in histori-cal narratives of a putative character.

Part 2 is devoted to exploring a variety of personal and creative commit-ments as they evolved at the time of the Yugoslav breakup. My focus in Chapter 5 is on the treatment of Balkan history in film. I focus my attention on some of the non-conventional cinematic approaches to historical material, by direc-tors such as Dušan Makavejev, Lordan Zafranović, Želimir Žilnik and Theo Angelopoulos. It is my intention to show how feature films that do not claim historical accuracy but choose to appeal to a shared historical imagination ulti-mately have influenced public perceptions of history more than its 'official' versions.

Chapter 6 is a case study of the controversy surrounding Emir Kusturica's *Underground*, which identifies a whole series of underlying moral problems that result from the mediated misperceptions discussed in the preceding chapters. This investigation is then continued in the following chapter, which is preoccupied with the inherent contradictions imposed by the need to take sides in the conflict. Here, I talk of the ordeal of those who had to live through involuntary ethnic parting, and of the peculiar twists that came about in the course of people's resistance to the forced taking of sides. I show how the logic of forced choices of ethnic belonging led to a situation where neutral-cosmopolitan or conservationist-nostalgic attitudes were rendered impossible and where integrity could only be preserved by making a choice against 'one's own'. My discussion of two Yugoslav films which attempted to point at indoctrination of all sides, *Vukovar* and *Pretty Village, Pretty Flame*, explores why an 'all sides are guilty' approach was deemed unacceptable. Here I also examine the role of those Western intellectuals who publicly committed to taking sides, particularly in the Bosnian conflict. I consider in this light Marcel Ophuls' epic documentary *Veillées d'armes: histoire du journalisme en temps de guerre/The Troubles We Have Seen: A History of Journalism in Wartime* (1994).

In Chapter 8 my focus is on the violent nature of the conflict. I draw on Arjun Appadurai's insightful discussion of the crucial role that mass mediation played in shaping the crisis in Balkan identities, and identify it as an underlying factor for the specific ideology of preventive aggressiveness.

Part 3 is devoted to a range of representations of various groups, some directly involved in the conflict, some affected by it. In Chapter 9 I look at a range of representations of villains, portrayed in much more individualised detail than the victims. I then turn my attention to the blurred image of the victim, which dwells in anonymous obscurity. Chapter 10 discusses a series of gender-related issues of representation. I begin by discussing the mass rapes of the Bosnian war and the main issues which came to determine the public discourse on these: victims and perpetrators, rape warfare and the subtle balances required when interpreting the rapes at the intersection of feminism and nationalism. I then move on to explore a range of cinematic representations of rape, and investigate how the social and cultural context is taken to influence the specifics of such representation within the wider discourse on gender and nationalism. I talk in most detail about Mandy Jacobson's *Calling the Ghosts*, a documentary which, taking the case of two Bosnian women, raises issues of universal concern on violence, survival and witnessing. In Chapter 11 my focus is on the way in which the Balkan cinema, itself marginal, depicts and conceptualises marginal communities. Here, I look mostly at the Balkan cinematic representations of the Roma (Gypsies), which I interpret within the framework of 'projective identification'.

Part 4, 'Spaces', looks at two examples: in the first a remote Balkan place, Sarajevo, becomes cosmopolitan as a result of its tragic fate. My focus is on

Sarajevo's cultural resistance, on the role of the intellectual and on the reincarnation of the city in film and other forms of artistic expression. I critically explore the concept of 'cosmopolitan' Sarajevo, as well as the palpable tensions between outsiders' perception of Sarajevo and the way the city's inhabitants believed it was to be represented. The politically correct blockbuster *Welcome to Sarajevo* comes under my scrutiny in this context. My second exploration of space is focused on the cinematic treatment of the migration of Balkan people during the past decade – the gradual reconceptualisation of displacement and the construction of a new, expanding universe created by the migrating mind. I show how the trademark atmosphere of lost homelands and shattered identities is gradually replaced by new visions that permit the migrants to gain control over their otherwise disrupted lives and to see themselves as subjects of new and fulfilling experiences.

This book aims to be of interest to audiences beyond narrow specialist circles, and is addressed to all those concerned with the critical exploration of the cross-cultural dynamics that characterises our times. The imagined community of my readers includes the growing number of students of transnational cinema, for whom my discussion of the international effort of film-makers to preserve and reconstruct a troubled culture will be of interest. It includes the growing number of students of South-East European culture who feel that traditional avenues for research are nearly exhausted and for whom my approach to the Balkans may open up new spheres for exploration. It also includes all those people in the international media who are led by a genuine concern for the troubled Balkans but are restricted by the 'parachute' and 'sound-bite' manner that their *métier* imposes. The book is, therefore, for those who have felt at one time or another that an understanding of the complex and delicate configuration of images and messages circulated globally is a necessary part of conflict resolution. Once my text reaches these readers, it will have the chance to create an impact by changing unproductive approaches and entrenched patterns of thought.

Notes

1. Panait Istrati (1884–1935) is a Romanian-born author of Greek descent who wrote in French and whose winding life path is described in autobiographical works such as *Kyra Kyralina* (1926) and *Codine: The Childhood of Adrian Zografi* (1929, no English translation). He was encouraged to write by Romain Rolland.
2. In defending my decision to describe these countries as 'Balkan', I do not want to repeat discussions which have been carried out by other authors and would only divert me from the main line of my investigation. But for those who are interested to learn more on the Balkanist discourse, I recommend

that they refer to Michael Herzfeld's (1987) authoritative work on the self-perception of modern Greece, as well as the commentaries of Slavoj Žižek (1994, 1995) on the Balkan 'imaginary'. Maria Todorova's 1997 book *Imagining the Balkans* is, still, the best introduction to the way the Balkan concept, with fuzzy geographical borders and blurred cultural referencing, has been constructed in the past and still functions today.

3. I have been criticised for speaking of mutual resentment between the Balkan nations and thus repeating a harmful cliché. I, however, believe that such resentment is a fact of life. While I recognise that journalists have stressed the resentment far too often and have turned the concept of intra-Balkan hostilities into a stereotype, I myself have seen variations of this resentment acted out far too often to overlook them. Even in academia, in spite of the prevailing tone of mutual respect, one can still observe academics arguing that their respective national culture is unique and utterly incompatible with the cultures of the neighbouring Balkan countries. A recent positive trend is the interest of some younger scholars in exploring the mutual image-making and stereotyping within the Balkan space, which has the important political effect of exposing the underlying preconceptions.

4. In 1994, the Bulgarian weekly *Kultura* published the results of a survey conducted with a number of Bulgarian intellectuals on the question of identity. In their replies, only about 15 per cent identified culturally with the Russian tradition, while all the rest indicated they were mostly influenced by some West European tradition, the German one gaining about 30 per cent. I asked myself how I would answer if surveyed, and immediately knew I would be another one who would speak about German cultural influence. No wonder, I had written my doctoral dissertation on the philosopher Schleiermacher, and had translated two books from German into Bulgarian. Only now, however, did I realise that my choice of German cultural history was conditioned by a complex set of educational influences which had an impact not only on me but on many others like me. I have since discussed the issue of identity formation with acquaintances from various Balkan countries. What I heard led me to the conviction that the orientation given to a West European cultural tradition, different in the case of each Balkan country, is an attitude deeply embedded in education and popular ideology, and is not a declining or disappearing trend.

5. In the course of the 1990s there have been over twenty such co-productions. Examples include films such as *Burlesque Tragedy* (Bulgaria/France/Yugoslavia, 1995), *The Slaughter of the Rooster* (Greece/Cyprus/Bulgaria/Italy, 1996) and *Balkanizateur* (Greece/Bulgaria/Switzerland, 1997).

6. Serb Radovan Tadić came from France to shoot *Living and Dead in Sarajevo* (1993). Croatian Lordan Zafranović was able to complete his *Decline of the*

Century: The Testament of L.Z. (1995) only after leaving for the Czech Republic in 1992.

7. *Warheads* (Germany, 1993), *Dogs of War* (UK, 1992). The war in Bosnia was shown through the eyes of a Western mercenary also in the feature *Savior* (USA, 1998).

8. *Bosnia Hotel* (France, 1996), *Safe Haven: The Betrayal of Srebrenica* (UK, 1996), *A Cry from the Grave* (UK, 1999) and the feature *Warriors* (UK, 1999).

9. *Yellow Wasps* (1995), *Serbian Epics* (1993).

10. *Mythmaking: The Balkans* (1995), *Prime Time in the Camps* (1993), *Truth under Siege* (1994), *The Troubles We Have Seen* (1994).

11. *Ordinary People* (1993), *Spansko Refugee Camp* (1993).

12. *The Island of Serbia* (Russia, 1996), *The Original of a Forgery* (Yugoslavia, Ministry of Information, 1995).

13. *Predictions of Fire* (1996).

14. *The Year after Dayton* (1997).

15. *The Punishment* (1999), *Moral Combat* (2000).

16. An international co-production with the majority participation of the USA, UK and France. 150 min. Documentary in four parts. Production: Brian Lapping Associates. Co-production: BBC (UK), Canal+ (France), Discovery Channel (USA), ORF (Austria), VRPO (the Netherlands), RTBF (Belgium), SVT2 (Sweden), NRK (Norway), Denmark's Radio (Denmark) and ABC (Australia). Exec. producer: Brian Lapping. Narrated by Robin Ellis. Directors: Angus McQueen and Paul Mitchell. Consultant: Laura Silber.

17. References have been made to two more types of videographic material, but the information about them cannot be systematically acquired. The first includes the many hours of videotaped testimonies that the commission, appointed by the UN to investigate the war crimes in former Yugoslavia and chaired by DePaul University's law professor Cherif Bassiouni, has collected. Some of these videos are currently being used in the work of the Hague tribunal, but it will take time before access to them for research purposes is granted. There are also the allegations of videotaped rapes made by feminist writers such as Catherine MacKinnon and Beverly Allen, who report that such tapes are being sold at clandestine pornographic markets in Romania and other Central Eastern European countries. I, however, have not found any evidence of the existence of such tapes.

18. Ironically, the only reference to Bosnia in *Arizona Dream* is one that rejects the concern about it: at the very beginning of the film, the protagonist (played by Johnny Depp), is asleep on the back of a truck in New York. The news bulletin on the radio starts with an item about 'The Bosnians ...' Depp wakes up and shuts the radio down.

19. Besides festivals, there have been various efforts to provide more exposure for

the films. Many human rights activists, academics or ad hoc groups have undertaken to produce and distribute video materials to raise consciousness about the war. Television stations have also had an input. Channel 4 in the UK, for example, held the well-publicised 'Bloody Bosnia' season for a week in August 1993 – an example that was followed by other television stations in the West (see Gow *et al.*, 1996).

20. *We Are All Neighbors* (1993), *Going with the Flow: An Anthropologist among Bosnians* (1997).

21. Even though I consider the concept obsolete, I have also worked in the field of Eastern European cinema, with my editorship of *BFI's Companion to Eastern European and Russian Cinema* (2000) and my 'College Course File: Eastern European Cinema' (1999d).

Part 1

Europe: Location or Destination?
Narrative and History

Chapter 2
Are the Balkans Admissible?
The Discourse on Europe

Hungarian director István Szabó's *Redl Ezredes/Oberst Redl/Colonel Redl* (1985) is set in the last years of the Austro-Hungarian empire and tells the life story of Redl, a career soldier of lower-class origins who progresses in an army dominated by the aristocracy. When at military school, young Redl befriends von Kubiny, the heir of a rich aristocratic family. One snowy day the von Kubiny boy takes the Redl boy to visit his family's estate. The lackeys take the boys' hats and gloves, and a minute later they are seated at a table set with porcelain dishes and silver utensils. The Redl boy is very careful in manipulating the fork and knife, keen to act as an equal as far as table manners are concerned. Yet he is surrounded by so many unfamiliar things that he cannot help feeling clumsy: the lady of the house addresses the Dalmatian in an unknown language ('Sit down!'); then Redl is asked by the grandfather if he is a Pole. The question about his background triggers a jumbled explanation, in which Redl elaborates that his father was a Ruthenian from the Ukraine, but that he is also descended from an impoverished family of German aristocrats. His mother, however, was Hungarian, and to prove this superior line in his pedigree, Redl starts singing a Hungarian song, which reverberates incongruously in the embarrassed silence of the room. Then Redl abruptly shuts up. Despite his awkward manner he seems to have managed to establish some credentials and claim admittance to the higher social circle of the von Kubinys. However, his hosts quickly re-establish control, switching to French, a language of which Redl is ignorant, and the boy is now effectively excluded. The grandmother declares, 'Il est charmant, ton copin' ('Isn't he cute!'). The von Kubiny boy tells her that Redl does not speak French, to which she responds: 'Il fault on apprendre, mon cheri. S'est aussi important, pas seulement le chevals' ('One needs to learn it, my dear. It is equally important, not just the horses'). Finally, the grandfather paternalistically pats Redl's hand.

Admissibility is the subject of the film from this moment on. Admissibility in this case is based not on dress code, knowledge and demeanour, but on presumptions about belonging to an ethnicity and a class.

Yet Redl, in spite of his unsatisfactory background, is situated on the territory of Austria-Hungary, and is standing face to face with the *European*. Even
though he is the son of a provincial station-master, he has an inborn European
legitimacy, similar to the Europeanness of the marginal personages of Joseph
Roth's classical Austrian novel *Radetzkiy March*. Redl faces directly those from
whom he must claim his admissibility, a situation full of subtle clashes and
inequalities.

If one moves somewhat further to the south-east, to the Balkans, the
encounter with the *European* looks different. The desire to be closer, to be
admitted, is there but the encounter with the *European* normally does not occur
face to face as it does in *Colonel Redl*. Yet, issues in the Balkans are often conceptualised by reflection on *Europe*, by placing things in a *European* context.

The events of a Bulgarian film from 1967, *Privurzaniyat balon/The Attached
Balloon*, are situated entirely in a remote Balkan village. The opening scene,
however, features a drummer, who reads aloud announcements to the villagers:
'As of today, in order to coordinate the local time with the Axis powers, European time will be introduced in the Kingdom of Bulgaria. Everybody is to set
their clocks an hour back.' Then the camera shows the early morning routine
in the village – ducks and hens, goats and cows waking up, and a rooster crow-
ing at first light – which now translates to 5 a.m. European time. From there on
everything will be taking place within the small universe of the village, and it
is only the crow of the rooster that makes the claim of admissibility to Europe.

Another Bulgarian film, *Lachenite obuvki na neznayniya voin/The Patent
Leather Shoes of the Unknown Soldier* (1979), is also set in a small Bulgarian
village, and also, from the beginning, positions the whole story in relation to
Europe. The film-maker, Rangel Vulchanov, is shown in front of Buckingham
Palace, where he is shooting the majestic changing of the guard. Three minutes
into this sequence, the footage of the Queen's guards is suddenly intercut with
scenes from Bulgarian peasant life, and the sound of a prolonged Bulgarian folk
song merges with the sounds of the British brass band. The images of the British
soldiers begin to overlap with the images of the Balkan peasants dancing at a
wedding, and the action gradually moves to the native village of Vulchanov. From
there on the film-maker will be telling a story from his childhood and all events
will take place in his native Bulgaria. But for an opening he chooses *Europe*.
Another one of Vulchanov's films, the 1984 *Posledni zhelaniya/Last Wishes*, opens
with scenes depicting clashes between soldiers on the battlefields of World War
I. A ceasefire is announced, and European dignitaries appear in glamorous attire
on the battlefield. It becomes clear that a short-term truce has been negotiated
so that the annual golf match of the European excellencies can take place.

Unlike *Colonel Redl*, in these Balkan films the relationship to Europe is not
shown within the same cinematic frame, but constructed through juxtaposi-

tions which automatically render the construct questionable. Moreover, the construct of 'Balkan in relation to Europe' heavily relies on the mediation of selected images and concepts, and thus opens up space for misperceptions. Nevertheless, the self-image of the Balkans is always constructed within a conditional *European* framework, and this is the framework which I would like to problematise and examine in this chapter.

Europe here is the cultural and socio-economic entity which overlaps approximately with the values that are believed to provide the basic principles for the cultural and social life in the Western part of the continent that goes by the same name: democracy, freedom of enterprise, free speech, respect for human rights, individualism. But most of all it is synonymous with prosperity and power that ensure respect. *Europe* is the opposite of everything associated with the Third World – for example, Africa. In the Balkan imaginary, Africa is associated with the foolish, Europe with the sophisticated. Africa is tribal, Europe is civilised; Africa is poor, Europe is affluent; Africa is incompetent, Europe is efficient; African affairs are messy, European interests are stringently managed; Africa is waste, Europe is cultivated; Africa is unattractive, Europe is beautiful; Africa is an overgrown jungle, Europe is a landscaped park. In the Balkan imaginary, Balkans may appear associated with all the characteristics that describe the Third World, but it is just an appearance. Their 'European-ness' is a profound characteristic of their inner essence that has been taken away from them and that is to be reclaimed.

Here Europe often stands for 'the West' in general. Terms such as *Europe* and *European* are used qualitatively, and are endowed with a glare of superiority, actually signifying the West in general and often including North America. Linguist Victor Friedman observes this 'ambiguity of the term *Europe*' even on the level of everyday language use, resulting in frequent discrepancies between the geographical and the political/cultural terms articulated even at the level of linguistic tropes. For example, in spite of being an American, in Macedonia he is commonly introduced as someone 'from Europe', Europe here being synonymous with the West. He also quotes the Greeks who say, 'I am going to Europe for my vacation', as if Greece were not part of that entity (Friedman, 1996, p. 128). The West is also often synonymous with 'the world', and when one claims that Balkan problems are problems of the world, or that the world does not care, one is actually implying only that Western Europe and North America are indifferent.[1]

The main question I ask in the course of this exploration is: How does it come about that belonging to *Europe*, a paramount element in their own public discourse, turns out to be so problematic and even improbable for the Balkan countries?

I would claim that the answer is to be found in the elusive nature of the concept of *Europe* itself, which facilitates the series of misperceptions ensuing from the positioning of the Balkans in relation to the ideal (*Europe*).

I will first identify and critically examine some of the implicit tropes of the ideology that aims at securing a *European* standing for the Balkans within their own present-day cultural and political discourse. I should immediately under-line that this discourse is carried out country by country, most often building up on specific national distinctions rather than on commonalties with the other countries in the region. The cohesive element is that while each Balkan country only negotiates for itself, the subject of the plea – recognition of an inherent *Europeanness* – is identical transnationally, as are most of the arguments.

Second, I will explore the tropes in which the *European* standing of the Balkans is being problematised within the present-day Western cultural and political discourse. I will focus specifically on the substitution of the socio-political approach to the Balkans with a culturist one, and on the ambiguous and even controversial role that mediated representations play in this process.

As a third step I will put these two discursive lines side by side, which will allow me to point out a series of sensitive issues and discuss the ambiguities which come about as the mediation of the discourse unravels.

In relation to the Balkans, the concept of *Europe* has a double function – first as an inclusive and then as an exclusive one. The inclusive function can be quickly summarised: geographical proximity and shared historical past are in the roots of the extended rhetoric which views the Balkans as inherently *belong-ing to Europe*. The exclusive function states the opposite case: geographical remoteness and idiosyncratic historical experience are in the roots of the cul-turist argument that sees the Balkans as inherently *unfit for Europe*. In either case, the discourse is built on a deep-seated perception of the Balkans as a cul-tural entity which is defined in relation to Europe. Even if liable to negotiation, this very premise necessarily confines the discussion to abstract issues of suit-ability and admissibility, making any practical steps of political and economic coexistence dependent on the culturist perceptions of the region.

The Balkans within Europe

Geographically, the Balkans are part of Europe. This geographical location is something like their *habeas corpus*, hence the tremendous weight given to issues of territory – it is not just any territory, it is a guarantee of European presence. Cul-turally, as their history suggests, the Balkans are part of Europe as well. Or at least this is what is believed in the Balkans, where national ideologies depict the respec-tive nations not as a 'margin' but as a 'bridge' between the Occident and the Orient.

In the 1980s and 1990s, the discourse on Europe, dormant during the cold war years, re-emerged in the public sphere of all the former Soviet bloc coun-tries. This 'Europhoria' took a variety of shapes. The actual name 'Europe' now came into more prominent use than had ever been the case before, with all sorts of establishments now so called – a hotel and a café named 'Europe' appeared in every big Balkan city, and sometimes a cinema theatre (in Zagreb, it was the 'Balkan' cinema that changed to 'Europe'). The first operetta to be staged in Sarajevo in 1995 was titled *Europe*.[2] Primary and secondary school education, which had always been fairly Eurocentric (by which I mean concentrating on the developed world, including North America and the West of Europe, considering one's nation as inherently belonging to the tradition of the developed Western nations and largely ignoring the problems of the rest of the world), was becoming even more so in the 1990s, and the media's choice of which issues to cover would suggest proximity to Europe.

Realising that they 'are in Europe, but not quite' Aleko Konstantinov in 1898 noted that, another trope in the public discourse of the Balkan countries is the one of 'return to *Europe*'.

The return to *Europe* has been the major task on the agenda of all East European countries since 1989. However, the chances for the Balkans to 'return' are far more remote than for the countries of *Mitteleuropa* (Central Eastern Europe), and not simply because of geographical location or because of the socio-political situation and economy. Back in Yalta in 1945, no difference between the Balkan and Central Eastern Europe was deemed essential and most of the Balkan countries, including Yugoslavia, who broke out only later, were transferred to the Soviet sphere *en bloc*. In the 1990s, however, the re-admission to Europe, was made conditional and was carried out individually, country by country. During the decade, while Central Eastern Europe was being reconceptualised and 're-admitted' to the European realm, the Balkans became a chunk of the former Eastern bloc that would be left outside the cultural boundaries of Europe. Developments within Central Eastern Europe, such as the creation of the Visegrad economic alliance, the special provisions of the Partnership for Peace programme, and the appeal that their application for admission to NATO is given priority consideration, furthered the dissolution of Eastern Europe into Central Eastern European and Balkan parts.

New resentments between the Balkan countries appeared that evolved around the questions of their proximity to or suitability for Europe. Countries located geographically on the margins of the Balkans and closer to the West began struggling for the chance to be admitted to the Central European space, and public opinion in these countries abhorred any instance in which they were referred to as 'Balkan'. Romanians thought of themselves as an extension of the Frankophone who just happened to be located in the eastern part of Europe. (This explains Romania's outrage when in 1993 Bulgaria also applied for membership in the community of Frankophone countries claiming that 37 per cent of its subjects had French as their second language.)

Since their separation from Yugoslavia in 1991, Croatia and Slovenia have issued state documents explicitly stating their desire not to be referred to as 'Balkan'. In 'Why and Since When Are We Afraid of the Balkans?' Croatian anthropologist Dunja Rihtman-Augustin brings into discussion a number of examples from Croatian public discourse that demonstrate this abhorrence of belonging to the Balkans, revealing the trope as one of the main rhetorical figures of Croatian populist politics (Rihtman-Augustin, 1997, p. 35). This abhorrence has long been an element of Croatian politics. In the 1930s, for example, the leader of the Croatian Peasant Party, Stjepan Radić, insisted: 'Our duty is to Europeanize the Balkans, and not to balkanize the Croatians and Slovenes' (quoted in Cohen, 1993, p. 15).

'A return to Europe implies that Europe existed in the same form at the time of departure as it does today, on the eve of the return,' noted Misha Glenny in his *The Rebirth of History* (Glenny, 1990, p. 216). In other words, a precondition for the 'return' of various countries in the east of Europe would be to restore a Europe that resembled the one of which they used to be a part. Different countries of Eastern Europe and the Balkans, however, have 'departed' at different times, and therefore the time of departure which needs to be restored to justify an adequate place for those seeking re-admission to Europe varies from country to country. It is misleading to think that 'the point of departure' is the time when the Eastern bloc left *Europe*, i.e. at the end of World War II (an assumption made by many political scientists).

The continuing dissolution of the former Eastern bloc into, roughly speaking, two entities – Central Eastern Europe and the Balkans – is structured around two different points of departure, a distinction which was blurred by the cold war division lines. Re-establishing a cultural and social space for the 'return' of *Mitteleuropa* was a different project than the one for the 'return' of the Balkans.

To 'return' to Europe, the Central Eastern European countries needed a restoration of the status which they had enjoyed between World War I and World War II. For the Balkans, however, the point of departure was different, and the 'return' therefore depended on the restoration of a different set of factors. Most would set their 'departure point' as far back as the time of the Ottoman invasion in the fourteenth and fifteenth centuries, a conquest that effectively meant isolation and abandoning the modernisation processes that were to be shared by most of the other European nations. A more recent possible point of 'return' could be set at the end of nineteenth century or early in the twentieth century, when national liberation struggles succeeded in establishing new independent states. In a move to 're-enter' Europe at that time, many of the countries in the region established new royal dynasties, with monarchs often recruited from across the European courts. The popular pro-monarchist tendencies in many of the Balkan countries today are an expression of the desire to re-negotiate a similar set of circumstances for 're-admission', which they believe could be negotiated for them by the offsprings of their respective monarchs, expelled at the time of communist takeover and now living in various European locations.

The desired concept of a Europe which one could 're-enter' also varies from country to country in the Balkans themselves. In order to 'enter' *Europe*, Macedonia, for example, would need a different set of circumstances than Albania or Romania. This issue is explored in extensive detail in regard to Greece by Michael Herzfeld, who calls the Greeks 'aboriginal Europeans', and who concentrates in his study on the basic rhetorical trope of Greek identity – the secularised idea of the fall from Paradise (Herzfeld, 1987, p. 20): 'In a discourse of culture where the highest accolade is to be called "European," it proves a justification of the frequently alleged national failure to live up to that demanding model' (ibid., p. 22). In his view, the metaphor of a fall from cultural grace is an attribute of the national self-image. In this context, the interpretation given to Turks (and therefore Islam) becomes particularly relevant, as they are held accountable for the alienation from the 'European'. He writes:

> By the nineteenth century, the European standard of cultural excellence had become central to official nationalism. Perhaps the best measure of western cultural and political hegemony was its eventual success in persuading the Greeks to adopt the Turks as their natural enemies, and to treat Turkish elements in Greek culture as its worst failing – as a source of cultural pollution
> (ibid., p. 29).

Albanian Ismail Kadare makes the alienation from and the 'return to Europe', a leading motif. 'The Albanian nation, banished from Europe for so many years,' Kadare writes, 'knocks again, like the prodigal son, at its gate' (Kadare, 1995, p. 181). To Kadare, the return is unconditionally linked to denouncing Islam as an alien force, touting Christianity as an entry pass to Europe:

> I am convinced that Albania will most likely embrace Christianity since it is linked to the country's culture, and to a nostalgic memory of the time before Turkish rule. In the coming years, Islam, which arrived late in Albania in the baggage of Ottoman overlords, will weaken – first in Albania, and then in Kosovo. Christianity, or rather Christian culture, will hold its own throughout the country. In this way, one evil (the 1967 prohibition against religious practice) shall give birth to good. Albania will carry out a great rectification of history that will hasten its union with the mother continent – Europe.
> (ibid., p. 34)

To claim their re-admittance to Europe, other countries, like Bulgaria and Serbia, would need to go back to the time they received their emancipation from the Ottoman empire, or even further back, to the nineteenth century, when first evidence of the formation of a national consciousness can be discovered. The best guarantee of admission for them, however, would be a restoration of the circumstances in Europe at the time of the Ottoman invasion in the fourteenth and fifteenth centuries, as this is the only time when their identity as a part of Europe is not likely to be questioned.

As such a remote departure point can barely be restored, a different project is taking place in these countries: an ideological restoration of similar premises. The history of these countries, which were conquered by the Ottomans in the late fourteenth century but managed to preserve their specific Slavic cultural and national identity throughout five centuries, until the end of the nineteenth century when their European identity re-emerged, is being stressed repeatedly. Unlike the imperial legacy of Austro-Hungary in relation to Central Eastern European countries (a legacy which is considered to have boosted social progress and is responsible for their privileged status in today's Europe), Ottoman rule is considered to have been a major interruption in the development of the Balkan countries as a part of Europe, and is conceptualised as a significant impediment to the fulfilment of these nations' European goals. The border between Christian and Islamic civilisations is treated as a threshold between modernity and traditionalism.

With a substantial contribution from historians, media and politicians in Bulgaria and Serbia today, Europe is being reconceptualised as a fragile area living under the permanent threat of an Islamic invasion, against which they act as the south-eastern shield. Such a situation would undoubtedly restore the status of the Balkan countries as ones that are *within* the European realm, albeit as its outpost. Thus, stressing the clandestine present-day European fears of a possible expansion of Islamic fundamentalism becomes essential to nationalist ideologies throughout the Balkans. It is a commonly held idea that the Balkans can be important to Europe only if they find themselves in the path of another Islamic penetration of the continent. As a result, no matter how abstract, the scenario of such an invasion is being debated again and again, validated by the very fact that it is being discussed. The 'shielding Europe from the fundamentalists' trope becomes a major ideological line. The belief that Europe will not allow the creation of an Islamic state in the south-east (first Bosnia and later, Kosovo), for example, was often spelled out by politicians and journalists not only in rump Yugoslavia but also throughout the Balkans. The arrogance of many of the aggressive nationalists in Serbia stems not from the fact that they do not fear punishment, but because they believe that the only place from where punishment could come, the West (Europe and America), actually secretly sympathises with them. American and West European politicians who insist on human rights and speak up in defence of Muslims are, they believe, performing a public relations stunt.

Turkey has a special role in this 'shield against Islam' ideology. Although it is probably the least fundamentalist country when considered in a wider Islamic context, it is the only Islamic country which, until early in this century, had a substantial foothold in the Balkans. This explains the identification of Turks as 'natural enemies', as noted by Herzfeld in the case of Greece, or the huge ideological importance attributed to the battle of Kosovo in Serbia, or the outrage triggered by a 1990 statement by a Bulgarian politician, an ethnic Turk, who had claimed that 'the way to Europe goes through the Bosphorus'.[3]

Another specifically Balkan trope is maintained by historians and journalists from the region: our nations originally contributed to the project of modernity no less than any 'genuinely' European ones, and therefore we are as much a part of Europe as others. An example of this ideology is found in the popular art history theories of the 'proto-Renaissance' in the Balkans (a pictorial style manifested mostly in religious painting), which they see as bearing essential similarities to the masterpieces of the Italian Trecento (Bozhkov, 1969; Radojčić, 1969). The advancement of this line in the artistic heritage of the region was brutally interrupted by the Ottoman invasion at the end of the fourteenth century that cut the ties with the western part of Europe and led the Balkan cultures away from the general path of development that the West European countries, 'shielded' by the selfless sacrifice of their Balkan counterparts, followed. The point here is to prove that the Balkans were a cradle of European culture and that their history is intrinsically connected with Europe's development.

A further modification of this same argument is a trope which has become an intrinsic part of Balkan education and in the process of conceptualisation and re-negotiation of the inherent Europeanness of the Balkans – namely, that the Balkans are superior to the West of Europe. Back in 1933, when unsuccessfully tried by the Nazis on concocted charges of plotting the fire at the Reichstag, Bulgarian communist hero Georgi Dimitrov gave a well-publicised speech in which he quoted the media's description of him as a 'dark Balkan subject' and a 'barbarian'. He countered these slurs by saying that, at the time when German emperors were speaking Latin in public and only used German when talking to their horses, Bulgarians had a civilised nation-state and their own alphabet (Dimitrov, 1986). This trope of civilisational superiority and pride in one's higher (but flawed) heritage is one of the pillars of nationalist education throughout the Balkans, and is repeated even by the least educated in society. It is a trope used, for example, by a Serbian paramilitary, one of the peasant characters in the 1996 Yugoslav film *Pretty Village, Pretty Flame*, who, while holding a fork, delivers a monologue that describes how the Germans ('Krauts') were eating with their hands at a time when use of the knife and fork constituted basic etiquette for any ordinary Serb. Thus the argument that 'as we were civilised from early on, we are more European than you' is still actively used.

At the same time, a number of recent Balkan works reveal an inferiority complex about what is perceived as truly European. One example is the Bulgarian film *Traka-trak/Clickety-Clack* (1996), in which a runaway-train plot and an all-star cast are intended to provide an allegory of the present state of the marginalised Balkans. In a remote Bulgarian town near the Turkish border, a group of people board an international train with the intention of travelling to a nearby destination. The train, however, fails to stop and leaves the country, heading at full speed toward the West. It passes Serbia, Croatia and Hungary, to reach Paris and even goes beyond it. For the duration of the film one observes the reactions of the trapped passengers and listens to their discussions of the absurd situation. It is a metaphor of post-communist Bulgaria – headed for the West, but trapped in an accelerating train which is out of control. The whole menagerie of 'new' post-communist types is here – Gypsy small-time smugglers, Ukrainian go-go dancers, Russian diplomatic workers trading in Kalashnikovs, a Polish pimp with two prostitutes and Rambo-like paratroopers. In their seemingly ordinary dialogues the characters touch on most of the concerns of contemporary East Europeans – troubled vernacular economies, strict travel restrictions, black marketeering, racism, growing differences within the once monolithic Eastern bloc, violence, crime and nationalism. The attempt of the runaway train to penetrate the West serves as a metaphor of the failed effort by Bulgaria to enter Europe. In a symbolical move some of the passengers try to sneak into the special car carrying a group of European Phare experts, but a UN blue helmet rudely pushes them out. At the end, it turns out to have been merely a nightmarish dream, and the protagonists actually never left their remote little town. The concluding message of the film reads as a reassuring: 'East, West, home is best.'

The symbolism of impeded travel to Europe is also a basic premise of Greek Theo Angelopoulos' *Topio stin omichli/Landscape in the Mist* (1988), whose protagonists, two young children, set out to join their father, who is working as a *Gastarbeiter* somewhere in Germany, but never manage to leave Greece. But while in Angelopoulos' work the confinement in the Balkans is endowed with deeper metaphysical dimensions, another widely popular Greek film, *Balkanizateur* (1997), shows Greeks who freely travel to Switzerland only to feel like complete outsiders and outcasts. A similar treatment is given to the insecure Romanian officials in Mircea Daneliuk's *Senatorul melcilor/Senator's Snails* (1995) who, pressured by concern about their coverage in Western media, try to corrupt the French journalists by offering them an absurd snail feast. In the film, the ability to offer a snail meal becomes an allegory for the misunderstood superior refinement of Europeanness.

The Balkans outside of Europe

As Stuart Hall noted in the early 1990s, 'No sooner have the barriers collapsed but Europe is busy constructing a new set of margins for itself' (Hall, 1992, p. 52). Willing to admit their own limitations and preparing to be flexible in negotiation for admission to Europe, the Balkans were now presented with the even more overwhelming burden of feeling guilty about their cultural incompatibility with the rest of the continent.

During the cold war books on Eastern Europe regularly omitted chapters on one or more of the Balkan countries, citing the excuse that there were no specialists competent to write on Romania, Bulgaria or Albania. Scholarly books dealing with issues relating to the whole Eastern bloc were traditionally limited to examples from Poland, Hungary and Czechoslovakia, as if the other countries did not exist or were all the same by definition – an absence which soon thereafter became a good ground to declare the countries in the southeast of Europe different. The most popular scholarly work on Eastern Europe was preoccupied with the formation of the concept of Central Europe and rarely cared to include the Balkans, thus effectively working toward the conceptual exclusion of anything that could be described as a Balkan space. This trend is clearly visible in popular books which were often used as texts within the system of Western higher education on Eastern Europe, such as the works of Timothy Garton Ash (1989) or Jacques Rupnik (1990). The work of these and other East Europeanists established Central Eastern Europe as an area of a thriving intellectual discourse. Here, the Balkan space was regularly subsumed under the trends seen in the Central Eastern European countries. Apparently, nothing of intellectual value was happening beyond Czechoslovakia, Poland or Hungary; the Balkans were not interesting to them. In the 1990s, however, these same scholars gradually repositioned themselves as Balkan experts, and now frequently write on Balkan matters, thus filling the need for fluid-pen pundits at a time when newspapers badly needed coverage on Balkan issues.[4]

This attitude was further perpetuated by scholarship and journalism in the Balkan countries themselves: as Slavoj Žižek (1995) has observed, whoever happened to be located to the West of this eastern part of Europe was in a hurry to declare themselves a westernmost boundary, thus pronouncing everything to the east and the south a barbarian wasteland. American-based Romanian Andrei Codrescu (1990), for example, discusses issues of European cultural discourse and includes in this discourse his native Romania (a country traditionally excluded from the European), while at the same time remaining persistently turned to the West, apparently oblivious to the fact that a contribution to this discourse could possibly originate from further south and east of where he stands.

It would be too much to claim that in the second part of the twentieth century the West European countries and America have been involved in a systematic effort to maintain the image of the Balkans as primitive or inferior; one can speak instead only of a continuation of the routine use of primitive metaphors, not an intended vilification of any particular nation.

If one scrutinises the Western portrayal of the various Balkan countries before the advent of political correctness, examples of frivolous slander abound. See, for example, Thomas Meehan's 1971 hoax piece in *The New Yorker*, in which the author ridicules a non-existent Bulgarian author to indirectly criticise the elitist approach of the Swedish academy to world literature. In this piece the author, described as a regular contributor to *The New Yorker*, writes to express his outrage that little-known authors in the West, like Georgios Seferis and Yasunari Kawabata, had been awarded the Nobel Prize for literature in the last few years. He claims that this time the award has gone to a Gregor Drubnik, a writer about whom not only has no one in the West heard but who is also unknown even in his native Bulgaria, as he is a member of an ethnic minority and writes in an obscure language, comprising only 243 words in total: 'Pludnik, a frustratingly ambiguous Slovene dialect that has for centuries defied the translating efforts of some of the world's most eminent linguists, many of whom, after wrestling with Pludnik, have fallen victim to serious mental illness.' Drubnik's only book of fables, *The Sullen Swineherd*, was barely comprehensible to anyone 'unacquainted with the arcane traditions of nineteenth-century Bulgaria':

> If literary cognoscenti everywhere were surprised that the coveted award had gone to the obscure Bulgarian scrivener, no one was more surprised than Gregor Drubnik himself, who until winning it had never heard of the Nobel Prize for Literature. A squat, roly-poly man, with dark, melancholy eyes that peer owlishly out from behind rimless spectacles, Drubnik, who hides his bald pate beneath an ill-fitting carrot-colored wig, has for the past 55 years lived alone in a rude 12-room duplex upstairs over a bowling alley in the heart of downtown Plitznitska, a remote hill village in the mountains of central Bulgaria, where the principal industry of the glum and exceedingly hostile peasants is stringing goats' teeth on rubber bands to fashion souvenir ankle bracelets. In his humble duplex, . . . has for decades worked literally from dawn to dusk on his brief, 25-word fables, laboriously turning out no more than six or eight a year. In fact, so slow a writer is Drubnik that there are many days in which he produces fewer than five words during over fourteen hours at his IBM '100' Electra typewriter.   (Meehan, 1971, p. 87)

However, Meehan was writing more than a quarter of a century ago, since when there have been many changes, including the advent of political correctness in

the USA. It is perhaps too much to claim that in the second part of the twentieth century the West has been involved in a systematic effort to maintain the
barbarian image of the Balkans; one can speak instead only of a continuation
of the routine of representation as a primitive 'backyard,' not the intended vilification of any particular nation. Even more, during the years of Tito's rule a
pro-Yugoslavian rhetoric was extensively used for Russian-bashing of various
kinds. Since 1989, however, the barbarian image of the Balkans has been revived
and brought back into circulation, with the substitution of socio-economic and
political considerations for culturist ones.

The end of the cold war seemed to suggest that 'Eastern Europe' had ceased
to exist, noted historian Larry Wolff. He indicated, however, that this did not
mean an automatic deletion of the mental division of Europe. Either new
associations would be found to mark the differences, or the older pre-cold war
division lines would be re-established (Wolff, 1994, p. 14). In the case of the
Balkans, the re-mapping was taking place in both directions – the older associations with the barbarian Ottoman legacy were quickly brought back into use,
as were a plethora of new associations with the Third World, a process explored
in detail in Maria Todorova's work on 'imagining the Balkans' (Todorova, 1994,
1997). Even before the 'difference' of the Balkans was spelled out in the discourse of journalists and political scientists, it was mapped out by layout
editors, whose choice of pictures of drabness and chaos, of Gypsy street for-
tune-tellers and underage pickpockets in Bulgaria, of AIDS-infected babies and
environmental pollution in Romania, and of daunting crowds of Albanians
coming to the West, effectively suppressed any 'European-like' images of this
part of the world as irrelevant and non-representative. Yet the role of visual referencing remained unaccounted for. Looking at the changing dynamics of
international news flows, media scholars Johan Galtung and Richard Vincent
noted that in the post-cold war situation the reporting of First/Second World
relations was undergoing transformation and that the coverage of the Second
World was now comparable to that of the Third World, 'with Eastern
Europe/the Soviet Union (later the ex-Soviet Union) playing a role relative to
the European community not so different from the role of South America relative to North America' (Galtung and Vincent, 1992, pp. 3–4).

Older geopolitical division lines were presented as geographical common
sense.[5] In a 1994 RAND corporation publication prepared for the US army, for
example, Thomas S. Szayna explained that

> The term Eastern Europe, in reference to the non-Soviet former members of
> the Warsaw Pact and Albania and Yugoslavia, was a political term appropriate
> during the Cold War. Following the breakdown of the East–West division of
> Europe, the term has lost relevance. The geographical terms central Europe

and the Balkans are more accurate and preferable in the post-Cold War era.

(Szayna, 1994, p. 1)

The refusal to approach the Balkans by focusing on the real problems, and the substitution of economic and political considerations with rushed talk about profound cultural incompatibilities, is most visible in Samuel P. Huntington's 1993 popular theory of a 'clash of civilisations'. Huntington's definition of civilisation is as follows

> the highest cultural grouping of people and the broadest level of cultural identity people have short of that which distinguishes humans from other species. It is defined both by common objective elements, such as language, history, religion, customs, institutions, and by the subjective self-identification of people.   (Huntington, 1993, p. 23)

To Huntington, politics and economy are secondary to the civilisation divides which determine the deeply embedded fault lines that will ensure that people continue to oppose each other, precluding dialogue and cooperation and conditioning future conflicts. Not much can be done to avoid these future conflicts, as they are predetermined by non-interacting civilisation entities.

A professor of political science at Harvard, in his work Huntington addressed the global political dynamics of our times. His preoccupation was global, not regionally Balkan. Widely featured in the American media, however, his views were most often mentioned in conjunction with the Balkan conflict, as providing a suitable model with which to grasp the crisis – namely, to see it as a culturist one, ensuing from an inevitable clash between incompatible civilisations, and effectively waiving the need to look any further into its economic or political roots. In conversations I have had with political scientists, I have been reassured that Huntington's views have not been really influential within the discipline (with the exception of the numerous high-profile featured talks he has given at academic institutions across North America and Europe). Huntington's theories, however, were widely publicised by the mainstream US media; and the professor himself gave a number of media interviews elaborating on his views. His theories of the civilisational clash were often adopted as an underlying ideology of the American media understanding of international conflict, as I will show below with an example from the influential *Chicago Tribune*.

In his work, Huntington dismisses politics and the economy as grounds for future world conflicts, and proclaims clashes between civilisations the major source of conflict for the years to come. Looking at Europe, among the civilisations that Huntington distinguishes are the Western, the Islamic and the

Slavic-Orthodox ones. For the purposes of clearly indicating who the West's enemies might be, however, Huntington equates the Islamic and Slavic-Orthodox civilisations: 'As the ideological division of Europe has disappeared, the cultural division of Europe between Western Christianity, on the one hand, and Orthodox Christianity and Islam, on the other, has reemerged.' This cultural split, in Huntington's opinion, is 'the most significant dividing line in Europe'. Overcoming it would be unthinkable, because

> The peoples to the east and south of this line are Orthodox or Muslim, they historically belonged to the Ottoman or Tsarist empires and were only lightly touched by the shaping events in the rest of Europe; they are generally less advanced economically; they seem much less likely to develop stable democratic political systems.

By classifying Orthodox Christianity and Islam together and ignoring their differences and internal tensions, Huntington in one blow invalidates the whole elaborate ideology of a 'shield against Islam', which is seen in many Balkan countries as a crucial stake for their place in Europe. What is particularly problematic in Huntington's approach, however, is his rush to proclaim the cultural division as the only relevant point of reference in the new division of Europe. He makes no mention of economic or political dividing lines within Europe, or of the respective institutionalisation of such division lines in a number of pan-European or Western organisations (such as NATO, the EC or the G-7), which in this light are seen as bodies existing for the sole purpose of consolidating the cultural identity of the West against the dangers of hostile civilisations. One is left with the impression that the main function of these organisations is to preserve cultural identity, a view which found its ultimate expression in Tony Blair's claim that the 1999 NATO bombing of Serbia should be seen as an act designed to save 'the values of [Western] civilization'.[6] The idea of an essential division between civilisations is brought in to substitute for all other aspects of interaction, and is described exclusively in terms of hostility: Huntington talks of future enmities, clashes and conflicts, and never of cooperation or convergence.

Huntington's formula presents the reality of today's and the outlook for tomorrow's world along simple clear-cut lines and conveniently avoids the intricacies of economic and political interaction, making it particularly appealing to many Western journalists, who now do not need to do any extensive background research into these areas. The elegant binary clash of civilisations negates the necessity to examine a whole range of political and economic factors in reporting, as all these aspects can now be played down for the sake of focusing on the 'culturist' aspect. Many reporters perpetuated Huntington's approach in their coverage of the Balkans by ignoring political and economic background. Illustrations can be found, for example, in the influential *Chicago Tribune*, which, at the time of daily anti-Milošević demonstrations in Belgrade in the winter of 1997, reported that

> Centuries of domination by the Ottoman Turks and a cultural affinity with Orthodox Russia have not instilled an intuitive grasp of democratic principles among the Balkan peoples. What's happening now in the streets may look like a pro-democracy movement, but it isn't.

In the same issue of the *Chicago Tribune*, senior writer R. C. Longworth spells out this thesis in detail:

> In Eastern Europe, half of the former Communist countries – the Western Christian half, including Poland and Hungary – have reshaped themselves since 1989 into modern democracies with market economies. The other half – the Orthodox Christians such as Serbia, Bulgaria and Russia – have barely begun: without exception they have wasted the last eight years.

In an interview in this same section of the newspaper Huntington himself underlines this point:

> NATO membership for Central European states that historically have been part of the West seems to me to be absolutely essential to stability in that area. At the same time, we ought to reassure Russia that NATO has no designs on Bulgaria, Romania, or Ukraine, for instance, which historically have been Orthodox societies linked to Russia.[7]

Even in the annals of the daily news bulletin of a respected newscaster such as *Radio Free Europe*, which specialises in this region's affairs, one can regularly come across claims like this one by an Albanian expert, according to whom:

> The biggest obstacles to reform [in Albania] are probably the political and cultural ones. . . . Many state officials at various levels display little concern either for the work ethic or the responsibilities of their office. Such an attitude has roots in the Ottoman era and accounts for the low productivity of much of the administration.[8]

The effects of Huntington's views were initially apparent mostly in the workings of journalism. Since *Clash of Civilizations* was first published, however, an army of US scholars have perpetuated its message. Even those who disagreed included Huntington's essay in the core readings for their courses and thus gave publicity to his conveniently simplistic view. The American college population became the primary audience for his insight into the future of international conflicts, and Huntington reached out much further than one could have expected initially – his thesis became a core part of the world vision for those training for executive careers in public administration. Along with the culturally grounded rediscovery and re-admission of Central Eastern Europe within the European space, the Balkans were proclaimed a 'culturally incompatible' chunk of the former Eastern bloc and were now left outside European semantic boundaries. It did not take much to make these new division lines, offered under the disguise of a 'civilisational' discourse, seem plausible, and it worked particularly well for American students, most of whom can barely claim a solid background knowledge in area studies. It is realistic, therefore, to expect that the new generation of ambitious college graduates will increasingly embrace the civilisational division lines as a framework in approaching international policy issues later on in their professional lives.

These are only some of the many facets of the continuing process of the re-mapping of the East European space after 1989, which resulted in the division of former Eastern bloc countries into Central Eastern European and Balkan parts: the Balkans were separated from the other former Eastern bloc countries on the grounds that this was geographically appropriate. As a result, people inhabiting the lands beyond the Western Christianity boundary were declared to belong to a different type of civilisation (for which claim the differences between themselves were deemed unessential). The international media helped facilitate this project by simply accepting its premises and providing the relevant type of coverage.

Interpretation and identity: bickering around the image

The substitution of the cultural for the political, with the cultural assuming dominance, explains the crucial importance of all issues related to image and representation in the case of today's Balkans. While for Huntington the reduction to the culturist was a tool for estrangement and logically resulted in the exclusion of all other civilisations from the sphere of enlightened democracies (= 'Europe'), in the Balkans it triggered situations where local ideology used the reduction to the culturist for the purpose of enhancing the inherent-belonging-to-Europe argument. These last attempts were doomed, however, as they were building on premises that were better suited to justify exclusion rather than encourage inclusion. Once the discourse had moved into the culturist field, the battle for 'belonging to Europe' was half lost, as it was now effectively limited within a sphere which lacked firm criteria and allowed frivolous speculation, thereby creating a fertile ground for mediated misapprehensions and mismatched aspirations. It was now largely confined to discussions of representation and self-representation and involved acts directed to the attention of an imagined attentive global audience, one that remained undefined and obscure, as it was largely constructed to serve the immediate discursive needs.

The culturist substitution resulted in a number of concrete and sometimes controversial manifestations, some of which I would like to trace here.

Succumbing to the culturist argument

Paying meticulous attention to idiosyncratic features of Balkan culture and highlighting unfavourable traits of the Balkan character embodies an attitude shared by many intellectuals of Balkan extraction who, ironically, are the ones most ready to articulate and reiterate the culturist clichés and engage in a specific form of self-bashing. Many of the stereotypes about the Balkans are uncritically repeated and perpetuated by insiders, who, like Croatian politician Žarko Domljan insisted in 1991 that Yugoslavia was not a nation but 'a mixture of ancient tribes'.[9] Or like American sociologist of Croatian extraction, Stjepan Mestrović (1993b), who developed maverick theories on the barbarian habits of the Balkan heart.[10]

In the 1990s, it no longer takes aloof foreigners to problematise the Balkans, as the region is willingly problematised by insiders, who uncritically adopt and eagerly perpetuate the culturist paradigm. Dušan Makavejev, the best-known film director from Yugoslavia, ridiculed the Western envoys in Bosnia for applying rigid Protestant ethics to what he called 'a profoundly Byzantine culture', where the negotiators' 'funny maps and signatures [were] not honoured 15 times in a row' and where they could not achieve anything else but the 'collecting [of] meaningless autographs like teenage groupies on heat'. The efforts of the West failed, as Makavejev explained, because here one dealt with a profoundly different culture:

> An old partisan from Herzegovina, the late Vladimir Dedijer, who was not an
> innocent, told me how, when one has to sign an agreement that one is not
> intending to honour, the signatory, while signing with his right hand, has to
> keep his left hand in the pocket, holding his testicles. This gesture makes the
> signature invalid. This is what international negotiators, who are ignorant of
> the culture they deal with, miss.   (Makavejev, 1993, p. 6)

While not intended to damage, this stance nevertheless effectively enhances the claim that the key to understanding the Balkans is to look into the deviations found in their distinct culture. In film, the celebrated 1995 Cannes winner, *Underground*, offered an outspoken confirmation of the substandard ethics of its Yugoslav protagonists, while the celebrated 1994 Venice winner, *Before the Rain*, showed tribal mayhem that dauntingly reached as far as a tranquil London locale.

Bickering about the international image

The painful recognition of the fact that Balkan nations rarely enjoy a very favourable international image is often expressed in incidents where the blame over undesired representations is explained away as conspiracies masterminded by hostile Balkan powers. Take cinema. A recent controversy (1998) surrounded the failed project of British producer Tarquie Olivier to shoot a biographical film about Kemal Atatürk, starring Spaniard Antonio Banderas, with Australian Bruce Beresford set to direct.[11] Reacting to news of the planned production, hundreds of outraged Greek-Americans engaged in a massive letter-writing campaign condemning the project, which intended to depict Atatürk as a modernist politician comparable to Gandhi. To those letter writers, Mustafa Kemal Atatürk was 'a rapist, murderer, child molester and destroyer of Greek civilisation', a 'savage maniac' and 'a disgrace to human civilisation as we know it' – qualifications mostly earned as a result of Atatürk's forced expulsion of nearly two million Greeks from Anatolia in the 1920s.[12] This controversy bears direct reference to an older one which evolved around the British film *Midnight Express* (1978). Although the film was based on an American survivor's autobiographical account of the mistreatment of inmates in Turkish prisons, it was a popularly shared belief in Turkey that the film was commissioned by the Greek lobby in the UK with the clear intention of damaging the international image of the country.

Another aspect of discontent over the international image is the angry reaction of Balkan individuals who realise that, when it comes to the representation of the Balkans in the Western media, Third World depictions are often favoured over European-style images, with photo editors routinely preferring images of sloppy peasant women to those of high-heeled Sarajevan urbanites. A Sarajevo journalist featured in the documentary *Truth under Siege*, for example, expressed outrage that the Western media tend to show Sarajevan residents as primitives, as if they were 'from Kurdistan'. The sense of (even marginal) identity with the West is so deeply entrenched that Balkan intellectuals routinely dismiss the plight of other deprived peoples, as is visible in this case where 'Kurdistan' becomes synonymous of such a desperate case of primitivism that it cannot possibly be worthy of serious consideration, and any comparison with which would be offensive.

Holocaust as a favoured frame of reference

The Holocaust rhetoric and imagery have been appropriated and exploited to the utmost, and much in the conceptualisation of the Balkan conflict draws from the Holocaust trope. Zlata Filipović (1994), whose diary was published in the West, is referred to as a Sarajevan Anne Frank. The revelations of the existence of Serb concentration camps, where Bosnian men were held, triggered numerous comparisons to the Nazi death camps.[13] Court TV materials on the World Wide Web about the tribunal at the Hague feature direct links to materials about the Nuremberg trials.[14] Here the indicted war criminal Goran Jelisić is presented under his nickname, 'The Serb Adolf'. Duško Tadić, a supervisor in a concentration camp and the first one to be sentenced, is called 'Ivan the Terrible', which is a reference not to the Russian Tsar, but to the notorious Nazi camp guard who used the alias.

Issues of the use (and abuse) of Holocaust referencing were brought up in the so-called 'LM' controversy early in 2000. ITN reporters who had filmed Serbian detention camps in Bosnia in the summer of 1992 were accused in a 1996 article in *Living Marxism* ('LM') magazine of deliberately manipulating the footage to make it reminiscent of familiar Holocaust images of concentration camps. ITN sued *Living Marxism* for libel and won. One of the arguments was that ITN reporters had never stated that the footage was of a 'concentration camp'. In all fairness, however, I should mention that even if this was the case, the footage was used by others in documentaries which edited it together with documentary footage of Nazi camps, thus creating an unambiguous visual referencing.[15]

Most importantly, the metaphors of Jewish victimisation have been used (or abused) by virtually all sides in the Yugoslav conflict, and everybody – Serbs, Slovenes, Albanians and Bosnian Muslims – has represented themselves at one time or another as Jews in peril (Živković, 1994). The Holocaust became the scale by which events in Bosnia were measured.[16] Occasionally, those who introduced direct parallels to the Holocaust did so in the belief that such comparisons would have a powerful impact on the public opinion, thus reducing the Holocaust to a tool in a public relations strategy.[17]

In his book, *Sarajevo, Kashmir and Other Poems*, Pakistani poet Irshad Ulla Khan (1994) makes a dedication 'to the victims of the Holocaust'. In his view of the world, a universal anxiety starts in Kashmir and then moves on to Sarajevo, and these places are seen by him as equally valid dimensions of the shared suffering of humankind, summed up by the concept of Holocaust. At the same time, while commenting on the Balkans has produced innumerable references to the Holocaust, only rarely have other genocidal situations – like those in Armenia, Cambodia or Rwanda, for example, or other large population transfers, like the ones in Kashmir or Anatolian Greece – been referred to as a means of interpreting the Bosnian carnage, as if they were irrelevant here.[18]

The Eurocentricity and specific superiority of the Holocaust discourse has been problematised in a different context by black theorist Paul Gilroy, who quotes the writer James Baldwin:

> The Jew's suffering is recognized as part of the moral history of the world and the Jew is recognized as a contributor to the world's history; this is not true for blacks. Jewish history, whether or not one can say it is honored, is certainly known: the black history has been blasted, maligned, and despised. The Jew is a white man, and when white men rise up against oppression they are heroes: when black men rise they have reverted to their native savagery. The uprising in the Warsaw ghetto was not described as a riot, nor were the participants maligned as hoodlums: the boys and girls in Watts and Harlem are thoroughly aware of this and it certainly contributes to their attitudes toward the Jews.
>
> (Gilroy, 1993, p. 216)

Gilroy insists that it is not only possible but necessary to discuss the history of blacks and Jews together, and to see the Holocaust in the general context of the modern history of racial slavery and terror in the Western hemisphere. He goes as far as to claim that by refusing to allow a comparative analysis of the Holocaust, Jewish intellectuals, who reflect on racism but exclude the experiences of slavery and other races as irrelevant, have in effect consolidated the interests of Eurocentrism.

When this last view is applied to the use of the Holocaust trope within the discourse on the Balkan conflict, it is impossible to ignore the underlying Eurocentric motivation for the overzealous willingness to find comparisons to the Holocaust but simultaneously to deny comparisons to any non-European ordeals. The Holocaust trope is favoured so much, not only for its moral compatibility but also because it is a *European* experience. The very fact that these other examples of genocide are European is the ground on which they are rendered irrelevant.

Disillusionment with and bitterness at friends

In our age of global interconnectedness news reporting is no longer a one-way process. During the Bosnian war, all Western reporting had a twofold function, as print media reports and broadcasts were the main source of information not only for audiences in the West but also for the people of Bosnia itself. BBC, CNN and Radio France International supplied news not only to their audiences in Europe and the USA but also to besieged Sarajevo, and have often been cited by former Yugoslavs as their main source of reliable information. The situation is pretty much the same across the Balkans. The broadcasts of Radio Free Europe are still listened to by large loyal audiences across South-Eastern Europe. There have been instances when broadcasts that were not intended for

Balkan audiences have had a significant impact – for example, the Italian commercial television broadcasting which was received in Albania and was to a large
extent responsible for the decision that many Albanians made to emigrate.

Alongside the reporting of continuing developments, all unfavourable representations and allegations of impeded cultural legacy, found in the West
European and American media, are instantly transmitted back to the Balkans,
where they quite naturally trigger a specific public reaction, which is particularly strong among those who are trying to counteract the negative social
tendencies in their countries. Seeing themselves depicted as outsiders whose
movement to democracy is interpreted as an illusory and doomed one, liberal-
minded intellectuals in the Balkans often feel isolated and outraged. They feel
that they have been cast out of a process that began less then a decade ago with
a different promise – one of re-admission to Europe, not of exclusion from it.
Their reaction is one of disillusionment and bitterness.

Many in former Yugoslavia believed in vain that the West would rush to
intervene and put an end to the conflict there, and were puzzled for quite some
time when it did not: 'When the war started, for a long time we hoped that one
of the big powers would come and calm our small bickering nations', or 'The
world seemed so cruelly indifferent, merely because normal life went on (still!)
outside our borders' (quoted in Lešić, 1995, pp. 27 and 55); or 'From time to
time we see pictures on the television of the sleek, well-fed people in other parts
of the world, and it seems so absurd that they should sit there, not giving a
damn about the fact that here in Bosnia we are dying like flies' (quoted in
Cataldi, 1994, p. 66).

Early on in the Yugoslav conflict, one came across statements like this quite
often. Gradually, a disillusionment took over, and near the end of the 1990s one
rarely saw any further manifestation of these expectations, which came to
sound banal and naive even to people trapped in the Balkan quagmire. Opinions about a desired external intervention profoundly changed with the Kosovo
war of 1999.

The irony is that the dismay most often finds expression in bitterness directed
against those Western intellectuals who acted as advocates for the Balkans.
Their visibility turned them into the resentful target for those on whose behalf
they had tried to act. In one of his essays, for example, Sarajevan Zlatko Dizdarević describes the satellite-transmitted TV encounter between French and
Bosnian intellectuals during which prominent film-maker Costa-Gavras, director of such politically engaged films as *Z* (1969) and *Missing* (1993), promises
to premiere his new film in Sarajevo. Dizdarević comments bitterly on this 'generous gesture', and points out 'that he [Costa-Gavras] would also have to send
along a movie theater in which to show it' (Dizdarević, 1993,
p. 151). It is certainly strange that a personality like the outspoken French film

director of Greek extraction would come under such critical fire. But it is no wonder – the politicians and intellectuals who did not care were not visible in the media, and therefore were never criticised.

The paradox of this bitterness aimed at friends is best visible in the writings of Sarajevan Dzevad Karahasan, who was exiled to Austria during the war. In an essay entitled 'An Argument with a Frenchman', Karahasan (1994) talks of an encounter with a French journalist who seems to be genuinely interested in the Sarajevan situation but is receptive only to information that would fit within his preconceived framework. Thus, instead of an active role in the exchange with the Frenchman, Karahasan claims he was relegated to the position of a 'passive object' (ibid., p. 65), a situation which makes him comment acrimoniously:

> When my Frenchman entered my home I was moved, grateful, and prepared to do anything to show him how much this visit from the faraway world meant to me. When he entered my home, my Frenchman was overwrought by the tribulation of my city, filled with good intentions and determined to do something noble for me personally as well as for all of us. Our encounter was therefore elevated and graced by beautiful, noble feelings. Our attempt to communicate was similarly founded on an entirely sincere effort to understand each other, and to agree.
>
> Why was our parting so bitter, then? Am I indeed such an ungrateful scoundrel, because I wasn't suffering as much as my guest had expected and had decided for me to suffer? Was my guest truly so shocked by my suffering that his emotions obstructed his view of the causes behind that and other, much greater suffering? Was my suffering truly enormous, and have I become so numb that I cannot see its dimensions and feel its depths anymore?
>
> (ibid., p. 62)

The Frenchman remains unnamed, and soon after this encounter Karahasan directs his bitterness to 'the West' in general. In another instance, writing for German audiences (in Vollmer, 1995, p. 162), Karahasan identifies the individuals who, he feels, are responsible for the disparaging way in which people of the Balkans are perceived in the West. His targets become influential intellectuals publicly standing for the cause of Bosnian Muslims, like German poet Hans-Magnus Enzensberger, one of the intellectuals who spoke publicly about Bosnia's ordeal. Ironically enough, his sight is set not on those who remained indifferent but on those who tried to commit themselves.

The ironies discussed here – succumbing to a denigrating self-representation, readiness to exoticise oneself, bickering about the international image, abusing the Holocaust framework and bitterness directed to friendly minded supporters – are reactions to the contested Balkan admissibility to Europe and the problematised Balkan Europeanness. While the obsessive struggle for admissibility to Europe may at first glance seem an innocuous fixation, it is accountable for many of the gravest misdemeanours that characterise the Balkan region today.

It is doubtful if much could be done to change the positioning and the interpretations allotted to the Balkans. Would there be much change if the young Redl from Szabó's film was told not to bother singing Hungarian songs and if his hosts were asked not to talk in French? All we can do is point at the inherent inconsistencies within the discourse on Europe and maintain awareness about its uses and abuses.

Notes

1. In a book of short essays entitled *Children of Atlantis*, young displaced people from former Yugoslavia repeatedly ask the question, 'Why is the world so unfair to us?' (Lešić, 1995). A German publication carries the indicative title *That We in Bosnia Belong to the World* (Vollmer, 1995).

2. *Europe* was composed by the Briton Nigel Osborne, written by Sarajevan Goran Simić and directed by Dino Mustafić. Paul Harris, 'Opera against the Odds', *The Daily Telegraph*, 18 February 1995, p. 16.

3. Ahmed Dogan, leader of The Movement of Rights and Freedoms, an ethnic Turk party in Bulgaria.

4. Timothy Garton Ash had shown no prior interest in the Balkans, but towards the end of the 1990s he published a series of essays on issues like the Kosovo war and its aftermath in publications such as *The New York Review of Books*, *The Times Literary Supplement* and the *Guardian*. Jacques Rupnik gave a number of talks on Balkan issues, and wrote on the Balkans in a series of leading French periodicals. Why these (and other) non-specialists were encouraged to convert to the Balkans rather than give the floor to dedicated Balkan experts is an issue which merits investigation, particularly when one bears in mind that the record of cases when non-experts were preferred by the media (in the capacity of pundits) and by politicians (in the capacity of advisers) to the existing Balkan experts is indeed an extensive one.

5. The fact that many of the Balkan countries belonged to the so-called Eastern bloc (referred to by some other scholars as the Second World) had given them a status equal to that of the countries which are now referred to as Central Eastern European. A potential 'package deal' transferring the entire former bloc to *Europe* was thus contemplated as a desired post-communist

solution by these countries. On this, see my 'Media Coverage of Bulgaria in the West and Its Domestic Use' (Iordanova, 1995).

6. Tony Blair in an interview with Partick Wintour, *The Observer*, 16 May 1999, p. 17.

7. Tom Hundley, 'Balkan Reform Crippled by Communist Past, Impoverished Present', *Chicago Tribune*, 16 February 1997, Section 2, p. 8. The quote is taken from just one of several articles mostly devoted to applying Huntington's views to the processes in Eastern Europe and to revealing how desperate and ill-fated any democracy movement in the Balkan countries is. R. C. Longworth, 'Clash of Cultures: Realism Intrudes on Our Rosy View of the World', *Chicago Tribune*, 16 February 1997, Perspective section, pp. 1 and 10; Samuel Huntington, 'On the Record', *Chicago Tribune*, 16 February 1997, Perspective section, p. 3.

8. Fabian Schmidt, 'Albania's Government: Confusion, Incompetence and Lack of Vision', *RFE/RL Newsline*, 27 November 1997.

9. Quoted in Barber (1995, pp. 195–6). This particular quote is taken from Milton Viorst's 'The Yugoslav Idea', *The New Yorker*, 18 March 1991, pp. 58–79.

10. Mestrović's (1993b) theories about the barbarian Balkans should be regarded as a continuation of his general theoretical claim that the 'barbarian temperament' is a crucial construct of post-modernity. If applied to the barbarian wasteland of modern-day America, these theories may be seen as an amusing theoretical equivalent of moralistic televangelism. Applied to the Balkans, however, a region which barely enjoys a positive international image, these theories cannot just be dismissed, as their role can be seriously damaging.

11. Notably, the news about the failed film project was reported not on the culture pages but in the international news column of the *Guardian* (Joanna Coles, 'Ataturk Star Retreats in Face of Greek Rage', *Guardian*, 17 July 1998, p. 15).

12. The unprecedented scale of the 1920/21 forced migration has been the subject of a number of works of Greek literature. In cinema it is explored in Nikos Kunduros' *1922* (1978).

13. See texts by Gutman (1993), Vulliamy (1994), Schiffer (1993), Rieff (1995) and Hukanović (1996), among others.

14. Courtroom TV Network. Court TV Casefiles: Bosnia War Crimes Tribunal (© 1999). Available: <http://www.courttv.com/casefiles/warcrimes/> (10 May 1999).

15. See, for example *Crimes against Humanity*, produced by Worldnet, the film and TV service of USIA, in 1995.

16. Udovicki and Ridgeway, for example, approached the subject matter of

Yugoslavia's ethnic wars by asking the question: 'Was it as bad as Nazism or in some ways even worse?' (Udovicki and Ridgeway, 1995, p. 1).

17. James Harff, the manager of the Ruder Finn PR agency, was quoted as saying that he considered his greatest achievement to have been to win over the Jewish circles for the Bosnian cause. This enabled his agency to equate Serbs with Nazis in the eyes of the public (Peter Glotz, 'Der Fall Handke: Wie sich Intellektuelle und Journalisten über dem Serbien-Aufsatz heillos zerstritten', *Die Woche*, 16 February 1996, p. 17). An exhibit at the US Holocaust Museum called *Faces of Sorrow* triggered vocal protests from Serbian-Americans, who felt the effect of this equation with Nazis (Steven A. Holmes, 'Photographs of Balkans Draw Fire. Serb Groups Fault Holocaust Museum', *The New York Times*, 24 September 1994. p. L6).

18. With the notable exception of Robert Hayden's article 'Schindler's Fate' (1996), in which he approached the issues of population parting in Yugoslavia by placing them within the larger context of other compatible events worldwide.

Chapter 3
Narrating the Balkans

The modern-day post-colonial discourse which revealed 'that "East" like "West" is much more of a project than a place', and which originally seemed a theory only remotely relevant to the Balkans, is reinforced by a small but growing number of recent studies that explore the gradual Western construction of the concept of Eastern Europe as 'a work of cultural creation, of intellectual artifice, of ideological self-interest and self-promotion' (Bakić-Hayden, 1995, p. 917). In his work on Russia, Larry Wolff provided abundant historical evidence to show that 'it was the intellectual work of the Enlightenment to bring about that modern reorientation of the continent which produced Western Europe and Eastern Europe', and that, ever since, Eastern Europe has functioned as a 'structural boundary, in the mind and on the map' (Wolff, 1994, p. 1). The major part of this 'mapping' project had been carried out by travellers over the years, so Wolff explores numerous travel-related narratives that have been instrumental for the mental mapping that established Eastern Europe as an intellectual project of 'demi-Orientalization' (ibid., p. 5), of 'neither definitive exclusion nor unqualified inclusion' but constructed on a 'developmental scale that measured the distance between civilization and barbarism' (ibid., p.13).

On this scale, the Balkans were located closer to 'the depths of barbarism', functioning as a specific sub-category of Eastern Europe, as 'a synonym for a reversion to the tribal, the backward, the primitive, the barbarian', and as something that suggested further lower levels of 'nesting Orientalism'. Historian Maria Todorova specifically explored the works and accounts of travellers to the Balkans, and concluded that

> geographically inextricable from Europe, yet culturally constructed as 'the other', the Balkans became, in time, the object of a number of externalized political, ideological and cultural frustrations and have served as a repository of negative characteristics against which a positive and self-congratulatory image of the 'European' and 'the West' has been constructed.
>
> (Todorova, 1994, p. 453)

In her 1997 book, *Imagining the Balkans*, Todorova continued the discussion of the writings of travellers to the Balkans from the seventeenth century until the present day to show how the construction of this image has come into being. She focuses on the Balkan writings of Edward Brown, Robert Walsh, Henry Blount, William Gladstone, George Bernard Shaw and Hermann Graf von Keyserling, along with present-day authors such as George Kennan, Robert Kaplan and Lawrence Eagleburger. Her overall conclusion is that Balkanism and its subject are imprisoned in a field of discourse where 'Balkans' is set in opposition to 'West' and to 'Europe', and where 'Balkanism' is the darker other of 'Western civilisation'.

But while the work of historians is retrospective, it is one of the intentions of this study to show that the 'orientalist' construction of the Balkans is a process that continues today. What is even more important, the 'orientalisation' of the Balkans cannot be declared a purely Western project, as it is a process which has been embraced, internalised and partially carried out by many consenting Balkan intellectuals. It is not just 'the West' which constructs the Balkans as compliant to Western stereotypes, to a large extent this construction is taken up and carried further by 'the Rest', and in our case by Balkan writers and film-makers themselves. The result is a specific voluntary 'self-exoticism', which becomes the preferred mode of self-representation for many Balkan film-makers.

Through the exploration of a number of works of literature and films, mostly by Balkan authors, it is possible to make the following claims.

First, the distinctive travelogue-type narrative structure is characteristic of a large number of 'Balkan' plots. Second, by submissively accepting instead of critically challenging a narrative structure which inevitably positions and constructs them as objects of the Western traveller's gaze, recent films from the Balkans that aim to address the current troubles of the region largely cater to traditional stereotypes. By doing so, Balkan film remains uncritical and fails to recognise the controversial effects of the Eurocentric construct. Third, this lack of critical examination provides grounds for wider speculation about the paradoxical positioning of the Balkans as geographically part of Europe, but conceptually excluded from the European cultural space.

The journey to the dark Balkans: Snakes and ignorance

A brief summary of a short story by Ivo Andrić, *Snake*, will take us to the very heart of the problem (Andrić, 1969, pp. 207–23). *Snake* is set in 1885 and describes the experiences of Agatha and Amelia, two sisters from a high-ranking officer's family in Vienna, as they travel through Bosnia. Back home the sisters have an extensive record of involvement in charitable activities for the poor (Agatha is even dubbed 'Caritas' by her friends), serving hot meals for the hungry, and providing shelter and warm clothes for the winter. In Bosnia, however, the sisters encounter an unusual situation – their carriage is stopped by a small crowd of people surrounding a girl who has been bitten by a snake. The girl's parents know no better than to call the local charm healer, but the two charitable sisters are just as helpless as anyone else. Although, they have seen and dealt with 'illness and poverty in the slums of Vienna', what they face now is quite different. The sisters react with pained annoyance in the face of people who appear slower and uglier than the ones they are used to dealing with, people whose ways of suffering are unmanageable and coarse. The hardship they encounter here is very different from what they are used to, and does not fall within the specifically aestheticised dimensions of their charitable activities at home. Their sweet ways of soothing pain are not suited for this rough and challenging situation. This lack of style casts an overwhelming shadow over the whole incident.

Still, Agatha and Amelia manage to help the girl by administering alcohol to prevent the poison from spreading. Soon after, they leave angry and frustrated by an experience that has shattered their self-esteem and undermined the image they have of themselves – one of efficient and beautiful fairy godmothers. They have preserved their ethical integrity as charitable benefactors, but the messy aesthetic dimension that accompanied this unexpected experience irritates them enormously. The sisters leave, eager to get away from this cursed place: 'Oh, I told you in Vienna what kind of a country we were going to,' Agatha tells Amelia. 'Now you've seen what it's like. Not a wretched thing under the heavens! I kept telling you about the poverty and the wilderness – the ugly, indescribable squalour. I told you so, I told you so? But it's even worse, it's awful – absolutely awful! Bosnia is not worth crying for.'

The sisters of Andrić's story travel to the Balkans, become involved in an unhappy experience, and then leave – an ordinary and conventional development. This story, however, is among the rare instances when the attitude of the Westerner is subtly problematised within a traditional narrative frame. In most other cases, the Westerner is just an unquestioned measurement used against the backdrop of 'otherness'.

The framework in which the Balkans are represented and conceptualised is most commonly one of accounts presented by European travellers who visit, pass through, explore, or undergo controversial experiences, and who then report on these from the safety and comfort of home. At least, this seems to be the case with some of the most popular works on the Balkans. The best-selling recent paperbacks on the Balkans, for example, have been Penguin's reprint of the 1941 *Black Lamb and Gray Falcon* (subtitled *A Journey through Yugoslavia*) by Dame Rebecca West; Vintage's *Balkan Ghosts* (subtitled *A Journey through History*) by Robert Kaplan (1993), which is widely researched and based on the travelogues of other Western visitors to the Balkans, and Penguin's *The Impossible Country* (1994) (subtitled *A Journey through the Last Days of Yugoslavia*) by Brian Hall. The travelogue is also the preferred vehicle for documentary film-makers, who chose to retain the travel diary format when editing their footage.[1]

The Journey to the Greek Islands: zest and flamboyance

Works in fictional film – recent, as well as classical – have further constructed the Balkans in this direction. The structure of the plot and the narrative strategies used to tell stories that take place in the Balkans are regularly shaped as accounts of a trip, a journey, or a visit. Typically, a Western protagonist goes to the Balkans and encounters other, different experiences, experiences that are dynamically evaluated through a continual referencing back to the original, Western point of departure. Thus the presumed 'normalness' embodied by the Westerner serves as a measure of the degree of Balkan 'deviance'.

Two well-known 'Greek' films can serve as good examples here.[2] The first one is *Pote tin Kyriaki/Never on Sunday* (1960), written and directed by Jules Dassin (a French-born American), and starring Melina Mercouri. In the film, Dassin casts himself in the role of a proselytising American, Homer, who comes across this cheerful Greek prostitute, Ilyia (Mercouri). Rather than being converted by him to the 'right' way, however, it is she whose influence proves stronger and who makes Homer reconsider many of his beliefs and puritan morals.

Even though the intent of *Never on Sunday* is to ridicule the rigidness of the West and to celebrate the zeal of the Mediterranean spirit, the formal structure of the narrative features a Western traveller and events that unravel in response to his presence; it is he and his experiences that are the first and last point of reference. Presenting Greece as a country of eternal sunshine and its people as joyous bon vivants, *Never on Sunday* is credited with pushing the tourist boom

In *Pote tin kyriaki/Never on Sunday* (1960), Jules Dassin casts himself as a naive American scholar who comes across an aggressive pub visitor and a cheerful prostitute (played by his wife and the future Greek Culture Minister, Melina Mercouri) whose situation he sets out to change

in the early 1960s and establishing Greece as a favourite holiday destination, a jolly alternative to the rigid routines that holiday-makers are escaping from.

The intensity of the encounter between 'stiff upper lips' and the exotic Balkan is taken a step further in the second film, *Zorba the Greek*, a 1964 20th Century-Fox adaptation of the 1946 novel by Nikos Kazantzakis. Scripted and directed by Cypriot Michael Cacoyannis, the adaptation claimed to capture the main moments of the novel's narrative. The film is, nonetheless, a prime example of concessions to Hollywood standards in reiterating self-inflicted stereotypes. Cacoyannis' changes to Kazantzakis' literary source reveal the way the consensual self-exoticising works.

The narrator of the story is a British writer (Alan Bates) who, during a visit to Greece, comes across this incredible individual, the flamboyant and colourful Zorba (Anthony Quinn). Whatever Zorba does in the film (and he does a lot of wild and exotic things), it is always conveyed to the audience through the aloof reticence of the Briton. Many of the scenes between the two protagonists take place within a cinematic frame that features Zorba at its centre (dancing wildly, mimicking mischievously or delivering a showy speech), and Alan Bates in the corner, observing Zorba's overexcited behaviour with restraint.[3]

The numerous challenges presented by Zorba's non-standard moral judgment are supposed to provide a learning experience for the Briton and to give him a chance to re-evaluate his rigid attitudes. But it does not work this way. Instead, Bates remains the onlooker. The Briton is intrigued, but he is far from abandoning his own moral standards, which he 'sacrifices' only occasionally in order to 'adjust' to local ways when circumstances dictate. When he leaves, he is enriched by his exposure to the curious Balkan mores, but he remains essentially unchanged.

Many scenes in *Zorba the Greek* (1964) feature Zorba (Anthony Quinn) doing something wild centre screen while critically watched by the restrained Briton (a young Alan Bates, cast here against the wild type he will come to be associated with later in his career)

Zorba the Greek opens with a shot taken from a descending aeroplane. In the closing shot, the camera moves away, leaving the scene of action by ascending back into the air. The very arrival of the Briton seems to have animated Zorba, as his life before the appearance of the foreigner and after his departure is deemed irrelevant and is left out of the narrative: he only exists in relation to the Western protagonist. The only reference to Zorba's past in the film is made in order to explain his command of the English language – he mentions that he has been to the USA. In the novel, however, the language of the exchange is Greek, not English: Zorba has not been to the USA, he does not know English and it is the Briton, of mixed ethnic background, who speaks Greek. In the film, all explanations of why and how Zorba has become what he is are deleted: he only exists in the present tense. The novel, on the contrary, abounds with references to Zorba's past, which establish him as a rich and complex character. The film ends with the departure of the Westerner, at which point Zorba ceases to exist. The novel, however, features an epilogue, which tells us what happened to Zorba after he parted with the Briton.

The changes that Cacoyannis made when adapting for the screen are indicative of some of the basic premises of the voluntary self-exoticism which characterises many other works by Balkan authors meant for Western audiences: Balkan individuals are represented as flamboyant and excitingly dismissive of the restrictive norms of Western civilisation; their lives before and after their contact with the Western protagonist are irrelevant and are better left out; their existence is of importance only in relation to contact with the foreigner. It is in this way, for example, that the Greek character of Ben Kingsley in *Pascali's Island* (1988) appears out of the blue and approaches an Englishman who has just arrived on the island. It is a Berkeleian 'esse is percipi' situation, as these characters seem to exist only when a foreigner who needs their services comes to town.

If the local Greeks' lives are referred to in some way beyond the Westerner's presence, it is merely to confirm the Westerner's fears that they differ substantially from the act they put on in Westerner's presence. Such is the situation with Tom Conti's Greek protagonist in *Shirley Valentine* (1989): he manages to seduce the British holiday-maker, played by Pauline Collins, only after investing substantial time and effort, and he appears to be genuinely devoted to her. But soon after, when she returns unexpectedly to check on him, he is revealed to be nothing more than a philanderer, who will work equally hard next week to seduce the next Western single female tourist he happens to come across.[4]

The journey to the gloomy Balkans: Blood and bullets
Today, little has changed, and the travelogue narrative continues to enjoy a prominent presence in recent films about the troubled Balkan lands. Again the

brokerage of a Western narrator is needed to validate the story. In *Welcome to Sarajevo* and *Comanche Territory* the story evolves around Western journalists covering the Bosnian carnage.[5] In *Gamebag* it is two Italian hunters who witness the madness of ethnic hatred which sets father and daughter against each other. In Godard's *Forever Mozart* it is a group of Parisian intellectuals who set out to stage a Musset play in embattled Sarajevo, venture into the war zone and suffer at the hands of local thugs. In Predrag Antonijevic's *Savior* it is a Western mercenary fighting for the Serbs who witnesses the guilt of all sides in the conflict. Even *Gadjo Dilo/The Crazy Stranger* (1997), directed by Tony Gatlif, who usually manages to tell stories about his gypsy people without recourse to this narrative device, is structured around the journey of a young Frenchman who ends up in a Romanian gypsy settlement in his search for fervour and authenticity.

The list of films structured around the same plot – of well-balanced and presumably sane Westerners who venture into the Balkan realm of barbarity – is much longer. What is common to all these films is that their protagonists seem to be searching for the madness, longing to get some exposure to it. And they are rewarded, as the Balkan lands always provide the excitement that they have come looking for. The closer the films are to the action-adventure end of the narrative spectrum, the stronger the thrill that the protagonists are exposed to.

There are many other more recent examples of the specific structuring of the Balkan narrative in the tradition of the travelogue. However, I will concentrate on just a few films that repeatedly reveal this pattern. What is special about the next three films – the Romanian *O primavara de neuitat/An Unforgettable Summer* (1994), the Macedonian *Before the Rain* and the Greek *Ulysses' Gaze* – is that they are all feature films made by Balkan film-makers. Unlike the examples listed above, these are films of self-representation. Nonetheless, as we will see, they deploy the same narrative devices as the Western films about the Balkans, and make full use of the travelogue tradition and of the figure of the visiting Western protagonist.

Thus, the 'otherness' of the Balkans, which may have originated in the West, is gradually taken up and internalised by local directors who claim to represent the Balkans 'from within'. Despite wishing to unravel the intricate logic of Balkan tensions, in these three films the directors prefer to present the events from a foreigner's point of view (seen as the only possibly objective one), thus relegating the people whose lives they want to explain to the position of being watched (and judged) by strangers. The result is consenting self-exoticism: the practice of Balkan directors to depict their own cultures as compliant to the Western framework we discussed.

The story of the Romanian film *An Unforgettable Summer*, directed by veteran Lucian Pintilie, takes place near the Danube's delta, in the border region of Dobroudja. Populated by Romanians and Bulgarians, the area has continu-ally been the subject of territorial disputes, has changed hands in the past and is currently divided between the two countries. The film's events unravel in 1925, at a time when most of Dobroudja belongs to Romania. The protagonist is an officer's wife, Marie-Therese von Debretsy, the offspring of an impover-ished Austro-Hungarian noble family. She marries below her status and readily accompanies her husband to his new posting at this remote border outpost – a sign that shows she is ready to give up higher society for the sake of love and family unity.

But she is ready to go even further than that. Once stationed at the border, Marie-Therese displays a readiness to merge with the barren landscape, which she tries to poeticise whimsically. The grey overtones of the peasants' clothes supplement the impressionistic pastels of her fading expensive outfits.

Seemingly out of boredom, she grows compassionate for the members of the victimised local minority. Such sympathies, however, are ill-positioned against her position as an official's wife, which requires her to keep distance from the locals and not to take sides even when she witnesses injustice perpetrated by the authorities. Marie-Therese, however, refuses to play along and persists in her caring attitude, ignoring the warnings of her military acquaintances not to get too involved with the locals. As a result, the officers ostracise her.

The fragile union that develops between Marie-Therese and the oppressed Bulgarian peasants does not last long, however, neither does it have much weight. Her compassion can barely help the peasants; indeed, it only makes things worse. Soon Marie-Therese and her husband are forced to leave, shunned by the officers and disliked by the locals.

The choice of Kristin Scott-Thomas, cast by Pintilie for the role of Marie-Therese, is barely accidental. She is an actress who embodies refined Europeanness. Her very presence keeps the viewer interested in the plot, and the Balkan subject matter. This casting of Western actors is not an isolated case, but is characteristic of most of the Balkan films discussed here. For *Before the Rain*, director Milcho Manchevski cast French actor Gregoire Colin and British actress Katrin Cartlidge, once again faces familiar to viewers both in the West and the East. In a similar way, Greek Theo Angelopoulos regularly uses actors with an established European reputation – Jeanne Moreau and Marcello Mas-troianni in *To meteoro vima tou pelagrou/The Suspended Step of the Stork* (1991); Harvey Keitel and Erland Josephson in *Ulysses' Gaze*; Bruno Ganz in *Mia aiwniothta kai mia mera/Eternity and a Day* (1998). The presence of these familiar faces in a Balkan setting sends out a specific message: these are the actors who have inhabited the intellectual universe of directors such as Luchino Visconti, Ingmar Bergman, Federico Fellini, François Truffaut, Andrei Tarkovsky, Martin Scorsese, Jane Campion and Wim Wenders. They have been cast as apprehensive and sensitive people, and their appearance in films about the Balkans is meant to ensure they are unconditionally recognised as such by the audiences. Once such recognition has taken place, the problematic of the Balkan universe is more likely to be recognised as immediately pertinent to the European one.

The recent Balkan features of Greek Theo Angelopoulos also unfold in the travelogue narrative form: in *The Suspended Step of the Stork* it is a Westernised documentary film-maker who visits a refugee settlement on the Albanian border; and in *Ulysses' Gaze* it is a celebrated film-maker, who has returned to his native lands after thirty-five years in the West, and who now travels across the shattered Balkans on a pensive and melancholic journey.

This narrative form is so typical of Angelopoulos that it is even encoded in the basic morphology of his unique film vocabulary. In *Ulysses' Gaze*, the mostly hand-held camera of his cameraman, Yorgos Arvanitis, moves very slowly and is often positioned in such a way that it reveals actions taking place in two different semantic layers of the screen space. For example, a typical shot for Angelopoulos would involve a long and elaborate sequence in which a torso or a side close-up of the protagonist occupies one corner of the screen, overlooking whatever events develop. As a result, the events lose their objectivity and are actually constructed through the gaze of the onlooking protagonist. Thus, it is not only the plot (which has taken the narrative form of a travelogue) but also the basic components of the film language that ensure that the account of the Balkans is provided through the gaze of a stranger.

Our third example is *Before the Rain* by Milcho Manchevski, a Macedonian-born, American-educated director. His non-linear tale of today's Macedonia, filled with elaborate twists in time and space, is told through the gaze of a displaced native, Aleksandar, a cosmopolitan photographer, who returns from London to his native village after eighteen years of absence only to find that the ancient enmities are stronger than ever. Aleksandar comes from the civilised and rational West, and encounters a world taken over by ugly and violent intolerance. He does not want to take sides and makes an attempt to rise above the irrational rivalries, but in the end his worldly ideas of humanist reconciliation cost him his life – he is killed by his own people. In *Before the Rain* contemporary Macedonia is shown as a land governed by a medieval ethos, where tribal mores mercilessly destroy everyone who dares to stand up against the primitive mentality of an 'eye for an eye'. The film moves within a prescribed framework that mirrors the long-standing stereotype of the Balkans as an exotic and attractive people who are impossible to deal with. It continues the line of representing the Balkans as a mystic stronghold of stubborn and belligerent people, and asserts the existing Balkan trend of voluntary self-exoticism.

These examples suggest that Balkan film-makers prefer to depict their own cultures through the eyes of Westerners (or locals who have spent sufficient time in the West) and that travelogue style of narration is still prevalent in Balkan film-making. Ingenious imagery is offered, but the way it is used often just mirrors established stereotypes. At first glance, it seems that these films are pioneering the treatment of a non-traditional and difficult subject matter, but in fact they do little more than perpetuate and facilitate the Eurocentric gaze, both through their chosen narrative structure and in many of their basic textual elements.

The journey to the poor Balkans: Raki and bunkers

Lamerica (1994), Italian director Gianni Amelio's film set in Albania, is yet another Balkan travelogue. Again, the story is told from the point of view of a Western traveller. What is substantially different here, however, is that the direction of the movement, and thus the gaze of the narrator, which traditionally is positioned from West to South-East, changes at one point in the narrative and is redirected from South-East to West, as we see the situation from the 'inside'. With its change of viewing point, *Lamerica* challenges the established hierarchy which guarantees the Westerner an untouchably higher standing, and thus subverts the Balkan travelogue construct itself.

The subversion is achieved by taking the protagonist, the Italian Gino, from his initial position as Western onlooker, and throwing him into the ultimately deprived position of a local Albanian outcast.

Initially, Gino is the assistant to Fiore, a businessman who arrives in Tirana to establish a joint venture with the locals using an Italian government grant. A shady enterprise, its main objective is to collect the grant money and then rapidly go bankrupt, a deceit which Fiore has performed on numerous earlier occasions in Africa. Gino (Enrico Lo Verso) is a young Sicilian with little education but full of energy. He is eager to make it into business and thus ready to

Gianni Amelio's *Lamerica* (1994) subverts the established Balkan narrative by depriving the Italian protagonist Gino (Enrico Lo Verso) of his privileged Western standing and making him endure the unfavourable condition of an Albanian outcast

work devotedly under Fiore's guidance. He starts off as the typical Westerner, who goes to the Balkans with the intention of leaving as soon as possible. But the circumstances change, and he experiences a forced journey through the country, during which he undergoes several stages of loss which gradually change his position – from a superior foreigner in fashionable shades to a rugged Albanian sailing on a crowded ship to Italy.

Gino is sent into Albania to chase a dim-witted Albanian man who happens to be a crucial element in the registration of the enterprise. While driving east into the interior, he encounters endless columns of hitchhikers, hopeful emigrants who make their way to Albania's ports in the hope of sailing to the West. Soon after, when Gino has completed his mission, which has taken him to the heart of Albania, he has to turn round and drive back to the western shore of the country. This simple physical reversal proves a turning point in the narrative. Gino began this journey as the ultimate foreign traveller, a superior onlooker, who, until just a while ago, was moving in the opposite direction to all these desperate wannabe émigrés. A simple change in direction, however, makes Gino's destination the same as theirs, and from this point in the story they all move in one direction. This is the first step in Gino's 'downfall' – the change of direction is automatically a change in the way his 'gaze' is positioned.

The next reversal occurs when the tyres are stolen from his car. Left without a vehicle, he now has to use the same means of transport as the Albanians – crowded buses, crowded trucks, hitchhiking. Even though his own sense of superiority is still unshattered, Gino now has to literally rub shoulders with the Albanians, to feel their bodies, to be among them, although still not one of them. When the crowded bus is ambushed by policemen who want to prevent the Albanian men from reaching the port, Gino makes it through by uttering a key password: '*I am an Italian*'.

During the journey, Gino finds out that his boss's fake business venture has gone bust. Stripped of his position of a 'businessman', he feels almost as disinherited as the Albanians. The final blow, however, occurs in Tirana, where Gino is detained and thrown into a cell with other Albanians. By the next morning, he has been forced to trade his Western clothes for a tattered hand-knitted sweater. With his scruffy face, he looks like an Albanian now. His superior status has gone, along with his glossy Western appearance.

Gino is released, but the authorities refuse to return his Italian passport. He is now one of the crowd, wandering the streets and thinking of exactly the same thing as all Albanians around him – how to get himself to Italy. He has nothing at his disposal but the same limited means.

At the end of the film Gino boards a ship bound for Italy: among a thousand hopeful refugees from Albania, he is indistinguishable from any one of them, and thus identical; from an onlooker he has turned into one of those who were originally looked at. The camerawork stresses this reversal in his positioning. Initially Gino appeared in the foreground of many shots, standing proud of the surrounding greyness in his trendy dark-blue suit and shades. Gradually, his appearance became less contrasting, as he is shown among other people more often, thus questioning whether his superior Western looks were an attribute of his personality, or just a volatile shelter which swiftly crumbled as fortune changed.

The plea for admission: Journey back to Europe?

Some Albanian intellectuals perceived *Lamerica* as a hostile, damaging and harmful depiction of their country. Ismail Kadare, the Paris-based Albanian writer, led a vocal campaign against the film. According to him, Amelio maliciously chose to stress the impoverishment and to suppress any positive features in representing the country.

These critics certainly have a case. Albania is so close to Italy (it is 'in the heart of Europe'), just a few hours cruise on the blue waters of the Adriatic, and yet it is represented as a world that is centuries apart. The architectural forms dominating the desolate mountainous landscape are the paranoid, crumbling bunkers of Enver Hoxha and the graffiti-covered monuments of partisan battles. The hills are decorated with surreal ruins and 'cluttering thousands of concrete domes' (Fonseca, 1995, p. 76).[6] The only buildings that the camera explores in more detail are a monstrous plant in the centre of a former labour camp and a shoe factory, all dust and greyness. The people inhabiting these structures are either shadow-like disabled figures who wear rags and chase rats, or worn-out weary women dressed in grey or black. All look alike, and all look hungry. In the bars there is no food, only raki, and the closest thing to food you can see is an oxen's head that the innkeeper chops up with an axe. Wherever a car stops, flocks of noisy, raggedy children who pass the time squatting on street corners immediately surround it (they also inhabit *Zorba the Greek* and *Before the Rain*). Toothless Albanians drink 60 per cent proof raki and grin dimly. Loud stereos play North African rhythms, and Italian television entertainment plays to an all-male, wide-eyed audience in jammed rooms. In the rare instances when the protagonists happen to eat, they keep their hands in front of their mouths, as if to protect the rare experience of chewing.[7] An emaciated young man dies silently; he is bare-footed.

The critics, however, failed to see the real worth of *Lamerica* – its subversive power, its critique of the Western gaze of the Balkans. *Lamerica* is among the rare instances when the Western attitude is subtly problematised within a traditional narrative frame. While in most other cases, the Westerner is just an unquestioned measurement used against the backdrop of 'otherness', here the Westerner is turned into one of the 'others' and left to experience life their way.

Starting off as an observer, Gino ends as one of the observed. With this radical change in point of view, Amelio's film undermines traditionally unquestioned hierarchies and calls for legitimisation of the 'other's' point of view.

The images of underdevelopment ask the painful question: is this really Europe of the 1990s? Barren hills, poor peasant houses, women in black and scruffy, raggedy men? Somehow, it does not fit into the traditional mental image of Europe. Neither, for that matter, does it fit into the traditional mental image of a grey industrialised Eastern Europe. It does fit, however, into a newly carved corner of the mental map of Europe: the Balkans.

The paradox of geographical proximity and common historical background, on the one hand, and the implicit but rarely articulated exclusion from what is believed to be truly European, on the other, makes the Balkan type of marginality particularly interesting to investigate. If used in the Balkans, the concept of *Europe* is a comprehensive one, which includes them as well. If used in the West, however, the notion admits a Balkan element only as a neglected 'backyard', which one needs to maintain, albeit reluctantly, according to the minimal standards.[8]

Balkan intellectuals are faced with the difficult question of how to combat this exclusion: aware that their lands are geographically located in Europe, and yet feeling that somehow they are not a desirable partner within the European realm, they believe that their standing could improve if they made an effort to 're-enter Europe'.[9] In order for this re-entry to take place, they feel obliged to be apologetic, and they are prepared to mirror stereotypical representations of themselves as part of an admission bargain which they believe they can negotiate. This voluntary self-denigration takes various shapes, of which the self-inflicted exoticism easily discovered in cinema is just one manifestation. There are also other examples, some of which are more mundane than the ones we have discussed here – for example, the widespread practice of self-bashing when interviewed by Western journalists, or the eager acceptance of the allegations of primordialism. In a recent work, which continues the tradition established by Jovan Cvijić back in 1918, an expatriate Croat scholar offered an elaborate conceptual scheme which is supposed to replace the tribal image of the Balkan people with more refined concepts such as, among others, some peculiar 'habits of the Balkan heart', which would help the West to better understand the 'power-hungry tendencies' of the Balkan people, who quite often happen to be 'mountain-dwelling herdsmen' (Mestrović, 1993b, pp. 4, 56 and 57). Self-criticism of this type is actually meant to help the dialogue – turning to the West with such disarmingly honest and unflattering admissions about themselves, Balkan intellectuals secretly hope that the West will respond in a similar way, admitting its own wrongdoings. In fact, the only result of this voluntary self-bashing is that the issue of the Balkans' 'admissibility' to the superior *European* sphere becomes even more problematic and conditional.

Without realising it, numerous works of Balkan cinema contribute to the project of exclusion and 'Third-Worldisation'. With their articulated preference for 'authentic' indigenous imagery, with their meticulous attention to the traditional and the patriarchal elements of the cultures depicted, with their outspoken confirmation of the peculiar moral standards of the locals, with their willingness to 'legitimise' the Balkan narrative through use of the travelogue structure and the figure of the visitor from the West, the effect of these films is to emphasise difference. Once admitted, however, this difference becomes an argument against the presupposition of affinity, as the 'otherness' is readily accepted, and the desired negotiation of terms for re-entering the European realm cannot take place, as there are no grounds on which it could be negotiated.

No works in Balkan cinema can be deemed equivalent to the subversive masterpieces of Third Cinema, such as Ousmane Sembene's *La Noire de ... /Black Girl* (1966), Nelson Pereira dos Santos's *Como era gostoso o meu francês/How Tasty Was My Little Frenchman* (1971) or Carlos Diegues' *Xica da Silva* (1976), which effectively challenge the dependency on the benevolence of the Eurocentric worldview. The film-makers of Third Cinema had an alternative ideology to propose to counter the dominant Western model. They resisted it; they wanted to subvert it. All the Balkan film-makers seek, on the contrary, is to be admitted. But subversion and resistance do not grant admission. Consessions work better for them.

It would be a step too far to expect that the Balkan film-makers whose recent work was discussed here would engage in any sort of critical discourse aimed at 'unthinking' Eurocentrism, a project conceived by Ella Shohat and Robert Stam, who insisted that 'an awareness of the intellectually debilitating effects of the Eurocentric legacy is indispensable for comprehending not only contemporary media representations but even contemporary subjectivities' (Shohat and Stam, 1994, p. 1).

It is most likely, instead, that the Balkan intellectual discourse will continue moving within the established framework of concessionary self-denigration and lack of self-confidence. Balkan film-makers will most likely continue to think of themselves as devotedly belonging to Europe, even though they may doubt that *Europe* is as nurturing and sheltering as they would like it to be. Although they may begin to criticise some attitudes, this will only scratch the surface, and they will most likely fail to question radically the symbolic meanings of traditional narrative structures and representations. They would be reluctant to engage in subversion, as any deep questioning may lead to an alteration of 'the conceptual object itself'[10] (Bhabha, 1990, p. 31,: namely, belonging to the sphere of European. It seems more convenient to perpetuate the practice of consenting self-exoticism, which somehow seems to work better for them in times when dialogue is sought.

Notes

1. Examples include, but are not limited, to: *Balkan Journey* (Canada, Brenda Longfellow, 1996), *Pancrac Diary* (USA, David Galessic, 1994), *Urbicide: A Sarajevo Diary* (UK, Dom Rotheroe, 1994).
2. I use 'Greek' in quotation marks here, as neither of these films is truly Greek – *Never on Sunday* was written and directed by a Westerner; *Zorba the Greek* was produced by an American company (20th Century-Fox), starred British actors and by financial and other criteria is clearly an American film.
3. The casting of Alan Bates for the role of the restrained and reticent Briton is a particularly curious choice, considering the way Bates' own artistic reputation developed. If *Zorba the Greek* was remade today, Bates would be a likelier choice for the role of Zorba.
4. The same morally questionable but nonetheless intriguing sexual politics have been the subject of other films exploring the encounters of the Western with the Balkan. In Dušan Makavejev's *Montenegro* (1981), for example, an affluent but frigid American-born Swedish housewife ends up in a sleazy immigrant bar in Stockholm, where she is initiated into a range of wild and exciting Balkan sexual practices.
5. In another (now abandoned) Hollywood project, *Age of Aquarius* (USA, Phil A. Robinson), the protagonist (Harrison Ford) was also an aid worker who is sent to Sarajevo and becomes involved with a Bosnian woman.
6. Fonseca's *Bury Me Standing*, a book about the Eastern European Roma, received quite a lot of publicity, and is another example of a travelogue narrative, researched by the author in the course of several trips (during one of which she even 'lived' with an Albanian Roma family). Fonseca observantly notes a Third-Worldisation context in relation to the gypsies in Eastern Europe – a Romani ghetto is described as 'as black as India' (p. 123), and another one is called 'Bangladesh' (p. 118). At the moment of writing, the author is back in the West, and is presented in the short biographical note with the appropriate credentials, 'educated at Columbia University and Oxford University', and 'lives in London'.
7. Alexander Sokurov's characters in *The Lonely Human Voice* (1978), a classical cinematic treatment of hunger, eat in exactly the same way.
8. I should note, however, that there are Balkan film-makers who occasionally become quite critical of the questionable qualification of the Balkans as Europe's backyard. Such a critical stance is found particularly in the films that address the Yugoslav crisis. As many in the Balkans believe that the West has done very little in response to their plight, a representation of this alleged

indifference is to be found, for example, in the portrayal of UN deployments in former Yugoslavia. In *Ulysses' Gaze* the presence of UNPROFOR's blue helmets in Sarajevo is shadow-like and absurd. In *Before the Rain* white UNPROFOR vehicles pass by, as if aliens have landed unexpectedly. In Srdjan Dragojevic's *Pretty Village, Pretty Flame* (1996) the Chetniks make fun of the UN soldiers, while in Emir Kusturica's *Underground* (1995) it is even implied that the UN forces are the main facilitator of illegal arms' smuggling.

9. I speak of 're-entering Europe' and not 'entering', as having legitimately belonged to the European cultural sphere until their takeover by the Ottomans, circumstances forcibly removed them from the development that took place in the rest of Europe, is a major trope of Balkan national ideologies. In the Balkans, the project of modernisation is conceptualised as one of 'return'.

10. 'To study the nation through its narrative address does not merely draw attention to its language and rhetoric: it also attempts to alter the conceptual object itself.' (From the preface to *Nation and Narration.*)

Chapter 4
Narrative and Putative History

Back in 1992 two media scholars, Canadian Gina Stoiciu and Israeli Dov Shinar, highlighted a phenomenon which they called a 'reality-construction' and which they had encountered when analysing the Western media coverage of the 1989 Romanian revolution. It consisted in privileging dramatic reports which were making it into the news without the appropriate verification, even when these reports contradicted the information supplied by stringers. A 'reversal of roles' seemed to have taken place in the relationship between those reporting from the spot and the newsroom editors. Traditionally, it was the newsroom desk that would cool down the enthusiasm of reporters in the field. In the Romanian case, however, this relationship had been turned around: the reports filed by the correspondents were phrased more carefully, while the imaginative interpretation was supplied by the newsroom, and there had been numerous cases of delay or omission of material that did not fit the editors' expectations.[1] As long as they fitted under the general heading of massacres and of evil Securitate forces plotting nasty revenges on civilians, unverified rumours were treated as favourably as the reports filed by the agencies' own correspondents. There were even cases when vampire fantasies were offered instead of news: the French first channel, for example, had run an item that stated that Ceauşescu was suffering from leukaemia and needed monthly blood transfusions, and that lately corpses of bloodless young men had been discovered in a Carpathian forest (Stoiciu and Shinar, 1992, p. 60).

Why was this happening, wondered Stoiciu and Shinar. In their view, it was a case of voluntary self-deception regarding the nature and the scope of the events, bordering on what they called newscasters' 'self-manipulation', and part of the overall newsdesk euphoria about the Eastern European revolutions that had led editors into a situation, where

> the realities they constructed were perceived and encoded by them even before correspondents in the field started to file their stories. These realities were constructed through the use of materials obtained from Eastern European sources that fitted the desk editors' psychological pre-dispositions of drama and of bloody tragedy. (ibid., p. 59)

But what about the professionalism of Western editorial desks? Unless they were doing it willingly, these experienced news editors could not possibly be fooled by distorted and blown-up information that clearly favoured some interested parties in Romania. And then, why all the stress on the violence? The fall of the Berlin Wall and the recent events in Prague had certainly created euphoria, but the reporting had all along stressed the 'velvet' style with which this revolution had opposed the forces of the dark. How come the editors' 'psychological pre-dispositions of drama and of bloody tragedy' only emerged when it came to Romania?

One of the possible answers (and my preferred one) is that the 'drama' and 'bloody tragedy' mindset is an essential part of the general Balkan narrative of which Romania is a part. After ten years of Balkan conflict, albeit concentrated in former Yugoslavia, we have seen the 'psychological pre-disposition' to discover 'bloody tragedy' and 'drama' re-enacted again and again. Be it Romania, Yugoslavia, Albania or Bulgaria, the narrative on the Balkans is of an area doomed to cyclical conflict, an area which can never escape the shadow of its own history.[2]

In this chapter I will discuss some of the ways in which the negative Balkan narrative was sustained, sometimes consciously but most frequently unacknowledged, in documentary and feature film. First, I will identify how elements of the past were used selectively to maintain a Balkan narrative of violent cycles in history. Often seen as 'first drafts of history', journalistic books and documentaries contributed the most to creating and maintaining this narrative. By focusing on the films, I will identify several trends: the articulate preference for using 'historical evidence' in interpreting the present; the frequent use of such 'lessons of history' to justify speculative coverage of the region; the proliferation of 'instant history' which, serving day-to-day news production needs, impulsively substantiated the sound-bite reporting on current affairs with selective references to past events. All the problematic uses of 'history' come down to the journalistic dominance (as opposed to scholarly expertise) over the Balkan discourse: the persistent discovery and reiteration of 'cycles' of violence; the overwhelming neglect of economic and current political factors and their substitution with 'historicised' tropes like 'clash of civilisations' and 'ancient enmities' as explanations for the conflict; and the role of the narrative of violent conflict, now supported by the newly construed historical evidence, in shaping popular and ultimately scholarly perceptions of the Balkans.

Second, I will show how the Balkan discourse, dominated by speculation based on these 'first drafts of history' found in the areas of journalism, documentary and even fiction film-making, has grown into a continuous conjecture of impending war in Macedonia. In this light, I will discuss the making and reception of the acclaimed Macedonian film, *Before the Rain*, trying to answer the question of whether the film was yet another putative prediction of Balkan trouble, or a cautionary fable of a possible future meant to warn and prevent.

With this discussion I hope to show how the 'Balkan narrative', nourished by the continuing construction of putative history, helped to re-establish the 'Balkan imaginary' as a dark and primitive periphery doomed to eternal trouble. As we have seen, in 1989 a number of newsdesk editors had sacrificed sober field reports on Romania for an intriguing vampire story and exaggerated rumours. Throughout the 1990s, the Balkan imaginary was sustained in a similar way, by forfeiting the earnest analysis of economic and political factors for a narrative that privileged the explanatory power of fables about bullheaded people beset by historical enmities and mystical cycles of violence.

Teleology of Conflict: The Traps of 'Instant History'

In discussing historical film as a corrective to 'real history', Robert Rosenstone (1995b, p. 6) distinguishes two main approaches. The explicit approach is dictated by the political and social context in which the film is made, while the implicit one pursues the creation of a cinematic text, which is then judged by historical criteria. Due to the narrative character of the medium of film, Rosenstone underlines, history is inevitably represented as a story with a beginning, middle and an end. The story, however, depends on the ending that has been chosen, for it is the ending that determines what is used in the beginning and in the middle. If the ending is one of bloody conflict, the beginning and the middle are likely to match the bloody narrative and to contain elements that highlight the seeds of forthcoming strife. If the story ends in peace, it is more likely that other elements, hinting at forthcoming peace, become the main points of the narrative.

When we apply this approach to international films about the Balkans, we would immediately classify them as following the explicit approach: most of them were made in response to immediate concerns about the conflict in the 1990s. In most of them, the ending of the story is one of violent conflict, thus determining the choice of material that is employed in the middle and at the opening.

Likewise, most of today's historical writing on the Balkans is done teleologically, seeking to explain the current state of things, and in particular, the 'bloody demise' of Yugoslavia (Lampe, 1996) by reference to past conflicts.[3] The past decade witnessed a sudden burgeoning of historical writings on South-East Europe, until recently an obscure branch in historical research. This writing flourished with the conflict in the Balkans, and its proliferation has been nicknamed, quite appropriately, 'instant history' (Stokes *et al.*, 1996).

Finding the roots of today's conflict is also the driving force behind the majority of Balkan-themed documentaries, which makes the undertaking teleological by default. Once there is 'fire', all preceding events are likely to be interpreted as *Predictions of Fire*, as in the title of Michael Benson's documentary on the Slovenian rock group Laibach and NSK. Once there is 'death', all preceding events are suitably interpreted as leading to the death, as in the title of *Yugoslavia: Death of a Nation*. The making of such films is premised on the belief that there is a direct causal link between the present-day state of affairs and concrete past events. The question is: which events precisely? In such interpretative endeavours, one is compelled to make provisional choices about which events from the past fall in line best with the later developments, and it is these choices that then become the foundations of 'first drafts of history'. It is the degree to which past events fit the explanatory needs of the present that matters the most in such a selection process, and the reconstruction can easily turn into manipulation. That it is not about history but about the use of historical remembrance is a distinction which is rarely explicitly acknowledged. Or, as Michael Ignatieff puts it: 'It is not how the past dictates to the present but how the present manipulates the past that is decisive in the Balkans' (Ignatieff, 1993, p. 21).

Catering to the explanatory needs of the moment, many documentaries end up as nothing more than projects of the 'instant history' type. Their teleological approach to history becomes the decisive factor in decisions as to which images will be recycled for use in the reconstitution of the historical backdrop to today's events, and which ones will be laid to rest. An American documentary, *Yugoslavia: Origins of a War* (1992), tells the story from the point of view of Slovenia's struggle for independence, and suggests a historical ground for the rise of a civilised independent Slovenia in contrast to the barbarian rest of Yugoslavia. Another documentary, entitled *From Yugoslavia to Bosnia* (1993), is a similar account of what led to the Bosnian crisis, but this time narrated from the point of view of Croatia's struggle for independence. Numerous Serbian-made documentaries go as far back as the Battle of Kosovo to explain current events. The teleological approach of many documentaries about the Bosnian war led Balkan expert Susan Woodward to describe them as 'ahistorical' narratives, which 'seem almost obsessed with identifying these conflicts as historical' but in fact remain either 'consumedly presentist in relation to the author's own personal experiences and network of acquaintances' or simply and speculatively 'draw direct inferences about current behaviors from life centuries ago' (Woodward, 1997, p. 1).

The construction of a voice-over commentary is easy, but things become more complicated when it comes to supplying supporting images. One can make statements, for example, about the reawakening of 'ancient enmities', but what is the appropriate image to go with it? One way has been to use clips from Balkan feature films in documentaries. For the purpose of authenticating the interpretation that is offered, these dramatised representations have been used as documents testifying to the historical factors influencing today's outcomes. That it is about feature clips and not documentary footage does not seem to make much difference. Scenes of the official Yugoslav feature production *Boj na Kosovu/Battle of Kosovo* (1989), depicting a dramatic and violent clash between Ottoman and Slav forces at the famous battlefield, were used, for example, by the British Channel 4 news as a background image for their daily piece-to-camera reports on the Kosovo crisis in 1998, thus providing a clash-of-civilisations visual reference, even though such an interpretation was not directly present in the commentary. While identifying the mythology of the Kosovo battle as one of the leading pillars of Serbian nationalist propaganda and then renouncing it, the visual referencing was building on the imagery produced by this same Serbian propaganda.

Even the absorbing documentary series, *Yugoslavia: Death of a Nation*, an authoritative international co-production, in which the story is structured around the 1987 rise of Milošević to political leadership, is not immune to selectivity dictated by the teleology of conflict. The lavishly financed documentary (and the accompanying book by Laura Silber and Allan Little, published in the same year) tells the story through well-selected footage, and features numerous interviews with various parties involved in the conflict. It puts together a convincing account of how the recent tensions mounted, and of the claims, the misunderstandings and the reactions of the main actors. Although historians questioned some of the narrative choices, the overall view was that the book and the documentary had granted all sides the opportunity to speak, thus making the bias negligible and remaining an 'accessible guide to the immediate causes and the detailed course of the wars' (Stokes *et al.*, 1996, p. 147). However, Susan Woodward argued that the seemingly minor inaccuracies were accountable for the most serious troubles.[4] She criticised the film, as well as a whole group of other documentaries and journalistic writing, for taking nationalism out of its concrete politico-economic context, for misunderstanding and misreporting the blanket-labelled 'Titoist period' and its immediate aftermath, and for selectively paying attention to nationalist tendencies and outcomes. But the causes of nationalism, she claimed, could never be correctly identified if they were only explained by reference to incidents of 'rising nationalism' in the past. By not making the effort to identify the roots of nationalism in the concrete changes in domestic economic powers of the republics, in the changes demanded by the International Monetary Fund and in the profound impact that economic reforms had had on employment and income practices during the 1980s – all reasons that led to a rebellion against uneven redistribution across the Yugoslav republics – the real factor behind the rise of nationalism remained unidentified.[5]

Films made at a later date, when the story had developed in one of many possible ways and a quick explanation was needed by reference to a simple causal link with the past, brought into consideration facts and footage that had earlier been deemed useless, the complex picture of the 'past' thus flexibly adjusting to the changing 'telos'. The footage of earlier unrest in Kosovo, for example, was only occasionally used until 1998.

But does not the persistent reference to past conflicts make the new ones look inevitable, as though they have just been waiting to emerge? Has not this body of works resulted in the perception of war no longer as an aberration but as a norm for the Balkans?

Projecting Trouble on Macedonia

These questions become particularly important in regard to a country like Macedonia, where the trouble is not an actual one but only a projection. Since the early 1990s, Macedonia was extensively discussed in the scenarios of journalists and political analysts as the real 'powder keg', from where uncontrollable violence could spill over into a conflict that would bring the neighbouring countries into the war as well. Presumptuous freelancers, who travelled to this new republic in the south-east of former Yugoslavia in search of stories, could not help expressing surprise at the peaceful and even sleepy atmosphere they found there, which they could only interpret as deceptive. In addition, there was the long record of violence and terrorism associated with the innumerable Macedonian uprisings, conspiracies, kidnappings and other violent disputes. In anticipation of a new wave of violence, preventive peacekeeping units were stationed in Macedonia in 1993.

Some Western-made documentaries on Macedonia made the putative speculation about forthcoming conflict their selling point. The text displayed on the cover of a documentary called *What about Macedonia?* (1994), for example, tells us that the reason for making the film was fear 'that the ethnic bloodshed and human rights violations now taking place in neighbouring Bosnia and Croatia may spread to Macedonia and lead to a new world war'. According to the Ikarus/First Run promotional materials of another documentary, suggestively entitled *Macedonia: The Next Bosnia?* (1995), the film sets out to explore the present-day state of affairs in the country with the conviction that 'Macedonia is set to follow the disastrous path of Bosnia, and that civil war in Macedonia would almost certainly embroil neighbouring countries'. The film contains 'secretly' shot footage of ethnic tensions, interpreted as a 'badly kept secret'. In the film, director Julian Chomet uses footage of empty restaurants and hotels in the tourist region around Lake Okhrid, shot out of season, to imply that the tourist industry in Macedonia is in decline because of the impending trouble. A sequence of a semi-destroyed building is supposed to show the devastation that has befallen the economy (the shots are, in fact, of the old Skopje train station, torn in half by the devastating earthquake of 1963 and left standing as a monument to the disaster).[6] Thinking of Macedonia in the framework of trouble, conflict and war, which was set about a decade earlier, was sustained throughout the 1990s in commentaries of the type. 'Of course, war in Macedonia would be nothing new' (R.Cohen, *The New York Times*, 1995).

In 2000, the tensions are still contained and the apocalypse has not yet happened. Instead, the country somehow manages to maintain a good record in spite of all the apocalyptic predictions, and to survive the crisis of 1999 when it had to accept an unprecedented number of refugees from Kosovo. Nonetheless, most of the commentary on Macedonia in the West is an anticipatory one – if there isn't a war yet, it is just around the corner.

Like other Balkan specialists, Macedonian scholars have tried to rebuff this coverage of the country as a putative 'powder keg'. Here is what a Macedonian media scholar, Dona Kolar-Panov, has to say about it:

> Not only is international expertise on the country limited, but it is also derived from perceptions of its instability generated by its proximity to the war, its ethnic composition and the plethora of stories initially of a 'first Bosnia, next Macedonia' type, and more lately of a 'first Kosovo, next Macedonia' type as the continuing conflict between Albanians and Serbs is assumed to have similar consequences for Macedonia. These putative predictions continue to be made despite the involvement of the Albanian party in the coalition government, the number of state ministers and deputy ministers of Albanian extraction, the existence of affirmative action policies, and the careful attention paid to balancing Albanian and ethnic Macedonian peoples in government posts.
>
> (Kolar-Panov, 1999, p. 39)

Such commentaries, however, have rarely made it to the mainstream press and broadcast media. Only specialised publications and independently made documentaries give them a tribune, 'for the record'. Thus, the critical views remain locked in the confine of alternative opinions, never to become determinative ones.

Before the Rain

It is in the light of this putative reporting on Macedonia as a land of impending trouble that I would like to discuss *Before the Rain*, a beautiful and absorbing film which won the Golden Lion Award at the Venice Film Festival, was then widely distributed across Europe and North America, and which came to be seen as one of the most insightful cinematic documents about Yugoslavia's breakup. The main focus of my investigation is how this film, set in the present and intended as a discussion about intolerance in principle, came to be seen as one that prophesied future Balkan troubles. My answer is – because, even if the film carried a different message and was intended to be nothing more than a 'cautionary fable' (Friedman, 2000, p. 135), it could not be perceived and interpreted independently from the overwhelming coverage of Macedonia as a land bound for trouble.

To what extent this coverage had influenced the film's creator, writer and director Milcho Manchevski is one of the questions that will cast light on the more general issue of the film's reception. The answer is found in Manchevski's own testimony. The Macedonian-born, American-educated director revisited his native country in the early 1990s, after years of absence. He experienced the atmosphere of the early post-Yugoslav years as pervasively tense; everything seemed to be overtaken by a sensation that something enormous and fearsome was about to strike. This feeling was compounded by 'the reports from other parts of Yugoslavia – which I mainly read in *The New York Times* before and after my one-month trip home'. The combination of personal encounters and background readings 'created an impression of something bad about to happen. It was a matter of feeling rather than rational analysis' (Manchevski, 2000, p. 129).

The feeling of impending trouble was combined with yet another feeling, the painful but exciting foreboding of the birth of something new. Manchevski resolved to make a movie about this moment of uncertainty, to supply images and sounds, and to communicate to others the twofold apprehension that he experienced himself. But the film was not meant to comment on Macedonia, as Manchevski felt he simply did not know enough about the real situation there. The film was about violence and intolerance in principle:

> I didn't want the film to comment on any event or events happening right now. You see, I don't know enough about the war. I haven't lived there for years. I wanted rather for my story to be pulled out of those events in its style, music, and in its content, too ... What is important is that I do not mean my film to be taken as a documentary of actual events.[7]

Back in New York, Manchevski wrote a six-page outline for the film, and a year later he was lucky enough to secure the support of British Screen for the project. The British financial commitment was enhanced by French financing, and, last but not least, the new Macedonian ministry of culture committed to the project. The people who gathered to work on the film were as cosmopolitan as they come, starting with writer and director Manchevski himself.[8] Shooting took place at a variety of locations across Macedonia in 1993, and the film was finished and released in 1994. Due to the European support for the project and the familiarity of the director with the mechanics of North American distribution, unlike other Macedonian films that rarely make it beyond the festival circuit, *Before the Rain* was widely distributed in the West, theatrically and on video. It is one of the few 'Balkan' films that are seen internationally, and certainly the only Macedonian one. If asked about Macedonia, Western viewers are likely to have exclusive images from this film flashing in their minds, as they simply have never seen another one from the region.

Before the Rain's narrative is non-linear, and structured around three slightly overlapping parts, entitled respectively 'Words', 'Faces', and 'Pictures'. What is particularly fascinating about the narrative is that those elements of the story that overlap are located in such relation to each other that even at a later point they never add up to a coherent linear narrative. Some events must have happened earlier than others, which we know actually happened before them, and so on. As this is about minor discrepancies which do not stand in the way of putting the general story together, the disjunctures actually create the effect of fascinating uncertainty, leaving a nice feeling of ambiguity, and enhanced by the sentence which is repeated several times in the film – 'the circle is never round'.

The first part, 'Words', is set at an Orthodox monastery in Macedonia. An Albanian girl, Zamira, is found by a young monk, Kiril, hiding in his cell. She cannot speak Macedonian, and Kiril himself has taken the vow of silence. But even without talking to her, Kiril immediately knows that this is the girl sought by a bunch of local rogues who claim she killed their brother. Kiril gives Zamira temporary shelter. They quickly become close, and the next night leave the monastery together. Their aim is to reach London, where Kiril's uncle may be able to help them. But as the day dawns, they are apprehended by the hostile members of Zamira's family, who try to separate her from Kiril. When Zamira attempts to escape, her brother kills her.

The second story, 'Faces', takes place in London, and is inhabited by different people with other concerns. Anne, a layout editor at a news agency, has had an affair with Aleksandar, a world-weary acclaimed news photographer, but she is now hesitant to go on. Aleksandar, a Macedonian cosmopolitan expatriate, has just returned from an assignment in Bosnia, and is deeply disturbed by an experience he lived through while there. He feels he needs to go to Macedonia immediately, and offers Anne the chance to join him on a trip to his native country. Anne refuses. Aleksandar abruptly leaves before Anne has shared with him the preoccupations which keep her behind. She is pregnant, and has to stay in London to confront her estranged husband about a divorce. Later that evening, Anne meets the husband at a restaurant. Their difficult conversation is brutally interrupted by an argument between a waiter and a noisy customer, both swearing loudly in Serbian. The quarrel leads to a shoot-out, in which the husband is absurdly killed, leaving Anne shattered and distraught.

It is only in the third part of the film, 'Pictures', that the first two story lines come together. Aleksandar returns to his native village in Macedonia, a place he had left eighteen years earlier. Although he is welcomed by members of his extended family, he soon learns that the village, once a peaceful haven where Albanians and Macedonians lived together, is now divided along ethnic and religious lines, and that the atmosphere is one of silent hatred and self-imposed segregation. Aleksandar crosses the check-point into the Albanian quarter to visit an old flame, Hana. As he comes from abroad, he is treated with respect, but it is made clear that his demonstrated neglect to the newly established ethnic divisions is seen as an exception and will not be tolerated on a regular basis.

Only now do we realise that Hana is the mother of Zamira, the girl who had escaped to the monastery, and that Aleksandar is the London uncle whose help the young monk Kiril was hoping to enlist. We also learn the details of the shattering experience that Aleksandar lived through while in Bosnia: while taking pictures of detained men, one of their guardians had singled out a prisoner and promptly killed him in front of the camera, just for the sake of supplying Aleksandar with sensational and newsworthy material. Aware of the explosive news value of the photographs, Aleksandar also realises that if it had not been for him, the killing would not have happened. Even if not carried out by his camera, it was for the camera that the murder took place.

On his return to Macedonia, Aleksander is soon to learn that where Albanians and Slavs once lived together, now the atmosphere is one of silent hatred and self-imposed segregation (*Pred dozhdot/Before the Rain*, 1994)

Aleksandar feels complacent. It is this shattering moral experience that has brought him back home, determined to do whatever he can to put an end to the intolerance. And what is he confronted with here? Everywhere he sees the signs of this same intolerance, still in an early phase, but equally implacable. But he already knows what its damaging consequences will be. Now it is about a divided village, inhabited by people who refuse to talk to each other; later on it will be about strife and war, and about meaningless and indiscriminate killing.

And everything Aleksandar encounters here confirms his worst fear. One of his relatives is stabbed with a pitchfork. It seems he sexually violated Zamira, who retaliated by stabbing him. The family members pursue the Albanian girl, determined to take vengeance. Hana, Zamira's mother, secretly comes to Aleksandar, pleading for his help. Aleksandar reacts quickly and manages to find the girl. But as he is securing Zamira's escape to the nearby monastery, he is caught by members of his family, in whose eyes he has become a traitor, and is shot.

The movie depicts the growing hostility between Albanians and Macedonians in a region with a mixed population. At the end of the twentieth century, the principle of an eye for an eye still prevails here. Time has stopped. There is an intense atmosphere – mystic Orthodox Christianity, chants, black robes, humid monastery cells, candlelight among the crumbling frescoes of hollow-cheeked saints, old houses, nostalgia, the smell of homecoming – all permeated with the scent of stalking danger. The story develops against a magic backdrop that pulls together a deep starry sky, the blue waters of Lake Okhrid and the tiled roofs of Macedonia – a composed and complex image. And a touch of magical realism evokes impasse and decay: golden tobacco strings dry on the cracked walls, there are no cars on the stone-paved streets. Only the state-of-the-art automatic weapons in the hands of local scoundrels remind us that it is a present-day situation.

And yet it is all so beautiful – the intense colour of the sky over the barren hills, the wind over the lake, the little chapel nestled on the shore, the large drops of warm rain – as the camera's gaze glides across the landscape to the accompaniment of prolonged music. And the enchanting ambiguity about the sequence of events, which do not quite come together in a straightforward time frame, leaves the viewer with a slightly dizzy feeling of open-endedness that supplants the confining circularity. The circle is not exactly round. We know that some events in the film could not have happened when they did. But as the narrative comes together fairly coherently, the discrepancies become part of an intoxicating and dazzling riddle that is better left unresolved. To overcome the disjunctive feeling the viewer turns the circular motion into a cyclical one by applying 'a carefully designed quirk in the chronology' (Manchevski, 2000, p. 129).[9]

Ultimately, it is the third part of the film which brings the story together and gives the film its meaning, thus making Aleksandar's experiences the focal point of the whole story. He returns to Macedonia haunted by the memory of his own ordeal in 'taking sides'. He has witnessed the death of an innocent man; but it is not just about witnessing – it was a death which he inflicted, albeit inadvertently. Aleksandar has lost his peace of mind and keeps repeating remorsefully: 'I took sides, I killed.' So when he comes back to Macedonia, it is not just for a visit; he returns armed with a superior consciousness of the devastation that rages nearby. He comes prepared to take sides against his own people, if needed, determined to counter the growing intolerance. What he finds is not encouraging – the old enmities have grown stronger than ever. Soon, even he will perish in the impending turmoil.

In comparison with the local people, Aleksandar belongs to a higher order, as he is in possession of a superior knowledge: he is aware of the devastating consequences of their behaviour, of the sweeping destruction into which their petty belligerence can lead them. They are inferior to him, not because they cannot know what he knows, but because they do not want to know. They would ask him for advice, but refuse to accept the wisdom he offers.

Aleksandar, the weary expatriate, represents the West. He could be welcome back home only if he chooses to turn his back on the West and become one of them; as a Westerner he is rejected. Aleksandar represents modernity, but he is killed.[10] By stubbornly rejecting him, his murderers make it clear that they will not accept the solutions offered by the West. His destruction is their symbolic denial of reason, their rejection of modernity.

Upon its release, *Before the Rain* became one of the most celebrated films to emerge from the Balkans. Many Western viewers responded to the film with straightforward admiration. To them, I was told, the film was of 'educational' value: only now could they grasp the deep roots and the absurd logic of the Balkan conflict. It was also a prophecy of things to come: as they knew from the media, the countdown had already started, slowly but surely heralding an inescapable bloody conflict. Had a conflict erupted in Macedonia at the time, it would have confirmed the image of the region and its people that Western audiences had seen in the film.

My own reaction to the film was not as clear-cut. The atmosphere and style of *Before the Rain* were fascinating, but still, something was wrong. As an expatriate concerned with the impending trouble in the Balkans, I just could not take the fatalism at face value. Other people, likewise concerned with the Balkans, reacted to the film in a similar way: they were 'deeply moved and impressed, but also deeply disturbed', as they quickly realised that Western audiences would probably interpret the film 'as a kind of documentary about the Yugoslav wars of succession that were then still being fought rather than as a cautionary fable set in Macedonia' (Friedman, 2000, p. 135).

To this day, a number of questions about the film's intended and actual reception remain open. What was the intended message of the film? Was the film an educational glimpse into the 'real' state of Macedonian affairs and a tool to understanding the logic of ethnic strife as the perennial motor of the country's history?[11] Or was the film a 'cautionary fable', a new kind of historical film, which predicts a grim future in order to warn against it? And if so, was the film read as intended? Was not *Before the Rain* simply translating the media reports of impending trouble in Macedonia into images and stories of a beautiful but tormented land, where the atmosphere is suffused with premonitions of trouble?[12]

Many critics read it as a film about tensions and taking sides in the Balkans. In *Before the Rain*, Macedonia was depicted as a medieval-feudal culture divided into the hostile ethnic-religious camps of Muslim Albanians and Orthodox Macedonians, where everyone is killed by their own people and from where violence spreads as far as a quiet London restaurant. According to *Variety*'s Deborah Young, Manchevski was presenting ethnic hatred as 'endemic to the region' (Young, 1994, p. 78), while for *The New York Times*' Roger Cohen, the film was undoubtedly conveying 'a haunting evocation of a Macedonian society on the verge of final fracture'(Cohen, 1995, sect. 2, p. 1). *Before the Rain* supplied fictional narrative and images to a story which historians had tackled in hefty volumes and journalists had already 'reported' on so many times. The director himself claimed that his film was not about Macedonia: 'The story was inspired by events unfolding in Yugoslavia, but it was *not about* them. It was about people in any country who stand in front of large events that are about to engulf them' (Manchevski, 2000, p. 130).

But only some viewers read the film as a 'cautionary fable set in Macedonia'; most of them just took it literally, as a film about Macedonia. Even when perceived as an allegory, *Before the Rain* had its concrete location in historical time and space: namely, the 1990s, the time of Yugoslavia's breakup, in the Balkans. The same literal reading was given just a couple of years later to another film that also wanted to speak about intolerance at large rather than a particular community: Russian Sergei Bodrov's *Prisoner of the Mountains* (1996) neither named the country where it was set, nor defined the historical period. Nonetheless, it was widely perceived and interpreted as a film about the Chechen war.

Before the Rain's apprehension of a possibly grim future led Robert Rosenstone to claim that Manchevski had created a new category: although not a strictly historical film, *Before the Rain* had addressed historical concerns by pointing to the 'history of what has not yet happened'. It was a conditional projection, a 'history of the future', which was meant 'to warn against that future in order to prevent it from happening' (Manchevski, 2000, p. 191).

The ultimate answers in regard to *Before the Rain* are also to be found in the future: if peace and goodwill prevail in Macedonia, it may well be that *Before the Rain* has accomplished the sublime mission which was attributed to it, namely to soothe the conflict and prevent it from reaching an explosive stage. If a violent conflict in Macedonia comes about, however, the film will go down in history as a grim and fatalistic prophecy.

For many Western viewers, *Before the Rain* merely confirmed a seemingly unstoppable cycle of events. The picture effectively contributed to the perception of Macedonia as a deceptively quiet but potentially explosive powder keg. Its message was widely perceived as a fatalist one: nothing can be done to stop these people from destroying themselves, to help the Balkan 'other' solve their own problems. But seeing grim outcomes where no fatalism was meant, Victor Friedman argues, was 'not a failure of the film but of the gaze' (Friedman, 2000, p. 143). I think he is right. Once again it concerns the 'psychological predisposition' that we encountered at the opening of this chapter to see 'drama' and 'bloody tragedy' everywhere. It seems it is about bringing it all together under the general Balkan narrative, one that evolved around 'drama' and 'bloody tragedy', and around history that endlessly repeats itself.

Notes

1. Many of the reports of massacres in Timisoara, Stoiciu and Shinar noted, were aired without awaiting confirmation from the reporters stationed there, thus creating 'the impressions that crews in the field sometimes lagged behind their headquarters desks'. A story entitled 'I Saw Nothing in Timisoara' by a veteran reporter of Third World wars and revolutions was shelved in the editorial room (Stoiciu and Shinar, 1992, p. 60).

2. In order to investigate this phenomenon in depth, one would need to rely on a confluence of two critical traditions – cultural studies should come together with this part of media studies that analyses the mechanics of news production. It is a task which is beyond the scope of my current undertaking.

3. The teleologism of historical writing is certainly not endemic to the histories of the Balkans. There is a degree of arbitrariness in every logical operation that links cause and effect in history, a problem which is the foundation of the sceptic view of historical reconstruction, a line of thinking that can be traced back to Aristotle and Hume, and which has had its main representative in the work of Richard Collingwood.

4. Woodward claimed that in *Yugoslavia: The Death of a Nation*, 'facts that did not fit the narrative are frequently abused, and behaviors that are quite

similar in different parts of the country are recorded with quite different sympathies' (Woodward, 1997, p. 3).

5. All these aspects are analysed in detail in Woodward's own *Balkan Tragedy* (1995), a book which has enjoyed the acclaim of the scholarly community. Her analysis of the international economic and political factors of the last two decades that led to the grave conflicts around the breakup of Yugoslavia remains the most serious and systematic one published to date.

6. I am indebted to Victor Friedman for some of these observations.

7. Quoted in Horton, Andy. 'Oscar-nominated "Rain" to screen at Tulane,' *The Times-Picayune* (New Orleans, LA), 22 February 1995, p. E5.

8. Had the director depended solely on domestic finance and subsidies, I doubt that such film could be made in Macedonia. The Paris-based producer, Cédomir Kolar, is of Yugoslav background and has since worked on co-productions with Burkina Faso, Kyrgyzstan and on an acclaimed Holocaust feature directed by a Romanian (Radu Mihaileanu's *Train of Life*, 1998). The cinematographer Manuel Terán was responsible for the dynamically shot AIDS biopic *Savage Nights* (1992). Other crew members came from South Africa, the UK, Bulgaria and the former Yugoslav republics.

9. Manchevski's non-linear tale appeared at the time when Tarantino's *Pulp Fiction*, another non-linear film, was occupying the minds of wider audiences. But while all elements of Tarantino's jigsaw puzzle added up together nicely, the 'carefully designed quirk' in Manchevski's chronology was a step forward in the development of non-linear narrative, as it built up on temporally ambivalent elements that do not fit together and yet make up for a coherent narrative. Manchevski's next film, the forthcoming *Dust*, is expected to go even further in this direction, by combining narratives that take place in Macedonia around 1903 and in present-day New York.

10. Robert Rosenstone sees Aleksandar as a figure located between the West and the Balkans, and discusses the particularities of his position within his conceptual framework of 'living in two histories':

> Aleks, our Macedonian hero who has lived in Western Europe for years and now has returned home, keeps saying: 'My eyes have changed.' What has changed them? His years abroad. His adoption of the belief, shared with the doctor in his village, in the Enlightenment project – in the very meaning of history. Or perhaps it is more accurate to say he is a man caught between and yet part of two notions of history that coexist and struggle in the modern world, history as an inclusive and history as an exclusive story. History as all of us or history of us and them. Living in two histories blinds Aleks to what is happening before his eyes: the fact that old hatreds are, for whatever reason – and the film provides no reasons – alive

again. For years, Aleks accepted a metanarrative of progress. News photography was part of that metanarrative, and yet, ultimately, it led him to commit a crime. Now he has come home to embrace the counter narrative of an Eden. But he learns you cannot go home again, learns that if you are not careful, a metanarrative can kill you. The only way out is death, a meaningful death based upon an act of love ... Aleks sacrifices himself and welcomes death, a way into and out of history.

(Rosenstone, 2000, p. 190)

11. Even though Rosenstone preferred to read the film as a 'history of what has not yet happened' (Rosenstone, 2000, p. 191), he supplied a testimony to the film's 'educational' value:

I struggled through parts of some standard [Macedonian] histories, books that contain the names of too many people and movements, the details of endless and apparently similar events ... Sitting in the library, my eyes grow heavy and I want to snooze. But *Before the Rain* has no trouble keeping me awake as it cuts through those complications to give me some sort of past in the present, to make me feel something for the (perceived) problems of the region precisely where books have left me swimming in a sea of details.

(ibid., p. 189)

11. All these questions about *Before the Rain* were raised at a two-day workshop at the European University Institute in Florence in April 1999, organised by Robert Rosenstone and Bo Strath. In the presence of director Milcho Manchevski, a number of scholars discussed a range of issues pertaining to the relationship of film and history. Among the participants were theorists Hayden White, Reinhard Koselleck, film specialists Ian Christie, Anton Kaes, Thomas Elsaesser, Robert Burgoyne and the Balkanists Victor Friedman, Bengt Holmen and Keith Brown. As a result of these discussions, Rosenstone put together a special issue of the journal *Rethinking History* (Rosenstone, 2000), which included some of the contributions.

Part 2

Commitments Amid Strife

Chapter 5
Balkan Film and History: The Politics of Historical Collage

While historians claim they work with a firm set of criteria to secure objectivity, film-makers have no illusions that in historical reconstruction there is an intricate selectivity as to what is remembered when, and what aspects of the past are left to gather dust in remote corners. In this chapter, I will look at the work of film-makers who, each in their own way, tackle various aspects of historical memory.

To work primarily with material from Balkan history means becoming aware of the existence of multiple points of view. It often means becoming sceptical about the possibility of a unified metanarrative that would tell the history of the region in a way that was acceptable to all of its actors. To seek consensus on many details of Balkan history is difficult, as details are interpreted differently across the region.

When translated into cinema, the multiplicity of narratives finds expression in two types of works. On the one hand, we have historical films that are strictly rooted in a particular national narrative and perpetuate it. On the other, however, we have films that recognise the conditionality of all narratives and acknowledge that reconciling them may not be possible unless one builds upon their relativity. It is this second type of film that I will discuss here. They often offer an intentionally fragmented, and even facetious picture of history.[1]

In my discussion, I will look at the work of several film-makers – Dušan Makavejev, Želimir Žilnik, Lordan Zafranović and Theo Angelopoulos – each one of whom has offered examples that work against the uniformity of firm explanations in their approach to historical material. These directors have approached historical material by creating a picture of multiple, fragmented pasts, and have relied on discontinuous narratives, most often with the intention of commenting on the present. They all have created an original and unique perception of shared historical time and space, of historical signification, of fate and power, of the role of personalities and masses in history, and the work of each one of them can be described as a specific collage.

If told in a straightforward narrative, structured around a clear-cut causality with a beginning, middle and an end, the history of the Balkans either comes across as impossibly volatile and complex, or simply remains restricted to the postulates of just one of the many national narratives that are intertwined here. The attempts to seek consensus on a Balkan historical metanarrative are continuously undermined by the multiplicity of conflicting interpretative frameworks. But if told as a post-modern collage, by superimposing multiple stories and lines, Balkan history becomes a dynamic entity. To approach history without attempting to create a definitive narrative, instead preserving the contradictions and the diverse character of the material, has been the choice of the most influential film-makers from the region. Dušan Makavejev, for example, whose leading line of work has been the creation of subversive historical collages. Or Theo Angelopoulos, who has been continually preoccupied with the creation of a cinematic language capable of translating subtle historical concerns into extended and elaborately structured takes. By approaching history as a continuous interchange of assertions and negations, by constantly switching angles, and by intentionally leaving the narrative open-ended, these film-makers have transcended traditional historiography and have managed to address radical concerns and to comment on the meaning of history.

It has been an imperative for Balkan historical film-making to find an appropriate approach to the conflicts and contradictions of the past. In such a context, satire has often been the preferred genre in representing earlier Balkan clashes. No one has been spared – neither the bickering Balkan nations, nor the interfering European powers. In Rangel Vulchanov's *Last Wishes*, set during the wars of the 1910s, we see soldiers crossing bayonets and warring sides clashing without ever being clear about who is fighting whom in a series of Balkan wars, fighting that is, nonetheless, put on hold at a decisive moment so that a previously scheduled golf match between European dignitaries can take place in their Balkan estates. In *The Patent Leather Shoes of the Unknown Soldier*, another feature by Vulchanov, the brief interruptions in these same wars are treated as intermissions, during which the soldiers hastily rush home to check on the animals and to impregnate the wives. The war only comes to an end when an irate granny, fed up with all the wrangling, goes to the battlefield and scolds a diverse band of raggedy soldiers. Satirical devices of this type are widely deployed by Makavejev, and, as we will see, by Želimir Žilnik, who confronts uncritical popular beliefs of history and conflict by staging paradoxical pranks for the camera.

Personalised interpretations of history have a particularly strong presence in Balkan cinema. Such personal films allow the director to problematise and critically examine the complex relationship between individual experience and national fate, and tackle a whole sphere of issues that usually remain excluded from the officially sanctioned memory. These films have a strong impact on

Past Balkan conflicts have not escaped the film-makers' attention: Serbian actor Rade
Markovic in the Bulgarian classic *Kradezat na praskovi/The Peach Thief* (1964). A film
depicting the fatal infatuation of a Bulgarian officers' wife with a Serbian POW
during World War I

public perceptions of history. By superimposing personal narratives and commonly held historical beliefs, they ultimately define the scope of a shared
historical imagination. We will encounter such personalised approaches to historical material in the work of Lordan Zafranović, who personally takes the
witness stand in his documentary *Testament*, and of Theo Angelopoulos, who
reconstructs the history of Balkans as an intimate identity quest in his feature
Ulysses' Gaze.

My discussion is influenced by the views of Robert Rosenstone, a theorist of
film and history, who believes that historical film-making should be seen as an
alternative to the standard historical discourse. Unlike written history, which
tends to be uniform and creates a grand narrative that explains everything, film,
Rosenstone notes, is much more like the oral tradition, because it 'works against
such uniformity and opens up the discourse once again'. It tends to create 'multiple, fragmented pasts, a series of discontinuous stories that never fit together
into a metanarrative' (Rosenstone, 2000, p. 185). Cinematic accounts of history
give us the chance for a much richer and multidimensional grasp of the past
and its extended influences on the present.

Historians have often treated historical film prescriptively, as a tool for illustrating existing and established views on historical events. Rosenstone is trying

to correct this attitude: 'Rather than theorizing about what film should do to or for the past,' he writes, 'we should study what historical filmmakers have been doing in order to understand the rules of engagement for history as it is rendered on the big screen' (ibid., p. 185). What transpires when such study is undertaken is that historical cinematic texts are often structured as fragmented alternatives juxtaposed to the official narrative of historians. Rosenstone drafts a list of the characteristics of what he calls 'post-modern historical filmmaking'. It includes features found in films that

> (1) Tell the past self-reflexively, in terms of how it has meaning for the filmmaker historian. (2) Recount it from a multiplicity of viewpoints. (3) Eschew traditional narrative, with a beginning, middle, and end – or, ... insist these three elements need not necessarily be in that order. (4) Forsake normal story development, or tell stories but refuse to take the telling seriously. (5) Approach the past with humor, parody, absurdist, surrealist, dadaesque, and their irreverent attitudes. (6) Intermix contradictory elements: past and present, drama and documentary, and indulge in creative anachronism. (7) Accept, even glorify in their own selectivity, partialism, partisanship, and rhetorical character. (8) Refuse to focus or sum up the meaning of past events, but rather make sense of them in a partial and open-ended, rather than totalized, manner. (9) Alter and invent incident and character. (10) Utilize fragmentary and/or poetic knowledge. (11) Never forget that the present is the site of all past representation and knowing.
>
> (Rosenstone, 1998, p. 206)

I believe that most elements listed here, turning film-making into an alternative to uniform historical narrative, can be found in the examples that we will consider.

Dušan Makavejev: History as Associative Collage

Incorporating documentary footage in feature film is usually accomplished by adding the documentary as an extension to the fictional narrative, normally to contextualise the fictional part. Only rarely have film-makers ventured into the realm of associative montage – bringing in familiar visual documents for re-examination and placing them in non-conventional combinations for the purposes of creating new context by association. Here, a widely accepted reading of given documentary footage is subjected to questioning from the individual perspective of the film-maker, who uses the footage to create a personalised and sometimes subversive vision of 'truths' about a given historical period or social order. In such a highly personal context, footage from documentary and feature film usually has equal status, as it is the subjective perception of the film-maker and not the 'objective' record that is the focus of the examination.

Andrei Tarkovsky's *Zerkalo/The Mirror* (1975), in which the director inter-cuts newsreel footage from the Spanish Civil War with clips from a Soviet feature about World War II in a context of narrative re-creations of intimate childhood experiences and dreams, is considered to be a classic example of such an approach. But years before Tarkovsky ventured into crafting his personalised vision of childhood under Stalinism, there was Yugoslav Dušan Makavejev, who since the mid-1960s had extensively experimented in creating complex film messages by intersecting feature clips and documentary footage of concrete his-torical events. Makavejev's visual commentary on the world's political and historical process, straight out of the counter-cultural zeal of the 1960s, was a profoundly subversive one, aiming at anxieties on the intersection of libidinal and ideological indoctrination. He had a taste for combining Soviet and Nazi propaganda with counter-culture material from 1960s America. His unique style of political collage, rich in historical references, impacted on radical film-making worldwide.

Combining documentary footage and fictive images in associative arrange-ments is an enabling approach. It allows the director to make important points

Makavejev not only uses existing stereotypes, but enjoys creating new ones like the one of the Serbian simpleton-strongman in *Nevinost bez zastite/Innocence Unprotected* (1968)

that could not be made through either purely scholarly, or purely fictive, formats. One could quote many other examples of the associative usage of documentary footage in the Yugoslav cinema tradition.[2] But there is nothing as brazen as Makavejev's daring montages. He does not hesitate to impose his own associations in a cross-referencing that disregards standard dimensions of historical time and ideological doctrine. Neither is he constrained by the numerous occasions on which he uses, and even creates, stereotypes – like a Serbian simpleton-strongman in *Nevinost bez zastite/Innocence Unprotected* (1968), a stiff Russian lover in *WR – misterije organisma/WR: Mysteries of the Organism* (1971), a hygiene-obsessed Texas oil tycoon or a sensually glamorous Latino singer in *Sweet Movie* (1975), and a sexually inhibited Swedish housewife in *Montenegro* (1981). In fact, Makavejev defies all the stereotypes he uses by placing them amid a non-traditional associative sequence of cultural icons and signifiers. His work proves that it is possible for a film-maker to subvert commonplace pillars of historical imagination and to seriously shatter ordinary mentality by confronting it with seemingly frivolous, but in fact intentionally provocative, visions.

Makavejev's innovative approach culminated in *WR: Mysteries of the Organism*, a film about, besides other things, American bigotry, counter-culture, Yugoslav communism, world revolution and sexual liberation.[3] Unconventionally structured, among other overlapping subplots that can qualify as documentaries by themselves, *WR* included a more or less straightforward fictional narrative featuring a tense love affair between protagonists symbolising two communist powers at odds with each other – a young Yugoslav female communist and a Soviet male ice-skater (named Vladimir Ilich, after Lenin). Even this story, however, was cut through by complex associative montages – a passionate speech was collated with footage of cheering crowds during Mao's cultural revolution and with scenes from a feature glorifying Stalin, under the accompaniment of the musical score of a song from the Nazi era, 'Lili Marleen', to footage of electroshock treatment administered in an American psychiatric hospital.[4]

The reaction against the provocative *WR* within Yugoslavia had been so adverse that emigrating seemed the the easiest solution for Makavejev. Once in the West, however, he realised that he had exchanged the repressive censorship of communism for the subtler one of capitalism. In the first case, he had made films which were shelved. In the second, nothing was shelved, but many of his projects never materialised. Makavejev's work enjoyed such a strong reputation of controversy that only a few of his numerous projects came to completion, mostly because of difficulties with financing.[5] He gradually abandoned the daring political montages, returning to his associative collages only in *Gorilla Bathes at Noon* (1992), a dissection of post-communist ironies, rich in contro-

The dedicated Yugoslav, female, communist, protagonist of *W.R. Misterije organizma/ WR: Mysteries of the Organism* (1971), seen here trying to win over a Soviet ice-skater (named Vladimir Ilich after Lenin) with the help of her sexually liberated room-mate

versial historical cross-referencing. Here, Makavejev combines two lines of signification juxtaposing the triumphal arrival of Soviet forces in Berlin in 1945 with the present-day story of a Soviet army major, who, determined to stay in the West, deserts the army at the time of its withdrawal from Germany in the 1990s.

Specifically Balkan issues have been explored by Makavejev only in the context of his general concerns with historical irony. Only his *Manifesto* (1988), set in Slovenia early in the century, was structured around a fictional historical episode evolving in a place where shady Austro-Hungarian interests had regularly intersected with the equally dubious ambitions of other political forces from the region. But in the 1990s – a decade which the director spent mostly teaching at various universities in the USA, from Harvard to Berkeley – there was increasing evidence that Makavejev was becoming more interested in the Balkans. Besides regularly talking to the media on various issues regarding the conflict, he had mobilised a number of Yugoslav émigré intellectuals in helping him with the research for a film centred on symbolic blowing up of a bridge, and had sought financing for a feature project tentatively entitled *Yugoslavia*.

In *Hole in the Soul,* an autobiographical documentary which he made for Scottish BBC in 1994, he even included footage of a half-drunk vagabond who addresses Western viewers from a barge on the Danube: 'Why don't you, affluent guys, give some money to Dušan, the director, only $2–3 million, no more, so that he can make a movie called *Yugoslavia.* He is one of the few who can tell you what the Balkans are all about! You've gotta' give him money . . .!'

With his taste for grotesque satire, Makavejev would have a thing or two to say about his native corner of Europe. But so far, he has not succeeded in getting the funding to make the film. In 2000, Makavejev helped to curate a Balkan film panorama at the Venice Biennale, and authored a piece in which he described the Balkans as a place where 'the rivers flow over the bridges', evidence that the symbolism of the bridge continued to haunt him. By now he was no longer speaking of a feature, only of a dream to make a 1-minute animation that would play around the endlessly changing Balkan map (Germani, 2000, p. 13).

Even though Makavejev has not yet made a film directly related to Yugoslavia's breakup, his influence on every politically committed film-maker from the region is so profound that we cannot possibly understand it without referencing the work of this master of historical irony. It is Makavejev who defined the politics of historical collage, and even though film-makers may not follow strictly his cinematic recipes, it is his trademark subversive and satirical techniques that have set the definitive standards for Balkan critical film-making.

Želimir Žilnik: Subverting the Tito-Icon

Želimir Žilnik's highly original works, mostly docu-dramas, re-enacted documentaries and provocative satires, have secured him the unique position of a master of subversive film-making within Yugoslav cinema. His radical-liberal political orientation and daring explorations of social taboos make him somewhat comparable with Makavejev, if not even bolder. In the late 1960s, Žilnik came to prominence with his experimental feature *Rani radove/Early Works* (1969), named after the highly contested Hegelian writings of Marx, a film which is now considered a prime example of the Yugoslav Black Wave.

Disillusioned with West European democracies during a short-lived emigration to Germany in the 1980s, Žilnik returned to Yugoslavia where, in the 1990s, he became an outspoken critic of nationalism and worked on a number of dissident productions realised jointly with Belgrade's Studio B92. His internationally acclaimed 'mockumentary' *Tito among the Serbs for a Second Time* (1993) questioned Tito's cult of personality and effectively weakened the overwhelming referencing to Tito as the source of all Yugoslav troubles.

The versatile Tito-icon has been used to symbolise rather too many things –

the glory of the struggle against fascism, the achievements of well-managed socialism, the possibility of independent foreign orientation in the cold war world, and the suppression of ethnic animosities. Even in the dreary aftermath of his exploits, the Tito-icon remains in place, this time to compensate for the intensely experienced lack of leadership, and to provide a consoling outlet for a range of passions. Žilnik radically questions this practice of bringing everything down to Tito.

Although politically Tito had been perceived as a figure who opposed rather than imitated Stalin, the personality cult of both leaders rested on a very similar visual inventory. Tito's native house in Kumrovec, Croatia, was turned into a museum comparable to the ostentatious residence of Stalin in Gory, Georgia. Tito's picture was displayed in all public institutions – like Stalin's. Tito's image – again, like Stalin's – was re-created in all kinds of conceivable hand-crafted artefacts, such as embroideries, mosaics, woodcarvings, enamel ware and stamped metal. Tito's portrait on transparent material – like Stalin's – was flown over cities, cultivated into shaped box shrubs and conifers by landscape workers on hillsides and alongside railway tracks, and evolved in living pictures composed of thousands of raised flags during celebrations at stadiums. According to the lyrics of a song about *druže* ('comrade') *Tito* sung in *Underground*, 'wherever he touched the earth, blue violets sprang up'. Similar claims about quasi-magic powers are found in many songs dedicated to Stalin.

Unlike Stalin, however, of whom not much archival footage is left, Tito liked to be photographed.[6] The 'Titoville' web-site (http://www.titoville.com), put together by two Slovenian students, lists nearly two hundred propaganda documentaries and archival reports containing live footage of Tito. During his lifetime, Tito was featured in innumerable weekly newsreels, and thus a wide range of his public appearances are accessible on tape and available to filmmakers for conceptual recycling.[7]

The most exploited footage of Tito, however, seems to be one in which he himself is not present – namely, the 1980 train journey that transported his body across the country, from Ljubljana to Belgrade, for his funeral.[8] Thousands of crying people gather alongside the rail tracks to bid a last farewell to the leader, and groups of children leave flowers on the rails where the train is to pass. Politically, the actual funeral was a curious event, as set in midst of a deeply divided Europe it was attended by a maverick group of dignitaries – Nikolae Ceauşescu and Willy Brandt, Leonid Brezhnev and Kurt Waldheim, Margaret Thatcher and King Hussein of Jordan – each one of them having made some use of the living Tito for their own political advantage. Ironically, it is Tito's absence that brings them all together.

It is the contestation of the heavily emotionally charged ideological sphere opened up by Tito's absence, an absence which has granted various political powers the chance to project a range of interpretations onto the Tito-icon, that Želimir Žilnik undermines with greatest intensity in his hilarious *Tito among the Serbs for a Second Time.*[9]

In the film, yet another political collage, Žilnik boldly examines the uses and abuses of Tito's absent father-figure. He lets a well-known Tito impersonator, comedian Micko Ljubicić, spend a few hours on the pavements of Milosevic's Belgrade wearing the Marshall's uniform and pretending that Tito has come back to life. The impersonator emerges from Tito's museum, and is taken by chauffeur-driven car to the city centre, where 'Tito' is to socialise for a day with his former subjects. During the ride, the driver briefs 'Tito' on the disastrous Yugoslav developments since his death and on the contradictory popular sentiments toward his personality today. The resurrected 'Tito' then takes a stroll through downtown Belgrade and readily stops to chat with passers-by on the pavements.

Even though they realise the conventional absurdity of the staging, a surprisingly large number of people accept the mischievous challenge and take up the chance to converse with the leader and speak their minds. 'Tito' asks them all sorts of questions, nods appropriately, listens with concern to their answers and occasionally questions the policy line of the powers that be. 'Whom do you hold responsible for today's situation in Yugoslavia?' he asks in a paternalistic tone of voice. To which many timidly reply by repeating the popular cliché of the 1990s that it is he, Tito, who is to blame. 'Why me?' 'Because you died,' they explain, leaving the people behind without a guiding star; you created the nation, sustained it, and then left it orphaned. A woman admits: 'I cried so much when you died!' but she is now angry at him for having deserted them all. Many of the idle men on the streets attack 'Tito' verbally – depending on where they stand politically – for a variety of alleged wrongdoings. After a few hours, 'Tito' realises that he is unable to offer a solution to their concerns, and retreats to the museum to rest in peace.

These improvised street exchanges are intercut with an array of documentary references – footage of Tito gloriously emerging from an aeroplane, of his meetings with Brezhnev and the Pope, and of thousands of cheering youths. This intercutting of archival reels with the footage of street encounters with the 'resurrected' leader keeps reminding the audience of the iconic quality of Tito's personality, both in the past and in the present. But this is all done to subvert. In Žilnik's film, 'Tito' is confronted with the dismal consequences of the myths that sustained his quasi-divine status, a confrontation which the resurrected 'Tito' could easily resolve by uttering a simple iconoclastic disclaimer. Instead of confronting the anxieties, however, he chooses to withdraw to the museum and to continue his paternalistic caring for the masses from the safe distance of his shrine. The orphaned nation, he seems to believe, will be better off retaining him as an object of worship than being left fatherless and faithless.

Lordan Zafranović: Testimony of a Century in Decline

Croat director Lordan Zafranović, a graduate of FAMU and a member of the so-called Yugoslav Prague Group, has worked on historical topics throughout his career. His films are not marked by the exuberant humour or the biting irony found in the work of the directors discussed above. Zafranović's main preoccupation has been to explore the pressures experienced by ordinary people under extreme historical circumstances. His films challenge the deepest foundations of nationalism and question the justification of historical violence.

Zafranović's masterpiece, *Occupation in 26 Scenes*, set in the old Dalmatian city of Dubrovnik during World War II and impressively shot by cinematographer Karpo Godina, told the story of the confrontation of three former friends – a Croat, an Italian and a Jew – who end up on opposite sides after the fascist regime is established in Croatia. Formally influenced by Italian denouncements of fascist moral decline found in films like de Sica's *Il giardino dei Finzi-Contini/The Garden of the Finzi-Continis* (1971) and Pasolini's *Salo* (1975), Zafranović investigates the relation of foreign occupiers (German and Italian) and domestic collaborators. His indictment is directed against the domestic villains, even though on the surface it is the arrival of the foreigners that sanctions the violence and makes the butchery possible.

Residents of Dubrovnik salute the arriving Nazis in Zafranović's *Okupacija u 26 Slika/Occupation in 26 Scenes* (1978)

The culmination of the film is a scene of extreme violence which evolves in broad daylight: on the hills above Dubrovnik, overlooking the beautiful Adriatic coast, a group of thugs are shown to cruelly maim and then kill a busload of detainees – a couple of Jews, several Serbs, an Orthodox priest and a blind street musician. The perpetrators are local thugs, and it never becomes clear if they were acting on orders or if the 'cleansing' was their initiative.[10]

Occupation in 26 Scenes, which won the FIPRESCI prize at Cannes in 1979 and an Academy Award nomination, exposed the dark sides of the Ustasha regime in Croatia during World War II, a line of investigation which Zafranović continued in his subsequent films *Pad Italije/The Fall of Italy* (1981) and *Vecernja zvona/Evening Bells* (1986), forming a loose trilogy with *Occupation*. The director's investigation of this shameful and violent period of Croatian history continued in the impressive documentary *Krv i pepeo Jasenovca/Blood and Ashes of Jasenovac* (1985), which looked into the history of the notorious extermination camp.

In 1988, Zafranović started work on another documentary exploration of Croatia's history, which was to become his *Testament*, yet another enquiry into the concerns of earlier films with fascism, power, violence and historical memory. Back in 1986 he had filmed during the trial of one of the Ustas leaders, Andrija Artuković, and was allowed to visit him after sentencing. At the time, Zafranović enjoyed the support of the local television network and was able to access a wide array of archival footage.

But in 1990, after Tudjman's ascent to power, things rapidly changed. Zafranović's inquisitive excavations of dark historical episodes came to be seen as adverse to the resurrected national ideal and were no longer tolerated. A campaign in the Croatian press accused him of plotting an intentionally unpatriotic work, and the accusations of disloyalty were soon transposed onto his entire oeuvre. Zafranović became a *persona non grata*, and had to finish his work in exile in Prague, where he still lives.[11] It was here, with Czech and Austrian assistance, that he was able to complete his epic three-and-a-half hour investigation into Croat history, *Decline of the Century: The Testament of L. Z.* (1995). An impressive collage, which makes use of a variety of material – archival footage, clips from the director's own historical features, excerpts from other documentaries and news chronicles – Zafranović's film was a powerful indictment of past and present-day Croatian nationalism.

The documentary loosely follows the history of the Ustasha movement, from its beginnings in the early 1930s, through its rise to power during World War II, to the demise of the regime in 1945. This history is told by collating extensive footage from news chronicles – cheering crowds welcoming the Nazis and the Italian fascists, the destruction of a Zagreb synagogue, a friendly encounter of Ustasha leader Ante Pavelić with Adolf Hitler, the horrors of Jasenovac, the controversial trial of Archbishop Stepinac of Zagreb – all inviting us to revisit unpleasant historical episodes of Ustasha terror. This is intercut with extensive footage from the war-crimes trial of the 87-year-old Andrija Artuković in 1986.[12] Supposedly one of the arch-villains, known as the 'Balkan Butcher', at his trial Artuković appears frail and senile. In the film, we see Zafranović visit Artuković in the jail hospital, where the old man lies on his deathbed, no longer able to talk or communicate coherently. No commentary is provided (or needed) to these shattering scenes, raising the same range of questions that Marcel Ophuls and Claude Lanzmann have been investigating in the West of Europe: of delayed justice and postponed accountability, of the blurred definition of guilt for genocidal crimes and of the reluctant but predictable pardoning in the face of advanced age.

The film's narrative is intensely personal: Zafranović includes numerous scenes where we see him working on the film's research and montage in the 1990s. But this is only one dimension of the director's personal presence. We also see him as a young man, in footage from a 1960s documentary, seeking answers to these same troubling questions that will become his lifelong preoccupation. Yet another line of personal commentary is set up by the collated footage from Zafranović's features, most of which have examined the same overwhelming historical concerns.

Zafranović's complex investigation of history and memory is a truly postmodern work. It makes meaning of the past in new, non-traditional ways, and treats history by adopting many of the approaches described in Rosenstone's categorisation: telling the past in a self-reflexive way, recounting it from a multiplicity of viewpoints and utilising fragmentary and poetic knowledge.

Only the short epilogue of *Decline of the Century* makes direct references to the present-day clashes, featuring footage of the 1991 war and framing the whole narrative of the film in relation to today's violent intolerance, which Zafranović sees as a repercussion of reconciliation that never happened.

As a Croat, Zafranović feels he has no choice but to examine Croatia's fascism and its alliance with the Nazis. He recognises that the film is 'very troubling and painful for Croats in some parts' (quoted in Smale, Associated Press, 1993). But, as Daniel Goulding notes, it is not only the powerful indictment of Croatia's wartime regime that emerges from the film, 'but a potent warning against the dangers of narrow ethnic nationalist ideology of any stripe' (Goulding, 1998, p. 2). Zafranović's work is one of the few films related to Yugoslavia's breakup that attempts to seek reconciliation by first admitting guilt.[13]

Theo Angelopoulos: Travels at the End of the Century

Theo Angelopoulos' treatment of Balkan history lies at the opposite end of the Makavejev–Žilnik spectrum, and is cerebral and introspective. Having established himself early on as a titan of Greek historical cinema, with films like *Meres tu '36/Days of '36* (1972), *The Traveling Players* and *I Kinigi/The Hunters* (1977), which explore the complexities of modern history with the means of complex cinematic language and non-conventional narrative, in his mature period the director grew more concerned with the problems of Balkan history and identity.

All characters in Angelopoulos' Balkan cinema of the 1990s are on a quest for the ultimate. The documentary film-maker from *The Suspended Step of the Stork* goes to a refugee settlement on the Albanian border to investigate the disappearance (or alleged voluntary withdrawal) of a prominent politician, whose book, suggestively, is entitled *Despair at the End of the Century*. Similarly, 'A.', the protagonist of *Ulysses' Gaze*, a film-maker again, travels across the bleak Balkan winter, searching for lost film footage that is supposed to document the conviviality of happier times. The writer-protagonist of *Eternity and a Day* is also on a quest for the ultimate, restlessly scanning his memory back and forth in an attempt to put together the scattered pieces of past happiness and present anxieties.

The Suspended Step of the Stork is about invisible borders that can never be crossed, and forsaken people who want to be elsewhere but who are stuck on the margins of a transition that goes on for ever. *Ulysses' Gaze* carries out a nos-

Angelopoulos' treatment of Balkan history in *O Thiassos/The Traveling Players* (1975) is cerebral and introspective, exploring the complexities of modern history through a complex symbolic language

talgic reconstruction, in vanishing flashes, of peaceful and colourful ethnic cohabitation at the crossroads between Orient and Occident. *Eternity and a Day* continues the painful search for lost harmony and elusive tranquillity.[14] Angelopoulos' characteristic atmosphere – lonely wandering through a misty landscape – prevails in all three films. All three are co-scripted by the legendary European screenwriter Tonino Guerra, and all three move entirely within the physical and semantic space of the Balkans. Questions about the seeds of conflict, of guilt and of misunderstanding are not explored here. Instead, the themes are the distortion of universal accord and shattered identities. And in this way, Angelopoulos attributes a universal humanistic dimension to the idiosyncratic Balkan problems.

Of these Balkan films, however, it is only *Ulysses' Gaze* that is exclusively preoccupied with the problems of historical reconstruction. The narrative of the film is a complex and frail framework that breaks away from the linear not only temporally but also spatially, providing an ultimately subjective account of the personal experience of history and regionality. The protagonist, a successful American film director named 'A.' (Harvey Keitel), has returned to his native Florina in Greece after thirty-five years of exile to attend the local premiere of his acclaimed new film. The world-weary A.'s sojourn in Greece was intended to be brief. But he remains in the region for much longer. While in Florina, he hears of several film reels, now missing, that were shot early in the century by the legendary Manaki brothers.[15] 'They have registered all the pains and sorrow of the Balkans, and have actually been interested in the people and not in the politics,' somebody tells him. The brothers seem to have recorded all the ambiguities of the past, and the key to healing the present-day intolerance may well be found in their films. The memory of happy multicultural coexistence is presumably recorded on the missing reels. A. sets off to search for the footage, and gradually grows obsessed with the belief that tracking it down and restoring it is the key to overcoming the confrontations of the Balkans. He hopes that finding evidence that harmonious coexistence was possible in the past may help him pacify today's hostile and alienated world. Moments from the legendary reels of undeveloped footage shot by the Manakis flash across A.'s mind, depicting women and men in innocent and peaceful togetherness.

A. may have hoped that coming back to his native lands would put his anxiety to rest and reconcile his internal doubts; that the short return to Greece would mark the end of a long journey. Now, however, he realises that it is only the beginning of a penance. He has to continue, to go on, to travel across the Balkans, searching not only for the footage but also for his own roots.

The journey takes him on a winding road – from Greece to Albania, Macedonia, Bulgaria, Romania, Serbia and, finally, to Bosnia. The return to places A. has known in his childhood is painful. While some of the locations are explored in their real geographical dimensions, others are present in the film only as memory sites of distant times and events, now called back into the mind of the protagonist. It is notable that it is difficult to identify the places where the action takes place, often because of a change of name, or the different names used in various Balkan nations for the same place. Macedonia's Monastir is today's Bitola, Bulgaria's Philipopolis is Plovdiv, and Koritsa in Albania is Korçë. Using the old names of cities is important, once again hinting at the relativity which placing the events in historical time inevitably entails. A whole universe of languages is spoken here. Besides English, one can hear Bulgarian, Macedonian, Greek, Romanian, Albanian, Russian and French.

Wherever he goes, A. bears witness to the volatility of present-day history. When he drops an old woman off in Korçë, he sees hundreds of expelled Albanians silently and grimly returning from Greece. In Romania, he comes across a giant statue of Lenin, erect and glorious until yesterday, but now deconstructed and transported up the Danube to Germany for rich collectors. During a brief visit to Belgrade, a friend takes him to a madhouse – a symbol of the state of affairs in this once vibrant city.

As well as travel in space, there is travel in time. First, there are A.'s personal memories. An episode that develops in his childhood home in the Sephardic neighbourhood of Bucharest spans several years within a sequence that lasts only a few minutes. The static camera, placed in the corner of a reception room, shows a prolonged New Year's Eve celebration in the tumultuous post-war years, starting in 1945 and running through the mid-1950s. The scene is one of a family reunion. A. is present in two ways – once as an adult spectator on the side, and again, as a child, taking part in the action. We watch as policemen in civilian clothes rush in and take the father away; we then see the family members discussing a return migration to Greece; we see the servants quitting, and requisitionists removing the piano. Each minute of screen time seems to equal a year – an approach which Angelopoulos has used before in his famous reversal of time in *The Traveling Players* in a scene that opens in 1952 and gradually goes back in time to 1939.

Second, there is the gradual identification of A. with the Manakis. He experiences their lives: their fascination with the magical moving image machine, the Bioscope, their excitement about the cinema theatre which they operated in the Macedonian town of Monastir (Bitola) and which was burned down in 1939, their controversial Kafkaesque encounters with the authorities in the Bulgarian town of Philipopolis (Plovdiv), and the Balkan animosities which throw their lives into disarray. It is all told in a masterful combination of re-enactment, actual archival footage and a series of flashbacks from the Manaki brothers' own movies.

A third extension in an imaginary trip takes A. to the banks of the mystical

Evros River, near the Yonian Sea. Here he ends up with a woman dressed in the black garb of a war widow. The ascetic landscape contrasts with the intensely blue waters, and abandoned, burned-out houses stand all around. Against the background of distant shooting and in an alienated voice, the woman speaks about armies that have passed through here, of endless suffering and loneliness. The protagonists spend their time together either in the room or near the water, in the eternal dimension of an unidentified historical time, and we see them in silent scenes of awkward lovemaking among crumbling walls.

Throughout the film, in an extended monologue, A. addresses a mystical woman, who appears in various reincarnations, all metamorphoses of Penelope to whom A. (Ulysses) is longing to return.[16] She is a silent shadow walking by in Florina, Greece. She is a museum curator in Monastir, Macedonia, who then travels with him to Romania, only to vanish and then reappear in a new identity during his fictional journey to Philipopolis, his Bulgarian exile. She is the widow in the burned-out house on the Evros River, and she will reappear in Sarajevo towards the end of his journey. She embodies in one all the mythical women surrounding the classical figure of Ulysses.[17]

All these historical explorations of the mind, all these personal trips, are constantly and continuously referenced back to the present. Angelopoulos is very clear about where things stand today, and in this context the obsessive 'I have to go to Sarajevo!' is not simply the next step in A.'s search for the lost reels. It is necessary to go there: Sarajevo, the heart of the conflict, is A.'s goal. No other place can substitute for it. And, indeed, the culmination of the film is his arrival in the city, where, among the shelling, he finally finds the lost footage and the man who is able to give him access to the cherished images informing his dream-like journey.

Sarajevo is the kingdom of war: the old buildings are destroyed, dark clouds cover the horizon, all cars are either burned-out or still burning, and people run beneath a soundtrack of distant shelling.[18] The deserted streets are reminiscent of a painting by Giorgio de Chirico. Amid the darkness and the sirens, A. meets Ivo Levi, the dedicated Jewish film curator, weary and wise, who has revealed the secret of the reels. It is a moment of sublime tranquillity: the two men have finally found each other, and are both relaxed, because now, it seems, they have all the time on earth for each other, and for an all-embracing conversation about restless longing and universal despair. They go out for a walk in the foggy but peaceful day, not suspecting that only minutes later Ivo and his family will be killed, while A. remains staring incomprehensibly into the thick blanket of fog that surrounds him.

For quite a long time, a few minutes maybe, the only thing that we actually see on the screen is the white fog. But this is the moment in which the most dynamic events take place – we hear a car stop, a conversation takes place, we sense that something terrible is happening, we hear shots, yet we see only the fog, then we hear someone throwing bodies into water (presumably in a nearby river), and a car leaves ... The screen is almost white the whole time – nothing changes, there is no movement, no action in the cinematic sense. The camera is subjective to the extreme. What we are offered here is the protagonist's point of view. His vision is obstructed, but he is no longer an observer; he is the one telling us the story now. He is no longer gazing from the corner; we are now watching through his eyes.

Only minutes ago they were walking amid protective heaps of sandbags, surrounded by silent male silhouettes. But now A., after running across the screen, leans over the dead bodies of Ivo, his wife and his daughter. He cries helplessly, realising that for the short time he spent with them, they have become his family, his home and his happiness. He seemed to have completed his quest. But so soon after the sublime moment of finding them, he is alone once again, helplessly confronted with the absurdity of death.

A. has nowhere else to go but underground, to the reels he still possesses. A few moments later, he has already seen the revered footage, and we watch as he sits in front of the moviola, which turns on in empty rounds. A. stares at the white screen, a scene echoing his staring into the blank white fog outside. Whatever may have been on these tapes is no longer of importance to him. He cries, dejected and desolate. All suffering is now gathered on his expressive face – maybe the only close-up in the film, as Angelopoulos never looks closely at the actors' faces and works exclusively in medium-close and long shots.

In the background we hear the monologue of Ulysses: 'When I return I will be wearing someone else's clothes, will be bearing someone else's name, and my coming will be unexpected.' The film has been about the desire to, and the impossibility of, recognising one's own true self. By the time A. reached what he was searching for, so much had happened and so many illusions had been destroyed, that he is no longer interested in possessing the secrets of the past that he believed would hold the key to harmony. The reality he has to confront proves so overwhelming that it barely makes sense for him to expect that answers or inspiration would come from revealing the past secrets that the lost tapes contain. By rejecting the hope that he willingly maintained while searching, he is finally reconciled with the demons that haunted him.

Ulysses' Gaze is a deconstruction of self-perceptions and identity believed to be firmly rooted in space and time. Nothing can be certain any more, however, and the search for a stable identity turns out to be in vain. Even if one is willing to adopt a conditional identity, the choice is easily invalidated. The return to one's roots can take place, but it makes no sense: by the time one arrives, everything that mattered in the past is over, and things will never be the same again. The nostalgia is meaningless, and all that remains is the longing for something that is impossible to attain. In the context of this existential pessimism, Balkan troubles are seen as problems of the world, as part of the tiresome recognition of its deterioration.

Angelopoulos approaches history as lived in personal destinies. By the time he made *Ulysses' Gaze*, he had created, with the assistance of cinematographer Yorgos Arvanitis, the perfect cinematic language, which allowed him to talk of the individual experience of history as one superseding time and space.[19] The remarkable use of elaborately manipulated long takes enables him to convey complex subtleties. In Angelopoulos, the camera may at one point identify with the protagonist who narrates the story, and then, by a single tilt within the same shot, continues telling the story from someone else's point of view while the protagonist, now relieved of the narrator's responsibilities, enters the frame and appears entangled in events that he watched from the side until a moment ago. This seemingly frivolous narration tells us a lot about how history is experienced in the Balkans, where one is only too aware of the volatile changes of being an actor and being an observer of one's own fate. Older historical interpretations intersect with the perceived significance of newer ones; one wonders what is left and what has become of us, and where one is going. Angelopoulos does not have the answers, but the way he asks the questions sets in motion a much-needed introspection.

Angelopoulos' Balkan films are also historical collages, raising issues of displacement and lost homelands, and trying to go beyond the geopolitical intricacies that dominate the approaches of other film-makers. His trademark atmosphere of lonely wandering through the mist prevails in all his films which deal with issues of universally distorted harmony, irrecoverable identities and *fin-de-siècle* sadness. He is the only one daring enough to claim that problems of universal identity lurk from within the peculiar Balkan universe.

Notes

1. A correct understanding of these issues can only be achieved if one abandons the one-country approach and looks at the cinema of the Balkans comprehensively. Only a consideration that would investigate historical films from the region in a comparative light will allow us to pinpoint the clusters of historical disagreements, and will lead to meaningful interpretative results. Such an approach, however, is in its infancy in cultural studies that focus on the region, and is still to materialise in film studies.

2. The controversial *Plastic Jesus*, the diploma film of director of Lazar Stojanović made in 1971, goes even further in its bold cross-referencing of musical score and documentary sequences. This boldness eventually led to a jail term for the director. Following in Makavejev's footsteps, Stojanović had used footage of the Croatian Ustasha, which was one of the reasons the film

was incriminated at the time; it may also be the reason that conditioned the timing of its official release in 1991 in rump Yugoslavia.

3. The first part of this film is a 20-minute documentary devoted to the American period in the life of the controversial radical psychoanalyst Wilhelm Reich. Later in the film at least three other documentaries featuring characters from American counter-culture unravel parallel to the main story line.

4. The feature is Mikhail Chiaurelli's *The Vow* (1946). In this particular case the 'Lili Marleen' score has not been added by Makavejev but figures in the Chiaurelli original, a detail which was brought to my attention by Herbert Eagle.

5. For a discussion of Makavejev's films after *WR*, see Daniel Goulding's essay on Makavejev in *Five Filmmakers* (1994), and Andrew Horton's piece from 1991.

6. A very limited choice in archival footage of Stalin is available to film-makers. The cinematic image of Stalin is linked rather to the performances of Georgian actor Mikhail Gelovani, who specialised in playing Stalin in the films of Mikhail Chiaurelli from the late 1940s, such as *The Vow* and *The Fall of Berlin* (1949). Most of the visual references to Stalin in later films have been not to archival footage, but rather to his portrayal by Gelovani.

7. Tito enjoyed such a powerful screen presence that some documentaries on the period focus on him exclusively, neglecting any other political figures and presenting post-war Yugoslavia more or less as his personal creation. A number of feature films depicted Tito's partisan struggles, one even starring Yul Brynner (*Battle of Neretva*), and another one Richard Burton (*Sutjeska*). Scenes depicting the reverent allegiance to Tito can often be found in other Yugoslav movies, such as Kusturica's *When Father Was Away on Business* (1985), for example, where the young protagonist is brought up as a devoted worshipper of Tito – both at home and within his pioneer organisation. In Goran Marković's *Tito and I* (1992), a coming-of-age film structured around the mockery of the cult of personality, Tito appears in dream-like sequences wearing his white Marshall's uniform, emanating brightness. His very appearance makes the child-protagonist fall, albeit momentarily, under the spell of his overwhelming charisma.

8. Footage of Tito's funeral is used in *Underground, Pretty Village, Pretty Flame* and in many documentaries.

9. The title of the film parodies the title of a classical work of Serbian satire from around the turn of the century (Radoje Domanovic's *Krajevic Marko/ Among the Serbs for a Second Time*).

10. The nightmarish brutality and sadism of this scene has had a profound impact on several generations of Yugoslavs. Elements of it have been almost

literally reproduced in the American film *Savior*, directed by Serbian-born
Predrag Antonjević.

11. Driven by anti-nationalist sentiments in the early 1970s, Zafranović had also
    temporarily moved out of Croatia (to Belgrade) to protest against the rising
    nationalism (Goulding, 1998, p. 5). Both Goulding and Smale (1993) testify
    to the ban imposed on Zafranović's films in Croatia in the 1990s.

12. Artuković has served as Minister of the Interior and Minster of Justice in
    Ante Pavelić's Ustasha republic, and is widely seen as the dictator's right
    hand. After the war, he emigrated to the USA via Ireland. The 1951 Yugoslav
    government's request for his extradition is contested by the American
    authorities, and only after a 35-year legal battle is he extradited to Yugoslavia
    in February 1986. At his four-week trial, Artuković pleads not guilty. He is
    sentenced to death but dies of old age in prison in 1988.

13. In 1997 Zafranović was said to be working on a project for a Sarajevo-themed
    feature, *The Balkan Island*, based on Vidosav Stevanović's *The Snow and the
    Dogs*. No further information on the project has been made public, however.

14. Angelopoulos was said to have been disappointed when he was not awarded
    the Palme d'Or at Cannes in 1995 for *Ulysses' Gaze*. But only three years later,
    in 1998, he received the main Cannes award for his next film, *Eternity and a
    Day*. While undoubtedly a serious intellectual film, this later work is
    essentially a compendium of Angelopoulos' film language devices, images and
    narrative interests, and can barely be considered a superior piece of work
    within the oeuvre of the director.

15. The Manaki brothers are considered patriarchs of film-making in the Balkan
    region, and the Bitola Film Festival in today's Macedonia is named after
    them. The brothers Miltos and Yannis Manaki lived all around the Balkans in
    the first half of the century, mostly in Macedonia, Bulgaria and Greece, and
    made films about the region. Angelopoulos' treatment of the Manaki brothers
    as exclusively Greek came under fire from critics in Macedonia, who pointed
    out that the director had misappropriated a number of historical details
    about these pioneers of cinema which would show them as people of a
    different ethnic background and different political allegiances (Blagoja
    Kunovski, 'Festival Parallels', *Kinopis, 14* (Skopje), Vol. 8, 1996, pp. 106–24).
    While I do not have enough information to be able to make a competent
    judgment on these and other Macedonian allegations, I do feel that I should
    mention that the Manaki brothers were of Vlach ethnicity, a fact which is not
    mentioned in *Ulysses' Gaze*, a puzzling omission considering the film's focus
    on the multi-ethnic society of the Balkans.

16. All the major female roles in the film are played by the same actress,
    Romanian Maia Morgenstern.

17. These female figures have been identified by Andrew Horton as Penelope,

Calypso, Circe and Nausicaa (p. 158). For an extensive discussion of the mythological references in *Ulysses' Gaze*, see Andrew Horton's *The Films of Theo Angelopoulos* (1997a).

18. Ironically, the scenes depicting Sarajevo under siege were shot at an empty aeroplane hangar near Belgrade (see interview with Angelopoulos with Andrew Horton, in Horton, 1997b).

19. I belong to those critics who, like Penelope Houston, trace the origins of Angelopoulos' visual style to Hungarian Miklós Jancsó. Angelopoulos' pronounced preference for staging complex shots featuring groups of people moving in different directions represents a direct continuation of stylistical devices used by the Hungarian master in earlier works such as *The Round Up* (1965) or *The Red and the White* (1967). A specific aspect of Angelopoulos' language is the stylisation and multiplication surrounding identical objects, often used as colour accents – the black umbrellas of the people in Florina, the blue bags carried by the Albanian men and the white water containers used by the Sarajevans.

Chapter 6
Kusturica's *Underground*: Historical Allegory or Propaganda?

In 1995 *Underground*, a film by Emir Kusturica, won the Palme d'Or at the Cannes Film Festival.[1] Controversy followed. For some observers, the film was nothing less than Serbian propaganda. Writing in *Le Monde*, French intellectual Alain Finkielkraut (1995) alleged that Kusturica had betrayed his own Sarajevan roots and put himself at the service of Belgrade. Here I will try to evaluate the film, the controversy and Kusturica's position as a Bosnian-born film-maker working in Belgrade.

Many of the films made in response to the Balkan conflict of the 1990s were surrounded by controversies and accusations of being Serbian propaganda, most notably *Vukovar* and *Pretty Village, Pretty Flame*. Often the propaganda message was only legible to members of the ethnic groups involved in the

Kusturica and Angelopoulos at Cannes, 1995. Angelopoulos had expected a Palme d'Or for *Ulysses' Gaze*. He didn't get it this time, but was compensated in 1998, for *Eternity and a Day*

conflict. The criticisms raised by Croatian-Americans or displaced Bosnians were barely within the grasp of Western audiences, and thus the controversies remained self-contained.

At first glance, the controversy surrounding Kusturica's *Underground* would appear to be the same: the accusations against the director seem too intricate to comprehend and quickly deter even those people who are prepared to look into the case. Still, *Underground*'s case should not be regarded as just another one of the convoluted Balkan arguments; it is a symptomatic moral case worth discussing beyond the narrow scope of the Balkan conflict. It has an importance of its own. The range of reactions to it, however, was quite disconcerting – from a display of moral fatigue to open encouragement of exclusive and relaxed moral norms for the artist.

This is why I believe that the 'Kusturica problem' is worth revisiting. By doing this separately from my discussion of *Underground*, I hope to be able to point out more effectively the underlying problems which I see here.

Apropos *Underground*
The Film

In *Underground* Kusturica plays with lengthy, elaborate scenes, ornate, dark props, a haunting musical score and a reality that refers to François Rabelais, Hieronymus Bosch, Terry Gilliam and Federico Fellini. The viewer is taken on a trip into the bizarre, the absurd and the deformed. Visually, the film is very dark, shot mostly in various shades of brown. There is even a shot taken from an unborn baby's point of view, peering out of the darkness of the womb. The camera prefers unusual angles and purposefully seeks the aesthetics of the cellar. The film leaves a lasting and unsettling impression on the viewers.

If one leaves aside the visual particularities, *Underground* is a historical film which offers a framework for interpreting the current violent state of affairs in the Balkans.[2] The film is set in clearly defined historical time, with a linear narrative that spans five decades, highlighting particular moments that take place in 1940s, 1960s and 1990s. Real events are called by their actual names, along with fictional historical encounters and occurrences. Documentary footage of selected moments of Yugoslav history is used as an element that triggers the narrative. The fictional protagonists mingle with real historical personalities, as seen in *Forrest Gump* (1994).

Underground is screenwriter Dušan Kovacević's and director Emir Kusturica's personal take on Yugoslav history.[3] In the film they closely follow the lives of three protagonists – Marko, a tireless, cunning cynic, Blacky, a pugnacious, artless dunce, and Natalia, an opportunistic, vivacious blonde – who are shown at various stages of their lives, which largely coincide with the highlighted moments of Yugoslav history. Early in the film it becomes clear that

Marko and Blacky both have a crush on Natalia and many of their further actions are determined by this rivalry, while Natalia herself, following a 'diamonds are a girl's best friend' approach, shifts loyalties incessantly. The film is not a romantic comedy, however, because the sombre backdrop to these passionate and sensual affairs is a war with no end. The three parts of the film are called 'War', 'Cold War' and again 'War'.

In the first part, which opens with the Nazi bombing of Belgrade on 6 April 1941, Marko Dren (Miki Manojlović), an energetic black marketeer, takes a large group of friends and relatives to a cellar which he has equipped as an air-raid shelter. Marko himself does not hide but remains at large, which casts a shadow of suspicion on the whole rescue operation and hints at the subsequent victimisation and exploitation of the people in the cellar. Above ground, Marko and Blacky complete a series of reckless assaults under the auspices of the communist Resistance – acts that they represent as motivated by anti-fascist zeal but which in fact are just a series of burglaries. After performing a daring anti-Nazi stunt (which is nothing else but another manifestation of a philanderer's showmanship), Marko gets rid of Blacky by sending him to 'hide' in the cellar as well. Having eliminated his rival, Marko can claim Natalia, the shared object of their affection, for himself.

The events of the second part, 'Cold War', take place in 1961. In post-war communist Yugoslavia, Marko has become a cherished poet and an influential *aparatchik* close to president Tito. He has married Natalia, and together they have created the myth of themselves as brave anti-fascists. Blacky is now celebrated as a courageous martyr who perished in the resistance fight. A film, *Spring Comes on a White Horse*, is to be shot about their heroic experiences in the struggle. At the same time, Marko and Natalia continue the duplicity and still hide a large number of people, Blacky included, in the cellar. They trick them into thinking that the war is still being fought by playing soundtracks of Nazi bombings and Hitler's speeches, and by occasionally appearing made up as if just having escaped the torturers at the local Gestapo headquarters. The people in the cellar are used as slave labour to manufacture arms that Marko promptly exports to a network of international customers.

One day Marko and Natalia descend to the cellar to attend the wedding of Blacky's son. Sweaty drunkenness reigns over this claustrophobic celebration and the wedding guests, all intoxicated, end up fighting over unsettled accounts from the past. In the turmoil, the walls of the cellar crumble and accidentally reveal an elaborate system of tunnels, mostly running from the East to the West, and carrying a heavy traffic of clandestine migrants. The members of the wedding disperse in disarray and most of the enslaved inhabitants of the underground run away. Blacky and his son climb above ground and end up at the shooting site of the *Spring Comes on a White Horse*, the film which was supposed to glorify Blacky's heroic past. Mistaking the set for reality and believing that World War II is still going on, they kill all the extras wearing German uniforms. Soon after Blacky's son, unfit for life outside the cellar, drowns in the Danube, and Blacky is captured by the police. Sensing trouble, Marko and Natalia escape, blowing up the house and the remains of the arms factory in the cellar.[4]

The third part, again called 'War', is set in the 1990s at an unidentified battlefield, where all the survivors cross paths one final time.[5] Marko, who has grown old and is now confined to a wheelchair, and Natalia, still pretty and practical, have become arms dealers of international stature, wanted by Interpol.[6] Blacky, still mourning the loss of his son thirty years earlier, is now in command of paramilitary forces shelling the city nearby. Amid the ruins, an Orthodox church with a big wooden cross burns.[7] Marko's brother, Ivan, one of the people formerly confined in the underground, is also here. It has taken him thirty years to realise the monstrosity of Marko's deception; his belated rage is so strong that in an outburst of retribution he beats Marko to death and then hangs himself on the church bell.[8] Blacky's paratroopers shoot Natalia, who dies in Marko's lap. The wheelchair and the two bodies are then set on fire and made to circle around the cross like a torch amid the apocalyptic scenery of the battlefield wasteland. Blacky passes by his former friends, and ends up desperately banging his head against a statue of a crucifix hanging upside down.[9]

The film's epilogue offers a sharp contrast to this apocalyptic, dark ending. In a utopian wedding scene, all the dead protagonists come back to life and gather together for a wedding feast on the Danube's sunny shores. As they cheerfully celebrate, however, the piece of land where they stand breaks apart from the mainland and quietly begins to float away. The wedding guests are too busy cheering to notice that they are being carried away to an unknown destination. Dancing and singing, embracing and kissing each other, they float further and further away from the mainland.

This final scene was the main image that screenwriter Kovacević and director Kusturica had in mind in the early stages of the project. While other individual sequences scattered throughout the film can also be seen as extremely effective, witty and revealing satire, the authors were determined to use this particular scene as the defining metaphor of Yugoslavia. The rest of the film – plot twists, characters and imagery – was gradually added to this image. Although the epilogue appears quite artificially attached to the main narrative, it affords an opportunity to juxtapose an optimistic view with the film's overwhelmingly grim story of betrayal and self-destruction. And indeed, while *Underground* contains many haunting images, this final one is the most distinct and memorable scene. 'There is still an energy in these people,' Kusturica claims in an interview with David Robinson:

They go away never really knowing what has happened to them. That is the way of the Balkan people. They never rationalize their past. Somehow the passion that leads them forward is not changed. I hope some day people may find better ways to use the passion they have so far persistently used to kill one another. (Robinson, 1996, p. 12)

The Controversy

One wonders what target audience Kusturica had in mind when making *Underground*. The film certainly intended to impress Western European fans by exploiting lesser used gloomy imagery and lesser explored aesthetic territories – an approach that had already proved successful.[10] For this target audience the film worked as expected – at the 1995 Cannes International Film Festival *Underground* was awarded the Palme d 'Or.

It is particularly notable that *Underground* was preferred by the jury to the other main contender, Greek Theo Angelopoulos' *Ulysses' Gaze,* which examined the same issues of the Balkan conflict in a similarly, if not more enhanced, epic manner. One can only speculate what had won the jury over in favour of Kusturica's film – my guess is that this was the rarely articulated but nevertheless vital desire of European film connoisseurs to cultivate further traditions that are in distinct dissonance with the straightforward and simplistic worldview of Hollywood. Kusturica's cultivation of cinematic equivalents of the bizarre and the untidy as aesthetic categories, his provocative imagery and unpredictable plots and his insistence on narratives that do not fall within preexisting frameworks were particularly appreciated. According to Kusturica himself (in an interview with H. G. Pflaum), this unorthodox worldview was at the very core of his artistic roots:

I am a Slav – in my contradictions, in my closeness to a black-and-white world view, in my affinity to the comical and in my humor, and in the quick change of moods – as well as in my understanding of history. I was born at this extremely painful border between the East and the West, and I bear the mark of my parents' heartbeat. At school the influence of Russian writers was added to all this, Chekhov and Gogol in the first place, and then came the cinema of the West. (Pflaum, 1995, p. 16)

The Cannes award carried weight with critics, most of whom praised *Underground*, while at the same time warning the audiences to be prepared for an unusual cinematic experience. J. Hoberman, for example, adjusted his language to fit the excessive, baroque atmosphere of the film to better describe it to his *Village Voice* readership:

A nearly sustained marvel of convoluted takes and choreographed energy that
never once loses its sardonic brio, *Underground* is truly maniacal. This is the
sort of movie in which characters break bottles of *slivovitz* over their heads.
The oompah rhythms could drive even the members of the New York Institute
for the Humanities to do the Zorba, critiquing Kusturica while pounding on
the closest seat.   (Hoberman, 1997, p. 75)

In the *Guardian*, Derek Malcolm simply suggested that the film should be
approached as an 'Alice In Wonderland rewritten by Franz Kafka' (Malcolm,
1995, G2, p. 13).

The overall critical reception of the film classified it as an esoteric piece of
elitist cinema. The tone of most reviews was evasively positive – critics were discussing a cinematic experience which had proved unusual even for them. But
since the film was coming from a revered director, the 'Balkan Fellini', and had
received the Palme d'Or, it was to be endorsed. *Underground* played at arthouse
cinemas across Europe, and later on across North America.

Underground, however, came under ardent critical fire from people who
claimed to be able to penetrate beyond the staggering imagery and to decipher
the arcane historical and political propositions upon which the film was built.
The main accusation was that the film was actually a well-masked version of
Serbian propaganda in times when Serbia was largely believed to be the aggressive force in the war that ensued from the partition of what used to be federalist
Yugoslavia. The most outspoken critic of Kusturica was Stanko Cerović, a Paris-
based journalist of Montenegrin extraction, who claimed that it was not by
chance that in *Underground*

the revolution is led metaphorically by a Montenegrin and a Serb; two
archetypal Belgrade figures, who together represent the cliché image of Serb
heroes created by nationalist writers. These are people who fight and make
love better than anybody else in the world, doubtless thanks to some genetic
and spiritual superiority – but who sometimes also happen to sin or do wrong
precisely because of this spiritual generosity and naivety. Even their violence
only adds to their irresistible charm.   (Cerović, 1995)

Furthermore, Cerović claimed, it was not by chance that Kusturica had selectively chosen the documentary footage used in the film to depict the Croats and
the Slovenes as Nazi collaborators and thus indirectly glorify the brave Serbs.[11]

Kusturica indeed uses footage of Slovene crowds cheering the arrival of Nazi
troops in Maribor around the time of the April 1941 Nazi bombing of Belgrade
in the opening of *Underground*. When asked about this in an interview (with
H. G. Pflaum), Kusturica admitted that he intentionally represented the Croats

and the Slovenes in an unfavourable light, because: 'I was against the selective humanism. I cannot stand the ethnic cleansing [carried out] by the bosnian Serbs, but neither can I stand the ethnic cleansing [carried out] by the Croats' (Pflaum, 1995, p. 16).

Beyond the narrow circles of Yugoslav experts, however, Cerović's opinion on *Underground* did not get any publicity – his very name was sufficient to immediately classify him as a biased ethnic. No matter how knowledgeable he may have been, Cerović did not have the much-needed aura of 'objective credibility'. Luckily, a French intellectual, Alain Finkielkraut, writing in *Le Monde* on 2 June 1995 and using quite strong language, became a mouthpiece for essentially the same criticism, causing quite a controversy. He wrote:

> In recognising *Underground*, the Cannes jury thought it was honouring a creator with a thriving imagination. In fact, it has honoured a servile and flashy illustrator of criminal clichés. The Cannes jury highly praised a version of the most hackneyed and deceitful Serb propaganda. The devil himself could not have conceived so cruel an outrage against Bosnia, nor such a grotesque epilogue to Western incompetence and frivolity.   (Finkielkraut, 1999, p. 184).

This attack challenged a number of well-known Western European intellectuals to debate whether Kusturica's *Underground* was in fact something more than a well-crafted piece of Serbian propaganda. Other high-profile figures such as André Glucksman (who had travelled to Sarajevo), Bernard-Henri Lévy (who had made the documentary *Bosna!*) and Peter Handke (who publicly defended the Serbs) got involved in the heated media discussion, which was covered on the pages of such prominent publications as *Le Monde, Libération, Journal du Dimanche, Süddeutsche Zeitung, The Independent,* the *Guardian, El Pais, Corriere della Sera,* as well as in *The New Yorker.*[12] Besides claiming that the Cannes award was a disgrace for the West, Finkielkraut criticised Kusturica for representing the western parts of Yugoslavia as pro-Nazi, thus supporting the Serbian claims that the present-day Croatian state is fascist in its nature. At the time he launched his criticism, Finkielkraut had not yet seen the movie. But he had already publicly committed himself to the Croatian cause. He had also recently visited the Croatian city of Dubrovnik – an embarrassing revelation which made his objections sound as if they had been influenced by his Croatian friends.[13]

Although the media noise was significant, the topic of the debate nevertheless remained quite cryptic to larger audiences in the West, and even film critics made little out of it. It seemed that nobody much cared whose side of the story was being told in *Underground*: the film was perceived as a gargantuan metaphor of the messy state of Balkan affairs rather than as a finely crafted

propagandistic insinuation that would work in favour of one of the warring
sides. In addition, in the midst of the controversy involving Serbian versus
Croat versions of historical truth, *Underground* was consistently described by
Western critics as a 'Bosnian movie', even though the film was a French, Ger-
man and Hungarian production, shot in Prague, Belgrade and Plovdiv, set in
Belgrade, dealing with Serbs and Croats, and not touching directly on anything
Bosnian.[14] In the minds of reviewers, these Balkan nations were all the same.

The Message

It is difficult to sustain the conspiracy theory and to prove that *Underground*
contained carefully planned pro-Serbian propaganda. Even if it did, the propaganda was so cryptic that it barely did much to improve the shattered popular
image of the Serbs. By concentrating on the issue of alleged pro-Serb bias, however, the critics of *Underground* failed to pay attention to some other important
and just as controversial messages.

With the exception of the final, bright image of joyful peace, *Underground* is
a dark film about the legacy of communism. The very dedication of the film –
'to our fathers and their children' (i.e. 'to ourselves') – suggests that the film is
addressed to and is best understood by those who lived during communism
and experienced its downfall. Challenging the popular argument about the
tribal nature of the Yugoslav conflict, *Underground* undertakes to show that the
roots of the present-day war are to be found in the moral nihilism that prevailed under communism. The film's setting is comparable to the state of the
Yugoslav people, who for the last fifty years have been kept in the cellar of communism. Even if they had been above ground, so to speak, they would have been
manipulated. Yugoslavs related with gratitude to leaders like Tito who were
eventually internationally compromised, which is similar to the way the
enslaved underground inhabitants look up to their 'saviour', Marko. The hypocritical demagogy of the communist system is accountable for the present
state of affairs, claims Kusturica, who said in an interview with David Robinson that *Underground* was:

> a film about manipulation, [about] the way that one or two people can keep
> large numbers of others in their power. In Tito's time people were kept in a
> kind of metaphorical cellar, isolated and believing that they were living the
> best of lives. And in recent years the people who had kept the others in cellars
> announced themselves as democrats and promptly created new cellars.
>
> (Robinson, 1996, p. 12)

If we undertake, however, to investigate which of *Underground*'s heroes' unsettling characteristics are accountable for what, we will see that most of their

wickedness is a result of the absence of clear moral standards. The film, however, does not offer any clear-cut evidence to suggest that it was communism that caused such amorality. Rather, the protagonists of *Underground*, as we first encounter them in the early 1940s, are already people with no morals. Communism only comes *post factum*. It may well have enhanced their amorality, but it does not seem that it created it.

Failing to prove communism accountable for the low morals of his characters, Kusturica ultimately attributes it all to impaired moral standards innate in the Balkan social character, an approach which is nothing else but a refined version of the primordialist argument, according to which the passions that are being played out in the Balkan conflict are of a pre-moral level.

'Living in a nation that was burning in a terrible war, I wanted a story that might answer not just questions about our history but about the nature of our people,' Kusturica said (Robinson, 1996, p. 12). He wanted to examine a group of interesting but unappealing characters and investigate what made them into such nasty human beings. Such an investigation would result in revelations about the profoundly unsettling meanderings of the south Slavic soul, a self-styled continuation of the fearful exploration of all-permissiveness and the infinite questioning of boundaries of moral order *à la* Dostoyevsky.

Whereas in Kusturica's earlier work (*Sjecas li se Dolly Bell?*/*Do You Remember Dolly Bell?*, 1981; *When Father Was Away on Business*; and *Dom za vesanje*/*Time of the Gypsies*, 1989) the director's attention was on the simple people who were being manipulated and abused, the subject of *Underground* is the manipulators, the perpetrators whose amorality is beyond any political system. Screenwriter Kovacević is quite clear about this, particularly as he avoids using the 'communist legacy' rhetoric:

> The war that never ends is the war between the parent and the child, the father and the son. The only solution is love and compassion. In our families we have fought too often over ideologies. Private wars have led to real wars. This is our fate.[15]

For Kovacević and Kusturica, the essence of the Balkan soul seems to be an omnivorous vigour. The poor light underground dims any clear ethical standards. Tunnels appear to be the only adequate setting for the Balkans, both today and for all times. A Byzantine mentality and opportunism cancel all rigid ethical considerations in these insecure lands. There are no clear boundaries between a swindle and a business venture, between victimisers and victims, and no moral limitations for those who have decided to survive, even at the cost of appropriating the survival instinct of others. The people victimised by Marko do not seem to dislike him; they think of him as a saviour. The survivors justify the total moral permissiveness by the fact that, even when above ground, they are still marginal, insignificant and neglected.

Underground looks at people who keep themselves busy by betraying each other. It never becomes clear what exactly are Marko's driving motives for the exploitation scheme. He does not seem to be connected to any social movement, and his declared involvement with communism is shown as a purely opportunistic one.[16] It seems that Marko just has more energy than the others to plot and carry out his conspiratorial undertakings. He is involved in shady dealings with whomever happens to be in power at the time. He enslaves a group of people, appropriating their lives for decades by playing their saviour while in fact acting as their master in the cellar where he has kept them in 'hiding'. Marko is not to blame, however, since in his world, swindlers are the only reliable entrepreneurs. They can play by the rules if needed. But they also have the energy to discard the rules whenever necessary to keep themselves on top of the volatile fortune. An indictment of moral irresponsibility would be inappropriate in this case: it is not about deceit, but husky survivalism. And it is not about communism; it is about the Balkans.

Blacky, the only one shown as a direct perpetrator of the aggression in the 1990s war scene, claims that he only represents himself, defending his country (without ever specifying which country it is). The exquisite, Western-looking, self-promoting entrepreneur Marko, in his dark, well-pressed suit and elegant, golden frames – the real villain – also only represents himself. Only, he would never allow himself to be caught with dirty hands and always would prefer to pull the strings from behind the scenes. Both Marko and Blacky are individualists, and so is Natalia, whose opportunism is driven by an equally egotistic impulse.[17] Their lack of ethical standards creates monstrously deformed personalities that cancel moral norms in the name of personal benefits.

How much of this amorality comes from communism? The answer is: very little. The communist system provided fertile soil for the substandard morals of the protagonists, but it did not create them; the low standards were already an inherent part of their untidy Balkan personalities.

Underground presents the practices of official Yugoslav historiography in a satirical light. Kusturica correctly shows how communism grossly tampered with historical memory. Incidents of drunken womanising are represented as heroic deeds to serve the needs of communist mythmaking. The wheeler-dealer affairs of the protagonists during the war are later beautified in a heroic light, their significance enhanced by Marko in his memoirs.

But while exposing the communist tampering with history, Kusturica himself grossly abuses historical time. Consider, for example, the lengthy leap between the second and the third part of *Underground* (from 1961 to the 1990s), itself revealing a fairly frivolous approach to time and history. In fact, such a leap is equivalent to a period that exceeds the life of the Berlin Wall, which was thought of as a symbolic embodiment of the communist grip over Europe. Kusturica uses extended documentary footage from Tito's funeral, a curious event in international relations which brought together a whole range of incompatible political figures, from Nikolae Ceauşescu and Todor Zhivkov to Margaret Thatcher and Kurt Waldheim, to make a (quite disputable) point about the relativism of all politics and ideology. Another relativistic metaphor, this time fictional, is the busy network of underground tunnels that exists below Europe, which suggests that what happens on the surface (stagnation and cold war) has been effectively lessened by the lively clandestine traffic. Things are not what they seem, and the existence of communism or any other political system makes little difference.

In such a relativist context, the personal politics of parasitism are easily cultivated. Add the unstable and insecure economic and political situation in the Balkans, and the politics of petty survivalism will be seen not only as justifiable but also logical. *Underground*, indeed, makes the point that talking about tribal intolerance is inadequate. This corrective point, however, is made by only slightly shifting the focus – the 'primordial' is rejected, but peculiar morals are admitted instead. Not a big step forward, provided relativist morals are as deprived of underlying rationality as are the primeval passions that are being denied.

Apropos Kusturica

The rest of my discussion will switch focus from the film to the issue of Kusturica's position regarding the controversy that followed.

The Background

Sarajevo-born Kusturica is a Bosnian Muslim by origin. He, however, dissociated himself from the Bosnian Muslim government, since he saw it as a perpetrator of extremism, and, as a matter of principle, refused to endorse any nationalist doctrine. Early in the 1990s Kusturica indicated his desire to stay 'non-aligned'. He was promptly proclaimed a Yugo-nostalgic, a category which described the political stance of numerous other intellectuals who refused to take sides.

Kusturica moved to the West before trouble started at home. By the time he left Sarajevo, he was still under forty and very successful. He had won the Palme d'Or (1985) and Best Director (1989) awards at Cannes, as well as numerous other international awards, and was the most acclaimed director to emerge from the region. Once in the West, statements he made to the press made it clear how painful the Yugoslav breakdown was for him. He went to New York and took a teaching job at Columbia University, where he worked under another prominent émigré, Czech expatriate Milos Forman. In 1992, he made *Arizona Dream*, a film which was well received in Europe but was a flop in the USA, effectively diminishing his chances of a high-profile American career. In 1993–4 he returned to Europe, settled officially on a farmhouse in Normandy and spent a substantial time in Belgrade working on *Underground*, which was released in 1995.

The Problem

Underground was shot between October 1993 and February 1995. The war in Bosnia had started in April 1992, and by the time the shooting of *Underground* began, the director's native land had lived through two years of ethnic cleansing. Thousands of lives had been wasted. The inhabitants of Kusturica's native city, Sarajevo, who were also subjects of his earlier award-winning films *Do You Remember Dolly Bell?* and *When Father Was Away on Business*, had been routinely exposed to mortar shelling and sniper fire and had lived as hungry and captive hostages of the siege for two winters. Of the highlights of the Bosnian ordeal, only Srebrenica was still to come. Back then, the international public opinion believed that Milošević's regime supported the terror in Bosnia, a belief which has not changed since.

In this context, the problem with Kusturica's *Underground* comes down to several simple and straightforward questions (and their respective answers):

Q.: Did the Yugoslav government endorse this film?

A.: There is evidence that the project was supported and endorsed by government-controlled cultural institutions in Milošević's Yugoslavia.

Q.: Had Kusturica, by accepting such an endorsement and making the choice to work in Belgrade, taken the side of the aggressor?

A.: Long before making *Underground*, Kusturica was successful enough not to need mentors or to plead allegiance to anyone. Provided he had expressed his disapproval of Bosnian Islamists long before *Underground*, it would not be logical to expect him to be a mouthpiece for their cause or to return to Sarajevo. One would rather expect to see him dissociate himself from politics altogether, as was the case with many of his displaced compatriots. He could have stayed in New York or Paris as a secular 'Yugo-nostalgic'. However, he chose to go Belgrade. By taking up the *Underground* project with a substantial Serbian involvement, he lost his neutral position and could no longer be described as impartial.[18]

Q.: Was the film Serbian propaganda?

A.: We should distinguish between two lines in the film's criticism. Finkielkraut attacked *Underground* for alleged anti-Croatian elements, which, I agree, can be found in the film. The criticism of Cerović was of a different category: he thought that Kusturica had identified with the Serbian point of view to such an extent that he uncritically idealised the Serbs and vilified all others. As far as the film's international reception is concerned, even if *Underground* could be read as pro-Serbian propaganda by audiences within the borders of former Yugoslavia, it barely worked as such in an international context, since the alleged pro-Serbian message was 'lost in translation'.

Q.: People in Sarajevo were being shelled by thugs who confessed allegiance to the same government that was sponsoring Kusturica's film. By making *Underground*, was Kusturica betraying his compatriots?

A.: This is the way people in Sarajevo interpreted it, and it is easy to see why.

Q.: What else could he do? What were his alternatives if he really felt this film had to be made?

A.: Making movies in Belgrade when you have the choice of making them anywhere else is to take sides. Unlike Dušan Makavejev, Kusturica has no problems securing financing for his projects, and can make films outside Yugoslavia without financial involvement and other forms of support from Belgrade. Such films, however, would certainly be different. *Underground* could not be made elsewhere.

The moral issues related to the making of Kusturica's *Underground* are somewhat comparable to the moral issues of Leni Riefenstahl's work of the 1930s. I should underline, however, that I use this comparative framework primarily because the Riefenstahl case provides a well-known, familiar background against which I can make Kusturica's case clearer. Riefenstahl claimed she did not intend to glorify the Nazis, that all she wanted to do was to celebrate beauty; Kusturica claimed he did not intend to make propaganda for the Serbs, that all he wanted to do was to realise his artistic vision. The Nazi regime happened to be there to give Riefenstahl the chance to work, a fact which she believed was coincidental and secondary; the Milošević regime happened to be there to welcome a Bosnian Muslim of Kusturica's stature, providing him with a supportive working environment, which Kusturica similarly regarded as coincidental and secondary to his work. In Roy Müller's documentary *Die Macht der Bilder: Leni Riefenstahl/Wonderful Horrible Life of Leni Riefenstahl* (1993), the director keeps asking Riefenstahl if she feels any remorse for being involved with the Nazis, and she persistently replies that she can think of nothing she may have done that would make her feel remorseful. In reply to similar allegations, Kusturica (1995) ridiculed his critics as paranoiacs.

True, unlike *Triumph des Willens*, Kusturica 'can hardly be said to have produced a piece of unalloyed Serb propaganda'.[19] But there was another
complication. Leni Riefenstahl did not need to cross front lines – she was German, and so were the Nazis; she did not choose them, she just did not reject
them. Kusturica, on the contrary, travelled half way around the world to find a
nurturing atmosphere in Belgrade. That Belgrade was leading a war against his
native Bosnia was seemingly irrelevant and secondary to him. The only thing
that mattered was his creative drive.

The Evidence

Underground was released as a French–German–Hungarian production. So
why, then, all this talk of Belgrade's involvement? The film was shot on locations
at Barrandov, Belgrade and Plovdiv.[20] Three production companies had
invested in the project – the French CiBY 2000, the German Pandora Film and
the Hungarian Novo Film. The credits of the film and the production dossier
also list production participation by Radio-TV Serbia (RTS) and a Belgrade-
based production company, Komuna, but for some reason these are not
commonly mentioned or translated.

The question of Serbian financial participation in the film has only been
raised in the media occasionally, mostly due to the firewall approach to the issue
taken by representatives of CiBY 2000. In reply to allegations voiced by journalists about the rumoured 5 per cent financing from Radio-TV Serbia, a CiBY
executive claimed that there had been no direct financial participation, and that
it was purely a pre-sale arrangement. Kusturica himself claimed that the
services rendered by RTS had no monetary value at all and were limited to
services-in-kind, lending studios and equipment in exchange for the right
to show the film on Serbian television.

This issue is tackled in detail by Florence Hartmann (1995), who notes that
the producers (CiBY 2000) kept the information on the circumstances of the
film's financing as confidential 'as a state secret'. She discusses the alleged Serbian government financing for *Underground* and whether such financing
represents a violation of the international economic embargo against Serbia at
the time of production. She quotes a number of embargo-related resolutions
under which the film should have been criminalised had the embargo been
strictly enforced.[21]

The deliberate downplaying of Serbian government participation in the production of the film makes it impossible to estimate precisely how much has
been invested by the Serbs. Different sources quote different figures, ranging
from 5 per cent of the production costs to $10 million.[22]

Insiders talk about a personal friendship between Kusturica and Milorad
Vucelić, who was at the time director of Belgrade TV and majority whip in the

Serbian parliament.[23] Besides the close involvement with the project, Vucelić was rumoured to have led what amounted to an (un)official Serbian delegation, which included the then-minister of culture Nada Perišić-Popović, to the Cannes Film Festival, where they attended the showing of *Underground* and the awards ceremony without causing much public outcry (Hartmann, 1995).

Only a month later, on 19 June 1995, *Underground* premiered in Belgrade. It was also serialised for RTS and aired in six parts later in the summer of 1995. By the end of the year, Yugoslavia had entered it into the Academy Awards competition for best foreign-language film, but it was soon withdrawn by the French CiBY producers. No exact explanation of the withdrawal was ever given.[24]

Since Kusturica was spending time in Belgrade anyway, in 1995 he became a co-director of the Belgrade Film Fest, and accepted the honorary chair of the new Balkan Film Board.[25] In 1996 he worked on *Crna macka, beli macor/Black Cat, White Cat*, a Gypsy story shot entirely in Belgrade. Initially conceived as a short, the film was then extended to feature length and was released by CiBY 2000. It received an award at the Venice Film Festival in 1998.

Around that time, Kusturica also made public statements that reiterated the 'ancient enmities' arguments. In an interview for *Cahiers du cinéma*, he compared the war in Yugoslavia to an earthquake.[26] In other instances, he was quoted as saying: 'In my film, I tried to clarify the state of things in this chaotic part of the world. It seems that nobody is able to locate the roots of this terrible conflict' (Žižek, 1995, p. 37). Oudran cites another instance:

> The Balkans are a slippery region, it is nothing like the CNN show as seen by certain French intellectuals. This is a country where in the course of 4,000 years people have struggled to live at the point where the biggest empires (Roman, Ottoman, and Austro-Hungarian) collapsed, a fragile region where the earthquakes may be more important than elsewhere.
>
> (Oudran, Agence France-Presse, 1995)

The 'earthquake' trope struck critic Stanko Cerović as outrageous. He wrote:

> He [Kusturica] described as a natural disaster a war which was politically and militarily prepared in detail for months in Belgrade; which was started by special units sent from Belgrade to Bosnia; and in which the worst crimes, rapes and deportations of population have been executed according to a plan and without the least spontaneity, all with the aim of creating ethnically pure territories in Bosnia. ... If this is an earthquake, then Kusturica is indeed the spontaneous and naive artist he pretends to be – just as spontaneous, naive yet

all-powerful as his heroes, who destroy and kill all about them out of
generosity of spirit and love of Yugoslavia, its other people and nations.

(Cerović, 1995)

Essentially, Kusturica was telling the world that no one could be held accountable for the deplorable state of Balkan affairs, that it was all bound to happen
in a region with high seismic activity.

In all fairness, I should mention that a similar stance to the war was adopted
by Dušan Makavejev, who insisted that 'professionals who deal with natural disasters' are called in to cope with the 'storm' raging in Yugoslavia (Makavejev,
1993, p. 6). As a Sarajevan, however, Kusturica did not seem to think that the
question of who was shelling Sarajevo at the time was of much relevance.
Shelling or earthquake, it seemed to be all the same to him – beyond human
control, coming from profundity.

Although Kusturica had earned the resentment of his fellow Sarajevans long
before these statements were made, the situation was rapidly deteriorating.
Even former close friends and colleagues (many of them Serbs) who had stayed
in Sarajevo of their own free will no longer wanted to listen to him.[27] Long
before *Underground* was released, many had promised never to see another film
made by him.

The director was one of the people who had created the image of Sarajevo
as a multi-ethnic city, only to desert it in difficult times and declare that the
only multicultural city in the region was, in fact, Belgrade (in Pauli, 1996, p.
135). In an interview he even recalled in detail the moment when he realised
that Sarajevo was 'no longer my city'. It happened during his last visit, in 1992,
when, walking down Sarajevo streets with his friend Johnny Depp, he realised
that he had grown irretrievably detached from this place, where 'the young
population was extremely defeatist and in a very aggressive mood' (ibid., p.
135). To Kusturica, the despair in the air was repulsive, something with which
he could not possibly be associated. In spite of his publicly articulated intention not to resume residence in Sarajevo and to make France his official home,
in another interview Kusturica indicated how displeased he was to hear that his
apartment, now vacant, had been confiscated by the state and given to someone else: 'In the name of creating a multi-ethnic Bosnia they are looting our
places' (quoted in Turan, 1997b, p. F1).

No doubt Belgrade was eager to welcome the dispossessed Bosnian director,
and to provide him with shelter and a supportive working environment. While
working on *Underground* and exposing how the legacy of communism was to
blame for the present situation, Kusturica enjoyed a treatment very similar to
that loyal film-makers received under communism. He did not even know the
cost of the services that Radio-TV Serbia had provided for the production. The

disposition of the powers that be was so benevolent that it had not set a monetary ceiling on its support.

The Reaction

Kusturica tried to reply to the international criticism in the autumn of 1995 by ridiculing his critics as rigid sectarians. Among the people who attacked him, besides Finkielkraut, were documentarian Dom Rotheroe, director of *Urbicide: A Sarajevo Diary* (1993), and Robert Yates.[28] Some of the voices in defence of Kusturica and artistic freedom were Mr Busy (an editorial pseudonym) in the February 1996 issue of the British film magazine *Sight and Sound*, Harald Pauli in the German magazine *Focus* (1996), Serge Rigourd in the French *Le Monde* (1995) and, most notably, Austrian writer Peter Handke (1997), in a series of articles which were subsequently published in a book format.[29]

In a reply published in the 26 October 1995 issue of *Le Monde*, which also carried a number of articles very critical of him, Kusturica confronted his critics by offering absurd images of himself collaborating with the aggressive Belgrade regime. For instance:

> Image Nr. Two: Sunset. Red from the East. Lit in an impressionistic manner à la Monet, my wife and I distribute propaganda materials (videocassettes of *Underground* and icons of Milosevic) to the poor and middle-class peasants, agricultural workers, and little schoolchildren in Normandy.

He also expressed fear that all Francophone humanists were preparing to lynch him.

It seems that Kusturica expected his critics to respond with remorseful statements in the media. It did not happen, however, and soon after he was again in the public spotlight, this time to announce his retirement from film-making. Kusturica declared that he would quit cinema altogether in December 1995, as a reaction to the unbearable scrutiny to which he was subjected by French intellectuals.[30] Was he not overdoing it? Journalists from *Süddeutsche Zeitung* wondered if Kusturica was indeed so used to praise and awards or so sensitive that he deemed it necessary to quit rather than face the critics.[31] Writer Peter Handke, the most vocal Kusturica defender, blamed his critics for trying to impose sectarian morals over creative liberty. For Handke, who claimed that *Underground* exhibited a Shakespearean force, artistic expression always prevailed over moral considerations (Handke, 1997, pp. 7–8).

Many Serbian directors have abstained from taking a public position on Kusturica's case. Srdjan Karanović and Paris-based Dušan Makavejev routinely decline to answer questions about him, wary of making statements that might be interpreted as sectarian calls to limit artistic freedom or as issuing

from envious peers. To my knowledge, apart from scattered references to the
past when he envied the better financial support Kusturica had received for a
similarly themed movie, Goran Paskaljević has also abstained from commentary in the mainstream media.[32]

Only Srdjan Dragojević, the young Serbian director who had referenced *Time
of the Gypsies* in his debut feature *Mi nismo andjeli/We Are No Angels* (1992),
publicly defended Kusturica. According to him:

> Kusturica did the right thing. Sarajevo expected he would stay and would
> make propaganda for Muslim people during the war. The artist has his own
> rights and his own place in the world. It's not necessary to choose one side in
> a conflict; if you do that, you stop being an artist.
>
> (quoted in Turan, 1997b, F1)

In a sincere effort to give Kusturica at least some credibility, most journalists
made sure to mention that, in spite of all his public commitment to Belgrade,
his declared place of residence was in France. Like other Bosnian refugees,
Kusturica had found a refuge in the west of Europe, albeit in somewhat
better conditions. When he was not in Belgrade, his home was a Normandy
farmhouse.

Kusturica, however, did not live up to the image of the exiled martyr for very
long. Only three months after his public retirement from film-making, in

Shortly after quitting film-making,
Kusturica released his apolitical
*Crna macka, beli macor/Black Cat,
White Cat* (1998)

March 1996, he was in the news again – he was in Belgrade, shooting his *Black Cat, White Cat*, which was released in 1998.[33]

The Acquittal

After Kusturica's retirement from film-making, *Underground* finally found an American distributor (*The New Yorker*) and was shown at arthouse cinemas across North America. It was reviewed in all major US newspapers, where critics often expressed reservations. But since the film was endorsed by a European cinema institution like the Cannes Film Festival, they recommended it. *The New York Times'* Janet Maslin first described *Underground* as a 'feverish, whimsical allegory elevated by moments of brilliant clarity', and on another occasion as 'exotic and elliptical'.[34] *Film Comment's* Katherine Dieckmann talked of it as 'sprawling, noisy, and extremely complicated', while *Variety's* Emanuel Levy called it a 'steamroller circus'.[35] There were even some straightforward instances of American ingenuity. David Elliott of *The San Diego Union-Tribune*, for example, wrote: '*Underground* received the esteemed Palme d'Or at the 1995 Cannes Film Festival. May I respectfully suggest that the jurors were drunk?'[36]

If mentioned at all, the European controversies were only touched on in passing by reviewers. The general attitude taken by American critics was that it was difficult, if not nearly impossible, to understand the allegations and the controversy surrounding the film; this probably explains why many referred to the film as 'Bosnian'. In her extensive portrait of Kusturica in *Film Comment*, Katherine Dieckmann chose to ignore the controversy altogether. J. Hoberman's advice to New Yorkers was that they use their own judgment: with the film finally released they could 'have their opportunity to denounce Kusturica – or not'. His own reaction was that none of it really mattered, since the 'passions of the early 90s already may be more passé than Yugoslavia itself' (Hoberman, 1997, p. 75). In general, critics believed that it was somehow irrelevant, or even bad taste, to bring up the issue of Kusturica's politics.

Adam Gopnik's 1996 piece in *The New Yorker* probably remains the only one to discuss the *Underground* controversy, but in a way that was most symptomatic of the manifestation of the *a priori* acquittal attitude. Entirely dismissing the underlying issue about Kusturica's political allegiances as something irrelevant, it focused on the Paris critics instead, exploring their scuffle around Kusturica as a manifestation of the extravagant and whimsical nature of French intellectuals. Diagnosing that Kusturica was the meat in another man's sandwich, Gopnik concentrated his entire discussion on the behaviour of the liberal French philosophers. He noted that they were different from 'their merely nihilistic British friends and from their downtrodden American cousins' in their belief that 'what they say matters, and that what they think today the world will think tomorrow' (ibid., p. 32).

The interest in this subtle case of Western intellectual subterfuge effectively diverted attention from issues of culture and politics that did not affect the West. The Balkans (or any other remote part of the world, for that matter) could not possibly be of interest; they were somehow too heavy-handed and insufficiently sophisticated. The *Underground* controversy was looked upon as representative of the whole Balkan conflict, incomprehensible and annoying. The politics of the French were the only ones to merit discussion, not Kusturica's politics, which reflected 'a quarrel in a far away country between people of whom we know nothing.'[37]

International academic celebrity Slavoj Žižek, one of the few from the Balkans (Slovenia) whom intellectuals in the West are willing to listen to, tried to indicate that Kusturica was an exemplary case of 'Balkanism', functioning in a similar way to Edward Said's concept of orientalism, as a timeless space onto which the West projects its phantasmatic content:

> Together with Milche Manchevski's *Before the Rain*, *Underground* is thus the ultimate ideological product of Western liberal multiculturalism: what these two films offer to the Western liberal gaze is precisely what this gaze wants to see in the Balkan war – the spectacle of a timeless, incomprehensible, mythical cycle of passions, in contrast to decadent and anemic Western life.
>
> (Žižek, 1995, p. 38)

While *Underground*'s Balkan origins were the reason for indifference, the prevalent treatment of Kusturica was the benevolence that an artist of his stature seemed especially entitled to. 'There is only one reason for me to make movies,' Kusturica said in his acceptance speech at Cannes. 'To be loved by you!' Turning to the international scene for approval and love, Kusturica indicated how much he needed to continue enjoying the special status of an exceptional *enfant terrible*. Repudiated by earlier admirers, he was still granted his wish, if not by all, by most – by the jury at Cannes, by high-profile patrons like Peter Handke who saw 'a Shakespearian force' in the film, and last but not least, by benevolent film critics.

Kusturica's quest for a relaxed and permissive moral standard revived the somewhat forgotten romantic concept of a special moral code for the artist to whom traditional norms cannot apply, but who rather lives in a state of perpetual self-assertion, playfully casting aside firm commitments and violating rules in the name of sustaining a frivolous, creative personality. First proposed by the early German romantic Friedrich Schlegel, further developed by F. W. J. Schelling and later critiqued by G. W. F. Hegel, the concept of special moral standards for the artist is also known as romantic irony. According to this principle, the only mode in which the genius can exist is one of asserting something, only to negate it soon after, and then to reassert it again in a playful, immediate return, a frolicsome refuting of oneself in a generous artistic gesture that cancels all known rigid morals, an *Aufhebung* which allows a return to a higher level.

Kusturica's career since *Underground* has been a good illustration for the theory of romantic irony. His next film, the intentionally apolitical *Black Cat, White Cat*, was meant to be a complete negation of the intricate politics of *Underground*. A compendium of Kusturica's exotic imagery, it received an award at Venice and a wide release, but was dismissed by serious critics as 'a swirling and pretty meaningless two-hour amalgam of bits and pieces from all his other movies' (Malcolm, 1998, G2, p. 11). For a while, the director's next film was supposed to be an adaptation of D. M. Thomas' *The White Hotel*, a challenging undertaking which seemed to contain the promise of a return to a higher level, as postulated in the romantic framework. But this project was cancelled. Most recently, Kusturica acted in a film, and has been busy touring with a rock group.

Notes

1. *Underground* (1995). CiBY 2000 (Paris)/Pandora Film (Frankfurt)/Novo Film (Budapest). 167 min. In Serbo-Croatian. Director: Emir Kusturica. Script: Dušan Kovacević. Cinematographer: Vilko Filać. Composer: Goran Bregović. Cast: Miki Manojlović, Lazar Ristovski, Mirjana Joković, Slavko Stimać.

2. Kusturica's hermeneutic approach to history was previously revealed in his *When Father Was Away on Business* (1985), subtitled 'A historical love film'. It focuses on an extended Sarajevo family to make an allegorical statement about the state of affairs in Yugoslav society of the 1950s.

3. The script is based on motifs from Kovacević's plays from the 1970s, *Spring in January* and *Meeting Point*.

4. This part concludes with extensive documentary footage of the grandiose funeral of Tito in 1980. According to the commentary, it was, in fact, the 1961 'mysterious disappearance of Marko Dren, the revolutionary and poet' that led to the end of Titoist Yugoslavia, since we are told: 'Comrade Tito got sick, suffered for twenty years, and died at the end.'

5. Most viewers of non-Yugoslav origin, including myself, take the battlefield in this part to represent, presumably, a Bosnian location. However, in a personal exchange with a man from Novi Sad, I was recently told that 'to a foreign eye it is presumably Bosnia, but for a person with some living knowledge of pan-Yugoslav geography and landscapes that battlefield is in Slavonia (eastern Croatia). It is not explicitly stated but one can sense it because of the flat land.' While I do not feel competent enough to judge precisely the location of the war zone, I should agree that the landscape of the battlefield is certainly

not the typical Bosnian (mountainous) one (which Kusturica, as a Bosnian, would be able to present very well). If the battlefield is in Slavonia, however, then Blacky's revenge in the following scenes is actually aimed against Croats, a consideration which makes one more argument in favour of those who, as we will see, claim that the film is deliberately anti-Croatian (and thus pro-Serbian).

6. In this part Kusturica appears in a cameo as a local thug and arms dealer, together with musician Nelle Karajlić, the leader of the rock group Zabranjeno Pusenje (No Smoking), in which Kusturica himself played during his Sarajevo years.

7. The aesthetics of this scene is reminiscent of the fires on the river in Kusturica's *Time of the Gypsies* (Yugoslavia, 1989), and seems to be directly influenced by scenes of fire and devastation characteristic of Russian cinema, in particular, Elem Klimov's *Come and See* (1985) and Andrei Tarkovsky's *The Mirror* (1975) and *Sacrifice* (1986).

8. A suicide attempt of the same kind is carried out by the protagonist of Kusturica's 1989 *Time of the Gypsies*, Perhan, only here it is presented in a comic light.

9. The Jesus figure hanging upside down is an image utilised in a similar setting of destruction and desolation by Andrzej Wajda in his classic *Ashes and Diamonds* (1958).

10. The underground wedding scene repeats imagery exploited in *Time of the Gypsies*. A number of visual motifs from *Arizona Dream* (1992) are also developed and deployed in *Underground*. The same is the case with the Romani music score by Goran Bregović, who also composed the music for earlier films by Kusturica.

11. Cerović works for the Yugoslav section of *Radio France Internationale*. The article appeared in print in the August 1995 issue of *Bosnia Report*, an independent publication run by the London-based journalist Branka Magas and is available on the World Wide Web.

12. A detailed account of the dispute surrounding *Underground* can be found in Adam Gopnik's discussion in *The New Yorker* (1996). Peter Handke's *A Journey to the Rivers* (1997) is the only text written as part of the original *Underground* discussion to have appeared in an English translation. It was originally published in 1996 in *Süddeutsche Zeitung*.

13. Finkielkraut was well known as a public defender of the Croatian cause from earlier on. Before the Bosnian war, he had published a book entitled *How I Became a Croat* (translated into Croatian and published in Zagreb).

14. A few examples: Reuters and Associated Press covered *Underground* with material entitled 'Bosnian Film Wins at Cannes' (29 May 1995). Influential Chicago critic Michael Wilmington (*Chicago Tribune*, 21 December 1997, p.

C1) called *Underground* a 'Bosnian-set' film. Toronto critic Shlomo Schwartzberg (*North York Mirror*, 3–4 January 1998) described *Underground* as a movie from Bosnia and France.

15. Chris Hedges, 'Belgrade Journal: Scathing "Conscience" of Balkans Spares No One: An Interview with Dušan Kovacević', *New York Times*, 8 February 1996, p. A4.

16. An interesting exploration of a similar type of character in Yugoslav cinema is Rajko Grlić's *Charuga* (1990), which looks at a self-styled Croatian anarchist from early in the twentieth century. For this protagonist, standard morals barely apply, and he is also full of vigour and energy. The topic of fanatic communists consciously violating moral standards is a different one. Within the wider context of East European cinema it has been treated by Agnieszka Holland in her award-winning *Fever* (1981), a flagship film of Polish dissent.

17. It is not my task here to discuss the representation of women, but it does not take much scrutiny to discover that all women in *Underground* are considered only in relation to their men. It would be easy to show that Kusturica has always had problems in representing complex female characters and that most depictions of women in his work have been quite schematic.

18. Critics of Kusturica often make comparisons with situations from World War II to make the case clearer. A fellow Sarajevan, for example, puts it this way: 'It is 1940, you do not give a concert with the Berlin Philharmonic' (quoted in Turan, 1997b, F1).

19. Personal correspondence from Paul Coates, 1998.

20. A documentary, *Shooting Days* (1996), follows the director around during the work on the film. The gigantic set for the production created temporary jobs for many unemployed workers at the bankrupt plant for metal construction in Bulgaria's second largest city.

21. Hartmann points to resolutions 757 of 1992, 820 of 1993 and 942 of 23 September 1994 of the Security Council of the UN, which imposed an international embargo against Serbia and Montenegro for their role in the Bosnian war. It is particularly resolution 943 that explicitly asserts the sanctions in the field of culture. She quotes unnamed legal experts, according to whom a film production of this scale undoubtedly would have had a positive economic effect on the economy of Yugoslavia. The numerous financial transactions that accompany the making of an international co-production would fall under the range of financial activities banned by resolution 757, which imposes strict limitations on the transfer of funds to the country in question.

22. In Yugoslavia the financial involvement of RTS was not a secret and was discussed in the media before the film's release in publications like the Montenegrin magazine *Monitor* and Belgrade newspaper *Politika* (Lazar

Stojanović at the American Association for the Advancement of Slavic Studies
convention, November 1995, Washington, DC).

23. Vucelić is discussed in detail by Stanko Cerović in his essay. According to a
    Belgrade informant, 'Vucelić has a long history. In his younger days, he was
    considered a kind of dissident. Believed very intelligent, Milošević had not
    liked him at first, but then Vucelić in some way has managed prove his
    loyalty. Suddenly he became a very close friend of the ruling pair. For a while
    he was the party whip in parliament as well as director of TV. His affair with
    folk singer Vesna Zmijanac was a big thing during 1994. She was constantly
    on TV these days. Then when the big turn came and Milošević "betrayed"
    Karadžić, he was reputed to have rebelled as a "hawk" and was removed
    quietly. But he is back now in the limelight.' Most recently, Vucelić has been
    the leading contender in the race to take over the leadership of the Socialist
    Party of Yugoslavia, after Milošević's deposition in 2000.
24. The entry was reported first in *Le Monde*, 26 October 1995, but was not
    covered in the US media. The subsequent withdrawal of the film from the
    Oscar competition was mentioned only in passing in the American press
    (Josh Young, 'The Usual Spats Over Nominees for Foreign Films', *The New
    York Times*, 11 February 1996, sect. 2 p. 18).
25. Kusturica became a general manager of the Fest alongside critic Nenad Dukić
    in February 1995 and had excerpts of *Underground*, then still in production,
    screened at the festival (Debora Young, 'Belgrade Revives Fest', *Daily Variety*,
    6 February 1995, p. 16; Debora Young, 'Belgrade Fest Taking Cues from
    Peace', *Daily Variety*, 29 January 1996, p. 28; Debora Young, 'Local
    Filmmakers Launch Balkan Board', *Variety*, 12–18 February 1996,
    p. 19).
26. 'Propos de Emir Kusturica', *Cahiers du cinéma*, No. 492, June 1995, p. 69.
27. One of the most outspoken friends turned critic was Sarajevan poet Abdulah
    Sidran, who had scripted Kusturica's *Do You Remember Dolly Bell* (1982) and
    When Father Was Away on Business. (Sidran eventually scripted Kenović's
    Perfect Circle.) For an extensive discussion of the resentment of Sarajevans,
    see Remy Oudran's 'A Sarajevo, les souvenirs amers des anciens amis d'un
    enfant de la rue', *Le Monde*, 26 October 1995; Jean-Michel Frodon's 'Sarajevo
    a l'aube incertaine d'une renaissance culturelle', *Le Monde*, 13 April 1996; and
    Turan (1997b).
28. Rotheroe in a letter to *Sight and Sound* (March 1996) and Yates in 'Gone
    Underground', *Guardian*, 7 March 1996.
29. Serge Rigourd, 'Underground, Alain Finkielkraut et Jdanov', *Le Monde*, 9 June
    1995.
30. 'Emir Kusturica annonce qu'il arrive le cinema', *Agence France Presse*, 4
    December 1995.

31. 'Resignation: Vertragen Künstler also keine Kritik?' *Süddeutsche Zeitung*, 7 December 1995.

32. In 1998, however, when both Kusturica's new *Black Cat, White Cat* and Paskaljević's *Powder Keg* were to be screened at the Venice Film Festival, the old animosity sparkled again. While Kusturica's film won an award at the festival, Paskaljević's film was only screened outside of the main programme (which did not prevent critics like Derek Malcolm declaring it the best film at the festival). In an interview which described the current state of affairs between the two directors as a 'feud', Kusturica blamed Paskaljević for accusing him 'of being a mouthpiece of Milošević just to get attention for himself'. In response to which Kusturica made it clear to the 'producer we shared' that 'he would have to choose between me and that jerk in the future' (in Fiachra Gibbons, 'He Duels, He Brawls, He Helps Cows to Give Birth ... and Makes Films', *Guardian*, 23 April 1999).

33. CiBY 2000 also backed a project (which was later abandoned) called *The Swedish King on a Bicycle One Friday Afternoon*, a romantic comedy with Daniel Auteuil. Another project, an adaptation of D. M. Thomas' novel *The White Hotel*, produced by Robert Geisler and John Roberdeau from a script by Dennis Potter (and reworked by Dušan Kovacević), was expected to be Kusturica's next film. But after the producers ran into financial troubles in 2000, the director withdrew from the project. He has now said he will make a film called *The Nose*, about a New York actor who gets into trouble with the Russian mafia.

34. Janet Maslin, 'From Former Yugoslavia, Revelry with Allegory', *The New York Times*, 12 October 1996, sect. 1 p. 18; Janet Maslin, 'Dangers and Jitters of Life in Sarajevo', *The New York Times*, 26 November 1997, p. E5. In the first review Maslin had claimed that 'There's no hidden agenda to this robust and not terribly subtle tale of duplicity.'

35. Katherine Dieckmann, 'When Kusturica Was Away on Business', *Film Comment*, Vol. 33, No. 5, 19 September 1997, p. 44; Emanuel Levy, '*Underground*', *Variety*, 29 May 29–4 June 1995, p. 55.

36. David Elliott, 'Overrated "Underground" Is a Mishmash of Balderdash', *The San Diego Union-Tribune*, 15 January 1998, p. 23.

37. As put by British Prime Minister Neville Chamberlain about Germany's annexation of the Sudetenland (*The Times*, 28 September 1938).

Chapter 7
Taking Sides

Aleksandar, the protagonist of *Before the Rain*, returned from the West to his Macedonian village and found everybody there in the powerful grip of frightful intolerance. He was above irrational ethnic rivalries and opposed the obsessive madness which he saw perpetuated by the members of his own extended family. In his outright rejection of the violence, he even helped a victimised Albanian girl escape the rage of the men who chased her. This act, coupled with the protagonist's ideas of non-violent conflict resolution, cost him his life. He was killed by his relatives, whose militant stance he refused to adopt. The first lesson: refusing to take sides only works in the tolerant West. You can be a 'Yugoslav' only away from the Balkans. The second lesson: the pacifist intellectual ends up taking sides against his or her own people.

As in the famous animated allegory of Canadian Norman McLaren's *Les Voisins/Neighbors* (1952), as soon as a fence line is drawn between neighbouring houses, one has to choose to be on one side or the other; each crossing of the line, and later on each look across the line, is a good enough reason for a fight. The neighbours' earlier friendship turns overnight into an intolerant rivalry. In such circumstances hatred grows into an all-consuming passion, and even though one may resist taking sides, ultimately it is impossible to avoid becoming embroiled in the conflict.

But was everybody in Yugoslavia ready to take sides; did everybody want to? How about those who were born into mixed marriages and had to choose between two inherent ethnicities? Or what about those who simply resented the idea of making a choice about something that did not concern them and who would prefer 'not to be considered a member of any of the world's tribes'?[1] No matter how unwillingly, everybody was requested to undergo this imposed re-identification – from the inclusive concept of 'Yugoslav', which had been cultivated for decades but was now abandoned overnight, people had to switch to a restrictive concept of belonging, confined to a clear-cut ethnic identity. Making the choice and taking a side was treated as a matter of life and death.

In this chapter, I will talk of the ordeal of those who had to live through such involuntary parting, and of the peculiar twists which came about in the course of people's resistance to the imposed taking of sides. The whole logic of parting alongside the newly erected divides of ethnic belonging implied choices that many had to make against their will. I will show that while some willingly stayed on 'their own' side, for others it was a matter of integrity to make the choice against 'one's own'. I will discuss in more detail the production and reception of films that reflected the forced 'parting'.

In the process of this violent parting, the attempts to take an 'all sides are guilty' stance, while welcomed internationally, did not work with the groups within former Yugoslavia. I will illustrate this by looking at the reception of two films that proposed that all sides should take a share in the blame: Boro Drašković's *Vukovar* and Srdjan Dragojević's *Pretty Village, Pretty Flame*.

In the second part of this chapter, I will examine the role of those Western intellectuals who were publicly committed to taking sides, particularly in the Bosnian conflict. For many, it was a commitment which largely coincided with their chosen path of public dissent. The Bosnian war simply provided another chance to continue the line of social critique with which they were already engaged in their given contexts. To many of them, already outspoken critics of Western attitudes to the rest of the world, Bosnia was just another example, and as such it pushed the critical discourse on Western ideas of conflict resolution, peacemaking and media a step further. In my discussion, I bring up issues concerning the nature of modern-day cross-cultural political commitments and the difficulty of engagement with political cultures outside of one's own immediate environment. In this light, I will consider Marcel Ophuls' epic documentary, *The Troubles We Have Seen: A History of Journalism in Wartime*.

Whose side?

The dilemma of mutually exclusive ethnic identities meant deprivation of individual freedom of choice. To many, the imposed taking of sides resulted in disillusionment with the meaning of commitment.

There were, of course, people whose personal stance seemed to fit the clearcut model of ethnic purity and who did not need prompting to choose sides, stepping in quickly to stand by those whom they considered to be 'their own'. For the warlords, the choice was easy: the late Croatian Goyko Sušak, for example, returned from his adoptive country, Canada, to run the armed forces of his native Croatia. The late Serbian Kapetan Dragan returned from Australia to run the paramilitary units in Serbia. In the summer of 1998, many expatriate Albanians returned from abroad to take up arms in the struggle for Kosovo.

While others did not take up arms, they outspokenly sided with 'their own'. In Belgrade, Milic od Macva, a celebrated naivist painter, became an outspoken militant nationalist.[2] Turbo-folk singer Baja Mali Knindja chose to appear in his music videos in a Chetnik uniform. A number of Serbian documentarians and feature film-makers chose to tell their side of the story, which often meant working on propaganda-style films,[3] while some expatriate film-makers also got involved in similar projects.[4]

In Sarajevo it was even easier to commit, as many intellectuals felt that the survival of the city depended on their physical presence there. Theatre director Haris Pašović, for example, a secular Muslim from Sarajevo, had risen to international fame while working for the stage in Belgrade. Pašović had initially left Yugoslavia for a career in the West and had settled in the Netherlands. But, in the autumn of 1992, 'while working on a spectacle called *Sarajevo* in Antwerp, he decided that he could no longer remain in safe exile, and at the end of the year managed to crawl back past UN patrols and under Serb gunfire into the freezing, besieged city'(Sontag, 1994, p. 94). Film director Ademir Kenović and poet-screenwriter Abdulah Sidran stayed in Sarajevo and collaborated on *Perfect Circle*, which was to become the first Bosnian post-war feature.

These people remained on the side of the ethnic group to which they belonged willingly. For many others, however, taking the side of the ethnic group to which they nominally belonged was not such a straightforward choice but one made rather reluctantly. In this process of the imposed taking of sides, the media were often instrumental and partial. In his account of the Bosnian war, Prijedor Muslim Rezak Hukanović (1996) describes how everybody in town was urged to take sides, as the local media proclaimed that all Muslims were Islamic extremists – what else could he, the Muslim, possibly be then? In Croatia, actress Mira Furlan was attacked by a journalist in her home town of Zagreb for taking part in a theatre festival in Belgrade after the breakup. According to the journalist, Furlan 'was parading her naked breasts on a Belgrade stage while people were being killed in Croatia'. Furlan began to receive threatening phone calls and letters, was called a 'Chetnik whore', and eventually dismissed from the Croatian national theatre. She could either firmly take the side to which she was appointed by the media and public opinion, or be ostracised. Furlan chose to emigrate.[5]

The logic of 'identity politics', which made the partition an imperative for individuals, was, ironically, furthered by the way the Western media worked. For the purposes of telling a comprehensible story, journalists needed to have clearly defined actors. Everyone who had not taken one of the opposing sides was practically excluded and denied media coverage. In the BBC documentary *Urbicide*, Bill Tribe, a British scholar who worked at Sarajevo University throughout the 1980s, systematically shows how the world media gradually accepted and perpetuated the divide in ethnic categories, rendering invisible anyone who did not belong to the main groups of players, and thus effectively dismissing the very idea of diversity.[6] In *Truth under Siege*, an insightful documentary made by independent American film-makers Leslie Asako

Gladsjo and Nathalie Borgers, Sarajevan journalist Adil Kulenović, director of Radio 99, discusses the plight of those who resisted the nationalist madness by refusing to take sides:

> The great tragedy of this war is that even the most prestigious TV companies and journalists oversimplified events to make a story about three warring sides. They never wanted to acknowledge the fourth side, to which the largest number of people belong – those who really care for normal life in Bosnia and Herzegovina.

Within the tripartite scheme there was a place only for those who belonged to one of the nationalist factions. The effects of the journalistic technique of simplifying in order to secure a concise narrative was to take away visibility from those internal powers that could resist the fragmentation. Interviewed also in *Truth under Siege*, Petar Luković, of the independent Serbian magazine *Vreme*, points out that international media were wrong in their summary condemnation of all Serbs, as this ensured that all critical forces inside Serbia were denied international publicity. The collective media demonisation of the Serbs made it difficult to counteract the internal propaganda and 'delivered the Serbian population into the hands of Milošević and the nationalists', as the late Milovan Djilas claimed (quoted in Ignatieff, 1993, p. 52).

In a situation where choices were limited, the pressure to take sides grew stronger all the time. Those who did not want to cave in to the nationalists' hysteria realised that their only remaining choice was to side against their own ethnic group, as only such an act would expose the irrationality of the nationalist discourse. It was a difficult choice, but it seemed the only way to avoid succumbing to the dominance of ethnic rivalries. It was a choice against populism, a choice to preserve the individual's right of self-determination and to stand against mass madness.

Take the case of Lordan Zafranović, who left Croatia and settled in Prague in order to complete and release his *Decline of the Century*. Or author Slavenka Drakulić, a vocal critic of Croatian nationalism but also of nationalism and sexism of all kinds, who published numerous essays and two books in the West that relentlessly exposed the various disguises of nationalism. Or the leading Croatian novelist Dubravka Ugrešić, now living in Amsterdam, whose powerful essay collection *Culture of Lies* (1998) is probably the most insightful indictment of the mechanics of nationalist indoctrination at work not only today but also in the past, during the years of Yugoslavia's 'togetherness'. Both Drakulić and Ugrešić are high-profile feminists, derided by mainstream media at home alongside other feminists, like Rada Iveković, Vesna Kešić and Jelena Lović, all dubbed 'Croatia's witches', who just 'won't be silenced' (Tax, 1993,

p. 624). Another feminist should be added here, a leading academic figure in classics and cultural studies, Svetlana Slapšak, a Serbian who now works in Ljubljana. Throughout the 1990s, she engaged in persistent critical feminist work, exposing nationalist rhetoric across the Yugoslav successor states.

While Zafranović, Drakulić and Ugrešić enjoyed the freedom to travel, work and maintain a high profile in the West, there were many others who stayed behind, in rump Yugoslavia. Those working for various dissenting organisations in Belgrade – such as Anti-War Action, Belgrade Circle, Women in Black, Humanitarian Law Fund and other autonomous women's and anti-war groups – were often charged with promoting foreign interests. As none of these organisations receives domestic financial support, their funding comes mostly from abroad, a fact that is used by domestic nationalist critics to claim that they are actually involved in subversive work on behalf of foreign powers.

The journalists working at critical publications like *Borba* and *Vreme* conducted their own campaign against Milošević. While their work was celebrated by the intelligentsia, across the country it was perceived as antagonistic and subversive.[7]

Serb Gordana Knežević and her Croat husband stayed in Sarajevo to work respectively for the newspaper *Oslobodjenie* and for the Bosnian Muslim government.[8] In spite of the fact that this was one of the most difficult choices, many other Serbs stayed in besieged Sarajevo, where they were exposed on a daily basis to the shelling by what can be described as their 'own people' who occupied the surrounding hills. By not taking the side of 'their own' they had turned into enemies.

Kusturica's case was also about this same refusal to embrace narrow-minded sectarian identities. To stand against the madness of his own people seemed to be the only way to point out how wrong it was. But in order to make the valid point of reminding people in former Yugoslavia that 'once there was a country . . .', he had relied on support from a group which was no less sectarian than the one he wanted to counter.

Pretty Villages Burn Nicely

> Let me point out that I am not a nationalist, but if you take part in a war, then you must fight . . . Although I have many Croatian friends, I already said that war is war. When we are friends, we are friends, but when it comes to war, we will fight.
>
> (Srdjan Dragojević, 1996/1997, p. 16)

Srdjan Dragojević, a young Serbian director, emerged into the international spotlight with his second feature, *Pretty Village, Pretty Flame*, a film addressing the burning issues of the deadly confrontation that followed the parting along ethnic divides. Those in command of the Serbian language noted that the title of the film did not translate well, and that *Pretty Villages Burn Nicely* would convey a more adequate understanding of its focus on destruction. Indeed, it is the scale of meaningless destruction – of buildings, towns and people – that is the focus of the films discussed here: the destruction of the Bosnian countryside in the film of Dragojević, and the destruction of the thriving city of Vukovar in the film of Boro Drašković.

Both films proposed a scheme in which all sides were to share the responsibility for the devastating violence that accompanied Yugoslavia's breakup. Both directors claimed they were non-sectarian. But as they were both Serbian, their proposed 'all sides are guilty' trope came under critical fire: how could they, belonging to an ethnic group which was perceived as the aggressor, invite all others to share a guilt that was originally 'theirs'?

While Dragojević and Drašković's films were acclaimed abroad for trying to offer a balanced view of the conflict, critics in Yugoslavia did not accept the angle that the directors were proposing – it was not about guilt in principle, but about quantifying and measuring concrete crimes. The attempt to rise above the damaging side-taking by showing the madness of all sides, a proposition which looked promising from outside, was not really viable in the divided public space of former Yugoslavia. People there were not ready for an easy reconciliation.

Boro Drašković's *Vukovar: Poste Restante*, an international co-production with Yugoslav participation, uses the plot of Romeo and Juliet to tell the story of the Yugoslav breakup.[9] The honeymoon of Croat Anna and Serb Toma, residents of the Yugoslav city of Vukovar on the Danube (now in Croatia), is interrupted by the war. Toma is recruited into the army, and Anna, who has just become pregnant, remains alone to live among increasing violence. Toma gradually caves in to the growing madness that propagates irreconcilable ethnic differences, and sides with the Serb nationalists. Anna (played by *Underground*'s Mirjana Joković) grows estranged from Toma and falls into a deep depression. Her suffering culminates at the moment when, in advanced pregnancy, she is brutally raped by unidentified burglars. By the time the baby is born, Anna and Toma are irreversibly alienated from each other. The antagonistic forces at work have succeeded in separating them. At the end, each one of them is shown leaving the war-ravaged Vukovar for good. Symbolically, they set off in opposite directions. The bus station from which they leave is not a meeting point any more but a place for final separations. War proves stronger than love, and the imperative to take sides has taken its toll.

It is no wonder that in the context of imposed parting along ethnic lines, the metaphor of Romeo and Juliet comes into use so often.[10] Back in the 1980s, Prague Group's Srdjan Karanović had made *Za sada bez dobrog naslova/A Film with No Name* (1988), about the doomed love affair between a Macedonian and an Albanian, nowadays considered a work of visionary pessimism. More recently, the heartbreaking real story of a Sarajevo inter-ethnic couple, *Romeo and Juliet in Sarajevo* (1994), who had tried to escape the city but were shot down by snipers, was made into a TV documentary and shown by major Western TV stations. And even more recently, the New Zealand production *Broken English* featured a young Croatian immigrant who, after falling in love with a local Maori man, tried to break out of her ethnic enclave but was forced to stick to her own people. The story was replayed in *Preku erero/Across the Lake* (1997), where the Macedonian protagonist crosses the lake that divides him from his Albanian girl, to face accusations as a spy and to end up in a labour camp.

At the time of its US release in early 1996, *Vukovar: Poste Restante* triggered a controversy, not as noisy as the *Underground* one, but still noteworthy. Members of the Croatian-American community wrote letters to *The New York Times* and *The Washington Post* accusing the film of being biased in favour of the Serbs and intentionally vilifying the Croats, thus inciting critics to scrutinise the film for alleged pro-Serbian propaganda. A *Vukovar* screening at the UN was abruptly cancelled when the Croatian mission protested that the film failed to condemn the Serbs. The main objection was to the depiction of Anna's rapists, who were heard exchanging a few words in Croatian, which left little doubt about their ethnic identity for those who could hear the difference from Serbian in a language which used to be, until recently, called Serbo-Croat. Critics also had to take sides. Some saw little ground for the outrage, and thought the film was trying to offer a balanced view. Todd Anthony, for example, wrote that 'only a viewer blinded by partisan beliefs would disagree that Drašković's overriding intent is to realistically depict the repugnant brutality of war'.[11] Others gave full credit to the Croatian complaints, like *Newsday*'s John Anderson, who gave the film no stars and described it as 'Propaganda for the Serbs'.[12] The fact that *Vukovar* had been rump Yugoslavia's entry for the Oscars in 1994 barely worked in its favour. Croatia had also entered a Vukovar-themed film in the competition, *Vukovar se vraca kuci/Vukovar – The Way Home* (1994), which presented the story as it was supposed to be told according to the Croats, but the film never received a wide release in the West and the controversy attracted little attention.[13]

I do not think that malevolent Serbian indoctrination was the main problem with Boro Drašković's *Vukovar*. In the context of the controversy, the fact that the film was co-produced by Yugoslavia and directed by a Serb seemed to have more weight than the fact that it was designed for an undemanding audience and its narrative was painfully predictable. The question of alleged partiality created a buzz around the film which would otherwise go unnoticed simply by virtue of its artistic mediocrity. There is only one exception to the tearful *Vukovar*: the unique long aerial take of the city, a haunting image that reveals the horrifying scale of destruction inflicted on this once prosperous town on the Danube. All that is left after the war is a mile-long stretch of ruins along the river.

The imposed taking of sides had a damaging impact not only on couples in love. It was also experienced painfully by many who saw themselves standing on either one or the other side, along fault lines that they did not believe in. *Vukovar*'s declared goal had been to critique the absurdity and the damaging consequences of the partition. But it missed the chance to deliver the message as intended, once again raising the question of whether it was possible for someone who nominally belonged to one side to propose to the other that they both acknowledge the absurdity of the conflict and accept equal blame. The controversy around *Vukovar* demonstrated that even if those who made it were prepared to recognise their own fault, it was still deemed insufficient by the other side. The alternatives of remorseful recognition and analysis of responsibility remained deadlocked in a context where no side was really prepared to talk of their own guilt.

If we judge from the statement quoted at the opening of this discussion, Srdjan Dragojević, the man behind *Pretty Village, Pretty Flame*, seems to have no illusions that being neutral is possible, or even desirable. He is certainly a Serb and makes no attempt to disguise it. What he wants to do is to find a way to make Serbs confront their own wrongdoings, a much-needed act that is likely to have a therapeutic effect on the tormented souls of his compatriots. For Dragojević, this means once again pursuing the 'all-sides-are-guilty' approach.

As his project was meant to explain the story from the Serbian side, the director did not hesitate in turning to all politicians, even the nationalist ones, to ask for support. In an interview, Dragojević (1996) describes how he sought financing from all forces in Serbia – he first approached nationalist leader Vojslav Šešelj and liberal opposition leader Zoran Djindjić, but failed with both. Dragojević then turned to the Bosnian Serbs, and for a while Radovan Karadžić seemed sympathetic to the project, but it failed to get the approval of ideologue Nikola Koljević, who thought the script was slanderous to the Serbs.[14] The main subsidies came from Radio-TV Serbia and from the Serbian Ministry of Culture. The film was shot over seventy-two days in the vicinity of Visegrad in the territory of Republika Srpska in the spring of 1995. The crew heavily relied on cultivating contacts among the Bosnian Serbs, and they acquired tanks from the local army unit in exchange for 50 gallons of fuel per day.

The script is based on a true story that writer Vanja Bulić had first reported in a 1992 issue of *Duga*, a magazine sympathetic to Milošević. The story focused on a Serbian fighter who, along with others, was stuck in the Visegrad tunnel and surrounded by Muslim troops in the autumn of 1992. The original article, presenting the Serbs in a vulnerable situation, had been part of the typical state-sponsored media strategy to counter widespread Western depictions of the Serbs as the main aggressors in the Bosnian war. The film, however, transforms the original story from a straightforward boost of Serb spirits into a more sober and complex look at the controversial experiences of war.

The camerawork is dynamic, showing preference for non-traditional angles and shots taken from above. Stylistically, the film ranks alongside Wajda's *Kanal* (1957), Tarkovsky's *Stalker* (1979), Wolfgang Petersen's *Das Boot/The Boat* (1982), Josef Vilsmayer's *Stalingrad* (1993) and John Woo's *Broken Arrow* (1996), in all of which a claustrophobic confine endangers the sanity of the protagonists.

Here the tunnel, the history of which is outlined at the opening of the film, becomes a site for tragic confrontation. Inaugurated as a Tunnel of Brother-hood and Unity in 1971, it soon after falls into a state of disrepair characteristic of post-Tito Yugoslavia. It gradually becomes the subject for the spooky fantasies of two boys – Serb Milan and Muslim Halil – who believe that an ogre hides inside its shadowy depths. Twenty or so years later, during the Bosnian war, these two boys, now grown up, are thrown against each other, standing as main protagonists on the opposite sides in an ugly confrontation. Serb Milan

Director Srdjan Dragojević: 'When we are friends, we are friends, but when it comes to war, we will fight.' (*Lepa sela, lepo gore/Pretty Village, Pretty Flame*, 1995)

and a group of Yugoslav army soldiers remain trapped in the tunnel for days, surrounded by Muslim fighters, one of whom is Halil.

The tunnel setting gives the film-maker a chance to bring together a whole gallery of secondary Serb characters – from a delirious drug addict to a sentimental criminal, who ends up committing suicide, to a decorated army veteran and a simple-hearted peasant who endures a Christ-like martyr's death.

The non-linear narrative evolves around a patchwork of several flashback subplots, tracing the individual paths that brought these soldiers together in the tunnel. The leading protagonist, Milan, survives the showdown at the tunnel, but is seriously wounded. While recovering in a hospital, he recalls his life as a member of the Chetnik squad and the ten-day inferno in the tunnel. Nostalgic memories of his friendship with the Muslim Halil, overwhelm him.[15] The two of them were simple village boys, car mechanics who even once ran a garage together. During the war Milan was shown trying to defend Halil's house, until someone told him that Halil had actually killed his mother. There is no way to check who did what; it is war. The two friends meet again only during the stand-off, Milan inside the tunnel, Halil above it. The oath of eternal friendship has been broken and thrown into the mud of the Bosnian war. Even though they manage to exchange a few hasty words, in which Milan assures Halil that he did not burn down his house, and Halil swears that he was not responsible for the murder of Milan's mother, it is too late to reverse the course of events. A mortar blast puts an end to the attempted dialogue.

'You don't see a lot of Muslims in the film,' says screenwriter Vanja Bulić. 'They are in the shadows, but this is good because this is a movie we made about ourselves. The stereotype is that the Serbs are the best, cleanest, true heroes. We attacked this mythology' (quoted in Pomfret, 1996, p. C1). Indeed, the Serbs are in the main focus of attention and a variety of Serb characters appear, while the Muslims, even Halil, remain episodic supporting figures with little personal characterisation – referred to simply as 'Turks' throughout the film. Not that the Chetniks are spared – they are shown looting deserted Muslim houses before setting them on fire. Nationalist graffiti covers the walls – 'Serbia to Tokyo!' – and later on, in something like a dialogue, other graffiti appear on top – 'Bosnia to Tokyo!'

But it is clear that the film-maker's attention is focused on the Serbian characters, even if for the purpose of exposing the whole range of contradictory sentiments inhabiting the Serb psyche. It is a deadlock. None of the film's protagonists can bring the war closer to its end. A small group of intellectuals is shown demonstrating against the war in front of the hospital, but they appear comical and completely inadequate, highlighting the wide gap that exists between the intelligentsia and common folk in today's Yugoslavia.[16] It is clear that a newly emerged prosperous class of war profiteers has a vested interest in keeping the conflict ablaze. Serb Slobo's pub is thriving, and it is he who implies to Milan that his mother was killed by the Muslims – a lie that has tragic consequences. The opinion of the international community is represented by the young American female journalist who ends up in the tunnel with the trapped Serbs. At first she merely recites the familiar set of anti-Serb clichés, but during the confinement she gradually realises that there is more to these men than the simplistic black-and-white perceptions perpetuated by Western reporting. Although she gradually sympathises with these lost souls, she will nevertheless remain an outsider with a camcorder. The real attention is focused on the feelings and actions of the Serbian men at war.

In Visegrad, the Bosnian Serb town where the film was made, *Pretty Village* enjoyed a standing ovation. It was subsequently screened and warmly received in various Serb-held parts of Bosnia. 'I was glad to see that Bosnian Serbs accepted the movie well. That is real proof that what I and my colleagues produced was according to the actual events during the war,' said director Dragojević (quoted in Turan, 1997a, p. 89).

In Sarajevo, however, the film's approach, proposing a philosophy of mutual blame, was deemed unacceptable. Intellectuals here critiqued the 'all-sides-are-guilty' message: 'The idea that everyone is guilty on some level is unacceptable to me as a human being. Defending yourself and killing to make a bigger country and destroying all traces of another nation's culture are not on the same level,' said Sarajevan film-maker Mirsad Purivatra (quoted in Turan, 1997a, p. 89).

When the film was released in the West, it was met by the same mixed reaction. Although clearly a good candidate for the classification of 'Serbian propaganda', surprisingly it was not unanimously received in this way. A Yugoslav-made film, which did not conceal its identity behind international financing, it was clearly trying to make the case for the Serbs by superimposing a human face over the demonised international image they had acquired by then. But even though *Pretty Village, Pretty Flame* was one of the most successful Yugoslav productions, there was no consensus in its reception. Widely rumoured to have been the favourite film at the Thessaloniki Film Festival, *Pretty Village* was deemed too controversial, so the award went to a British film, *Brothers in Trouble*, instead. Acclaimed at many other festivals, the only award it actually received was from the remote and politically neutral territory of Brazil's São Paulo Film Festival. The director of Viennale, the Austrian film event, refused to screen it, claiming the film was a 'Serb fascist propaganda'.[17] In November 1996, *The Washington Post* had covered the film as one which had the backing of the Serbian government and was therefore a clear-cut propaganda piece (Pomfret, 1996). But just a year later, in November 1997, this same newspaper drew attention to the fact that the film had been boycotted by the

Bosnian Serb leader Radovan Karadžić and his government officials on its opening night, which made it more than a piece of clear-cut pro-Serbian propaganda.[18]

Pretty Village, Pretty Flame was, in spite of all the mixed reactions, an undoubtedly successful film, particularly in the USA. Two main factors can be identified to explain the film's overall positive reception.

First, many of the American critics liked it because it focused on the perpetrators, showing the complexity of their experiences and thus aligning it with many of the best Vietnam war sagas. *Chicago Tribune*'s Michael Wilmington even spoke of the film's 'truly audacious spirit'.[19]

Second, during the US promotion of the film, the people who were involved with its production lived through an intriguing adjustment process, depending on what the public opinion happened to be in the places where the film was shown. While in early domestic interviews Dragojević had not hesitated to come across as a committed Serb who would take up arms if needed, in the West he made sure to distance himself from the tarnished Serb reputation by stressing his identity as punk rocker and telling journalists that he has been branded a fascist in his country.[20]

The mixed international reception and the occasional criticism at home (accusing him of painting the Serbs too bleakly) made Dragojević vow never to make another film about the Yugoslav problems. His next film, however, *Rane/Wounds* (1998), which dealt with the devastating moral consequences of the war on the generation of Yugoslav teenagers, could be perceived as an indirect indictment of the regime. Around that time, Dragojević received an offer from Miramax to make films which presumably will keep him away from the controversial topic of Yugoslavia at least for the next few years. In April 1999 he left Serbia and landed with his family in New York, where, during the Kosovo bombing, he immediately became a focal point of interest for the community of independent film-makers and journalists. He now lives in Los Angeles.

Dragojević's example reflects an interesting learning curve. It is most likely that he had started off with a firm commitment to the idea of making a feel-good movie for Serbian audiences. But as a result of the international exposure and success, as well as the chances for a high-profile international career, his original allegiances lessened. Such an evolution – from a firm taking of sides to a cautious distancing – is also a realistic trajectory for those caught at the difficult intersection of post-Yugoslav dilemmas.

What Kind of Involvement?

When considering Bosnia, many in the West wondered why it had not elicited the same response from abroad that had greeted the Spanish Civil War back in the 1930s.[21] Why wasn't there a team like that of Joris Ivens and Ernest

Hemingway to make a documentary as powerful as *Spanish Earth* (1937)? Why weren't there people of the stature of George Orwell, André Malreaux, Dorothy Parker and hundreds of others who went to Spain to fight fascism? When so many writers went to fight on the Republican side in the Spanish Civil War, why had the Bosnian war and the herding of Bosnian Muslims into concentration camps not stirred a similar response?

The answer to all these questions is to be sought, I believe, not in hasty claims about indifference, but in exploring the controversial experiences of social commitment and the diminished public stature of the intellectual, all developments of the last several decades. But even if we dismiss the comparisons to the Spanish Civil War as invalid, the questions to those who got involved from abroad, remain: could taking sides help break the circle of violence? What kind of commitment was needed?

In fact, the numbers of Western intellectuals who took sides in the conflict arising from the Yugoslav breakup were by no means smaller than of those involved in Spain during the 1930s.[22] In the West, the story of the troubled Balkans was told by a number of writers and journalists who visited and revisited the region and offered their accounts of it. Some travelled across division lines with an investigative attitude, and tried to listen to all sides. Some had only one destination and were mostly interested in checking the reality against an opinion they already held. A few took the side of the Serbs – either to defend what they suspected was an internationally distorted image, or just to see for themselves.[23] Some even got involved in the actual fighting – in *Serbian Epics* (1994), for example, one can see the flamboyant Russian writer Eduard Limonov, at the time a cultural minister in the shadow Russian government of Zhirinovski, firing shots at Sarajevo from Serb positions in the heights overlooking the city.

Influential Austrian writer Peter Handke travelled to Serbia in the winter of 1995, and produced a series of essays collected in the book, *A Journey to the Rivers* (1997). Although conscious that his trip was somewhat 'comparable to the glorification of the Soviet system by some travelers in the West during the thirties' (ibid., p. 24) he is nonetheless determined to venture into Serbia, if it would help to overcome the 'mutual inflexible images'. No doubt, in Serbia there are people worth meeting. Milorad Pavić, for example, the author of the magical realist *Dictionary of the Khazars* (1988) is one, and it is him, and those like him whom Handke meets. In relating his conversations with these intellectuals and in giving accounts of his meetings with ordinary people, Handke attempts to show that Serbs have also suffered a moral devastation. His essays, however, remain just another piece of Balkan travelogue literature, which focus more on his physical presence amid the fields of Serbia, without reaching deeper than the mere registration of a gloomy and wintry landscape.

Handke's pro-Serbian writing caused a sensation in Germany, provoking a polemical firestorm. French writer Alain Finkielkraut (who himself had publicly committed to the Croat cause) attacked Handke for substituting serious political issues with an unjustifiable aesthetic approach. Finkielkraut was particularly appalled by the fact that, when discussing Srebrenica, Handke did not talk of the massacre but elaborated on his own associations on the concept of the *arabesque*. Finkielkraut calls this attitude 'monstrous', believing that it should be the intellectual's duty to address issues of moral responsibility rather than let themselves be carried away in inspirational daydreaming.[24] According to Croat playwright Slobodan Snaider, Handke deliberately avoided the discussion of political issues:

Of course, once he travels through Serbia, he meets many open-hearted people. I also know many ... But it is difficult to see the power structures, in Croatia as well. Could one see in 1935 that Germany lived under a totalitarian dictatorship? Mostly not.[25]

The issue of substituting political considerations for aesthetic ones is crucial. Unfortunately, it all came down to taking concrete sides – with the proponent of the problematic view occupying one side, and the critics firmly standing on the other. The important philosophical issues remained obscured by the continuing conflict, and never moved beyond Croats and Serbs, rights and wrongs.

Many got involved with the Bosnian cause. For those who came to know the Bosnian war first hand, remaining neutral no longer seemed possible. British journalist Ed Vulliamy and American journalist Roy Gutman, for example, not only took the side of the Bosnians but even decided to testify at the Hague. Vulliamy wrote about his decision:

I've had many discussions about testifying at the Hague. Some colleagues whom I admire greatly say it is a mistake, that by going into the witness box you take a step across a line inappropriate for a reporter. I argue on two grounds: legal and moral. Legally, if I saw an old lady mugged, I would expect to be called by the police to testify at the murder trial. The moral argument concerns neutrality. It is, of course, essential for a reporter to be objective so long as objectivity concerns the facts. Sometimes, however, those facts are so appalling that to remain neutral is not really neutral at all – there are moments in history when neutrality is complicit in the crime.[26]

It seemed particularly important to assign guilt, to fight the interpretation of the clash as a civil war and to argue that the Bosnian conflict is seen as a war of Serbian aggression (Mousavizadeh, 1996, p. 9). Nobel Prize laureate, Polish poet Czeslaw Milosz wrote a poem in support of Sarajevo's solitary resistance, and Nobel Prize laureate, Russian poet Joseph Brodsky wrote a strongly worded piece condemning the Serbs.[27] If such public commitment to the Bosnians was not taken, they believed, all sides would be deemed equally guilty, which effectively would mean it was impossible to apportion guilt.

Frenchman Bernard-Henri Lévy was one of the outspoken public figures in favour of the Bosnian cause, and his film, *Bosna!*, received more exposure than any of the documentaries made about the Bosnian ordeal.[28] His high-profile uncompromising attitude and passionate partiality were well noted by the critics. Lévy himself made an eloquent case justifying his commitment:

> There can be no question of making a balanced movie about Bosnia. We're living in crazy times. There's this growing cult of balance, of equidistance, as if the death of a torturer and his victim had the same value. They do not. Bosnia is a just cause and to respond, as we have, to its destruction with the delivery of humanitarian aid is like bringing sandwiches to the gates of Auschwitz.
>
> (Quoted in Cohen, 1995, sect. 2, p. 1)

Lévy glorified the Bosnian resistance while indicting Western democracies' indifference to the continuing conflict. He claimed that 'Europe died in Sarajevo'. His film was publicly perceived as a new 'j'accuse!'

The nature of Lévy's involvement with the Bosnians, however, soon came under severe scrutiny. Critics could not help noticing that he had embraced the Bosnian cause particularly passionately in 1994, precisely at the time when he was running for a seat in the European parliament. Some even called *Bosna!* a 'campaigning documentary'.[29] While enjoying a high profile for his Balkan commitment, Lévy also took significant blame for using his defence of Bosnia within his own political agenda. André Glucksman, another Frenchman who took the side of the Bosnians, was ridiculed for displaying bad taste in trying 'on his twenty-four-hour trip to Sarajevo, [to] explain to the people of Sarajevo who had come to his press conference, that "war is now a media event," and "wars are won or lost on TV" ' (Rieff, 1995, p. 123).

While the motives of people like Lévy were routinely scrutinised for hidden symptoms of compassion deficiency, the issue of the nature of the overall Western involvement has rarely been a major preoccupation of investigative journalism. Ilan Ziv's *Safe Haven: The United Nations and the Betrayal of Srebrenica* (1996) is one of the few films which did not hesitate to lead an investigation into what he interpreted as an attitude of criminal negligence among international politicians. The film attempts to analyse the reasons for the inaction that led to the tragic events of 1995 in the safe haven, where thousands of Muslims were massacred despite being in close proximity to the UN protection force. *Safe Haven* features some of the most outspoken critics of Western policies in Bosnia, like former UN envoy Jose Maria Mendiluce and former State Department employee George Kenney, each of whom resigned their posts to protest about the way the Bosnian conflict was being tackled by the West. Their critiques are juxtaposed to interviews with those Western officials who are believed to ultimately bear the responsibility for the failure of the West to prevent disasters such as Srebrenica – the UN's Boutros Boutros-Ghali, the USA's Lawrence Eagleburger, UNHCR's Yasushi Akashi and French general Bernard Janvier. A more recent British documentary, *A Cry from the Grave* (1999), once again powerfully reasserted the unresolved issues of the Western role in facilitating the Srebrenica tragedy on the public agenda. In *Welcome to Sarajevo*, UN Secretary General Boutros Boutros-Ghali is shown telling Sarajevans that around the world at the present moment there are at least thirteen other places where the situation is even worse than theirs, as if this could help them in any way (and as if the 'upgrade' would help people in these other thirteen places feel any better). This unfortunate statement is repeatedly and contemptuously quoted by the protagonists of the film, who remind themselves of it each time they are under sniper fire, shelled or amid blazing flames.

With their outspoken commitment, however, the Western intellectuals contributed to a project of a somewhat dubious character – the assertion of the trope of 'Balkans as an inextricable part of Europe'. Frenchman Daniel Schiffer entitled his 1995 book about Yugoslavia *Requiem pour l'Europe* (*A Requiem for Europe*), and German Raimar Wigger called his 1995 book *Verraten im Herzens Europas* (*Betrayal in the Heart of Europe*). By reasserting the claim of the 'Europeanness' of the Balkans they failed to convince anyone in Europe that this was really the case. All they achieved was to maintain the illusion of such 'belonging' in the minds of Balkan audiences.

Susan Sontag's (1994) account of a Sarajevo project she got involved with reveals the same pattern. Travelling to Sarajevo during the siege to direct Becket's *Waiting for Godot*, she indicated that for the people of the city staging this 'great European play' meant 'that they are members of the European culture'. Although during her mission to Sarajevo she only represented herself, the local Sarajevan press and radio inflated the fact of her presence as evidence that the world 'does care'. Back in the USA, confronted with a reality of indifference to the Bosnian cause, Sontag lamented the apathy. But she did not think she had made a mistake by maintaining the illusion of Sarajevans' belonging to the realm of the 'European'.

Neither Sontag nor the others, who with their acts of support for Bosnia asserted the trope of belonging to Europe, ever openly confronted the fact that in their dissent they had also misled audiences in the Balkans into believing that a wider Western public also firmly backed their aspirations to be considered a part of Europe.

London-based Michael Ignatieff (1995), who also travelled to former Yugoslavia to shoot *Blood and Belonging* (1993), was one of the few who admitted that 'a strong element of narcissism' was buried inside the more obvious motivations that led Westerners to Bosnia. According to Ignatieff, all that mattered was the 'discovery of an ideal image of ourselves'. It was not even clear 'whether Bosnia did in fact approximate our fantasy'. The question was not to save the Bosnians as part of Europe, Ignatieff wrote:

> but to save ourselves, or rather an image of ourselves as defenders of universal
> decencies. We wanted to show that Europe 'meant' something, stood for
> toleration within a peaceable and civilized civil society. This imaginary
> Europe, this narcissistic image of ourselves, we believed was incarnated in the
> myth of a multi-ethnic, multi-confessional Bosnia.   (ibid., p. 98)

Taking sides in the Bosnian conflict may have led to some sort of compassion fatigue among Western intellectuals, as the diminished public outcry about Kosovo in 1998 seems to suggest. While Kosovo was widely covered, one can barely find evidence of public commitment among Western writers and filmmakers comparable to that which evolved around Bosnia.

By the time of the Kosovo showdown, the nature of the sides had changed. It was no longer about Serbs and Bosnians, and not even about Serbs and Kosovar. The issue had relocated to the West itself, and was now about siding with NATO or against it. The concept of 'Europe' functioned quite differently in this new context.

The new configuration of 'sides' was clearly seen in the case of Michael Ignatieff. He gradually gave up the privileged position of an independent critical intellectual for another stance, which looked prestigious but was barely independent. By now considered a specialist on all things Balkan, Ignatieff became the expert of choice for American politicians, who regularly invited him to accompany them on their missions, and record their efforts and point of view. During the Kosovo conflict, Ignatieff wrote a number of pieces for *The New Yorker*, *Time* magazine and a range of newspapers, and was a vocal defender of the 'bombing of peace' cause. His writings on the Balkans from 1998 and 1999 read as if produced by a speech-writer for NATO. He also made numerous television appearances, in one of them even as an advocate for NATO (NATO on Trial, Channel 4, May 1999). During the Bosnian war it was possible to act as an independent Western observer; during the Kosovo conflict, Westerners found they had to take sides. And Ignatieff did.

The Troubles We Have Seen[30]

Even earlier on, the side-taking inevitably translated into the (quite different) categories and concerns of Western politics. Some, like Marcel Ophuls, think that this change in the focus of concern should be admitted clearly – every concern about others, he believes, is only an extension of a self-fixated interest. This is why, although its formal topic is Bosnia, Ophuls' post-modern documentary collage, *The Troubles We Have Seen*, (1994) is dedicated not to Bosnia itself but to a moral investigation of Western reporting and its underlying motives.

As far as the defined sides are concerned, Ophuls is on the side of the Bosnians. In an interview he explains why:

> Frankly, I can't understand how anyone could get involved, whether on the ground or as a journalist, in what is happening to these people in Sarajevo without choosing sides. Certainly the very few journalists I have met who tried to maintain the neutral stance or came out on the Serbian side seemed to me to be *agents provocateurs*; they're probably paid by the enemy. It's that clear cut.[31]

As far as the Bosnian dimension of the film is concerned, Ophuls never becomes too involved. The director is shown bound for Sarajevo on two occasions, on board what used to be called the Orient Express, and the two parts of the film are structured loosely around the two journeys. Once in Sarajevo, Ophuls spends significant time with various Western journalists, like *The New York Times*' John F. Burns and the BBC's John Simpson. While during his Northern Ireland investigation in *A Sense of Loss* (1972) Ophuls had talked extensively to the ordinary victims of terror, in Sarajevo his discussions with local people are restricted to occasional street interviews. Although present throughout the film, the experiences of local people remain outside the main narrative and do not integrate into the crucial line of investigation, which remains preoccupied with Western journalists' coverage of the conflict. Ophuls takes sides, but the only topic he really comments on is the Western discourse on Bosnia.

As a legendary film-maker, Ophuls enjoys privileged treatment and is given the opportunity to film in places where only a few lucky documentarians have managed to go. But, because his investigative focus lies elsewhere, he does not make much use of the rare material he has acquired. Only occasional footage from his conversations with perpetrators of the conflict like Nikola Koljević, Radovan Karadžić and Slobodan Milošević makes it into the film, although Ophuls is probably the only documentarian who has been granted exclusive interviews with all of them. He talks to Koljević and Karadžić in Pale against a background of clearly audible shelling, and with Milošević in Belgrade, where

they discuss the freedom of the press. The Serb leaders make extremely problematic statements – Milošević insists that the media in Yugoslavia enjoy an
unprecedented freedom under his rule, while Koljević says that he is uncon-
cerned by the shelling of Sarajevo. But this material is sidelined. The
perpetrators do not really interest Ophuls. They are thugs by default; his investigation is into the morals of Westerners.

Many of the issues discussed in *The Troubles We Have Seen* make sense only
in the context of the themes of history, remembrance and morality that Ophuls
has been exploring throughout his work. It is a context in which Bosnia functions as a case study, a background against which he can develop his views a
step further. Pursuing his own line of enquiry, the account of real-life suffering
is present in the film only as a backdrop for the moral investigation which
evolves around Western television coverage of Bosnia. Opening with evidence
of uninformed shallowness in war reporting, he explores throughout this
4-hour post-modern collage whether the superficiality in reporting is due to
intrinsic media patterns or to the deeply ingrained smugness of institution-
alised consumer culture. He remains sceptical about the possibility of
adequately conveying information across borders and cultures. Critics even
read his pessimism as a general 'radical skepticism about the moral decency of
any image-making'.[32]

The main line of enquiry in Marcel Ophuls' work has always been a moralistic one, from dissecting the reasons why ordinary people turn a blind eye to
historical horrors such as the deportation of Jews in occupied France (*Le Chagrin et la pitié/The Sorrow and the Pity*, 1971; *The Memory of Justice*, 1976; *Hôtel
Terminus*, 1988), through exposing the tragic consequences of the mismanaged
dialogue in Northern Ireland (*A Sense of Loss*), to dealing with the side-effects
of German reunification (*November Days*, 1992). Ophuls' mature brand of
investigative sarcasm also sets the tone in *The Troubles We Have Seen*, where he
once again looks into the question of why knowledge of injustice and atrocities does not change the outcome of conflicts, and why Western politics is once
again inoperative when confronted with abundant evidence of ethnic cleansing and terror.

In the film, Ophuls talks to more than thirty war journalists. The extensive
interviews with veteran reporter Martha Gellhorn, John F. Burns, John Simpson and France Presse's Remi Oudran are intercut with recorded appearances
of Christiane Amanpour, Martin Bell and Walter Cronkite, and with footage of
the Gulf war, which Ophuls takes as the ultimate mediated war event. Both in
Bosnia and in the West Ophuls questions the ethical tensions inherent in the
trade and the journalists' special attitudes to danger, courage and moral
responsibility. How do they feel using special security measures for themselves,

when ordinary Sarajevans cannot enjoy such levels of protection? Can they ever be dispassionate analysts? Should they ever champion a cause?

Another line of the enquiry is the indifference of French politicians and their strategy for public defence, dissected with a biting commentary delivered by actor Philippe Noiret and by writer Alain Finkielkraut. No one is spared – from General Philippe Morillon to François Mitterand, all are shown making compromising statements. The film uses abundant references to well-known Hollywood pictures – from the Marx brothers' *Duck Soup* (1933) and Max Ophuls' *De Mayerling à Sarajevo/From Mayerling to Sarajevo* (1940), to Mark Sandrich's *Holiday Inn* (1942) and Fellini's *8½* (1963) – all of which are meant to sharpen the contrast between a self-obsessed West and a forsaken Bosnia. A frequently employed ironic device, for example, is Bing Crosby's song from the film *Holiday Inn*, hummed by the war correspondents stationed at the infamous 'Holiday Inn' hotel in Sarajevo.[33] Ophuls does not spare himself either, and extends the satire by including a set-up scene in which he appears in a Viennese hotel room, having just left Sarajevo, discussing the Bosnian project on the phone, while in the background a naked woman sips champagne, waiting for him in bed. Ophuls does not make concessions even for himself; as a Westerner he is, by default, complacent about the attitudes he exposes.

While continuing his earlier investigations, Ophuls' criticism of news production deficiencies in *The Troubles We Have Seen* brings up more questions than it resolves. This may be the reason why Ophuls prefers to regard the film as an unfinished piece of work, and has been reluctant to show it publicly after it was aired on the BBC and at the Toronto International Film Festival.[34] He has said that this particular film should be regarded as a work-in-progress.

Notes

1. Or 'I was a Yugoslav, but now I am a Bosnian' (both quotes in Lešić, 1995, pp. 161 and 40). Numerous similar quotes can be found in the essays of displaced people from the former Yugoslavia.
2. A lavish and extravagant nationalist party at the home of the artist is described in detail by Florence Hamelish Levinson in her *Belgrade* (1994).
3. Like, for example, the Serbian-made documentaries, *The Truth Is a Victim in Croatia* (1994) and *The Original of a Forgery* (1995). In features, many films that do not bear a directly propagandistic message are made to show the suffering of the Serbian people. For example, *The Awakening of Spring* (1992), in which a 25-year-old man from Knin, wounded in the clashes in Yugoslavia in 1992, comes to Belgrade to recuperate from his trauma, obsessed by the death of his former classmate whom he has killed. Here he falls in love with a Canadian girl, an UNPROFOR officer who had saved his life. Or *Suza and Her Sisters* (1995), in which the wounded boyfriend of the protagonist

chooses, upon recovery, to return to the front line and is killed. The story is told in flashbacks triggered by the ghost-like appearances of the good-looking dead young Serb in the protagonist's dreams, who now sits sad and alone in Kalemegdan park on the Danube.

4. The American-based SerbNet, through its offspring Group for Truth in War Reporting, produced, for example, a documentary called *The Truth Is the Victim in Bosnia* (1995), distributed by the Chicago-based Truth in War Journalism Project. The film develops the Serbian point of view on biased war coverage and on the issue of 'civil' versus 'aggressor's' war. The comment mostly relies on the opinions of Western experts, who make the case about a lack of objective reporting, the demonisation of the Serbs and the one-sided portrayal of the war in the Western media. A similar production, this time telling the Croatian side of the story, is *The Truth about Croatia* (1992), which is available from the Consulate General of Croatia in Chicago.

5. The story is told by Slavenka Drakulić in 'An Actress Who Lost Her Homeland' (1993a, pp. 76–85). This imposed necessity of taking sides is commented upon by two more female writers – Croatian Dubravka Ugrešić, in 'ID' (1994) and by American Beverly Allen in her *Rape Warfare* (1996, p. 7).

6. Another documentary critical of the divides imposed by foreign media is Paper Tiger TV's *Mythmaking: The Balkans* (1995). The media construction of ethnic categories which efficiently obscures serious political and economic considerations is explored in depth by the contributors to *The Media of Conflict: War Reporting and Representations of Ethnic Violence* (1999) edited by Tim Allen and Jean Seaton.

7. In August 1998 *Borba* had to shut down operations due to financial difficulties. Only a few months later a massive crackdown on media was instigated by Milošević's government.

8. The issue of their understanding of allegiance and the necessity of taking sides against one's own nationalist-minded group is discussed at length by Tom Gjelten in his *Sarajevo Daily* (1995). Gjelten juxtaposes the decision of Knežević to stay committed to the Bosnians to the one taken by another reporter from *Oslobodjenie*, Serb Liljana Smajlović, who early on acknowledges that she may not have the determination to take sides against the Serbs in Bosnia and moves to Belgrade, where she ends up working for the dissenting press. In his comprehensive *The Serbs*, Tim Judah notes that later developments made Knežević give up the fight against ethnic nationalism and that eventually she was also forced to leave (Judah, 1997, p. 218).

9. Most reviews of the film made a reference to Romeo and Juliet in one way or another. In *Variety*, Allen Young talked of 'a Capulet–Montague combat'

('*Vukovar: Poste Restante*', 24–30 October 1994, p. 69). Stephen Holden's review in *The New York Times* carried the title 'Serb Is Romeo, a Croat – Juliet' (2 February 1996, p. C8). According to Jim Farber in *The Village Voice*, 'Drasković relies on the old Romeo and Juliet formula' ('Shrouding Bosnia in Confusion', 6 February 1996, p. 48). Zan Durbin described the film as 'a Romeo-and-Juliet story'('Film Fest Honors Serb-Croat Story', *Los Angeles Times*, 29 March 1996, p. F1) and John Hartl called it a 'powerful Romeo and Juliet story' ('Vukovar: Love Conquering', *The Seattle Times*, 3 May 1996, p. F4).

10. The list of Romeo and Juliet-inspired cinematic plots, in which the dividing line is enhanced by ethnic divides, may be quite long. Some of the films that immediately come to mind are *Mississippi Masala*, love story between an east Indian girl and a black man in the American South; *China Girl*, which describes the affair between a Chinese girl and an Italian boy in Brooklyn; and *Krima-Kerime*, which focuses on the affair between a Dutch boy and a Turkish immigrant girl.

11. Todd Anthony, 'Romeo and Juliet among the Ruins', *Miami New Times*, 22 August 1996.

12. *Newsday*, 2 February 1996, p. B11.

13. The two Vukovar films were submitted alongside a number of other Balkan and Balkan-themed works, such as *Before the Rain* (Macedonia), *The Awkward Age* (Bosnia), and *Lamerica* (Italy). The winner that year was Nikita Mikhalkov's *Burnt by the Sun* (Russia).

14. According to John Pomfret, the director 'met with Karadžić, who gave the project his verbal support and, Bosnian Serb sources say, some money – an allegation Dragojević denies. The only opponent was Nikola Koljević, then the Bosnian Serbs' vice president' (Pomfret, 1996, p. C1).

15. Dragojević explained that the friendship between a Serb and a Muslim that is presented in the film is an exception and not a rule: 'Especially in rural areas you couldn't find a Serb and a Muslim friends – don't even think about it, it's never happened.' (Dragojević, 1996/97, p. 15).

16. A similarly peaceful siege appears in the Croatian film *How the War Started on My Island* (1996), where on a small island in the Adriatic a Yugoslav garrison has barricaded itself in a stand-off against local Croatians who want to break away and claim their independence. Groups of friendly and intelligent local people gather outside the barracks and sing to the soldiers to make them withdraw peacefully.

17. In a personal correspondence from Misha Glenny, 2000.

18. Desson Howe, '*Pretty Village, Pretty Flame*: Ugly Truth', *The Washington Post*, 21 November 1997, p. N54.

19. Michael Wilmington, '*Pretty Village*: A Shocking Contemporary War Film', *Chicago Tribune*, 5 December 1997, p. CN1.

20. Nick Hasted, 'It Isn't Very Pretty What a Town Without Pity Can Do', *The Independent* (London), 16 January 1998, p. 3.

21. The question has been asked in different contexts by Susan Sontag (1995), by Roger Cohen (1995), by Bernard-Henri Lévy (in *Bosna!*, 1994) and Marcel Ophuls (in *The Troubles We Have Seen*, 1994). Ophuls even takes the allusion to the Spanish Civil War one stage further while extensively talking with correspondent Martha Gellhorn about romancing 'la causa', and about Robert Capa's famous photographs of the war.

22. It should be noted, however, that while in Spain the intellectuals' involvement became visible mostly in literary writing, in Bosnia a number of writers chose the medium of film to speak up. Examples would be Bernard-Henri Lévy with his *Bosna!*, Michael Ignatieff with the first part of his TV series *Blood and Belonging*, Bill Tribe with his *Urbicide: A Sarajevo Diary* and Susan Sontag, whose work on *Waiting for Godot* was filmed for a documentary by the same name.

23. Levinson (1994) describes an information session at the Belgrade Ministry of Information, attended by herself and many Western guests, including an American film-maker, Karl Haupt, who was about to make a documentary about the Serbs. Another American, Barry Lituchy, an adjunct lecturer in history at Kingsborough College, CUNY, has made a number of pro-Serb documentaries, which are now distributed out of Brooklyn. Titles include: *The CIA War in Bosnia* (1994), *Western Intrigue, Media Deception, and the Yugoslav Civil War* (1994), *America's War against the Serbs and the Dayton 'Peace' Talks* (1995), *Serbs Speak out against US Aggression* (1995), *The Truth behind the Pentagon's War in Bosnia* (1995), *The Dayton Accord and the International War Crimes Tribunal: Human Rights Defenders or Human Rights Abusers?* (1996). In a programme for TV Ontario (*Between the Lines*, 1993), journalist Steve Paikin also tries to tell the story from the point of view of Serbs travelling to Belgrade. In a discussion appended to the documentary and aired live, the makers of the programme were criticised by the panellists for presenting an idealised image of the Serbian side.

24. Alain Finkielkraut, 'Die Perversion der Scham. Alain Finkielkraut antwortet auf die Jugoslawien-Texte von Peter Handke', *Süddeutsche Zeitung*, 7 November 1996.

25. 'Macht kann man selten sehen: Der kroatische Autor Slobodan Snaider ueber Krieg und Medien', *Süddeutsche Zeitung*, 16 January 1996.

26. Ed Vulliamy, 'Death That Cheated Justice', *Guardian*, Tuesday, 4 August 1998, p. 9.

27. Joseph Brodsky, 'Blood, Lies and the Trigger of History', *The New York Times*, 4 August 1993, p. A/19.

28. *Bosna!* (1994). Bosnia-Herzegovina/France. Directors: Bernard-Henri Lévy

and Allain Ferrari. Script: Bernard-Henri Lévy and Gilles Hertzog. Co-production: Bosnian Radio/TV, France 2 Cinema, Canal+ and Centre National de la Cinématographie. *Bosna!* was preceded by another documentary by Lévy, *A Day in the Death of Sarajevo* (1993).

29. Kate Muir, 'Pretentious, Moi?' *The Times*, 16 December 1995. The tone of this British portrait of Lévy is more than sarcastic. Muir portrays Lévy as a profoundly vain intellectual. She insists that his motives for involvement with any public cause are seriously questioned: 'Lévy says he has witnessed renewal of energy and conviction among French intellectuals who have attempted to intervene in the situation. Particularly himself. Indeed, Lévy's views on Bosnia are considered so important by the French media that his declarations often make the front page.' To Josyane Savigneau, Lévy appears as one of the 'media intellectuals' ('intellectuels mediatiques') who may be seen 'touring Sarajevo' or making Bosnia a political ticket ('Chronique d'un monde deraisonnable', *Le Monde*, 9 February 1996).

30. *The Troubles We Have Seen: A History of Journalism in Wartime* (1994). A Little Bear Production (Paris)/Premiere (Germany), with participation of Canal+ and the BBC. Production: Bertrand Tavernier and Frederic Bourboulon.

31. Kurt Jacobsen, 'Memories of Injustice: Marcel Ophuls's Cinema of Conscience', *Film Comment*, Vol. 32, No. 4, July 1996, p. 61.

32. Phillip Lopate, 'New York Film Festival', *Film Comment*, Vol. 30, No. 6, November 1994, p. 74.

33. Ophuls and *The New York Times'* John F. Burns are shown singing the lyrics:

If the traffic noise annoys you,
If your nerves get thin,
Grab your coat, get your hat,
And come to Holiday Inn.

Another sequence of the film shows a woman and child running through a snowy square in Sarajevo to escape sniper fire. The background score that Ophuls has selected for this image is the song *White Christmas*, again from *Holiday Inn*, originally sung by Bing Crosby and Marjorie Reynolds.

34. Personal correspondence with Oliver Gaycken of DocFilms in Chicago, who was trying to schedule the film for a screening in 1998.

Chapter 8
Violence: 'Violated Trust', Indoctrination, Self-Destruction

Many depictions of violence can be found in the Balkan literary heritage, but it is no more than the violence found in other literary traditions from around the world. Even though aspects of the literary heritage were efficiently used for populist and nationalist propaganda during Yugoslavia's breakup, I am far from convinced that the heritage in itself can be said to play a definitive role in inciting today's violence. Still, I keep coming across situations where humanitarian scholars scrutinise the Balkan literary and cinematic tradition for examples of violence, and then use these to explain today's state of affairs. Looking at Montenegrin Vlatko Gilić's short, *In Continuo* (1971), about the ritualistic violence in a slaughterhouse, film scholar Vlada Petrić interpreted the blood-soaked imagery and the suggestive title of the film as a nightmarish vision of the violence that was to come to Yugoslavia twenty years later.[1] (Such an approach could declare George Franju's *Le Sang des bêtes/Blood of the Beasts* (1949), an equally violent and shattering documentary about a French slaughterhouse, to be a premonition of the Algerian war.) In yet other cases, literary scholars traced today's violence back to the wealth of violent scenes found in Njegos' folk poem *The Mountain Wreath* (1847), a classic of Serbian literature. Andrew Wachtel wrote: 'if we look at *The Mountain Wreath* through the prism of the 1990s, the conversations between the Montenegrin Moslems and their Orthodox brothers look chillingly prophetic' (Wachtel, 1998, p. 49). Branimir Anzulović extensively comments on Njegos' text and its reception over time as 'a call to genocide' (Anzulović, 1999, p. 67). Such a deduction is equivalent to explaining the Nazi extremities with the macabre aspects of the Brothers Grimm's fairy tales. The approach is clearly problematic, but as it is about the Balkans, it does not seem to have come in for significant criticism.

And while attempts to assert a direct lineage with the violent content of literary and folk inheritance persist, there is virtually no recognition that, in a globalised cultural environment, a Hollywood-style or Asian martial arts-style glorification of violence is likely to have an equal, if not even stronger, impact on the perpetrators of violent behaviour in the Balkans.

My exploration of violence looks at issues of representation and mediation. I discuss the specifics of violence as found in the Balkan cinematic tradition, which I then juxtapose with Western film representations of Balkan violence. I build on Arjun Appadurai's insightful discussion of the crucial role that mediation played in shaping the crisis in Balkan identities. Taking my lead from Appadurai, I develop a framework that evolves around two main tropes: the specific ideology of preventive aggressiveness and the concept of majority rights, both used to justify aggressive action on behalf of people who persist in seeing the aggression as self-defence. I explore the concept of Serbian victimhood in the context of cross-cultural mediation, identifying the paradoxical reversals that take place in the positioning of villains and victims, and highlighting some crucial aspects of the indoctrination at work.

Film Representations of Violence

When looking at cinema, it is difficult to sustain the Balkans' reputation for endemic violence. Compared to the gun-crazy tradition of the Western, to the elaborately choreographed martial arts movies, or to the bullet-ridden escapades of Hong Kong thrillers, Balkan cinema has exploited very little of the spectacular visual quality of violence. In relation to these high-profile traditions, Balkan film violence is a poor relative, deprived of glamour and excitement. Here, violence is not celebrated but condemned. Wherever present, the acts of violence are treated as ugly, meaningless and self-destructive.[2] The use of violent scenes is meant to make the viewer shudder in revulsion. Such is the effect, for example, of a scene like the shooting of the kitten on the monastery roof in *Before the Rain*.

In historical films, violence has been used mostly in defining the image of the enemy. Ottoman invaders, for example, are regularly depicted as rough and murderous. One should note, however, that such representation is not always black and white but is usually accompanied by a deeper and more complex treatment of the issues of power, and often the negative depictions of Ottomans (or other oppressors, for that matter) have been balanced by positive portrayals of individual Turkish rulers in literature and film.

Violence is also explored in films which contribute to a more recent discourse on political power, like Zafranović's *Occupation in 26 Scenes*, which contains a graphic sequence of savage atrocities committed by a bunch of the Ustasha during World War II.[3] The perpetrators in the film are local people who turn on their neighbours. The issue, however, is not the violence of one ethnic group against another, but the way in which violence is sanctioned and made legitimate under a particular social order – issues, therefore, not of ethnic rivalries but of political power. Similarly, political violence and lawlessness perpetrated by the powers that be is the bottom line in Yilmaz Güney's *Yol* (1982), a film full of violent encounters and endless background shooting. One should not forget that a classical and shattering condemnation of political violence like *Z*, a 1969 French production which takes place in an unidentified North African country, was adapted for the screen by Greek Costa-Gavras and was, in fact, based on a Greek novel (by Vasiles Vassilikos), the original action of which took place in Thessaloniki.

Some Balkan films, indeed, explore violence in its existential dimension, as a suppressed dark passion. The Montenegrin classic *Jovana Lukina* (1979), for example, is structured around the continuous struggle of the protagonists to survive within a hostile, barren landscape. Violence claims a well-established presence in the lives of the tongue-tied inhabitants of this stony region, where words are rarely used to settle disputes. Here violence is an extension of their daily struggle with the rough and unyielding nature that surrounds them – they deal with people in the same rough way that nature deals with them. The vendettas that frequently take place amid mountainous landscapes in Albanian films are another dimension of this same interpretation of violence, one which is not substantially different, for that matter, from the violence seen in the Corsica-set *Matteo Falcone* (1975), or the Taviani brothers' *Padre Padrone* (1977) and the recent films by Cipri and Maresco, *Lo zio di Brooklyn/The Uncle from Brooklyn* (1995) and *Toto che visse due volte/Toto Who Lived Twice* (1998), all set in Sicily.

The popular perception of Balkan violence involves ethnographic particularities, such as dagger-piercing, throat-slitting or roasting on a spit. It is a face-to-face sadistic fervour involving blood, spilled guts, severed limbs, tortured and mutilated bodies, and one that is certainly far from any hi-tech approaches like sniper-shooting or precision bombing. Many Western journalists, like Robert Kaplan (1993), but also other writers (like feminist Beverly Allen (1996), who devoted a special discussion to the particular enjoyment of Balkan individuals in killing with a knife), see the engagement with primitive torture as a culturally specific phenomenon. This concept of culturally specific violence is mostly defined through the enjoyment of bodily closeness with the victim. In some cases, as seen in a text by *The New York Times'* Roger Cohen there is even talk of a Jungian-style collective 'Balkan subconscious':

> In three years of traveling in Bosnia and the rest of former Yugoslavia, I have often heard such talk of people roasted on spits. . . . The point is that in the Balkan subconscious, the horrific image of human kebabs – like the specters of castration, rape, mutilation and beheading by ax – lives on. Many of these crimes have indeed been perpetrated during the wars of Yugoslavia's demise.
>
> (Cohen 1995, p. 1)

As seen in other instances, such Western views are readily corroborated by consenting Balkan intellectuals. Branimir Anzulović (1999, pp. 135–7) speaks of a 'cult of the knife'. He supports his view by reporting that one of the best-selling books of new Serbian literature was the novel *Dagger* by politician Vuk Drašković, the narrative of which contains horrifying scenes of a throat-slitting massacre as well as other equally bloody incidents.[4] Anzulović seems to believe that the popularity of the novel should be seen as a proof of the sadistic enjoyment of butchery by Serbian audiences. (It is believed that it is the graphic violent content of *Dagger*, seen as a work of a pathological mind, that has been the main reason for the reluctance of the West to support Drašković as a legitimate opposition leader in Serbia earlier in the 1990s.)

The mortar shells or the snipers of Sarajevo just do not fit the established image; they are somehow felt to be inadequate for the true face of Balkan violence. For the same reason, even though all killing in *Before the Rain* is carried out with modern-day automatic guns, it is the fork stabbing that remains most memorable.

In the Oliver Stone production *Savior*, a Serbian soldier, Goran, is depicted as a violence-crazed psychopath who cuts off the finger of an old Muslim woman just to get her ring. He then violently induces a young Serbian woman impregnated by the Muslims into labour, prepared to shoot the baby as soon as it emerges from the womb. The American mercenary who fights alongside is so deeply shattered that he kills the Serb. Not that this American opposes violence in principle: he has just killed a teenage Muslim boy with an optical sniper. Only, he practises the civilised and technologically superior way of killing from a distance. He is deeply disturbed, however, by the finger-chopping incident that involved rough bodily contact between victim and perpetrator.

Along these lines, most Western explorations of Balkan violence move within a representative framework, where the Balkans emerge as inhabited by violence-crazed and violence-craving people, who are explicitly shown to enjoy the violence they perpetrate. Images of the Bosnian wasteland as an eternal field of suffering under the control of sadistic warlords flash in DreamWorks' *Peacemaker* (1997) and in a series of the Canadian TV production, *La Femme Nikita* (1997). In the Italian film *Elvjs e Merilijn/ Elvis and Marilyn* (1998) everybody whom the protagonists come across while travelling through war-ravaged Bosnia – hungry and sex-starved soldiers, a suicidal cancerous officer, a pistol-carrying teenage boy – delight in cruelty. In Jean-Luc Godard's *Forever Mozart* the protagonists, also travelling through desolate Bosnia, are soon captured by heavily armed Serbs, whose sadistic leader mostly speaks in quotes from Robespierre. The primitives who act under the guidance of this insane individual rape the protagonists, force them to dig their own graves and finally allow them to be absurdly killed by exposing them to the fire of another guerrilla group (allegedly consisting of equally insane primitives). In the film, war is described as an act of 'sticking a piece of metal in flesh', again suggesting that bodily closeness is a crucial element in Balkan warfare.

The imagery of butchery is exploited even in a film set far from the war, the New Zealand production *Broken English*, which deals with the Balkan violence only indirectly, by looking at the violent male members of a Croat immigrant family in Auckland. In a memorable scene, the father (Rade Serbedzija), a domestic tyrant, and his devoted son, Darko, are shown skilfully skinning a lamb and sticking a thick spit through it, suggesting that their obvious enjoyment of butchery also extends to their relationships with the female members of the family and to society at large.

Not that these violence-crazed protagonists are absent from Balkan cinema. But if we scrutinise the works of directors from former Yugoslavia, we will see that when they address the issue of senseless brutality by depicting violent individuals acting on the verge of insanity, they are aiming to show first and foremost the pernicious self-destructiveness of their actions. The local militants in *Before the Rain* do nothing more than destroy their own people – the Albanian girl is killed by her own relatives, and so is Aleksandar, the photographer. The violent guy who terrorises the London restaurant in the second part of the film, presumably a Serbian and certainly a 'dark Balkan subject', resorts to chaotic shooting as an extension of his own helplessness. The protagonist-friends in Srdjan Dragojević's *Pretty Village, Pretty Flame* fight against each other and destroy nothing but themselves. In Gorćin Stojanović's *Strsljen/Hornet* (1998), the protagonist kills his own brother and then lets himself be killed. The violent protagonists of Goran Paskaljević's *Powder Keg* destroy friends and acquaintances, and, along the way, destroy themselves as well. Here, the ultimate repercussions of violence are suffered equally by perpetrator and victim; violence is as much self-destructive as it is destructive.

Appadurai: Violated Trust and Mediation

While Arjun Appadurai's work is well known among anthropologists and media theorists, his views on contemporary ethnic violence remain largely unknown in the circles of the political scientists and politicians who dealt with the Balkan crisis. I have found some of Appadurai's (1996) discussion, however, to be most useful in explaining the specifics of the violence in the Yugoslav breakup.

Speaking of contemporary conflict at large, Appadurai remarks that rape, degradation, torture and murder often happen between actors who know one another, and who belong to the same immediate community as neighbours, co-workers or fellow students. It is this intimate closeness of the enemy, this 'horror at the neighbor turned killer/torturer/rapist' that seems to hold the key to understanding the specifics of the conflict. We have to realise, Appadurai insists, that 'imagination and agency are far more vital to group mobilization than we had hitherto imagined' (ibid., p. 145), and that much of the national and group politics in the contemporary world has to do not with the mechanics of primordial sentiment, but with what he calls 'the work of imagination'. In the new ethnic wars it comes down to rifts in the interpersonal relationships of a small community and the projections of a mass-mediated identity which, once superimposed on the small-scale ones, put individual imagination to work in the creation of an exaggerated and demonic sense of threat, even where no such dangers exist. Appadurai notes that the worst incidents of violence today seem to occur in situations where there is a distorted relationship 'between daily, face-to-face relations and the large-scale identities produced by modern nation-states and complicated by large-scale diasporas' (ibid., p. 145). It is about undermined identities which grow increasingly dependent on media, state politics and global macro-events:

> The rage of those who kill, maim, and rape seems to be tied up with a
> profound sense of betrayal that is focused on the victims, and the betrayal is
> tied up with the relationship between appearance and reality . . ., a sense of
> deep categorical treachery, that is, treachery about group identity as defined by
> states, censuses, the media and other large-scale forces. . . . The rage that such
> betrayal seems to inspire can of course be extended to masses of persons who
> may not have been intimates, and thus it can and does become increasingly
> mechanical and impersonal, but I would propose that it remains animated by
> a perceived violation of the sense of knowing who the Other was and of rage
> about who they really turn out to be. This sense of treachery, of betrayal, and
> thus of violated trust, rage and hatred has everything to do with a world in
> which large-scale identities forcibly enter the local imagination and become
> dominant voice-overs in the traffic of ordinary life.   (ibid., p. 154)

Appadurai recognises the importance of multiple other factors – economic, political, religious and ethnic – which influence the overall dynamics of ethnic strife in concrete social and historical settings. Unlike other existing explanations, Appadurai's hypothesis links the violence to the sense of profound treachery, and hence to the sense of identity, shattered by the workings of the media. The sense of betrayal and increasing loss of control grows continuously stronger amid mediated 'revelations' about the secret conspiracies of ethnic minority members.

Appadurai's 'treachery' hypothesis seems best suited to cast light on the 'transformation of ordinary people into killers, torturers, and rapists and the re-presentation of friends, neighbors, and co-workers as objects of the deepest hatred and rage' (ibid., p. 155), which remains unexplained in other models. He writes:

> If the hypothesis of treachery is plausible, it has much to do with the large-scale identities created, transformed, and reified by modern state apparatuses (often in a transnational and disasporic field) and circulated through the media. When these identities are convincingly portrayed as primary (indeed as primordial) loyalties by politicians, religious leaders, and the media, then ordinary people self-fulfillingly seem to act as if only this kind of identity mattered and as if they were surrounded by a world of pretenders.
>
> (ibid., p. 156)

As a result of mediated indoctrination, ordinary people begin to feel even more threatened and insecure as they start to perceive their former friends and neighbours as enemies. These same ordinary people, then, turn into perpetrators of violence. In an act of aggression they are ready to claim that hostile action is necessary to prevent the perpetrators on the other side from committing the hostile acts they plan.

Indoctrination

Film has registered such illuminating moments when the 'treachery' that Appadurai is talking about is exposed in an act of revelation, as a result of which an 'enlightened' individual turns aggressive. It is a situation that often comes down to the workings of education and the media.

In a sublime moment of national pride in *Pretty Village, Pretty Flame* that takes place in the tunnel, a peasant protagonist holds up a fork and explains to the American woman how, while in earlier times when the 'noble Krauts' still ate with their bare hands, the Serbs were so civilised that they used forks. Many Western journalists cited this as one of the most amusing lines in the film. In fact, Lazo is just repeating a primary-school-level trope of Yugoslav patriotic education.

In another scene earlier in the film, this same peasant is seen sitting in his village home, watching 'telly' alongside family members. The news is, once again, about sabotages and the insurgence of hostile Croats and Islamic fundamentalists. The peasant cannot stand it any longer, and decides to go and fight for his country. He runs to the road, waving down vehicles for a lift to the conscription site. A truck stops, and he jumps in. Loud oriental music is playing inside the truck, and a variety of Muslim paraphernalia adorn the driver, himself a dark hairy man. The driver smiles in a friendly way, as he listens to, without understanding, the peasant's Serbian blabber about how he can no longer stand by and watch these horrible fanatics destroying his country ...

In the clear-cut worldview of the peasant protagonist, the Muslims appear as direct descendants of the one-time Ottomans and their expansionist ambitions; to him they are all as dangerous mujahedeens. Now it is time to avenge the five centuries of Ottoman oppression, and to stop the Islamic fundamentalist resurgence. In his mind, his Muslim neighbours (the only Muslims he has ever known, so no wonder he is unable to recognise that the foreign truck driver is also a Muslim) swiftly turn into perpetrators of dark fundamentalist plots. Until now he has simple-mindedly trusted them, unable to recognise their treacherous inner essence. But now, he has seen through their disguise and they can no longer fool him. He is ready to fight. He will take up arms to defend his endangered people.

The revelations of treachery are brought to the peasant protagonist and his like by the media. Thus, this feature film episode is a truthful account. Althought the media, in what is left of Yugoslavia, were full of anti-Muslim propaganda, many of those who took up arms against 'the fundamentalists' had no idea what fundamentalism actually meant. But reports of the Islamic fundamentalist menace were repeated so often, and always with such negative connotations, that the very word 'fundamentalism' came to be perceived as a synonym of horrible impending danger. The fear of Islamic fundamentalism was inflicted by the media, and it was the media that precipitated the ideology of preventive aggressiveness.

There is a wide consensus that without television, it would not have been possible to wage a war on such scale at the time of Yugoslavia's breakup, and that television was the key element in creating the inflamatory and irreconcilable fear of the newly found enemies. In the opening sequences of the documentary *Truth under Siege* passers-by are interviewed on the streets in Belgrade, Zagreb and Sarajevo; they all claim that the war was started by the media. They cannot explain why, they only give expression to an intuitive feeling that it was in the media that the roots of the conflict are to be found. The filmmakers travel across the three main zones of conflict – Croatia, Bosnia and Serbia – and talk to ordinary people and journalists, trying to put together a picture that would explain how such levels of indoctrination came about. What emerges is an ethnographic snapshot of disoriented and insecure media audiences. Disoriented, because they have continuously been exposed to conflicting signals of all sorts of impending dangers. Insecure, because there is nothing beyond the immediate mediatic environment to look to to counter the 'information' of treachery and danger. The role of international media coverage also comes under scrutiny here: it unwillingly perpetuates the indoctrination, as it takes the existing split and the 'warring sides' as given, and can barely transcend the logic of conflict to offer an alternative for reconciliation.

The reporting on danger and treachery, often irresponsibly exaggerated across the territories affected by conflict and war, has played a crucial role in the way the conflict evolved.[5] Marco Altherr of the International Red Cross claims that the propaganda of the warring parties has been so effective that 'If you talk to them, people on both sides are absolutely convinced that the other side is intent on killing them' (quoted in Stiglmajer, 1992, p. 41). In another instance, a Muslim doctor tells of a Serbian friend who genuinely believed that, as Banja Luka TV had informed him, 'the Muslims had lists with the names of Serbian children who were going to be butchered' (ibid., p. 89). Seeking protection from the UN forces, Bosnian Serb politician Biljana Plavsić based her claim on yet another one of Banja Luka TV's reports, namely that 'live Serbian babies are being fed to zoo animals in Sarajevo' (quoted in Rieff, 1995, p. 38). A Serbian soldier is quoted by Vulliamy as insisting that 'In the past weeks, we have seen hundreds of Serbian babies nailed to crosses' (Vulliamy, 1994, p. 100).

It is essential that this mediatic indoctrination, seemingly insignificant in the larger context of state-sanctioned violence, be seen as equally accountable for the violence.

Preventive aggressiveness/majority rights

As a result of mass-mediated indoctrination, each side is convinced that the other is intent on killing them as soon as an opportunity arises. A potential aggressive action would then seem justified, as it is seen as preventing a situation in which one is liable to be vanquished. It is only in this process of consolidating the pillars of national identity by cultivating the image of the enemy that the stress on tradition, history and culture becomes important.

As Renata Salecl remarks, 'the national identity serves as the basis upon which the specific ideology of the moral majority depends' (Salecl, 1994, p. 24). In the case under discussion, national identity is often represented as problematised, questioned and humiliated. It is this inferiority complex-ridden identity that becomes the basis for the ideology of preventive aggressiveness. Cherif Bassiouni, the law professor who investigated Bosnian war crimes for the Hague tribunal, discusses this issue:

> When I talked to soldiers from each of the three warring factions, I said: 'Look, I don't care about your politics, but you cannot rape, torture, and kill innocent civilians.' They replied, 'Yes, but we are only retaliating.' When I told them, 'You cannot retaliate in this way,' they replied: 'Well, then, what can we do? We must defend ourselves!'[6]

The vocal Western concern about minority rights triggers a corresponding adverse Balkan discourse on 'majority rights': everyone seems to care for the minorities, but is not our own position itself one of deprivation, isolation and marginalisation? If no one seems to care about us, we will take care of ourselves in the way we know best. While the internal, local minority is marginalised in the context of the given nation-state, the dominant group increasingly thinks of itself as a new type of deprived minority: weak and disinherited, vulnerable and threatened, culturally isolated in the wider European context.

If we expand Appadurai's argument and try to trace the global aspects of the mediation of large-scale identities as they are being transformed and inter- nalised in the workings of the group imagination, we will have to take into account not only the workings of the nationalist propaganda machine but also the unfavourable image of the Balkans found in the international media at large. Not much propaganda is needed: it is enough to reprint or re-broadcast Western coverage to convince the dominant ethnic group that no one could care less about them. This only adds to a tense situation where internal hostilities are exacerbated by external ones.[7] The sense of growing international marginalisation, contrasting with the international attention for domestic minorities, strengthens and deepens the sense of betrayal and treachery, ensures that the perpetrators feel even more threatened and intensifies their aggression. The marginalisation enhances the feeling of inferiority and triggers an adverse reaction: when we behave, no one cares. Whatever we do, we will always be kept in the backyard. Why, then, not become the bad guys, as no one takes us into consideration anyway?

Villains as victims

It is this conviction, that one acts violently only to prevent the other side from striking first, which is crucial to understanding the paradoxical interchange- ability of the concepts of villains and victims in the Balkan conflict.

Most international observers have indicated that Serbs bear the main burden of responsibility for the bloodshed in former Yugoslavia. Yet, in the age of satellite broadcasting and global networks, the Serbian propaganda has been so successful that many in Serbia see themselves as vulnerable victims. How is this possible?

It was the late Milovan Djilas who noted that by demonising the Serbs, the international media had made them more susceptible to nationalist propaganda. True, one of the most damaging consequences of simplified inter- national reporting on the conflict was the strengthening of nationalist propaganda in Serbia, which built on the feeling of victimhood among the Serbian population. The loss of the crucial Kosovo battle in 1389 was the pillar on which the mythology of Serbian victimhood was built. The reiteration of numerous experiences of defeat became a solid background sustaining the ideology of preventive aggressiveness. In addition, the vision of victimhood was strengthened by the exclusion from Europe. Even some of the war criminals standing trial at the Hague, are seen as martyrs victimised by the international anti-Serbian conspiracy. Needless to say, the NATO bombing over Kosovo, which apportioned guilt collectively, only strengthened the feeling of a comprehensive victimhood, reflected, for example, in the popular badge with the inscription 'target' which the inhabitants of Belgrade wore during the air raids.[8]

Notes

1. Vlada Petrić, director of the Harvard Film Archive, talking at the University of Texas at Austin, February 1996.

2. Senseless violence within the army, for example, is the subject of films such as the Bulgarian *Border* (1995) and the Romanian *Last Stop Paradise* (1998). Mircea Daneliuk's drab post-communist film, *The Conjugal Bed* (1991), could be described as an encyclopaedia of domestic violence and contains scenes which could be compared to the violence in Tarantino's movies, were it not that it exhibits less fascination with it.

3. The shocking violence of this sequence caused a stir in the Croatian studio responsible for the film. The film would have been censored or shelved had it not been for the nearly miraculous last-minute benevolence of the party comrade in charge, who granted it permission to be released without cutting out the scene. For more details, see Daniel Goulding's *Occupation of 26 Scenes* (1998).

4. The novel served as the basis for a film adaptation by Miroslav Lekić, made in Serbia in 1999. Even though the film contained graphic translations of the violent episodes, it was not a big hit with domestic audiences.

5. Even though approached from different angles, the mechanisms of nationalist indoctrination are well discussed by British journalist Mark Thompson in his book on the media in former Yugoslavia (*Forging War*, first published in 1995, 2nd edition 1999) and by the Yugoslav contributors to *Bosnia by Television* (Gow *et al.*, 1996).

6. Quoted in Dennis L. Breo, 'Cherif Bassiouni Condemns "Psychology" of Balkan Crimes', *The Journal of the American Medical Association*, Vol. 270, No. 5, 4 August 1993, pp. 643–4.

7. I have discussed at length the intricate workings of local media that selectively report on the international image of a country and create the background for such discourse in a case study on Bulgaria. See my work in Iordanova (1995, pp. 223–54).

8. A Hollywood production, *Peacemaker* (1997), offered an interesting image of a Bosnian Serb who, while villainous, also had the painful features of a victim. The protagonist is shown taking a stolen nuclear warhead to New York to launch a terrorist attack. There is a flashback explaining his motives – because his family was killed in a mortar attack in Sarajevo, he takes the irrational decision to take revenge on the West. He is alone and insecure, and

ultimately commits suicide. In a videotaped statement he repeats the familiar clichés about the long-standing hostilities and how the West has kept interfering, redrawing maps and deciding the fate of his people. In his desperate terrorist act he is shown simultaneously as perpetrator and victim.

Part 3

People

Chapter 9
Villains and Victims

Since the times of Romanticism, the Balkan villain has been an object of representation in a long line of works of Western writing, painting and film-making. There is a whole gallery of depictions of unruly Balkan subjects, which range from the romanticised to the barbarian, from the *voyvodas* and *hayduks*, to the partisans, the Chetniks, the Ustasha and others.[1]

The popular representations of Bosnia (or the whole of the Balkans, for that matter) that gained circulation at the time of Yugoslavia's breakup did not differ much. A recurrent trope in a range of low-budget action-adventure and exploitation films, Bosnia was seen as a land populated by passive locals, easy prey for the insatiably bloodthirsty paratroopers in balaclavas and ready for violent encounters at every step. In an episode of the Canadian TV series *La Femme Nikita* the heroes travel through a nightmarish winter landscape where murders of sheepish civilians are committed at every step and injustice accelerates in a way which gives the brave protagonists ample opportunity to engage in their respective shooting and martial arts routines. In *Black Punisher* (1991) Fred 'The Hammer' Williamson stars as a one-man task force out to stop a Serbian terrorist group. In these representations, ironically, the victims dwell in obscure anonymity. Their function is to provide a backdrop for the main actors, the villains, who perform in the spotlight.

This chapter is preoccupied with the mediatic and cinematic representation of villains and victims, based mostly on examples from the Bosnian war. I offer a typology of the Balkan villain, as seen in film and in the media: the ridiculed and diminished Balkan politician, the intriguing thug, the flamboyant warlord and the retarded killing machine. I then discuss the representations of victims – as martyrs, witnesses, ordinary people – almost all of whom are portrayed one-dimensionally and less compellingly than the villains.

The politician
Speaking of Soviet politicians in the 1980s, an American journalist had remarked that the fact they wore western style suits and ties was particularly misleading, as this tended to give the impression that they were Western in their

views as well. Were the Soviets dressed in caftans, their difference would remain obvious and any talks with them would be conducted in a much more vigilant manner, the journalist claimed.

This view can be transposed onto Balkan politicians, whose image is one of deceptive discrepancy. Usually, they are represented in Western reporting as European on the surface but intellectually inferior and inefficient beneath the façade. The Balkan politician is traditionally perceived as incompetent and uneducated, and there is a tendency to ridicule and disparage him. The legitimacy of Balkan leaders – be it monarchs or elected politicians – is always an issue: they can cease to be the powers that be at any moment. On the one hand, such treatment results from a long tradition of popular Western literary and filmic images of Balkan politicians. On the other, it is supported by facts: the Albanian King Zog was a commoner who single-handedly proclaimed himself a monarch in 1928; the Romanian dictator, Nicolae Ceauşescu, had worked as a tailor; his wife, Elena, was a poorly educated woman obsessed by a ridiculous academic ambition;[2] Todor Zhivkov of Bulgaria had worked in a typing pool and was known for his preference for peasant-style jokes.

It is not so much the background, however, but the unruly looks of Balkan politicians that are most exploited by the Western media. The populist Serbian leader Vuk Drašković, for example, a bear-sized man with a flamboyant bosomy wife, untamed beard and a pair of burning eyes, ideally fits the mental image of a Balkan politician, especially if one takes into consideration his quick-temper and his inclination to write novels tackling the rights and wrongs of all things Balkan.

As a rule, the Balkan politician is a man, with some rare exceptions, like the 'Iron lady' of the Bosnian Serbs, Biljana Plavsić, or Mira Marković, the wife of Slobodan Milošević. Interestingly, the underlying ridicule in the representation of male politicians only occasionally transfers to the treatment of women. Marković attracted substantial international media attention in 1999 but no consensus was reached about her precise role, even though everyone agreed that she played an influential part in Serbian politics. The media often used photographs of Marković wearing a flower in her black (dyed?) hair. The choice of this mature woman to have herself photographed as mischievous and girlish, once again hinted at the deceptive discrepancy between looks and essence.[3]

The deceptive discrepancy coverage also extends to those Balkan politicians who belong to the intellectual class. An intellectual politician from the Balkans is an oxymoron, something that cannot possibly exist, and the professional competence of such a politician is questioned or mocked, an issue analysed by Vesna Goldsworthy (1998).

In the light of the union of educated populists and uneducated butchers, most attention has been devoted to Radovan Karadžić, the 'ludicrous Bosnian

Serb leader, with his mane of graying hair and the psychiatrist's diploma on his office wall' (Simpson, 1998, p. 432). Karadžić's unruly salt-and-pepper forelock is a typical accessory of a Balkan *voyvoda*. Mediocre both as a psychiatrist and as a poet, disregarded and jeered, Karadžić fell victim to his own excessive ambitions, according to the two-hour documentary *True Stories: The Reckoning* (1998) that the British Channel 4 devoted to him. His poetry was derided in *Serbian Epics* (1993), in which he was persuaded to recite his own verses. His poetry-writing was the subject of discussion by psychiatrists, who examined its contents from a diagnostic point of view. The reports on the record sales of Karadžić's poetry book in Greece suggested an unhealthy curiosity. His incompetence as a psychiatrist was asserted by the narrator in *Urbicide*, a former client. Nevertheless, this foolish impostor remained the public figure who was constantly being interviewed and with whom the West negotiated over Bosnia until the time of his indictment, when he went into hiding. Karadžić's media image was never one of a real villain; rather, he was depicted as incompetent and obtuse.

Bill Tribe, the narrator of the BBC's *Urbicide: A Sarajevo Diary*, made a more serious attempt to identify the political villains. Standing in front of the ruins of the Sarajevo library in January 1993, he named first and foremost several nationalist professors from Sarajevo University. According to Tribe, they wanted to destroy all evidence that Sarajevo had ever had an oriental element, and so they planned the barbarian act of burning down the library and its priceless orientalist collection. One of them was Nikola Koljević, from the Comparative Literature Department, who was referred to as 'the archcitect of ethnic cleansing'.

Koljević, a man in his sixties in a grey suit, with a plain face and generally nondescript appearance, appears briefly in BBC's *Yugoslavia: Death of a Nation* and in Ophuls' *The Troubles We Have Seen*. He is believed to have been the intellectual who, while not having personally killed anyone, had incited others to do so in the name of the ideology he propagated. The fact that he was a Shakespearian scholar triggered well-worn associations with the images of cultivated Nazis. With a Balkan tint, however: *The New York Times'* John F. Burns claims in Ophuls' film that in Bosnia the people who quote Shakespeare are in alliance with the people who cut throats. In 1995, Koljević committed suicide. In the brief media reports on this event he was depicted as one of the moderate nationalists, and as an intellectual who helped draft and pass the Dayton Agreement, his villainous image suppressed and forgotten.

The deceptive discrepancy media coverage of Balkan political dignitaries extended to stressing the comical and kitschy elements in their behaviour and background. Articles about the late Croatian nationalist war minister, Gojko Sušak, for example, ridiculed his undercover life as a pizza-parlour operator in

Toronto.[4] The crazy actions of Bosnian Serb general Ratko Mladić received an abundant tongue-in-cheek coverage: he used to send threatening faxes to Paris warning the French that he would blow them up if they dared to attempt air strikes. Did ridicule help the situation, however? Did making fun of the villains prevent them from carrying on? In their preposterous ways they managed to do serious damage. No constructive exploration of their reasoning and motivation emerged, however.

The Thug

The colourful thug is well represented in media, documentaries and feature films within the Balkan region but is rarely explored internationally. In the Balkan context the thugs are more or less the same men in Bulgaria, Romania, Greece, Albania and across former Yugoslavia, and they all have some sort of link to the new internationally operating branches of the Ukrainian and Russian mafia. Here we will look in more detail at the cinematic portrayal of Serbian thugs.

The link between the criminal underworld and the nationalist paramilitaries is straightforward. Criminals have waived many of the stipulations of standard moral behaviour, but as far as patriotic feelings are concerned, they are often seen as brave men in possession of an inborn nobility, who care deeply about the national wellbeing. They have dared to take an unconventional and dangerous path in life, and they are equally daring in their patriotic commitment. In peaceful times they practise racketeering and trafficking and are regularly involved in coercion and violent showdowns. As soon as they hear the call of the motherland, however, they are ready to employ their gangland skills against the appointed enemy. The manner in which they once dealt with disobedient debtors is now applied to the members of an ungrateful and disobedient ethnic minority. The simple, violent boldness of everyday organised crime is transformed into heroism once transposed to the sphere of patriotic warfare.

It is in this context that the folklore surrounding thuggery is a subject of interest to ethnologists in Serbia. Ivan Colović, the leading Belgrade anthropologist, has extensively explored the specific fascination with the criminal as urban legend. He is particularly preoccupied with the cases of Ljuba Zemunać, a criminal who was killed in 1986 in Frankfurt and who eventually became a legendary folk hero, and with the slender paratrooper Kapetan Dragan, who fought in the war against Croatia (Colović, 1994a, pp. 5–21 and 61–70). Similar superior status is ascribed to other Serbian thugs-turned-fighters who become folk heroes imbued with an aura of the 'noble' or 'tender-hearted criminal' and grow into specific urban legends, as investigated by Marko Živković (1998).

A Studio B92 production, *Vidimo se u citulji/See You in the Obituary* (1995), focuses on the young thugs of the new elite of Belgrade criminals, a cross-over of international organised crime and small-town youth violence.[5] Most of the young men featured in the film live in the suburb of Novi Beograd. They are involved in racketeering and trafficking but think of themselves as business-men. They drive sports cars, exhibit overconfidence, talk of financial transactions only in Deutschmarks and have their specific views on violence and justice. Most are very young and well groomed. A scene from the film shows one of them in his Jakuzzi whirlpool, talking on a cellular phone and wearing a massive gold chain and crucifix on a hairy chest. Other elements of their B-movie-inspired styles include multiple golden chains and bracelets, sleeveless T-shirts, muscular bodies, expensive jogging suits, silk shirts, state-of-the-art pistols, well-shaven faces and trimmed hair, dark glasses, leather jackets and underage girlfriends. Their lives are fast-paced, and by the time of the film's release at least two of the people interviewed during the filming had been shot dead, killed by rival gangsters. By the time of this writing, none of the people featured in the film are still alive.

This Serbian thug subculture has enjoyed a good international exposure in the films of Srdjan Dragojević – fleetingly, in *Pretty Village, Pretty Flame*, where one of the Chetnik protagonists is shown in episodes of his civilian life as a gang-ster returning from affairs in Germany, and prominently in his next film, *Wounds*, which focuses exclusively on the teenage gangster subculture. In the first film, there is still a link between a life of crime and commitment to the nationalist cause. The prematurely tough protagonists of *Wounds* belong to a generation that apparently cares little for nationalist excess. It is clear, however, that it is the background of an intense nationalistic culture that has confined their accelerated lives to the orbit of glamorised brutality, shootings and drugs.

The cross-over between the lifestyles of the criminal underworld and the Chetnik paratroopers finds its best display in the turbo-folk videos:

'Turbo Folk' is a homegrown Serbian musical hybrid of Oriental and Slavic folk melodies, 'disco beats, and Arabic yowling,' according to Belgrade critic Petar Luković. Turbo-folk singers are generally leggy women dressed in short sequined mini-skirts, pushup bras and heavy makeup who socialize in the public spotlight with political figures and military thugs. Originally, in a period of particularly high Serbian chauvinism and xenophobia, the form was endorsed and even promoted by the official media as an all-Serb alternative to outer influences. . . . And while political boasting of the more hard-headed sort is actually part of Serbian tradition, as in songs such as 'Ko to Kaze Ko to Laze Serbija je Mala' ('Whoever says that Serbia is small is a liar'), never before have political themes been incorporated to such an extent into the songs of the country's pop stars.[6]

The appearance and the demeanour of one of the main stars of the genre, Baja Mali Knindza, an 'auteur' who writes his own lyrics, can be deemed representative of the phenomenon. In the music video compilation tape *War and Peace* (1994), the short-legged hairy-chested singer is first seen wearing a Hawaiian shirt, dancing amid girls in tight short skirts, all shot from below so that one can catch a glance of the girls' laced panties. It all takes place in an apartment, furnished in a *nouveau riche* style. Another song is set in a casino, where he is shown gambling, wearing dark glasses and a tuxedo. The video also includes clips from an interview in which the singer discusses his creative beliefs. For the interview he has changed into a tracksuit and a Reebok baseball cap, and wears a massive gold chain. Baja Mali Knindza then sings about 'the Serbs' in a video which uses images of Chetnik fighters training in the fields, presumably somewhere in Croatia, and the dispersal of a demonstration, suggesting that irresponsible protesting may destabilise the country. The visuals for another song consist of old Chetnik photographs, footage from glorious moments in the Balkan wars and bearded men with Chetnik hats, who sit at a table full of half-empty bottles, in front of a portrait of the Chetnik leader Draža Mihajlović, urging him to rise from the dead and take up leadership once again. We also see the singer being trained to shoot, and firing off a shot in an unspecified direction. All these jump cuts between past and present are there to suggest that from time to time it becomes necessary to take up arms to protect oneself and secure the enjoyment of life in a Hawaiian shirt.

Only rarely do films made by Westerners explore the figure of the thug as a perpetrator of ethnic cleansing. One of the few documentaries to explore this link between petty criminals and violent nationalists is Ilan Ziv's *Yellow Wasps* (1995). The film is an investigation into the violent activities of the paramilitary unit known as the 'Yellow Wasps' ('Zuta Osa'), named after a strong brandy. The film-makers investigate the paratroopers' involvement in the savage ethnic cleansing of the eastern Bosnian town of Zvornik in April 1992. The investigation begins with a photograph of a Bosnian man, naked from the waist up, with blood flowing from his mouth over his torso. Also in the picture is a man, allegedly the perpetrator, who wears a pony-tail and a Chetnik cockade, and whose back is turned to the camera.[7] After an extensive search, the film-makers manage to find the man in Belgrade, at the trial of the 'Wasps' bosses. Still sporting the pony-tail, he is identified as one of the leaders, along with his brother. The brothers are described as local New Belgrade thugs with a lengthy record of petty crime. Both brimming with self-confidence, they look like characters from a turbo-folk music video. Although the film-makers do not manage to get much out of them, at least *Yellow Wasps* marks an attempt to explore the ethnography of violence, tracing the villains and revealing the close linkage between the criminal underworld and the paratroopers.

The Glamorised Villain: Arkan

It was the disproportionate media attention given to the Serbian warlord Arkan that established him as a celebrity. He had always enjoyed coverage as a larger-than-life figure, so it is not surprising that the news of his mysterious Belgrade assassination in January 2000 made the headlines. His end was just as flamboyant as his life.

Arkan characterised a specific phenomenon – that of the glamorised villain – and he readily played along. It was not so much his crimes but his audacious aura that guaranteed the extensive coverage. But why were the media so preoccupied with him? I think mainly because he fitted so well into the preconceived image of what a Balkan thug should be.

Arkan was an alias for Montenegrin Željko Ražnatović, a Belgrade-based businessman, one of the leaders of Serbia's organised crime, one-time parliamentarian and founder and president of the Party of Serbian Unity. He was a man well connected both to Serbia's secret services and the mafia, and leader of the paramilitary unit known as the Tigers, which in 1992 had terrorised, looted and 'cleansed' a number of towns in eastern Bosnia. Arkan's official business was in sweets – pastries and ice cream – and he was said to have regularly

Arkan in a uniform on loan from the National Theatre in Belgrade, one of the several costumes he changed during his 1995 wedding

profited from trafficking fuel against the embargo. Later on he also bought a football team, Obilic, named after the Serbian folk hero of the Battle of Kosovo.

It was not for these activities, however, but for his exposure-conscious lifestyle and reckless attitude that he was regularly at the centre of media attention. His hacienda-style home in Belgrade was one of the landmarks of nouveau riche residential architecture. Well aware of the admiration of his devoted following, in 1994 he pleased his fans by publishing a calendar that featured a different photo of him for every month. His 1995 wedding to turbo-folk singer Ceca was played out as a popular media event, the lavish 'feast in times of plague' wedding of a charismatic warlord and a fabulous turbo-folk queen, which commanded international media attention.[8]

In *See You in the Obituary*, Arkan is identified as the inspirational role model for the younger gangsters of Novi Beograd. He appears to embody their ideas of style, with his army of bodyguards and his exclusive use of top-of-the-range four-wheel-drive vehicles. In the film, Arkan is shown campaigning for Parliament in Kosovo, and then, at his lavishly furnished headquarters, kissing the Serbian flag. Wearing an immaculate white suit, he tells the camera, in a close-up: 'I do not give a damn!' – a line which he delivers in English.

As a media phenomenon, Arkan began domestically. A Yugoslav media scholar, Milan Milošević, described him as the darling of the Serbian media from the early 1990s, a romanticised 'TV favourite' who 'was referred to as a "restless youth," with some of the aura of a Rambo'(quoted in Udovicki and Ridgeway, 1995, p. 116). Many legendary stories of Arkan's glorious past were in circulation – like his daring escape from a Swedish courtroom in the 1980s, where he was being tried either for drug trafficking or bank robbery, and from where he was abducted by his buddies who held the judges, clerks and court security at gun point. Consistent with the tele-novela style characteristic of the reporting of his exploits, late in 1997 documents concerning his criminal past in Sweden mysteriously disappeared from the car of a Swedish diplomat working for the war crimes tribunal, who was *en route* from Stockholm to the Hague.

Wanted by Interpol, at home Arkan was more than confident about his personal safety. Although his name would appear in the West almost every time paramilitary atrocities were mentioned, he was safe in that respect as well: his name did not appear on the list of those indicted by the Hague tribunal until 1999, when it was announced that such an indictment had come into effect, not least because of international media pressure.

In 1997, CNN aired a half-hour Arkan special with Christianne Amanpour, featuring appearances by Richard Holbrooke and Cherif Bassiouni discussing Arkan's war crimes and raising the question of why he had not been indicted.[9] His infamous statement, 'I do not give a damn!' was played again and again.

The narrative made use of existing footage, such as scenes of the terror in Vuko-var and Zvornik, to assemble a consistent indictment of the warlord. Survivors from Osijek, Zvornik and Bijelina were interviewed about atrocities commit-ted by Arkan's Tigers. Their testimonies were juxtaposed with footage of Arkan declaring to the camera in English, 'we came to help these people', a statement which is further intercut with images of slaughtered civilians and Arkan exclaiming that 'Muslims are like wild dogs'. Amanpour talks of Arkan's links to the Yugoslav state security and authorities, shows his pre-election posters and footage of his campaign for a parliamentary seat in Kosovo in 1993 and mentions that he is planning to run for the presidency in the year 2000.

Arkan reacted publicly to the documentary by threatening a libel suit.[10] He claimed that, provided no formal indictment was laid against him, CNN had committed libel. Irrespective of whether or not CNN had a case to answer, what is true is that Western and domestic media alike played an important role in blowing up the importance of Arkan by providing extensive coverage of all aspects of his shady activities in politics, business and crime. It is therefore dif-ficult to say now whether it was the crimes that warranted such media attention, or the extensive media coverage that ensured the continuing scrutiny of his crimes. The media coverage of Arkan always portrayed him as a thug. The coverage itself, however, happened not just because he was a thug – many others were – but because he was a charismatic and colourful one. And he was willing to play along and deliver what the media expected of him.

The best-known photograph of him was taken by American Ron Haviv, in which Arkan appears in his paramilitary uniform, standing in front of a tank and holding a baby tiger. He is surrounded by his boys, the Tigers, all wearing black balaclavas and wielding high-powered automatic rifles.[11] There is a macho, thuggish glamour in this photograph, and an audacity in Arkan's appearance that reminds us of John Wayne or Sylvester Stallone.

Another photograph of Arkan, from the publicity stunt of his wedding to folk-singer Ceca, was widely reprinted around the world: Arkan sits on a chair and holds his bride on his lap, her slender long legs on display; both look straight at the camera. This audacious, unblinking willingness to face the media seemed to fascinate and attract journalists, and they readily gave the attention that Arkan demanded.

When Belgrade was bombed in retaliation for Kosovo, Arkan was one of the first people Western journalists pursued, not least because they had declared him to be one of those who sought to 'cleanse' Kosovo, and now needed to ver-ify the story. True to his love of the media, Arkan readily popped up in person at the Hyatt hotel where most of the journalists were stationed. Once again net-works from around the world focused their attention on him and reported his presence in Belgrade. This last, widely covered Belgrade appearance, alongside

British tabloids ran this
photograph of Arkan and Ceca
during the Kosovo crisis under the
headline 'The Beauty and the
Beast', while *The Observer*'s reporter
noticed Arkan's weight gain

his glamorous wife, who was adorned in white fur for the occasion, gave him
prime coverage, particularly from the British tabloid press. Although the
essence of the coverage was supposed to be Arkan's attempt to refute Western
media reports that he was 'cleansing' Albanians in Kosovo, the tabloids simply
made good use of the images that the event supplied. Some ran a cover photograph of the couple with the headline, 'The Beauty and the Beast'.

It was at this time that the announcement of his indictment by the Hague
tribunal was finally made public. Always ready to talk to the media, Arkan was
interviewed by international networks. Soon after, however the buzz around
Arkan faded. As Maggie O'Kane described it in *The Observer* (16 January 2000):

> Later, as the nights of the Kosovo war dragged on and the press was confined
> to Belgrade and the Intercontinental, journalists stopped paying him any
> attention and he would have a slightly offended look in his handsome face
> when people stopped looking on from their late dinner to draw breath at his
> presence. Arkan was getting fat and becoming an old hat.[12]

While earlier she had described Arkan as 'a brilliant and charming TV per-
former who left interviewers struggling with his articulate defence of himself
as a "nationalist and servant of the motherland" ', now he no longer seemed to
matter. O'Kane and others noted that by 1999 it was Arkan who was seeking
out the journalists, particularly the new ones in town, and that it had become

somehow too easy to get an interview with him. He was desperate to impress, but it no longer seemed to work. Why was this? Because people no longer feared him? Or because he was getting fat? I am inclined to think that the early signs of obesity had a lot to do with changing media attitudes.

In such a context, it seems he had a timely death. The news of his assassination, besides making the front page, occupied whole pages of coverage in the leading newspapers of the world, and it was still not too late for him to be remembered as 'the most able self-publicist in Serbia'.[13] The details of his life were covered in more detail than any of the other war criminals responsible for the violence in the Yugoslav breakup. There was still interest in him and the media did not miss the chance to run a last round of pictures.

Media which rely on visuals, such as newspapers and TV networks, want their images to impress, to be memorable. So they tend to use pictures of distinctive-looking people rather than of those of a nondescript appearance. This is the case with criminals of all kinds – barely a media report on Charles Manson or Jeffrey Dahmer remains that does not include their photographs. This was also the case with the villains of the wars of the Yugoslav succession – pictures and footage of the good-looking perpetrators were more likely to appear in the media than pictures and footage of those whose faces did not intrigue. This was clearly true in Arkan's case. When in 1998 an indicted Bosnian Serb leader, General Radislav Krstić, known as 'the butcher of Srebrenica', was arrested and deported to the Hague, Western news media repeatedly showed a photograph of him that portrayed him as a proud warrior: a handsome, white-haired man with piercing blue eyes, in a black beret and uniform. The footage of Krstić's subsequent court appearance appeared only briefly in the media – maybe because he had been transformed into a balding and bland-looking man, stripped of glorious military paraphernalia and wearing a plain suit.

In 1999 when another indicted Serbian general, Tadić, was arrested in Vienna, very few papers and networks ran pictures of him – short and plump, he lacked a distinctive appearance. Similarly, the bland demeanour of one of the main thugs, General Mladić, granted him only peremptory appearances in the media. His face is well known around the world only because it has been shown so many times over a long period since 1992. The first man to go on trial at the Hague, Duško Tadić, the guard from Omarska, however, featured quite often in the media. Albeit short, he was in possession of a 'handsome' face (*The New Yorker*).

Arkan's coverage is the ultimate reminder that much more individualised attention was paid to the villains than to the victims in the Balkan conflict. Ironically, a good-looking criminal who fits the concept of Balkan thug stands a better chance of a career in public relations than any politician or victims' advocate. For only a few 'dark Balkan subjects' have managed to remain in the media spotlight for so long.

The Monster? Borislav Herak

One of the few well-publicised villains to go on trial early in the Bosnian war was Borislav Herak, a twenty-year-old Bosnian Serb simpleton who confessed to slaughtering scores of people and raping women. Herak, possibly the only one to plead guilty, was tried and sentenced to death in Sarajevo on 30 March 1993, in a trial which received extensive international media coverage. Close-ups of his semi-idiotic face hit the pages of all Western newspapers, a haunting image of a retarded killing machine. The photograph was taken with a wide-angled lens, further distorting his egg-shaped shaven head, and making him appear even more retarded. It was a memorable picture, difficult to erase from one's mind once seen.

The publicity that surrounded Herak's case was controlled and directed by the Bosnian government in Sarajevo – he was their captive, and it was they who were in possession of his story. Herak was the type of villain who was well suited for instant notoriety, so they passed on his story, along with its respective interpretation, to the international media. A short about Herak, *Ispovjest*

Close-ups of Herak's face taken with a wide-angled lens that further exaggerate his egg-shaped shaven head, hit the pages of Western newspapers: a haunting image of a retarded killing machine

Monstruma/Confession of a Monster (1993), was made by Sarajevan documentarians authorised by the Muslim government and was later included in the omnibus documentary *MGM Sarajevo: covjek, bog, monstrum/MGM Sarajevo: Man, God, Monster* (1992/4).[14] The film uses a dynamic montage of images, structured around conversations with Herak, who looks up to an invisible interviewer. He is a tall young man who comes across as clumsy and awkward. With his long arms and legs, he readily shows in front of the camera how he was taught to slaughter people by first practising on a pig, and then how he smashed skulls with the butt of his rifle. He describes how he ended up fighting because a friend called him, and how he gradually became a merciless killer. He talks of his taste in pop music, about his favourite radio stations and of a video-clip of four men in dark glasses and dark suits. He talks of more looting and killing. He claims he was always told what to do by others – to rape, to slaughter, to shoot. And he obeyed. He talks of his sister and his niece, whom he particularly loved and whom he would take out for ice cream. He describes how he passed his driving test. He talks about his father, and how much he wants to tell him what he has done and that he is now repentant. But, well, it does not really matter now, as he will not live much longer. No, he does not believe in the afterlife. He dreams of a speedy end. He looks nervously to the side, and we are shown close-ups of his shoes that have no shoelaces, and of his feet and hands. The camera shows us Herak's cell and bed, and we watch him sleeping. Then we see him taking lonely walks in the prison yard. Aeroplanes take off from the airport in the city, while Herak lies on the bed in his cell and smokes, waiting for the end.

Looking at Herak, clearly a retarded killing machine, I could not help asking myself if this, indeed, was the monster? He surely was, as far as his actual deeds were concerned. But wasn't it somehow too easy to blame it all on such a dim-witted figure, who had acted obediently and who then confessed? Wasn't he just a function of the monstrous? Undoubtedly a perpetrator, but wasn't he also a scapegoat?

Two other people were indicted and sentenced to life in prison based solely on Herak's testimony. One of them, Sretko Damjanović, had insisted throughout that his confession was beaten out of him. In 1997 it transpired that two of the men whom Herak had identified as Damjanović's victims were, in fact, alive.[15] Despite this revelation, Damjanović's conviction was upheld by a Bosnian appeals court. Both Herak and Damjanović are serving life in a Bosnian prison in Zenica.

Herak's trial and the associated media coverage are reminiscent of a story tackled by Bertrand Tavernier in his remarkable film *Le Juge et l'assassin/The Judge and the Assassin* (1976). Tavernier tells a story from early in this century, in which a mentally ill soldier terrorises the French countryside, murdering young peasant boys and girls. The villain is soon apprehended and incarcerated. The ambitious local investigator in charge of the case (Philippe Noiret) quickly realises that he is dealing with a criminal not competent to stand trial, but nonetheless chooses to proceed with the high-profile case, because to secure the execution of a cold-blooded villain is to his political advantage.

There are both similarities and differences between Tavernier's protagonist and Herak. In both cases, a dim-witted criminal protagonist provides a much-needed villain. In both cases, the insane one who repents is punished. In Herak's case, however, the sane instigators, those who always plead 'not guilty', remain at large. Unlike *The Judge and the Assassin*, which questioned the motives of the judge as a moral pillar of society, the mechanisms of justice that were applied in Herak's case never came to be examined.

Victims: A Blurred Image

In the Hungarian Holocaust classic, András Kovác's *Hideg napok/Cold Days* (1966), a group of officers, now in jail, remember the massacre of Jews from Novi Sad which they organised and carried out. The villains are shown as individuals living through experiences of moral reflection and deep remorse. Their victims, however, never appear as anything more than a group of people herded together on the icy shore of the Danube, and as a pile of dead bodies that will be thrown into the river just a few moments later.

The same approach to depicting the victims is found in the representations of today's Balkan conflict. What we can call footage of the victims most often shows groups of anonymous women herded on to the back of trucks, remnants of charred bodies found in the ruins of burned houses or decayed pieces of clothing dug out of muddy mass graves. Compared to the individualised attention which the villains receive, the media and film portrayal of victims is much weaker, highlighting the general difficulty of producing an individualised and strong representation of the victim, the one who is denied agency. One speaks of them in the plural. It is a bad thing to be victimised, and the victim is blamed for letting it happen. Thus the victims are suppressed twice – once in the act of violence to which they are subjected, and once again in their media image. Media portrayal of the victims not only does not restore agency, it takes it away one more time. Apparently concerned with the issues of trauma and painful witnessing, it nonetheless approaches victims as silhouettes or blurred images.

Camps and martyrs[16]

The Bosnian camps were extensively discussed by Western journalists, in particular, Roy Gutman (1993), Ed Vulliamy (1994) and David Rieff (1995). The accounts from survivors, however, are not as plentiful. Rezak Hukanovič (1996), a Bosnian Muslim poet and journalist from Prijedor, who was in his late forties at the time, was one of the few who wrote an account of his time in the camps of Bosnia in 1992, first published in Oslo and then in New York. The documentary narrative is delivered by a fictional protagonist, as the author believed that such an approach would allow him to transcend the confines of his individual story and best convey the horrible mixture of the macabre and mundane that reigned over the lives of Bosnian prisoners. He talks of Omarska and Manjaca, and of torture and atrocities. He talks of confinement sites where both prisoners and guards come from the same community, and where the camp population consists of 'men who know each other well, neighbors who greet each other in the street, friends of many years standing who, suddenly, poisoned by patriotic and ethnic fanaticism, become fierce and bitter enemies'. He talks of the awful helplessness, how he was unable to protect his own son, who was also held in the same camp. The man next to him, a diabetic deprived of his daily insulin injection, dies. Another one is tortured horribly, and yet another, whose ribs are broken, is killed on a bus and then tossed like a suitcase into the baggage department.

What is particularly noteworthy about Hukanović's account is that he talks of personal experiences, and that his protagonist, while herded in the camp alongside others, retains an individual identity. He only discusses his own individual story, acknowledging at the same time that this was a mass experience. While talking of himself, he talks for all the others – for those who have no chance to talk of themselves. It is rare for camp inmates to be individualised; in most other cases, camp populations are just a part of an anonymous herd, and their experiences are represented collectively.

It is the concern about those others who remain voiceless and anonymous victims that triggers the survivors to speak. This speaking up is framed in a way that has often been used in writing and film – the personal account of the survivor is intended to stand in for the collective experience of a mass of anonymous sufferers. Only the protagonists' personal suffering is explored in depth, while other victims remain as background extras.

But then, this is the depiction of oppressed ones in cinema at large. Such is the representation of the camp population in the Soviet Union, for example – from the adaptation of Solozhenitsyn's *One Day in the Life of Ivan Denisovich* (1970) through the award-winning post-*perestroika* tale of deprived camp childhood in *Zamri, umri, voskresni/Freeze, Die, Come to Life* (1990), to the remorseful portrayal of *Chekist/The Chekist* (1992), where the KGB victims are nothing more than piles of bodies and scores of anonymous young men lined up in front of an execution squad. Such is the representation of Nazi-run camps, where the most typical scene is the image of herded Jews being loaded onto transport or arriving at the camp, or, soon after, piles of anonymous dead bodies, shoes or clothes. Such scenes have appeared in numerous films, from the survivor's tales found in Andrzej Wajda's *Krajobraz po bitwie/Landscape after Battle* (1970), based on Tadeusz Borowski, and Francesco Rosi's *La tregua/The Truce* (1996), based on Primo Levi, to tales of perishing in the camps depicted in Wanda Jakubowska's *Ostatni etap/The Last Stage* (1948) and Roberto Begnini's *Life Is Beautiful* (1998).

Of course, it is almost impossible to create a narrative that would grant an equal level of agency to all victims. The only alternative to this denial is to resort to allegory, to focus on the attempted resistance of a select protagonist, like the two boys who escape from their transport in the Czech Holocaust classic *Démanty noci/ Diamonds of the Night* (1963), or the desperate moves to preserve dignity which Warsaw ghetto's orphanage director Janusz Korczak undertakes in Andrzej Wajda's film, *Korczak* (1991).

Witnesses

The traumatised witnesses are another blurred image. We mostly see them in films made in the West. Many of the people who have agreed to testify on camera either live in the safety of exile or prefer to give their evidence in darkened rooms, so that they can remain unidentified.

A rare exception, once again, is found in Ilan Ziv's *Yellow Wasps*. Not only has he tracked down the Wasp leaders, he has also managed to coax refugees from Zvornik to talk, even though they are still afraid to give their names and prefer to remain anonymous. Ziv even managed to persuade Ahmet Isic, the man featured in the picture that inspired the film's investigation, to come forward in plain daylight and talk about the beating he took, the results of which can be seen in the photograph. It does not seem, however, that giving testimony made much difference in this particular case. The film-makers cannot help noticing that none of the witnesses they interviewed for the film were summoned for the trial of the paramilitaries, and none of their testimony was heard during the trial of the perpetrators.

Similarly, the authors of *Calling the Ghosts*, a film in which victims of the Bosnian rape camps bear witness, mention in the epilogue that most of the rape victims who were supposed to testify at the court in the Hague decided to withdraw their testimonies. Nonetheless, the film evolves around the issue of witnessing, featuring two courageous rape survivors, determined to speak for the sake of others who perished. Film-makers feel that showing the individual quest for justice by taking up the difficult decision to testify is a way to empower victims. This is how documentaries like Channel 4's *The Unforgiving* (1993) come into being – a film which documents the desperate attempts of a Serbian couple to find out how their eleven-year-old son was murdered and where his remains might be. The only clues come from a Muslim prisoner, a family acquaintance before the time of ethnic cleansing.

Explored by Dori Laub and Shoshana Feldmann (1992), in respect of a
diverse range of Holocaust accounts, the importance of witnessing in literature
and history is recognised as a crucial approach in the process of recovery from
trauma. A wide range of testimonies from survivors of the Yugoslav wars in the
1990s are being collected by the Chicago-based project on trauma and witnessing, which worked with numerous victims from Bosnia, by the Bassiouni
investigation, which gathered extensive videotaped testimonies, and by the editors of various collections of texts by survivors (Cataldi, 1994; Mertus *et al.*,
1997). These testimonials, however, even if supplied with names, gain a real significance only in the wider context of suffering where, as we saw, the victim is
deprived of individual identity and becomes an allegory for the suffering of
others.

The human interest story
The generally shared critical opinion on the 'human interest' documentary is
that it tends to simplify or even avoid the debate on conflict. It is an approach
that shifts the focus and favours superficial emotionalism to in-depth analysis.
Journalist David Rieff, whose *Slaughterhouse* (1995) was a moving account of
the West's failure to intervene in Bosnia, spoke out against the 'human interest'
documentaries. Such films, he claimed, are of little use, as they cannot help to
produce an informed decision about what should be done:

> By remembering what happened in Bosnia through a series of cinematically
> compelling individual tragedies one has already lost the battle ... You can have
> a good cry and remain just as passive as you were before, unless you are forced
> to understand that what is at stake in our indifference is not merely justice but
> perhaps peace itself.[17]

True, as far as political action is concerned, witnessing sad stories has barely
motivated people to do something about atrocities. But other, more politicised
documentaries did not generate action, either. From various remarks that high-
ranking politicians have made in the media, it transpires that these influential
individuals have often been compelled to take action after seeing a shattering
human-interest documentary or a moving fiction film (convinced that such
films would allegedly have the same emotionally stirring effect on their popu-
lace). Watching critical documentaries that expose their vacuous political
rhetoric has rarely had the same effect.

It seems to me that when the context is one of general inaction, as it was in
Bosnia for a long time, the human interest documentary played an important
role. In particular, it gave individual identities to the victims, and made them
stand out from the blurred morass to which they were relegated in the context

of daily media coverage. The human interest documentary could not, indeed, compel the international community to intervene, and did not suggest what kind of intervention would be meaningful. Nevertheless, it did its quiet job of representing the victims' experiences as experiences of normal human beings with whom the viewer could identify, and for whom one could feel compassion and understanding. It took a closer look at the exotic Others and turned them into ordinary people with valid anxieties and concerns. This is what human interest documentaries like *Romeo and Juliet in Sarajevo, Elles s'appelent toutes Sarajevo/They Were All Called Sarajevo* (1994) and many more, managed to do.

These documentaries rarely went below the surface to consider the political dimensions of the war. Unlike the politically focused documentaries, however, those that addressed human interest stories looked into how individual human beings experienced the impoverishment, the loss of homes and livelihood. They also looked at aspects of the conflict that affected people's day-to-day existence: death, destruction and bodily harm. The human interest stories were the only ones to explore what war meant to ordinary people, the ultimate victims.

In such a context, well-researched works of visual anthropology came to play a specific role: once screened by mainstream networks, such ethnographic accounts turned into influential human interest documentaries. Such was the case of *We Are All Neighbours* (1993), based on the work of Norwegian anthropologist Tone Bringa, who had conducted her research in an ethnically mixed Bosnian village and was preparing to publish her timely account on *Being Muslim the Bosnian Way* (1996).[18] This documentary differed from the average human interest story in that it was based on serious research that made it much more compelling when showing the effects of war on human relations, families and friendships.

Shot in two stages in 1993, the film shows how conflict comes and destroys the communal life of a small village in Bosnia, inhabited by Croats and Muslims. During their first visit the crew registers still suppressed but mounting inter-ethnic tensions, while during the second one, just two months later, they witness how the conflict has grown into a full-blown war. The footage from the earlier visit shows villagers content with their simple lives. The women, Muslim and Croat, still gather for an afternoon coffee and cook together. By the end of the film, however, they will no longer talk to each other, separated by deaths, burned houses and destruction. But they still want to talk to the camera, allowing the viewer to grasp how their devastation is caused not so much by the destruction but by the feeling of betrayal and the loss of trust. New allegiances and agendas, hastily taken up by the people of different ethnicities within the village, have come to replace the traditional, ethnically indifferent community commitments. Forty-year friendships have come to an end within a day, replaced by mistrust. They all talk about treachery now. Nobody is sure where it is safe any more.

The concluding part of the documentary is built around four juxtaposed shots of before and after: women making burek in the kitchen/the same kitchen turned into rubble; women doing the dishes in the yard/the yard deserted; a child at the door of the house/the house shelled; women singing together in the living room/the living room destroyed. These are images to which any viewer could relate. It may be an irony that testimonies stood a better chance of entering the public discourse of the West when they were offered as human interest stories than when they appeared in the context of critical and analytical films. For all the criticism of the human interest documentary did not change the fact that it was influential, an issue that deserves a more extensive investigation into the wider contextual correlation of populism and media effects.

The fantasy of the victim

Those who need help are not always asked what aspects of the war affect them most and what kind of help they need. The people who come to offer assistance often use their own framework of suffering, and their own preconceived ideas about what the victim is like and the help he or she should receive. Here is one example that illustrates this projection of ideas about suffering and support onto the victims. In 1994 I attended a feminist gathering organised by activists of the Foundation for Compassionate Society in Austin, Texas. One of the speakers, a woman of seemingly affluent background, passionately spoke up in support of Bosnian women and appealed to all attending the gathering to join with her in a campaign to attest solidarity by sending these women personal packages full of rose petals.

Well, I must admit I do not think that the rose petals would make much difference to the lives of Bosnian women. But even when more practically directed, sometimes the approaches of helpers themselves are inappropriate, leading to a conflict in their own ranks. Such was the case with self-styled British relief worker Sally Becker, dubbed 'The Angel of Mostar', who, though wishing to give relief, had acted impetuously and hastily, thus risking the safety and wellbeing of those whom she was desperate to help. A BBC documentary about her, *Where Angels Fear to Tread* (1999), indicated that as a result, she only managed to help a select few.

Slavoj Žižek has produced one of the best analyses of the harmful aspects of projecting such generalised concepts of victimhood onto the Bosnian victims (Žižek, 1994, pp. 213–14). He spoke of 'universalization of the notion of the victim', where the concrete dimensions of suffering and the need for help were substituted by abstract ideas, and where a fantasy image of the victim thwarted the ability to act. It all results in an ethics of compassion that 'legitimizes the avoidance, the endless postponement of the act'. Such humanitarian activity was extremely limited in its effect, he claimed, as all it managed to do was 'obfuscate the urgency of the act'.

Functioning as a template for victimhood, the universalised notion was exclusive and privileges only those victims who could unquestionably pass the test of being pure victims and nothing else. This is why the suffering of children, presumably innocent, came under the spotlight and was featured more often than the suffering of adult women; and why the suffering of men, presumably guilty whichever side they were on, rarely attracted media attention (and when it did, only in the plural, as in the case with the victims of Srebrenica).

A documentary, *Sabina's Story* (1999), told of the efforts of a British cameraman to get a girl suffering from leukemia out of Bosnia; but he is too late and she dies nonetheless. In the feature, *Welcome to Sarajevo*, based on a documentary account, the protagonist, a Western journalist, witnessed the suffering of many children, men and women, but helped only one girl to escape. In the fictional *Savior*, the protagonist, a Western mercenary, did not try to help the mother but saved her angelic-looking baby.[19] One has to be innocent by definition, a baby or a child, whose motives cannot be questioned and whose allegiances do not need to be scrutinised, to fall within the universalised concept of victimhood and thus be considered a legitimate victim. Adults simply cannot qualify. Even if victimised, they are presumed to be capable of agency. Be it villains or victims, they are all tainted by the fact that they are embroiled in the conflict.

The mediated representation of the conflict evolved around a deeply ironic configuration of villains and victims. Those who acted adversely, the villains, were the action heroes who led the narrative and were granted individualised attention in the coverage of the conflict. Those who suffered adverse actions, the victims, were the passive extras whose only function was to enable the narrative to evolve as defined by its villainous protagonists. In this narrative the sufferers were relegated the supernumerary background of multiple blurred shadows.

Notes

1. These are explored in a number of studies on literature, most recently by Vesna Goldsworthy in her *Inventing Ruritania* (1998).
2. Elena Ceaușescu's well-documented ignorance of chemistry, however, did not prevent leading American and British universities from awarding her honorary doctoral degrees when the politics of the day seemed to demand it.
3. Photomontages of Milošević's baby-face, superimposed over pictures of the

burning oil refinery at Pancevo in April 1999, had a good run in international magazines, alongside family portraits of him and Mira Marković – he in a casual, sporty jacket, she wearing a flower in her hair – reminiscent of the set-up of family photographs of the Gorbachevs in Russia or the Blairs in Britain.

4. Patrick Graham, 'Canadian Warlord', *Saturday Night*, Vol. 112, No. 10, December 1997, p. 56.

5. The authors of the film preferred a different English version for their title and have translated it as *The Crime that Changed Serbia*. It is my belief, however, that the literal translation of the original Serbian title gives a more appropriate idea of the content of the film.

6. Kim Simpson, 'The Dissolution of Yugoslav Rock', unpublished paper, University of Texas at Austin, 1995. For an extensive discussion of the aggressive role of turbo-folk in the Yugoslav music scene, and on why genres such as punk, rock, etc. are considered antagonistic to turbo-folk in the Serbian context, see Gordy (1999).

7. Chetnik paraphernalia and hats are sold at the Belgrade train station and elsewhere. The normal hats worn by Serbian peasants are also acceptable, as long as the Chetnik cockade is attached.

8. I have discussed the mediatic aspects of this 'wedding of the century' in a special piece: see my 'Balkan Wedding Revisited' (1998c).

9. *Arkan: Alleged Serbian War Lord*, aired on CNN on 2 June 1997 in their *Profiles* series.

10. In a programme on Belgrade TV Arkan declared that he would file a libel suit and hired a Greek lawyer to represent him ('Arkan Denies Being Tito's Henchman', *BBC Summary of World Broadcasts*, TV Belgrade, 6 June 1997; 'Paramilitary Leader Denies CNN Allegations of War Crimes', *BBC Summary of World Broadcasts*, interview on Belgrade TV, 6 June 1997; 'Warlord to Sue CNN, to Announce News to "Astound" World', *BBC Summary of World Broadcasts*, 19 June 1997).

11. This photograph was even used by the designer of the book jacket for Cushman and Mestrović's edited collection (1996).

12. Maggie O'Kane, 'Swaggering Style of the Hard-Eyed Killer We Knew', *The Observer*, 16 January 2000, p. 3. O'Kane is the author of a Channel 4 documentary about Arkan and Milošević, *The Puppet Master of the Balkans* (1994).

13. Misha Glenny, 'Underworld Boss of Milošević's Murder Squad', obituary in the *Guardian*, 19 January 2000, p. 20.

14. Footage from *Confessions of a Monster* is also used in Bernard-Henri Lévy's *Bosna!*.

15. 'Two Bosnia War Victims Still Alive', *Chicago Tribune*, 2 March 1997, sect. 1 p. 7.

16. Here I am not discussing the representations of the violence and the victims of earlier infamous Balkan camps such as Jasenovac (run by Croatian Ustasha) or Goli Otok (run by Yugoslav communists), nor similar camps in Bulgaria, Romania and Greece. These camps have been the subject of numerous documentaries and feature films from the region.

17. Quoted in Judith Miller, 'Taking Two Bosnian Women's Case to the World', *The New York Times*, 23 February 1997, sec. 2 p. 36.

18. For a good discussion of this work of visual anthropology as a human interest documentary, see Peter Loizos, 'A Duty of Care? Three Granada Television Films Concerned with War', in Allen and Seaton (1999).

19. Noted by John Wrathall in his review of *Savior* in *Sight and Sound*, July 1998, p. 52.

Chapter 10
Representing Women's Concerns

In the 1990s, women across the Balkans were facing a range of grave social problems: unemployment, cuts in social benefits, deteriorating or unaffordable health care, inadequate contraception and denial of abortion rights, a rise in domestic violence and a decline in child-care options. In parts of Yugoslavia, however, women faced an additional set of problems. By the mid-1990s many of them had lived through the harsh experiences of war and rape, had become homeless refugees, had sunk below the poverty line and had seen their previously modest living conditions reach deplorably low levels. Many realised that their children's chances for a decent life were extremely limited, and many others chose not to have children at all. The representation of some of these coarse experiences merits a discussion.

I will begin by looking at the mass rapes of the Bosnian war and the main issues which came to determine the public discourse: victims and perpetrators, rape warfare and the subtle problems of interpretation which arose at the intersection of feminism and nationalism. I will then move on to explore a range of cinematic representations of wartime rape, discussing in detail Mandy Jacobson's *Calling the Ghosts*, a documentary which, taking the case of two Bosnian women, raises issues of universal concern – violence, survival and witnessing. My aim will be to show the confining nature of the specific 'feminisation' of the critical discourse on resistance to nationalism which established itself as an alternative to the popularly mediated perception of 'macho' Balkans.

The Bosnian rapes

In *How We Survived Communism and Even Laughed*, written in 1991, feminist Slavenka Drakulić talked about the deprivation of women under communism, and in *Balkan Express* (1993a), written in the period of Croatia's secession from Yugoslavia, she scrutinised the repercussions of rising nationalism in her country. But she could not foresee what the problems of Bosnian women were to look like only a little later. Her writing did not in any way anticipate the mass rapes and the violence that were soon to come. It was the same for all feminists from Zagreb, Sarajevo and Belgrade – all of them emancipated urbanites who now had to face one more, unanticipated, side of the war: the automatic guns and mortar shelling of Vukovar and Sarajevo and the knife-killing butchery that swept through the Bosnian villages. The reports of horror emanating from the patriarchal hamlets had become a fact of life.

In the late summer of 1992, along with the unravelling of the Bosnian war, reports of mass rapes of women started appearing in the international media. The first one to extensively investigate and report the rapes was the *Newsday* journalist Roy Gutman, who eventually received the Pulitzer Prize for journalism in 1993 for his *A Witness to Genocide* (1993). Gradually the mass rapes became a *cause célèbre* for feminists in Croatia, Serbia, Germany and the USA. Mainstream magazines such as *Newsweek* and *Der Spiegel* published reports on the rapes, feminist publications such as *Ms.*, *WIN News* and *Connexions* regularly reported on the evidence, and even popular women's magazines such as the Canadian *Homemakers' Magazine* joined in and ran a shattering report on a rape victim, a 59-year-old peasant woman.[1] Names of camps – Keraterm, Omarska, Manjaca, Trnopolje – emerged repeatedly, along with the names of 'ethnically cleansed' towns such as Zvornik, Prijedor and Doboj, and those of notorious wartime brothels such as 'Sonja's' near Sarajevo or the 'Vilina Vlas' hotel in Visegrad. Two feminist books dealt exclusively with the subject – a volume edited by Alexandra Stiglmajer (1994), and Beverly Allen's monograph *Rape Warfare* (1996) – reporting horror stories about the ordeal of women mostly with Muslim names. Documentary reports were compiled by the team led by the Chicago law professor Cherif Bassiouni, who worked on the preliminary report for the UN investigation into the atrocities of the Bosnian war, and eventually by the team led by the former Polish prime minister, Tadeusz Mazowiecki.

The estimates of how many women were raped contradicted each other. Moreover, it was almost certain that not all rapes were reported, as many women felt ashamed to come forward, fearing repercussions from the traditional mentality that puts the blame on the rape victim. Different numbers were reported by different sources, and these vary between 800 firmly registered cases to an estimate of 50,000.[2] In the report prepared by the European Community the number of rape victims was estimated at around 20,000.[3] It is certain that in at least 119 cases pregnancies had been forcibly induced.[4] Rape victims ranged between seven and sixty years of age. Human rights activists who collected information on the rapes spoke of a variety of patterns and settings – of cases like the rape of an elderly women, witnessed by a large group of villagers, the repeated rape of a twelve-year-old girl, and of many women who were forced into brothels to entertain soldiers and who were more likely to be killed than released.

The information on the perpetrators was scarce. The confessions of three mass rapists, all Serbs from Bosnia, were featured in Stiglmajer's book – Borislav Herak, Cvjetin Maksimović and Slobodan Panić. They all claimed they had acted under orders and that they had to commit the rapes to prove that they were 'real Serbs' to Serbian Chetnik paramilitaries who had crossed into Bosnia from Serbia and who, for the duration of the rape, would play turbo-folk tunes loudly. Most of the perpetrators, however, remained unidentified.

The reports seemed to suggest that while Croatian and Bosnian Muslim men were involved in rape, the majority of mass rapes in the territory of Bosnia and Herzegovina were committed by Serbs, mostly against women of Muslim ethnicity. Gradually, concepts such as 'genocidal rape' came into use, seen as part of the 'ethnic cleansing' policy systematically performed as warfare by the fighters for greater Serbia. It was now believed that women had been systematically raped with the purpose of driving them out of their home towns. While it was never possible to prove the existence of such an overall systematic rape policy, most reports indicated that many of the rapes could not have been carried out without some level of organisation and group activity.

Even though women of all national groups in former Yugoslavia were raped – Croatian, Bosnian Muslim, as well as Serbian – most of the media attention was focused on the Bosnian Muslim women. In her detailed account of the rapes, Alexandra Stiglmajer admits that the cases of Serbian women were rarely reported internationally and that there was little sympathy for Serbian victims, because these women were the

> wives, sisters, and daughters of the aggressors. There is hardly a journalist who feels motivated to seek them out, to check up on what has happened to them and thus offer propaganda material to the Serbian side – this is, the 'bad' side, the side 'responsible for the war.'   (Stiglmajer, 1994, p. 138)

The intense coverage of the Bosnian rapes led to a situation in which the Serbs more or less came to be perceived as the only rapists. The generalisation on this issue of the perpetrators of rape led to further stigmatisation of the Serbs.

Popular media offered a range of instances of preferential coverage of the rapes in former Yugoslavia, wherein the significance of some rapes was downplayed in order to stress cases and patterns that fitted into the respective nationalist agendas.[5] This was further enhanced by the writings of high-profile American feminists, such as Catherine MacKinnon (in Stiglmajer, 1993) and Beverly Allen (1996), who, in their efforts to construct a convincing interpretation of rape as a weapon of ethnic cleansing chose to focus on the prevailing ethnic pattern constituting the rapes (Serb perpetrators and Bosnian victims) and to neglect cases involving a different ethnic make-up (Bosnian or Croat perpetrators and Serbian victims).

The involvement of MacKinnon and associates, however, came under scrutiny by scholars with a first-hand knowledge of the region, who undertook to show the problems connected with the 'genocidal rape' interpretations. Elissa Helms criticised the rushed and generalised denunciation of Serbs as rapists and the almost complete neglect of the fact that rapes were also committed against women of Serbian origin by Croats and Muslims.[6] She pointed out that the preferential treatment of some cases and neglect of others could only distort the genuinely feminist cause, which cannot possibly exclude any rape. Helms pointed out that the Western feminist public advocacy for select victims of ethnically motivated 'genocidal rape' was immediately abused by those ethnic nationalists (like Bosnian Muslim or Croatian) who were spared criticism and who 'used rape testimonies to add fuel to their [nationalist] cause'.[7] Helms insisted that the Bosnian rapes should be understood as part of the larger context of ethno-nationalist ideologies dominant in all of the successor states of Yugoslavia. Robert Hayden also criticised the hasty reaction of American feminists in speaking about 'genocidal rape', noting that

> by viewing rape as 'genocidal' they have, in fact, accepted the message that coexistence is not possible, for how could anyone expect victims of genocide to live communally once again with perpetrators of that act? Thus labelling rape as 'genocidal' would seem to acknowledge its effectiveness as a tool for partitioning purposes.
>
> (Hayden, 2000, p. 13)

Hayden claimed that the disproportionate attention given to any case that fitted the criterion for 'genocidal rape' had effectively diverted attention from the equally important issues of loss and suffering experienced by women —lost relatives, lost children, displacement, homelessness, loss of the means of survival.

The Bosnian rape victims had hardly benefited from the feminist intervention. Even worse, they were objectified in the process, and thus victimised again, a situation occasionally described as their 'second rape'. Helms commented:

> The difficulties for feminists in taking the 'right' position vis–à–vis rape in Bosnia should not be surprising. The nature of critiques levelled at all types of feminist representations of the Bosnian rapes recall the objections of 'Third World' women, lesbians, and women of color to 'First World,' white, heterosexual, middle-class feminists who presumed to represent the interests of all women based on their own specific experiences with gender oppression. Nevertheless, ... feminists still attempt a 'global' approach, positing universals in women's experiences before the details and local contexts are known, rather

than after. The case of Bosnia shows how even the most well-intentioned advocates have served to undermine the very causes they seek to further.[8]

It was important that rapes were approached in a context where gender relations were analysed in their complexity and above ethnicity, because it was the 'gendering of nationalism' among all ethnic groups that had provided the ideological impetus for the use of rape as a strategy of war against ethnic others. It was precisely this nationalist gendering that was unintentionally endorsed by the vocal involvement of Western feminists.

Although I have no doubts about the sincere motives of MacKinnon and Allen's vocal involvement with the Bosnian rapes, I believe that their efforts were largely discredited, as they not only became entangled in nationalist bias but also occasionally rushed into unsupported and incompetent speculation. I will discuss only one example which illustrates the overall approach.

Even though they readily admitted that there was no supporting evidence, the number of extreme statements they made about the media use of the alleged videotaping of rapes was alarming. In her study of the Bosnian rapes, Catherine Niarchos claimed, for example, that 'some of the rapes have been videotaped and shown on Serbian television, with the Bosnian or Croatian victims presented as Serbian women and the Serbian attackers as Muslim or Croatian men' (Niarchos, 1995, p. 655). Similarly, Catherine MacKinnon repeatedly insisted that rapes were filmed and that the tapes were subsequently sold for the pornographic market. She concluded that 'in the conscious and open use of pornography, in making pornography of atrocities, in the sophisticated use of pornography as war propaganda, this is perhaps the first truly modern war'.[9]

In her book, Beverly Allen repeatedly stressed allegations of the videotaping of rapes and of the subsequent distribution of the videotapes throughout clandestine porn markets in Eastern Europe. In the footnotes of the same book, she admitted that she has never been able to find evidence of the distribution or even of the existence of such tapes. Nonetheless, Allen assumed the tapes exist (Allen, 1996, pp. 34–7), which permits her to frame the (alleged) practice of videotaping by referencing it to the Nazi use of media, and then conclude that in their 'escalated explicitness', 'the Serbs make the Nazis' efforts look comparatively primitive' (ibid., p. 80).

By relegating the admission of her lack of evidence to the footnotes, while reasserting the unsupported claims in the body of the main text, and by treating the question of proof as negligible, writers like Niarchos, MacKinnon and Allen (some of whom were trained as lawyers) consciously engage in an attractive conceptualisation which may fit well in the feminist discourse on pornography but which remains deeply problematic as far as the discourse on gender and nationalism is concerned. Such seemingly minor but disappointingly revealing instances of manipulation seriously taint the overall picture of feminist involvement with the grim legacy of Bosnian rapes.

Rape and representation in Balkan film

I will approach the issue of rape from another angle: in the context of the Balkan cinematic tradition. I will look at rape representations in feature films dealing with Yugoslavia's breakup, and then contextualise by widening the discussion to include representations of rape in Balkan and international cinema at large. It is my intention to show that in international film, gender violence has mainly been used as a metaphor for general deprivation and social disturbance.

When one looks at the cinematic representations of rapes from the time of the Yugoslav breakup, it becomes immediately clear that rape is treated by film-makers not so much within the discourse on gender but rather within the discourse on violence, despair and social turmoil. The spotlight is not on rape as a sexual act but on rape as another dimension of the brutal violence that reigns all around. This is probably the reason why, in the narrative films made in response to the Yugoslav crisis, rape has rarely been focused on exclusively. Rather, it has been explored as just one of the many violent aspects of the war. Rapes and their consequences are shown but rarely made a main focus in the representation of the conflict. In the cases when gender-specific violence is depicted, rape is conceptualised as just one of the means used for achieving the goal of driving people out – it is not so much about sexual overpowering but about homes, territory and control.

The plot line of *Savior*, a curious hybrid American–Serbian product of transnational cinema, is driven by a rape which the viewers are not shown, even though they are exposed to all sorts of other horrific scenes of violence.[10] The young Serbian woman in the film, Vera, has been raped and impregnated by Muslims.[11] When she is sent back home to Serbian territory in a state of advanced pregnancy, the reaction of Goran, the soldier who takes her back, is to blame it all on her. He calls her a whore, takes her to an abandoned tunnel and forces her into labour, pointing his gun between her legs so that he can shoot the baby as soon as it emerges. It is a scene of unsurpassed violence. Vera's miraculous escape is due to the intervention of the American protagonist, the mercenary Joshua. Later on in the film Joshua continues to help Vera, who is also rejected by her own family, and develops a tender relationship with her and the baby. Most of the time Vera remains numb, displaying complete resignation about the circumstances that produced the child, the stigma of her disgrace. She herself has accepted that it is all her fault, refusing to forgive herself for being violated; she never manages to come to terms with her own experiences and ends up a tragic victim, sacrificing herself in an intense situation during the next violent encounter with villains on the loose.

Boro Drašković's *Vukovar*, set during the 1991 war over Croatia's split, featured a brutal rape scene in which the Serbian protagonist, who is eight months pregnant, is raped in her own home by two looters disguised as nationalist fighters, who are speaking in the Croat dialect (this scene triggered the wave of protests among Croat-Americans). The sexual violence, again, is not at the centre of the film's narrative. It is just an added dimension in the overwhelming range of violence that reigns over the lives of the protagonists. The approach is similar in *Pretty Village, Pretty Flame*, where sexual violence is not explored as such but is shown as just one more aspect of the overall violence. The same spirit is apparent in the Serbian film *Powder Keg* – violating the self-esteem of women is shown on several occasions in the film as a routine form of sadism. In this, and in many other recent Serbian films, rape as such does not even happen; it does not really matter, however, as the air is saturated with the spirit of violence. It is an environment populated by people gone crazy, who experience bizarre pleasure in tormenting whoever they come across. Only Želimir Žilnik puts the subject of sexual violence at the centre in his *Marble Ass*, a re-enacted documentary film in which the protagonist, a male prostitute, claims that he is engaged in a noble project to divert and absorb the violent energy of his macho clients which, if not vented in this way, would find a more dangerous outlet. If made in the context of a consumerist Western society, such a claim would be treated as a metaphor; in the context of Belgrade in the 1990s, however, it may just be best to take it literally.

In the wider context of Balkan cinema, rape is often portrayed as a traumatic event that takes place within an ordinary setting. In Lucian Pintilie's *La balanta/The Oak* (1991) the protagonist is gang raped; but the rape does not even become the focus of cinematic investigation, which treats is as just one episode in the protagonist's continuous grim existence in Ceauşescu's Romania. In another Romanian film, Stere Gulea's *Stere de fapt/State of Things* (1996), set around the time of the 1989 'revolution', the raped protagonist tries to seek justice, only to become trapped in the limbo of a corrupt legal system. The shocking mess of disoriented people's lives is also explored in the utterly gloomy *Patul conjugal/The Conjugal Bed* (1991). Here rape is just an aspect (and not the worst one) of the dark picture of drabness and violence prevailing in the chaotic post-communist reality of Romania. The ruthless reality of Pintilie's *Terminus paradis/Last Stop Paradise* (1998) – a film exposing a merciless and mindless military machine and depicting a society where relationships are reduced to hasty copulations – is even more violent and bleak. Women are exposed to violent assaults and systematic sexual harassment on a daily basis;

A range of films featured assaults on fair-faced Orthodox women by hairy-chested
Ottomans: a scene from the Bulgarian *Koziyat rog/Goat's Horn* (1972)

they no longer even realise that they could oppose the seemingly endless circle
of brutality. The directors of these films seem to share the view that women
adapt better then men in tough times: their protagonists get bruised and bat-
tered but nevertheless handle the bleak post-communist realities; they will
manage to outlive whatever is to come. They are not victims, but survivors.

Rape as a metaphor has been extensively used in Balkan cinema, most often
for the purposes of historical discourse, where one's own nation is usually
identified with the rape victim. This is the case with films where the focus is on
the totalitarian past – here the communists are constructed as rapists and the
raped women, seemingly identical with the respective 'raped' nations, suffer
political oppression and deprivation. In such films, women are often subjected
to violent sexual assaults, even in relationships they have sought themselves.
They are silently and gradually tormented through their sexuality. The socio-
historical clash between good and evil surfaces as a clash between the sexes, with
innocent female victims and evil male perpetrators. Female sexuality is traditionally interpreted as passive and submissive, while male sexuality is
exploitative, violent and excessively carnivorous.[12]

Rape has been publicly acknowledged as a weapon of war only recently, but
in Balkan films which evolve around past clashes along ethnic divides, such

depictions of rape have been used for a long time. In a range of films, focusing on national struggles, rape is represented as one of the means foreign invaders use against local women, thus associating the image of the enemy with an over-whelming sexual violence. The Ottomans, the traditional enemies, have been shown as rapists in a wide range of Balkan films. One should note, however, that this representation is not always black and white, but is often accompanied by a deeper and more complex treatment of the issues of power and violence.[12]

When we try to contextualise the Balkan film representations of rape inter-nationally, it becomes apparent that the parallels with Hollywood depictions of rape are limited. Whereas all sorts of shoot-outs and other violent acts make up the Hollywood routine, images of rape are relatively rare. I am inclined to explain this by the impossibility of aestheticising rape in the way that Holly-wood has treated various other kinds of violence. Contrary to Molly Haskell's (1974) influential argument that Hollywood's portrayal of women is becoming increasingly disrespectful and violent, I believe that representations of rape are not as frequently exploitative as representations of other types of violent clashes. Shattering rape scenes found in recent American films, such as *The Accused* (1988) and *Last Exit to Brooklyn* (1989), are memorable exceptions which, as a rule, do not stand in for a wider context of social turmoil or oppression.

Graphic depictions of rape immediately linked to a troubled social backdrop, however, can be found in many films belonging to non-Hollywood traditions, where violence in general is conceptualised as something painful and ugly, and is depicted as such. These representations are found in the cinemas of coun-tries that have lived through the experiences of war and violent confrontations. Painful images of wartime rape are seen in the Italian neo-realist classic, *La cio-ciara/Two Women* (1961), in German war films such as *Die Btechtrommel/ The Tin Drum* (1979), *Deutschland Bleiche Mutter/Germany Pale Mother* (1980) and *Stalingrad*, as well as in the Russian war classic, *Idi i smotri/Come and See* (1985). In the recent Indian saga, *Phoolan Devi/Bandit Queen* (1994), a drama-tisation of the real-life story of a popular fighter for the rights of lower caste women, Phoolan Devi, rape was shown as a routine method of denigration and subjugation used against the rebellious protagonist.

In most of these films, Balkan and international, the rapists are clearly ident-ified, but are usually strangers. In many of the rape cases from Bosnia, on the contrary, the perpetrators were recognised and identified by the victims as their personal acquaintances. I am not aware, however, of a single narrative film which explores this type of situation. While in reality it was often neighbours or school friends who committed rapes and tortured women, sometimes wearing bala-clavas and sometimes not even disguised, the mainstream cinematic representation of rape remains an act committed by strangers, resulting in a treatment in which the image of the perpetrator is obscured. With a few exceptions, it seems that film-makers are not up to the challenge of looking and exploring rape situations where women not only endure rape but also, unless they leave, often have to face further encounters with the rapists within the same community, village or town. The painful aftermath, the stifling feelings of injustice and trauma, are topics that are treated almost exclusively in documentaries.

Calling the Ghosts

> Why would I rape a woman of forty-five when I am twenty-six, especially since the woman in question is bad and unattractive. The way she was, I would not have leaned my bicycle against her, let alone rape her.
>
> Željko Meakić, commander of Omarska camp, in response
> to rape allegations raised by Jadranka Cigelj in *Calling the Ghosts*
> (USA/Croatia, Mandy Jacobson and Karmen Jelincić, 1996)

How did this statement come about? Jadranka Cigelj was the first female survivor of Omarska to talk to journalist Roy Gutman, the American reporter who first wrote about the death camps of Bosnia in 1992. As a principled independent investigator who knows he has to confront the perpetrator and ask him to react to the allegations, Gutman sent Meakić an outline of Jadranka's testimony, and asked him to comment on her allegations that while she was detained at camp, she was repeatedly gang raped, and that on several occasions he personally raped her. Meakic's faxed response, sent through the Bosnian Serb press centre in Banja Luka, denied that women were ever held at Omarska, and that they were brought in for interrogation only occasionally if the course of the investigation dictated it. Nothing like rape ever occurred. And besides, why would he, a young stud, rape this old woman? He would not even lean his bicycle against her.

The disturbing arrogance of Meakić's reaction is not his denial of the rape. The reply is upsetting, because it takes rape from the realm of violence and transplants it into the realm of sexuality. He treats an act of ultimate abuse as if it is a casual sexual encounter. He is appealing to a common sense that equates sex and rape. Rape, however, is not about sexual impulses. It is about aggression and deprivation, and about the intentional humiliation of the victim. Meakić's response is a radical refusal to recognise a victim's distress. It is a rejection of the violent essence of the rape.

In this particular case, it was this reply that helped the rape survivor to take the difficult decision not only to admit the rape but also to discuss it in public.

Due to the nature of the subject matter, documentary films about rape like this one do not rely on a direct and graphic representation of the violence, but rather focus on the subtle realms of trauma and bearing witness. The best-known of this type of cinematic work is probably Helke Sander's celebrated documentary, *Befreier und Befreite/Liberators Take Liberties* (1992), which features numerous interviews with now elderly German women, raped by Russian soldiers in 1945, who recall and talk of these experiences forty years later.

Similarly, Mandy Jacobson and Karmen Jelincić, the authors of *Calling the Ghosts*, focus on trauma following the rape and raise questions about the chances of recovery and redemption. 'We wanted to make a film not so much about what it means to have been raped,' Jacobson said, 'but about how these women made sense of what had happened, and how they were going to reconstruct their lives'.[14]

Calling the Ghosts tells the story of two former school friends from the Bosnian town of Prijedor, Jadranka Cigelj, an ethnic Croatian and a lawyer, and Nusreta Sivać, an ethnic Muslim and a civil judge. Both women are survivors of the Serbian camp at Omarska. The film documents their stories two years later, at a time when they both live as refugees in Croatia and are recovering from traumatic camp experiences. The women are shown in everyday situations which emanate calmness: sitting near water, looking into a river and even riding on a merry-go-round. The tone in which their testimony is delivered is calm and controlled; they speak of humiliation and rage in an even voice, and the shattered side of their psyche rarely comes to the surface.

Unlike many others who shared similar fate but stayed silent, these two women have decided to speak in public. The decision has not been an easy one, and the protagonists are clear about the choice they are making: 'If I stay silent, is this moral? If I speak – how good is it for me? I would actually have to expose myself.'

Their narrative of the camp is straightforward and horrific: when Serbian paramilitaries take power in Prijedor on 29 April 1992, no one expects that the women would be targeted. About a month later, however, amid a full-blown ethnic cleansing campaign, which leaves people dead and houses on fire, a number of men and women are taken to the camp that has been set up nearby at Omarska, a place which is to become notorious for chilling killings and tortures. Many of the guards at the camp are local men, who now pretend not to know the prisoners. The commander, Željko Meakić, a man in his late twenties wearing paramilitary uniform, is also from Prijedor. At Omarska, the men are routinely tortured and the women routinely raped. Jadranka describes, in spare but shattering words, her own experience of repeated gang rape led by Meakić. Nusreta prefers to talk about how she hoped to survive.

Obviously concerned to conceal the fact that women were kept in the camp, the commanders release the female prisoners as soon as they learn of an unexpected visit by two Western journalists, the *Guardian*'s Ed Vulliamy and *Newsday*'s Roy Gutman. It is a miraculous development – if it were not for the arrival of the reporters, the women doubt they would be alive today. Jadranka drags herself for 20 kilometres until she finally reaches home, emaciated and barefoot, and drops exhausted on the threshold. 'We were stinking of death,' she says. 'Even my dog ran away from me.' Seven women remain in Omarska, locked up in the bath. They never return.

A few months later, both Jadranka and Nusreta manage to emigrate to Croatia, where they have lived ever since and where the film-makers meet and talk to them. They do not plan to return to Prijedor: the place is now inextricably linked to a series of horrifying flashbacks. Nusreta is reunited with her husband, and Jadranka with her teenage son. But while Nusreta has grown numb and talks little of her experiences with anyone, Jadranka has gradually managed to tell her son about her ordeal, mostly to prepare him for the day when, as she has decided, she will come to testify in public.

Jadranka admits that revenge was all that she thought about initially, and she believed that her own public testimony would grant her that revenge. Later, however, she comes to realise that the revenge would have a much stronger impact if supported by the testimonies of others. This is why she begins to work for the Croat Information Centre and other NGO's that are interviewing rape victims.

In order to explore the crime, you violate the witness, says Jadranka. Witnessing is an ordeal for all the women to whom she speaks, but they feel they have to do it, if just for the sake of the ones who will never be able to speak. As she turns into a confessor, Jadranka's own stance changes, her hatred gradually subsides. By listening to the witnesses, by collecting testimonies, she realises that she can accomplish more than simple revenge – she can give relief to the suffering. Jadranka now believes she has overcome every nationalist bias and is able to see violence against women as a crime regardless of whether it was committed against a Muslim, Croat or Serb. She lives for the day when the perpetrators of this violence are brought to trial.

Jadranka and Nusreta are bound to be disillusioned, however. They have put all their hopes in the International Tribunal. They even travel to the Hague to see the court's headquarters. But will the trial bring the justice they long for?

The epilogue is a grim one. By the time the tribunal starts working, many of the indicted ones, including Meakić, have not been apprehended. The scenes from the opening of the tribunal show a hall full of men. They begin work. One of the few women in the room, judge Gabrielle Kirk McDonald, reads the indictment of Duško Tadić, one of the guards at Omarska, whose plea is 'not guilty'.[15] In May 1996 the first scheduled witness from the camp withdraws her testimony because she is afraid for her own and her family's safety.

At the time of its release, *Calling the Ghosts* faced criticism from some proponents of the cause for intervention in Bosnia. Critics saw the film as just another human interest story lacking a broader political or historical context. The testimony given by the women may have played a cathartic role for the witnesses, but such testimony could have no real effect in preventing any further rapes or violence.[16] What was needed was intervention, not humanitarian concern, critics insisted.

But *Calling the Ghosts* was not a film that intended to call for intervention. It had an impact in a different and important way: one of the few films to be shown internationally, picked up for distribution by Women Make Movies, it was screened at special events around the USA, and is available for distribution on video. The testimony of the two women thus won an enduring presence in the wider context of issues such as trauma and witnessing.

Women's films, women's voices

Most of the documentaries which focus on women's experiences of hardship and conflict are made by women. Female activists from the Texas-based Foundation for a Compassionate Society visited refugee women in Croatia and made a film about them, *Spansko Refugee Camp* (1993). Two women – Norwegian anthropologist Tone Bringa and UK director Debbie Christie – brought the everyday concerns of several Muslim and Croatian peasant women to wider audiences with their ethnographic portrayal of a Bosnian village, *We Are All Neighbours*. American documentarian Jo Anders made *Black Kites* (1996), a film about art and creativity as a survival strategy, a dream-like spectral interpretation of the journals of Bosnian visual artist Alma Hajrić, who survived the Sarajevo siege in a basement shelter. Canadian documentarian Brenda Longfellow travelled to Belgrade, Zagreb and Sarajevo in the last months of the war to meet women activists she had encountered on the Internet, and showed these encounters in her *Balkan Journey* (1995). The women in this film were involved in different forms of resistance – underground radio operators, lesbian graffiti artists, feminist philosophers and members of Women in Black, who stood each Wednesday in Belgrade's Republic Square to protest against the war. The activists of *Frauen in Schwarz/Women in Black* (1997) were the subject of yet another documentary, the German full-length production by Zoran Solomun and Helga Reidemeister. Two other documentaries were made in francophone Canada. The first, *They Were All Called Sarajevo*, included testimonies from seven Sarajevan women from the time of the siege. They talked of their fear, of the cold, of the hunger, of the darkness, of the lack of running water, of deprivation and of a bleak future. Yet, despite these hardships, they tried to practise their professions and raise their children. The second, *Les Rendez-Vous a Sarajevo/Sarajevo*

Encounters (1997), brought two teenage refugees to Montreal back to their native Sarajevo.

For the film-makers who realised these projects, however, the journey was soon over, and they returned to Toronto, Montreal, Berlin or New York, to work on new projects looking at women elsewhere. Those who remained interested in the Yugoslav topic were mostly artists from the region.

The Zagreb-based feminist agency for healing through art, Nona, helped many traumatised refugee women to regain self-confidence. As the hostilities subsided, however, it gradually lost its funding and had to transfer its activities on-line, into the less expensive virtual space.[17] Marina Abramović, a Serbian performance artist based in Amsterdam since the 1970s, received a Golden Lion in Venice for her show *Balkan Baroque*, which was turned into a film in 1998: a deeply personal narrative, in which Abramović talks in Serbian and English about a cosmopolitan background, ranging from Balkan partisan stories and memories of a Yugoslav childhood, to soul-searching travels to Tibet. Vesna Ljubić, the director of *Ecce Homo* (1992–4), made her film in Sarajevo during the siege. The video experiments of Jasmila Zbanić, a young Sarajevo video artist, were seen and acclaimed at a range of international film festivals. Women film-makers from across the Balkans were given a forum at the feminist film festival at Créteil in 1997, where they were able to showcase their work.

Thinking not only of these film-makers but also of the writers, the journalists and the scholars, I am more and more often inclined to think that it is women who represent the viable and vocal critical alternative in former Yugoslavia today. This is due, in my opinion, to the questionable credibility of the men who occupy the public sphere in the Yugoslav successor states, and is certainly associated with the widespread perception that machismo and nationalism go hand in hand in former Yugoslavia. Women are spared such suspicion, so it is no wonder that during the Kosovo war in 1999 it was two Serbian women whose reports from Belgrade were the only ones to be seen internationally, and whose texts were translated and reprinted across Europe: feminist writer Jasmina Tešanović and the young playwright, Biljana Srbijanović.[18] Even earlier on, women were more vocal than men, and female voices from Serbia were internationally heard, such as those of academics Svetlana Slapšak (1997), Dubravka Knežević (1996), Nevena Daković (1997) and the radical activist Lepa Mladenović (1995). Similarly, Slovenian Renata Salecl (1994), Serbian-American Jasminka Udovicki (1995) and Milica Bakić-Hayden (1992, 1995), as well as the Serbian-British Vesna Goldsworthy (1998), authored internationally respected works in sociology and cultural studies. The polemical writings of Dubravka Ugrešić (1994, 1998) and Slavenka Drakulić (1996) have become internationally regarded as definitive accounts of the Balkans. Maria Todorova (1995, 1997), a historian by trade, is compelled to occasionally switch to high-quality polemical journalism in order to deliver knowledgeable and competent opinions on current Balkan-related issues to a wider audience (Todorova, 2000). The overall picture suggests that the leading figures of the Balkan critical intelligentsia are women – let's add here Romania's best-known dissident, Doina Cornea, and Bulgaria's Blaga Dimitrova, an internationally respected intellectual. These women have come to play an equally important role (albeit less recognised) to the one which the critical intelligentsia, comprising of men like Vaclav Havel, György Konrad and Adam Michnik, played in the self-definition of Eastern Central Europe throughout the 1980s. The influential writings of those men shaped the self-perception of, and redefined the discourse within, the countries of Eastern Central Europe. The influential writings of these women have the potential to do the same for the Balkans in the year 2000. My main concern is that these female voices are still better heard internationally than at home.

Notes

1. Sally Armstrong, 'Eva, Witness for Women', *Homemakers' Magazine*, Summer, 1993, pp. 19–33.
2. Allen (1996, p. 76), quoting Cherif Bassiouni, who worked on the preliminary report for the UN investigation into the atrocities of the Bosnian war.
3. The report for the European Community was prepared by former Polish prime minister, Tadeusz Mazowiecki in 1995.
4. This number is repeated by both Stiglmajer (1992) and Allen (1996) quoting Mazowiecki.
5. In a PhD dissertation entitled 'From Media War to Ethnic War: The Female Body and Nationalist Processes in the Former Yugoslavia, 1986–1994' (University of Nijmegen, Netherlands: Centre for Women's Studies, 1999) Dubravka Žarkov shows how government-controlled mass media in Serbia and Croatia have used specific textual strategies to exclude certain sexually violated bodies from territories where they do not belong, thus creating a specific 'sexual geography of ethnicity'.
6. Elissa Helms, 'Writing the History of Wartime Rape in Bosnia-Herzegovina (1992–95)', presentation at the 'Doing History in the Shadow of the Balkan Wars Conference', University of Michigan, Ann Arbor, 18 January 1997. A similar criticism is found in Vesna Kesić, 'A Response to Catherine MacKinnon's Article "Turning Rape into Pornography: Postmodern Genocide"', *Hastings Women's Law Journal*, No. 5, 1994, pp. 267–80.
7. Elissa Helms, 'Representations of Wartime Rape in the Former Yugoslavia: Nationalism, Feminism, and International Law', MA thesis in Cultural Anthropology, p. 38, University of Pittsburgh, 1998.
8. Ibid., p. 46.

9. Catherine MacKinnon, 'Turning Rape into Pornography: Postmodern Genocide', *Ms*, July/August 1993, Vol. 5, pp. 75 and 81.

10. The Americans involved in the project included producer Oliver Stone, writer Robert Orr and actor Dennis Quaid. The film was shot on location in Serbia by Serb director Predrag (Gaga) Antonijević and starred Serb actors Sergej Trifunović and Natasa Ninković.

11. In another 'hybrid' production, the British–Bosnian *Beautiful People* (1999), a Bosnian woman is impregnated by Serbs and wants to abort, but is persuaded to give birth to the baby. Once born, mother and her husband gradually bond with the child.

12. Some of the films which I have in mind for this discussion include (but are not limited to) the Bulgarian *The Well* (1991) and *The Canary Season* (1993) and the Romanian fantasy allegory *Hotel de Lux* (1992).

13. See, for example, the Bulgarian classics *The Goat's Horn* (1972) and *Time of Violence* (1988), two very different films which both feature assaults on fair-faced Orthodox women by dark-skinned Ottomans.

14. Judith Miller, 'Taking Two Bosnian Women's Case to the World', *The New York Times*, 23 February 1997, sect. 2 p. 36.

15. Tadić was eventually sentenced to twenty years in prison.

16. David Rieff, quoted in Miller, 'Two Bosnian Women's Case', p. 36.

17. Nona International can be found at http://www.applicom.com/nona

18. Jasmina Tesanovic, 'The Diary of a Political Idiot: Belgrade March 1998–June 1999', *Granta*, Vol. 67, 1999, pp. 39–87. Tešanović also made a documentary called *Jasmina's Diary* (Yugoslavia, 1999), which was shot in May–June 1999 in Belgrade during NATO's bombing. Biljana Srbijanovic, 'The Other Face of Serbia', *Guardian*, 31 July 1999, Review, p. 3. Srbijanović also appears as one of the main interviewees in Goran Rebić's *The Punishment* (Austria, 2000), a film about the legacy of the Kosovo war in Belgrade.

Chapter 11
Gypsies: Looking at 'Them', Defining Oneself

The complex relations between the Balkan nations and their respective ethnic minorities have been a topic of Balkan cinema since its very beginnings, as demonstrated by the early work of pioneer film-makers such as the Manaki brothers, members of the Vlach minority who lived in Macedonia and Greece.

Numerous ethnic communities are scattered throughout the Balkans. There are groups that live in minority condition near the borders of a respective nation-state – like the Greek minorities in Albania, Bulgaria, Macedonia and Russia. But there are also minorities scattered across the Balkans which do not have explicit links to existing states – like the Gagauz (Turkish-speaking Christians mainly concentrated in Moldova but also found all over the region), the Vlachs (speakers of Aromanian, a Romance language close to Latin, who live south of the Danube mostly in Macedonia and adjacent parts of Greece, Albania and Bulgaria) and the Sarakatsani (Greek-speaking transhumant pastoralists, who live in the same general region as the Vlachs, although they extend more into Thrace and Thessaly). They appear in film only occasionally and have mostly been the subject of traditional ethnographic documentaries, and their specific problems are known to only a handful of scholars (Winnifrith, 1995).

Like these groups, Roma (Gypsies) also live all over the Balkan lands and do not 'belong' to any existing nation-state. Unlike them, however, the Roma have consistently been the subject of cinematic interest. Films featuring Roma protagonists have been made in every Balkan country, and Gypsy subplots are present throughout the cinemas of the region. To name just a few examples, Roma women emerge as passionately romantic heroines in early Yugoslav features such as *Sofka/Impure Blood* (1948), *Anikina vremena/Anika's Times* (1954), *Ciganka/A Gypsy* (1953) and *Hanka* (1955). In the Greek *Laterna ftoheia kai filotimo/Barrel-Organ, Poverty, Dignity* (1955), Romani women perform a stylised dance for the travelling protagonists. In documentary, Gypsy life is the subject of the Academy Award-nominated Macedonian *Dae* (1979), the Greek *Stin akri tis polis/At the Gates of the City* (1975), *Rom* (1989) and many more.

For my discussion I will mostly consider the films about the Roma as an extension of the specific minority discourse on the relationship between nationhood and ethnicity. The leading lines of my investigation will supply evidence to support a number of claims.

First, that the Balkan Gypsy films are preoccupied with the excitingly weird lifestyle of the Roma and reflect the belief that encounters with this marginalised group are an enriching experience, leading to a healthy questioning of the rigid norms of mainstream society. Combined in one, the rough realism and the excessive exoticism, the endemic Balkan cinematic celebrations of free-wheeling Roma seem to be best understood if considered in the context of the broader Balkan preoccupation with marginality. Exploring the Roma in Balkan film-making has served not only to produce a romantic critique of the rigid premises of rationalism and morality (as has been the case with many Western treatments of the Gypsy topic), but has evolved around a specific 'projective identification', mostly carried out against the straitjacket of the remote and unattainable European standard. This trend is intricately linked with the problematic positioning of the Balkans in Europe which was extensively discussed earlier: as the Roma appear to mainstream society – marginal and poorly adapted but likeable for their vigour and non-traditional exuberant attitude – so the Balkans (would like to) appear to Europe.

Second, even though most films about the Roma are made by film-makers who do not belong to this ethnic group, it is the existing Roma representations in Balkan cinema that define the way Roma self-representation is tackled in the works of ethnic Romani film-makers.

Third, Roma are often portrayed in exotic terms but normally not as a hostile threat, possibly because they are seen as a transnational minority which does not have the backing of an expansionist power. As they are not perceived as a menace, they are not depicted negatively. This is not the case with the representation of various Muslim minorities, which as a rule are perceived as an extension of the potential Islamic threat. These perceptions condition the prevalent portrayal of Muslim minorities: in the cinema of the Balkans their representations range from hostile to paternalistic.

Finally, in the Balkan countries the discourse on minorities at large remains rudimentary, and even though film-makers make persistent efforts to address a range of important issues, it is the overall media and political context that poses an impediment to addressing directly the concerns of past and present minority relations.

If one examines the socio-economic aspects of the Roma condition, factors like the post-1989 large-scale migrations, the loss of benefits, massive unemployment and an increased crime rate, the variety of discriminatory measures, the growing anti-Romani sentiments, the skinhead attacks and the pogroms, as well as the fact that no nation or state power acts as an advocate for this ethnic group, all play a role – directly or indirectly – in the way they are portrayed in cinema. Most of the films made in the 1990s cannot be considered independently of the socio-political context in which they were made. One observes two leading trends in the new films with Romani themes, which I provisionally call 'correcting the record', and 'celebrating the non-conventional'. The first trend reflects the attempt of documentary and feature film-making to counter media vilification and show the social problems the Roma face. The second reflects the tendency to glorify the free-spirited, non-conventional lifestyle of the Roma. There are many examples where these two tendencies – social concern and exoticism – coexist.

Representing Roma or representing oneself?

It is important to note that the films which I will be discussing here are not, as a rule, made by directors who are members of the ethnic group being portrayed. With a few exceptions, the representation of Balkan minorities in film revolves around the viewpoint of the dominant ethnic group.

Balkan films abound with Gypsies but they are not made by Gypsies or for Gypsies but by and for the dominant groups. These films are not meant to 'represent' the Roma. As we will see, their ultimate function is to project concern about oneself. In such a context, the use of Romani protagonists, plots and subplots often evolves around the mechanisms of 'projective identification' (van de Port, 1998, p. 154). This use of Gypsies to define oneself contrasts interestingly to Ella Shohat's discussion of the representation of Sephardic Jews in Israeli cinema. She notes that films featuring Sephardic characters and plots are used within the Ashkenazim-dominated film-making mostly to distinguish and define oneself in positive terms. The representations of Sephardim in mainstream Israeli film is often denigrating, and, as Shohat underlines, it has actually

> camouflaged the actual historical processes by obscuring a number of facts: first, that the Ashkenazim, not unlike the Sephardim, had also come from countries on the periphery of the world capitalist system, countries which entered the process of industrialization and technological-scientific development roughly at the same time as the Sephardi countries of origin; second, that a peripheral Yishiv society had also not reached a level of development comparable to that of the societies of the 'center.'
>
> (Shohat, 1989, p. 119)

Not so in Balkan film-making. To a large extent, exploring the Roma serves as a means of self-representation, of admitting and reflecting on one's own marginality. When choosing Roma stories and characters, Balkan film-makers use them as a metaphor in a 'Balkans to Europe as Gypsies to us' sense. The fact that the Roma are considered to be the least integrated ethnic community in these parts bears direct parallels with the way the Balkans are seen in a wider context – as the least integrated group of countries within the greater European realm. Thus, the compassion exhibited for the plight of the Roma is often a parabolical expression for the (suppressed) self-pitying attitude of the dominant group, who may be dominant in one context, but feels subservient in another.

While the cinematic treatment of the Roma may have presented them in an unflatteringly exotic light, their portrayal in Balkan cinema remains, nevertheless, predominantly positive. In these films, the Roma are frequently seen to do things which are deemed socially unacceptable. But it is also clear they do not have the option to act in a different way. For example, they often end up as pickpockets, because they have no decent chance of employment or social benefits. Similarly, Balkan countries may engage in activities which are deemed unacceptable but which are considered justified given their limited chances to act differently – for instance, they may enter into shady political deals with even shadier groups because they, in their view, are deprived of decent opportunities to participate on an equal footing in international trade, and are hit by embargoes and political instability without being compensated.

That looking at the Roma is, in fact, an indirect and metaphorical way of looking at themselves is a view that has been developed independently by a variety of scholars over the past decade. Each has recognised and commented on different aspects of this phenomenon. Belgrade film scholar Nevena Daković believes that even though the analogy may not be sustainable throughout, Roma representations are preferred by directors who, while

> trying to avoid too harsh a slap in the face of the nation, elevate the Gypsy life to a magical, universal metaphor claiming that if we are to be cinematically translated as Gypsies, we certainly share their most valued, unique qualifications, and recognize the ground for the displacement of the most feared negative labels.   (Daković, 1998, p. 13)

Chicago anthropologist Marko Živković (1998) also believes that Yugoslav directors developing Gypsy plots are in fact interested in exploring their own plight within a larger European context. But he goes a step further and implicates the film-makers by speaking of a specific 'strategy', in which peripheral groups choose to present themselves in terms of the lowest element in their own internal civilisational hierarchies, which thus begin to function as 'reclusive replicas of the larger replicas imposed by the centres'. According to Živković, the 'Gypsies are a kind of cipher, a polyvalent trope that the dominant group, in this case the Serbs, use to tell something to themselves and to others about themselves'. Why would they do this? Because the Gypsies are

> exemplary pariahs, outcasts, the very bottom of internal hierarchies throughout Europe. If the Balkans are perceived as a pariah and at the bottom of European hierarchies, one can expect to see the demon of metonymic misrepresentation delcare Balkanites to be the Gypsies of Europe.
>
> (Živković, 1999, p. 1)

Živković believes that such use of Roma-related plots is consciously exploited within Balkan film-making, and is part of a specific marketing strategy targeting Western audiences. It is an extension of the consensual self-exoticisation that we discussed in the opening chapters. Making good use of the 'romanticisation of barbarity', Živković writes:

> A periphery would then metonymically present itself to the metropolis in terms of what is most denigrated in the overarching hierarchy while trying to reverse its value. And the metropolis is eager to see what it projected into the periphery reflected back to it. Why should a Paris urbanite be interested in the mundane problems of a Belgrade urbanite? Barbarity, violence and Gypsy exotica are much sexier. For the periphery, that can result in various material and immaterial benefits, from increased tourism revenues to Golden Palms at the Cannes Film Festival.
>
> (Živković, 1998, p. 17)

Dutch anthropologist Mattijs van de Port (1998) extrapolates the hypothesis of the Serb 'projective identification' with the Gypsies to discover it in various aspects of Serbian everyday life as well as in a large number of literary and cinematic works. The 'projective identification' of Serbs with the Roma, in van de Port's view, consists of the fact that 'Gypsies represent what we are although we are not allowed to be it' (ibid., p. 154). To him, interest in the Roma actually serves as a specific means that allows Serbs (or other dominant Balkan groups, for that matter) to 'approach the danger zone' beyond civilisation without actually entering it. For him, there is no doubt that the motivation of such interest is self-serving, and he is particularly careful to maintain the distinction between interest in the Roma and interest in oneself:

> This should not be taken that the Serbs are interested in the Gypsies themselves. When they shed a tear at the pitiful fate of the Gypsies in Kusturica's film, when they boisterously sing a strophe from a sentimental Gypsy song, when they reflect on a Gypsy poem by Glisić or Dretar, they find

themselves in contact with the implicit social knowledge for which the figure
of the Gypsy has become a repository.   (ibid., p. 162)

And indeed, all the recurring motifs of Roma plots – the non-compliance with
the straitjacket of Western social norms and lifestyles, the passionate and self-
destructive infatuations, the 'feast in times of plague' attitude, the extended
families and ensuing complex family relations, the stubborn persistence in
rebuffing the *gadjo* (outsider, foreigner) and the astonishing maturity of streetwise teenagers – found throughout the extensive 'Roma' filmography can easily
be seen as a repository for all those characteristics that might describe a suppressed, nice but uncivilised 'other'.

The use of Roma personages and plots is certainly not endemic to the Balkan
region. Discussing the long-standing tradition of West European Roma representations, cultural historian Katie Trumpener explains the Western attention
to the Roma with an underlying interest in questioning the Enlightenment definitions of civilisation and the nationalist definitions of culture. She is
concerned that the nature of this interest results in a specific 'cultural amnesia'
that neglects the real plight of the group, and that

> decades after the persecution of the Gypsies under the Third Reich, Gypsy life
> remains in the popular imagination as a carefree, defiant, disruptive
> alternative to a Western culture at once humanized by its history and
> restrained by the discipline of its own civilization. Moving through civil
> society, the Gypsies apparently remain beyond reach of everything that
> constitutes Western identity . . .: outside of historical record and historical
> time, outside of Western law, the Western nation state, and Western economic
> orders, outside of writing and discursivity itself.   (Trumpener, 1992, p. 848)

In the Balkans, film-makers have often used the subject of the Roma's ostracism
to express their own sense of exclusion from all these Western symbolic orders
and discursivity. It is never clear to what extent, however, they actually want to
be 'inside', as they recurrently reiterate that being outside of the rational sphere
of desired belonging (civilisation) may actually be seen as admittance to
another, esoteric sphere of enjoyment and gratification from which the civilised
nations are banned. Or, as Živković puts it, 'Gypsies are pariahs, but they are
also highly romanticized embodiments of freedom. Mud is backwardness, a
lack of civilization, but civilization could be seen as decadent, while backwardness could be seen as vitality' (Živković, 1999, p. 4).

Depicting Roma isolation from the mainstream of society gave film-makers
a chance to simultaneously address a wide range of instances of marginalisation – from personal experiences of ostracism to general statements about

Kusturica on the set of *Dom za vesanje/Time of the Gypsies* (1989), with actors Davor
Dujmovic and Elvira Sali

troubled nations in transition. Emir Kusturica, for example, who has to his
credit two films that exclusively focus on the Roma (*Time of the Gypsies* and
Black Cat, White Cat), compared himself to a Gypsy in a number of interviews
he gave in 1999 and 2000, alluding to the continuity of his own migration and
troubled attachments.

In *Black Cat, White Cat*, a film which was intentionally conceived and
executed as an apolitical one, Kusturica nonetheless makes a political statement
on the current Balkan state of affairs. During a prolonged wedding celebration,
one of the protagonists, an entrepreneurial crook, whose bossy attitudes are
hated by the entire family, becomes the target of a practical joke and ends up
collapsing into a latrine. Such ridicule is the only chance for the weaker Romani
to show how little they care for his authority. While, as this episode reveals, the
strong ones may impose their ways, it does not prevent them from diving into
shit. This may again be taken as a commentary on broader Yugoslav experiences
(here represented by the weak Roma) in relation to the 'international community' (represented by the bossy entrepreneur).

Sometimes these political parallels are explicitly acknowledged by the film-
makers. Such is the case with Macedonian director Stole Popov, who admits that
while focusing on the Roma in his *Gypsy Magic* (1997) his real intention was to
illustrate the condition of uncertainty experienced by his entire nation in the

early 1990s, when, after hurriedly declaring independence, it plunged into a period of transition for which it was not really prepared. According to Popov:

> This is a funny yet sad story of a Gypsy family of great dreamers making a last, desperate effort to find their way out of the Balkan labyrinth of absurdity, evil, and misfortune. In terms of atmosphere and associations which come to mind, the story explores a situation in which one set of social rules have suddenly disappeared while new ones are still being established. In another way of putting it, the lights are going out and in the new darkness you are responsible for finding your way around the best you can. The Gypsies serve merely as a picturesque backdrop for the more universal story of the rejected and the maladjusted, of those who don't know the rules and have trouble finding their way around in the dark.[1]

Bulgarian Georgi Dyulgerov's film *The Black Swallow* (1996) is yet another one of these self-reflexive Gypsy features – while looking at the complex social situation of the Roma in the periphery of today's Europe, the film seeks to address all the social sores of contemporary Bulgaria, ranging from the rise in violent crime, through the declining economy and growing corruption, to international isolation.

In addition, the increasing interest in Roma topics, particularly in recent years, most certainly has something to do with the sense of growing marginalisation which film-makers in the Balkan countries experience. The Gypsies are particularly vulnerable to abuse, because they lack the support of an established and powerful nation that would articulately define and speak up for their rights. Similarly, the Balkan countries feel orphaned and abandoned by the larger powers, none of which seem to have any interest in articulating their interests, and speaking up for them.

'Projective Identification' in Yugoslav Roma Classics

Roma plots and subplots have been present in Balkan cinema since its early stages. In Yugoslav cinema, the interest in the Roma has led to the creation of some most memorable films – the Cannes winner *Skupljaci perja/I Even Met Happy Gypsies* (Aleksander Petrović, 1967), the all-time Yugoslav favourite *Ko to tamo peva?/Who Is Singing Out There?* (Slobodan Šijan, 1984), the internationally acclaimed *Andejo cuvar/Guardian Angel* (Goran Paskaljević, 1987) and *Time of the Gypsies* (Emir Kusturica), winner of best direction at Cannes. All these films treat the Roma heritage with respect and feature memorable musical scores, with songs which achieved nationwide popularity. When scrutinised, all these films also reveal elements of this same 'projective identification' found in more recent examples.

Better known today from Kusturica's Gypsy films, the flock of geese first claimed a prominent cinematic presence in Petrović's *Skupljaci perja/I Even Met Happy Gypsies* (1967)

Aleksandar Petrović's *I Even Met Happy Gypsies* tells the story of Bora, a wheeler-dealer Gypsy who trades in feathers and is often cheated by his partners. Too involved in gambling and the pursuit of love, Bora can never get control of his business and fails in every undertaking, until the very end when he has to go into hiding after killing a man. Though the plot evolves around Bora's relationship with the young Tisa, the exquisite value of this film lies in the telling and authentic glimpses of the Roma community. The images of extreme poverty and dilapidated housing round out a picture which combines alluring stereotypes with the gritty realities of the Romani existence. The community consists of strong and flamboyant women, singing but also sometimes kicking and screaming, of philandering and drinking men, swindling and sometimes clashing and fighting, and of soiled and shabby children, puffing cigarette butts and chasing ducks. Much of the haunting imagery of the film is structured around the contrasts of Bora's white suit and Belmondo looks with the muddy lanes of the Roma hamlet, and of Tisa's burning eyes and swarthy silky skin with the rough texture of her threadbare clothes, alluding to the belief of many Yugoslavs that it is important to demonstrate prosperity even in the midst of crisis and near bankruptcy.[2] Van de Port even sees one of the Gypsy women of the film, 'a withered figure with a clutch of children', to whom Bora, following the tides of his own fortunes and misfortunes, generously gives a TV set one day, only to violently take it away on another, as a 'genuine monument to the recurring disaster that strikes the peoples of the Balkans' (van de Port, 1998, p. 138).

Released in 1984, Slobodan Sijan's *Who Is Singing Out There?*, scripted by *Underground*'s Dušan Kovacević, is considered by many Yugoslavs the quintessential metaphor of national fate. It is a road movie that follows a busload of travellers as they try to get to Belgrade on the same day that the Nazis bomb the city, the beginning of World War II in Yugoslavia.[3] Two Roma travelling musicians are also on the bus, amid a gallery of characters representing various aspects of Yugoslav society. During the journey, the Gypsies entertain the other passengers, but are soon accused of a theft they have not committed, and are savagely beaten up. Meanwhile, the bus reaches Belgrade and, right at the crucial moment of the violent assault on the Roma, is hit by a German bomb. All are killed, with the exception of the Gypsies, who are the only survivors. This symbolic ending, asserting survival for the marginal and oppressed, is believed by many to be a prophetic vision of Yugoslavia – a country busy fighting imaginary internal demons while vulnerable to destruction from the outside.

In *Ko to tamo peva?/Who is Singing Out There?* (1984), the social distinctions between the protagonists are largely defined through their relationship with the Gypsy musicians

The Serbian journalist Dragan, protagonist of Goran Paskaljević's *Guardian Angel*, investigates the fate of Yugoslav Roma children who earn a living as pick-pockets in Italy. For a large part of the film, the journalist's moves are identical with those of any concerned social worker tackling illegal trafficking. Only later on, as he bonds with a twelve-year-old Gypsy boy, does it become evident that the journalist's interest in the boy is ultimately defined by personal motives. Having allowed his own son to drift away from his life, his interest in the Gypsy boy fulfils his own emotional needs, in which the boy figures as a substitute. Thus, the story is not so much about the Gypsy boy's fate as the egotistic suffering of the narrator.

In contrast to *I Even Met Happy Gypsies*, *Who is Singing Out There?* and *Guardian Angel*, which have enjoyed only limited international exposure, Emir Kusturica's *Time of the Gypsies* has been seen more widely. The film, which also takes off from the story of illegal trafficking of Yugoslav Roma children to Italy, tells the story of Perhan, a Roma teenager with telekinetic gifts who gets involved with a flamboyant crime lord, and ends up running a crime ring of underage pickpockets and beggars in Milan. Avoiding idealisation and treating the Roma with sympathy, Kusturica nevertheless exploits to the maximum those elements in their lifestyle that are deemed exotic – relaxed attitudes to life, flamboyant tastes and quick-tempered intensity.

All these films feature fairly authentic ethnographic representations of Roma life. The poverty and squalor of Gypsy life is realistically portrayed, while any idealisation or stylisation is kept to a minimum. In this sense, it cannot be claimed that these films treat Gypsies unfairly and unjustly exoticise them, a claim which is fully justified in relation to many Western works of literature or cinema. As far as representations of Roma lifestyle are concerned, I would say that in these films we probably encounter some of the most truthful depictions of Roma life that have been created by non-Roma film-makers. The trouble with these films is not the authenticity of the ethnographic representation, but the fact that their very interest in the Roma is defined and driven by projective identification needs.

Intricacies of self-representation

After decades of being studied by someone else, Roma scholars are increasingly taking the exploration of Roma history and Roma representation in literature and media into their own hands. If one looks at film, however, the fact is that most of the cinematic works which feature the Roma continue to be made by non-Roma film-makers, and that only occasionally have there been examples of Roma self-representation. In contemporary international cinema, therefore, the issues of Roma representations repeatedly come down to discussions of authenticity versus stylisation, and the dangers of patronising and exoticising.

Rather than being encouraged to portray themselves, the Roma continue to be depicted by others. Unlike the numerous chances afforded black or chicano film-makers to make movies about African-Americans or chicanos, Roma film-makers have rarely been given the opportunity to portray themselves. Issues of self-representation, then, become even more acute in the context of current debates around minorities' cinematic self-portrayal. See, for example, the case of Native Indians, where works such as the American *Powwow Highway* (1989), *Incident at Oglala* (1992), *Thunderheart* (1992) and the Canadian *Clear Cut* (1994) and *Dance Me Outside* (1994) – all of which, while trying to be truthful to the Indians' problems, were made by non-native film-makers – were juxtaposed to Chris Eyre's *Smoke Signals* (1998), the only film made in a reservation setting by native film-makers, and thus elevated to a special status as the only genuinely authentic film made by Indians for Indians.

In the context of Roma representation and self-representation, a similar precedent was set by the work of Tony Gatlif, a French-based director of Algerian-Roma descent whose works became internationally known in the 1990s and came to be accepted as the definitive film representations of the Roma. Gatlif initially focused on the French Roma, then moved on to explore the transnational dimensions of the group, and most recently concentrated on the lives of the Roma in the Balkans.

Gatlif's first film was *The Princes* (1982), a bleak story of Gypsy family life in a Paris suburb. Only his *Latcho Drom* (1994), however – an unconventional and colourful musical history of Roma migrations as expressed in their songs, from Rajasthan and Turkey to France and Spain – attracted international attention. The film won numerous prizes and became a favourite on the arthouse circuit around the world. Gypsies from Turkey and Romania appeared in *Latcho Drom*, an indication of the director's growing interest in Roma from the Balkan region. Then, in 1997, came *Gadjo Dilo/The Crazy Stranger*, Gatlif's film of Balkan Gypsies, set in Romania.

The Crazy Stranger begins with the arrival of Stephane, the young Parisian protagonist, in the frosty Romanian Vallachia in mid-winter. The Frenchman, of whose background the viewers never learn much, is determined to track down a legendary Roma singer whose clandestine record he carries on a tape. He ends up in a Roma settlement, where he is given shelter by an old flamboyant drunk, Izidor, and becomes exposed to, and eventually involved in, the life of the Roma community. Initially the Roma regard Stephane as a curious object, a crazy stranger (*gadjo dilo*), but gradually they begin to accept him. These particular Roma are musicians, *lautari*, and they are shown singing and dancing on various occasions. Stephane grows attracted to the young Sabina, and his devotion to her grows into a devotion to Romani life. He never finds the singer but instead, guided by his new friends, travels around the region and methodically records samples of the local folklore, which he plans to take back to Paris. But soon the tensions between the Romanians and the Gypsies intensify, and the local Romanians raid the Gypsy hamlet, resolved to cleanse it thoroughly and indiscriminately. An accidental witness to the pogrom, Stephane is shattered. Back on the road, accompanied by Sabina, he destroys his tapes and performs a ritual dance on top of them, thus erasing the link to the Western world to which he will not return. He will remain where he is, in the forlorn lands of Val-lachia, with the Roma.

Made by a Rom about Roma, *The Crazy Stranger* is one of the few works that is intended to speak for the Gypsies. And it does. The only question is – to what extent? Journalists gave extensive coverage to Gatlif's work, heralding the arrival of this first authentic cinematic voice for the Roma. Critics who ventured into more serious examination, however, did not perceive *The Crazy Stranger* as a film that offered a different and more authentic portrayal of Gypsy life than the one found in the work of other, non-Roma directors. *Variety*'s Derek Elley noted that Gatlif, indeed, had 'veered from the bleak and uncompromising to the colourful and exotic in his various depictions of Romany life', but had nonetheless succumbed to a high degree of stylisation which impeded the claim for authenticity.[4] *Sight and Sound*'s Jonathan Romney did not see much authenticity, either. For him, the reality of *The Crazy Stranger* was reminiscent of the spirit of Jewish *shtetls*, as in the work of Chagall and Isaac Bashevic Singer – isolated and remotely beautiful – but barely presented from a radically different point of view.[5]

Gatlif's portrayal of the Balkan Roma in *The Crazy Stranger* is undoubtedly authentic. But so were some of the films of the other Yugoslav directors we have discussed. In addition, in his treatment of Romanian Roma, Gatlif uses a narrative technique which was critically analysed at length earlier in this book: he tells the story through the eyes of a stranger, a Western traveller. Although the protagonist does not return, but grows closer to the Roma than the usual onlooker, nonetheless, he is a stranger, even if a crazy one, and the narrative remains one that is mediated by a Westerner. In contrast to Gatlif's film, directors like Aleksandar Petrović and Emir Kusturica have made a step forward by disposing of this narrative device and leaving the narratives of films such as *I Even Met Happy Gypsies* and *Time of the Gypsies* entirely under the control of their Roma protagonists.

Writing on Russian Roma performers, anthropologist Alaina Lemon notes that while the Gypsy actors of the Moscow Roma theatre Romen happen to 'grumble among themselves at moments they feel their culture is misrepresented, they give way to the constraints of the conditions of their employment and attend to their future ability to be hired as performers' (Lemon, 1998, p. 160). It is an irony, indeed, that the Roma have no other choice but to conform

to the existing stereotypes. In such a context, Roma film-makers are also compelled to comply with existing representations. Even if confined by these, Gatlif
has, undoubtedly, achieved a lot by giving a Roma community an authentic
cinematic expression. But the best achievements of his work should not be seen
as an alternative to the existing representations. They all coexist and compel us
to look for the common ground in representation and self-representation.

There are other projects, like the one led by visual anthropologist Asen
Balikci in Bulgaria, that attempt to afford an opportunity for Romani self-representation. For *Roma Portraits* (1995–8) Balikci gathered together a group of
young Romani, who were subsequently trained in video filming techniques,
given camcorders and then allowed to make short films about their own community. The resulting compilation of shorts is one of the rare instances when
self-representation of Balkan minorities is encouraged and facilitated. The
material is devoid of any stylisation and exoticism; it is an ethnographic record
of the everyday existence of a poor but supportive and friendly community.
Projects like this, however, are barely seen beyond the narrow circles of visual
anthropologist seminars or human rights film festivals.

Muslim representations: from hostility to paternalism

Even when used to address one's own needs, the portrayal of the Roma is never
hostile. I believe that this is because Gypsies are not linked to any existing
nation-state, and their actions cannot be perceived as extensions of the policies
of an expansionistic foreign power. The situation dramatically changes, however, when an ethnic group is perceived as a Trojan horse implicated in a
conspiracy engineered by an intrusive or irredentist force. Such has been the
case with a variety of Muslim minorities, like the Albanians of Kosovo and
Macedonia or the Pomaks and Turks of Bulgaria, whose respective cinematic
representations have ranged from hostile to paternalistic. In a range of officially
sanctioned productions, they have been treated as hostile and dangerous in
the context of the nationalist discourse. At the same time, in films made by
dissenting intellectuals keen to counter-balance the damaging and hostile
mainstream image, their portrayal remains idyllic and idealised.

Balkan countries attribute their isolation to the fact that they were enslaved
by the Ottomans for centuries, and their international policies are often determined by a drive toward emancipation and getting closer to the West. Many in
the Balkans sincerely believe that the region's role today is to protect Europe
from yet another expansion of Islam. If this view was accepted internationally,
it would be particularly satisfying to a number of Balkan countries, as it would
legitimise their status as part of Europe. In addition, it would justify occasional
incidents of 'preventive aggressiveness' toward Muslim groups, who may or may
not be aggressive themselves, and would unmask the West's complaints about

human rights abuses as hypocritical by endorsing the view that any anti-Muslim crusade serves, after all, the West's interests. A British documentary, *The Valley*, which visits the warring sides in Kosovo in the summer of 1998, for example, has registered this ideology on tape. A Serbian man armed with a rifle is shown giving his interpretation of the conflict on camera: 'Islam on the one side, Christendom on the other. The Battle of Kosovo is not just about Serbia; it is important for England, France and Germany, too. Because Islam is trying to conquer all of Christendom.' One should underline that while these twisted ideological perceptions may be purely of local origin, various versions of such views are in circulation in the West as well. It is enough to recall Huntington's civilisational divides, which, in their essence, do not differ much from the view of the Serbian peasant.[6]

Muslims in Balkan cinema are often depicted as a menacing group, closely linked to the fears of Islamist danger. Mainstream media in the predominantly Christian countries of the Balkans often present such danger as imminent, sometimes by reporting on resurgent Muslim ethnic groups, and sometimes by running translated Western materials that express Western fears of an Islamic expansion. References to the detrimental legacy of Ottoman times abound, accompanied by the conviction that such an Islamic upsurge should be avoided at any cost.

The use of historical plots is particularly favoured by those expressing these concerns, as they serve the nationalist strategy of preventive aggressiveness well while remaining immune to accusations of directly inciting ethnic hatred. For example, to commemorate the 500th anniversary of the infamous Battle of Kosovo, which marked the beginning of Ottoman rule in the region, in 1989 Yugoslavia produced the historical dramatisation *Battle of Kosovo*. In the film, the Serb national hero, Milos Obilić, sacrifices his own life but manages to stab the Turkish sultan. Even if the death of the sultan does not decide the outcome of this battle, Obilić's words imply that it matters for the outcome of future confrontations. Over the bleeding body of the sultan, Obilić solemnly declares: 'Serbia is not a rug under your feet, and not a silk cushion to sit on ... Serbia is not a bowl of rice for every crow to feed on!' The scenes at the battlefield, where Orthodox and dark Muslim forces clash, are daunting, and the scary image of invading hordes reads as a warning that this should never be allowed to happen again.

A similar treatment of the clash between Islam and Orthodoxy was given just a year earlier in the Bulgarian superproduction *Vreme na nasilie/Time of Violence* (1988), a historical epic dealing with the forced conversion to Islam of parts of Bulgaria's population during the years of Ottoman rule. Here, the clash between Turks and Bulgarians is presented as a manifestation of an eternal conflict between Islamic and Christian civilisations. The two forces are juxtaposed through the use of a range of filmic devices – the dark colours of the Muslims' clothes are contrasted to the light ones worn by Slavs, heavy oriental music alternates with melodic Slavic tunes, and the grim, wrinkled face of a Muslim pasha is offset by the healthy complexion of a Slavic child. The violence perpetrated by the Islamic oppressors is cruel and merciless, and the distress suffered by the martyred Slavs, degrading and painful. The ultimate message of *Time of Violence* is that Muslims are responsible for centuries of suffering; this must not be allowed to recur.[7]

The film was set in the seventeenth century and did not appear to be directly related to the current situation. This current situation, however, was one in which the Muslim minorities were perceived as an extension of Turkish designs on Bulgarian territory. In addition, with a birth rate significantly higher than any other ethnic group, they were suspected of conspiring to enforce a possible 'demographic conversion', which, in time, could result in a minority status for the ethnic Bulgarians in their 'own' country. Such a context clearly suggested a desired reading for historical epics like *Time of Violence*: since the Turks have been slaughtering and oppressing the Bulgarians for centuries, a pre-emptive and reverse oppression is more than justified; the community of Bulgarians should consolidate, stay vigilant against the treacherous Islam, and not allow its resurgence. The frequent Serbian referencing to the defeat at Kosovo *polje* had a similar function.

The treatment of minorities in mainstream media indirectly reflects current public perceptions of the vested interests that their respective 'kin-country' may have in respect to 'us', and of the alleged interactions of minority members with this kin-country. As long as a country that represents a given minority is believed to be a hostile force, the minority is also perceived as a threat. The negative cinematic portrayals of Muslim minorities simply mirror these fears.

At the other end of the spectrum are the dissenting intellectuals, who regard the distrustful depiction of Muslim minorities as conspiring subversive forces as a manifestation of speculative paranoia. Film-makers who share the dissenting view aim to address unresolved nationalist legacies and produce films that contain much more favourable depictions of Muslims. As they make these films in reaction to a predominantly hostile environment, however, the resulting portrayal of minorities in their films is often idyllic and idealised, and the disposition patronising.

This patronising attitude is prevalent in a number of ethnographic films that pay tribute to beautiful handicrafts and unspoiled lifestyles. Viewers are shown a hybrid mixture of cultures, where minority members are seen equally respecting pagan, Christian and Muslim traditions. The idyll is well rounded, with images of respectful extended families, of the peaceful coexistence of animals and children, and of young brides on swings and merry-go-rounds. Only

occasional sobering hints point to the serious preoccupations of these populations: the destruction of the traditional industries that provide their
livelihood is mentioned, and an atmosphere of trouble is in the air. How are
they going to earn their daily bread from now on? The young ones all leave for
the cities, and tightly knit communities disintegrate from within, through
migration and impoverishment.

In one of these films, a caressing female voice-over concludes in a patronising tone: 'Is the Other really so different that we are unable to see the shared
characteristics?'[8] The question suggests that the film-makers are confronting an
adverse public opinion that sees minorities as threatening and hostile. But their
very message leaves an overwhelming sense of tutelage, reassuring the wary
public that the minorities in question are harmless innocents who live in a state
of primitive oblivion. Minorities are once again represented by members of the
dominant ethnic group in films made for audiences of the dominant ethnicity.
Once again it is more about 'us' than it is about 'them', with the leading concern of the film-makers firmly vested in 'us'. No wonder, then, that such a
portrayal is seen as offensive by the minority members themselves, and remains
as equally problematic as the hostile nationalist depiction.

Minorities: a rudimentary discourse

A specific feature of the Balkan situation is that, as far as film is concerned, we
can barely speak of an identifiable self-conscious minority audience. While
many films may focus on various ethnic groups, only a handful are made with
a minority audience in mind, and even fewer are seen by the respective minority audiences.

This unacknowledged but effective sidelining of minority audiences is an
impediment to any serious dialogue between the ethnic groups. In the case of
the Roma, the 1990s saw a proliferation of films exploring the difficulties and
marginalisation they experienced in post-communist times. A body of works
analysing the social roots of the Roma predicament emerged, a politically correct effort to counteract the ugly racist trends and vicious media campaigns
which often dominate public perceptions of the Roma across the Balkan countries. These films represented an effort by film-makers to challenge negative
public opinion, to question the vicious coverage of the Roma in the media and
to expose a negligent administration which not only ignores the needs of this
socially weak group but even silently encourages the segregation and the violence. In Bulgaria, for example, the social problems of the Romanis were the
subject of documentaries such as *Vrabchetata na choveshkata rasa/Sparrows of
the Humankind* (1990), *Tsigani ot vsichki strani saedinyavaite se!/Gypsies of the
World, Unite!* (1994), *Vassilitsa* (1995), *Za horata i mechkite/Of People and Bears*
(1995), *Kal/Mud* (1997) and *Zhivot v geto/Life in a Ghetto* (1999). Similar films,

both features and documentaries, made with a socially corrective consciousness, appeared all over Eastern Europe, approaching directly the issues of
poverty and social neglect.[9] A large number of mostly Western-made documentaries in the 1990s chronicled the plight of the Gypsy migrations
throughout the New Europe.[10] But even though all these films feature the problems of the Roma, they somehow remain absent from the public discourse.
Sidestepped as audiences, they are unable to enter the public spotlight to react
to their representations.

Numerous reports of anti-Roma violence originate from Romania, the
country with the most sizeable Roma population. The problems of the Roma,
however, have not been the central focus of Romanian-made feature films. The
Roma only appear in subplots: in Mircea Daneliuč's *The Conjugal Bed*, a group
of them mourn the death of the Ceauşescus and hope for a miraculous return
of the dictator, during whose times they enjoyed at least basic social benefits;
and in his *Senator's Snails* they become victims of a pogrom, but the focus is
on the town officials' concern about how to cover up the violence if questioned
by Western journalists. The leading films about Romanian Gypsies are made
abroad: Tony Gatlif's *The Crazy Stranger*, set in Vallachia, is a French production, and *Auf der Kippe/Wasteland* (1998), Andrei Schwartz's chronicle of half
a year in the life of a group of Romanian Gypsies living in the vicinity of a rubbish dump in Cluj-Napoca, is a German film.

It seems there is a certain reluctance to address the sores in the relationship
with minorities, and even less interest in addressing past instances of mistreatment. And this is confined not just to the Roma. In the Balkan traditions, there
is an abundance of films dealing with the resistance and the camps of World
War II, but only a handful that explore the Jewish Holocaust.[11] What I am trying to show here is that there is much more to expect from the public discourse
in the Balkan countries if we are to address seriously the issues of minority
relations, film-making included. It is not an easy task. The prevalent public
opinion on minorities is hostile, often defined by the work of mainstream
media and by political rhetoric supported by authoritative nationalist historians; in contrast, those who would like to see an open public dialogue on
reconciliation evolve only have alternative means at their disposal. Films carrying a populist message of hostile minorities enjoy a better overall reception than
ones that ask for remorse.

Lately, a new genre of 'minority' film seems to be emerging, one that evolves
around a nostalgic recognition of a beautiful ethnic harmony which existed in
the past but is now irretrievably lost. Such nostalgia is present throughout
Angelopoulos' *Ulysses' Gaze*, for example. In another 'nostalgia' film, the Bulgarian *After the End of the World* (1998), which is set in the 1950s in an
neighbourhood of Plovdiv, a variety of groups – Armenians, Turks, Jews, Roma,

Greeks and Bulgarians – are shown living alongside each other in perfect harmony. Such nostalgic referencing to the idyll of past times, however, effectively evades addressing present-day concerns.

Evidence supplied by strictly ethnographic film paints a different picture of minority relations. Investigating the concrete ways in which the numerous Balkan minorities have lived side by side, visual anthropology registers a coexistence which, while not overtly troublesome, has not been based on much mixing or interaction, either. Another project of Asen Balikci is especially interesting in this context. In 1993, Balikci gathered representatives of three ethnicities – Pomaks, Bulgarians and Roma – in the village of Breznitza in the Pirin mountains for an exercise in participatory visual anthropology. Like the young Roma who created the series *Roma Portraits* of which I spoke above, the group was taught ethnographic research methods and video techniques, after which they were supplied with camcorders and left over a period of three weeks to film whatever they considered of interest and importance. Contrary to the expectations, Balikci noted, their selection of themes did not lead to overt ideological controversies, and ethnic tensions practically never appeared in the filmic agendas of the minority members. There were numerous problems in the region at the time – overwhelming preoccupations such as impoverishment and unemployment, rising Bulgarian nationalism and a corresponding rise in Islamic influence, as well as a general rejection of the Roma – but no trainee had made an attempt to confront any of them. Most participants had chosen to film their own ethnic group, bypassing the others. Thus their perception of regional society had proved to be 'that of ethnic units who live close by, interact daily, but remain separate'.[12]

Notes

1. Popov's statement at the Montreal Film Festival web-site, 1997: <http://www.ffm-montreal.org>
2. See: 'My Friends, the Gypsies', an interview with Petrović for *Patrin: Roma in Culture and the Arts*, an on-line magazine for Gypsy culture (1996). Available at: <http://www.geocities.com/Paris/5121/culture.htm> (8 October 1999). Petrović's next film, *It Rains in My Village* (1969), also evolved around a Gypsy subplot.
3. Kovacević evidently has a preference for this crucial day of 6 April 1941 – it is also the date of the opening sequence in Kusturica's *Underground*.
4. Derek Elley, '*The Crazy Stranger (Gadjo Dilo)*', *Variety*, 8–14 September 1997.
5. Jonathan Romney, '*Gadjo Dilo*', *Sight and Sound*, August 1998, p. 40.
6. In Huntington's view, however, the Balkan conflict on the fault lines of Orthodox Christianity and Islam is not a truly 'civilisational' one – to him, Islam and Orthodoxy (even though they are different civilisations on his

scale) are closely grouped on the same side, and are positioned together against Western Christianity.

7. For a detailed discussion of the reception of the film, see my 'Canaries and Birds of Prey: The New Season of Bulgarian Cinema' (1998b).

8. Roumiana Petkova's *A World In-Between* (1995).

9. To mention just a few: Hungarian Ildiko Szabó's *Child Murders* (1993) tells the story of a teenage Gypsy girl who, when her baby dies accidentally, is treated as a murderess. Czech Petr Vaclav's *Marian* (1995) is an account of a young Gypsy protagonist who becomes a victim of a correctional system designed to encourage further deviance. Hungarian János Szasz's adaptation of Georg Büchner's *Woyzeck* (1994) is a study of humiliation and helplessness in a present-day Romani slum.

10. The German film *Gelem, Gelem* (1991) follows a group of displaced Gypsies travelling through Germany to the Dutch border where they hope to get asylum, only to witness them being thrown out once again. Two other German productions, directed by Nadya Derado in 1995 – *The Bones Are Thrown* and *Gypsies Go to Berlin* – visit Roma refugees from former Yugoslavia. The films focus on wartime trauma and life in the grey zone between integration and exclusion in Germany. The French film *Who is Afraid of the Romanian Gypsies* (1997) features Roma who have left their dilapidated houses in exchange for trailer-life on the margins of French society.

11. The initially reluctant, but later on heroic, support given to a Jewish girl by a Croatian man is the topic of the Yugoslav film *The Ninth Circle* (1960). The horrifying anti-Semitism of Italian fascists and Croatian Ustasha is the main focus of Lordan Zafranović's *Occupation in 26 Scenes* (1978). Bulgarian Jews were saved from deportation, an act explored in *The Echelons* (1986). But during this same time, under German supervision, it was the Bulgarian occupying forces that carried out the deportation of most Greek Jews from Thessaloniki, a topic developed in the Bulgarian–East German romantic drama *Stars* (1959) and revisited by Claude Lanzmann in *Shoah*. Under General Antonescu, Romania ran a well-organised system for the extermination of Romanian Jews. Prominent Holocaust survivor and author Elie Wiesel comes from a region which is currently in Romanian territory; his painful return to these parts is explored in Judit Elek's full-length documentary *To Speak the Unspeakable* (1996).

12. Assen Balikci, 'A Visual Anthropology Project in a Multicultural Setting', *Balkan Media*, Vol. 4, 1995, pp. 37–40.

Part 4

Spaces

Chapter 12
Visions of Sarajevo: The World Comes to the Balkans

As Sarajevo was systematically destroyed, the suffering of the city was systematically re-created in all conceivable art forms. Film-makers and visual artists played a major part in the project of keeping Sarajevo alive. Like Beirut, Sarajevo became a city-martyr, rediscovered numerous times and replicated as rubble.[1] The city's doomed reputation of having started World War I, thus making it a sort of jinxed originator of apocalypse, was soon forgotten and replaced by the image of a dynamic cosmopolitan location that had now fallen pray to dark forces.

In the mid-1980s, I passed through Sarajevo on my way from Dubrovnik to Belgrade. What I saw then was just an ordinary Balkan city, like any other in the region, with a large main street leading from the station to the city centre. The surrounding hills, familiar to me from the Yugoslav partisan saga *Valter brani Sarajevo/Walter Defends Sarajevo* (1972), were no more impressive than those circling other cities in the Balkans, which traditionally nestle in valleys among hills.

Seeing the real city, however, could not replace another definitive image of Sarajevo which had retained a more vivid presence in my mind. It was from a German adaptation of Thomas Mann's *Doctor Faustus* (1982). Following a moment of crisis the protagonist has a brief respite in Sarajevo, where he gets involved with a local woman. Sarajevo appears for just a few moments, but its presentation leaves a powerful after-image: morning fog pierced by the ghost-like needles of the mosques, steep curved streets, a background soundtrack of prolonged oriental singing and people's breath crystallising in the chilly blue air.

I would argue that this image, or a similar one, was largely the image of Sarajevo with which the West operated. Were it not for the war and the siege, it would have remained the definitive image of the city. Even if for some other reason Sarajevo's image had changed, so that the city was no longer to be perceived as a deeply provincial, sleepy oriental town, there is little reason to think it would be replaced by anything else but the summary image of large Balkan cities: urban monsters symbolising the impotence of all communist undertakings, littered with depressing housing projects and marked by the characterless urban architecture of socialism.

Certainly the cinematic image of Sarajevo from before the war differs significantly from the elevated one which emerged during the times of siege and conflict. The change came about mostly due to the work of various visual media. The suffering of Sarajevo granted this city an exposure which it would not have received had it been spared by the war. This exposure resulted in appreciation and respect for Sarajevo's martyred citizens, with a degree of attentiveness not normally granted to inhabitants of the region.

Depending on the narrative point of view, earlier city photographs of Sarajevo would stress either its European looks or its oriental character. Gradually, panoramic shots of the city started focusing on the diverse architectural landscape of cohabiting mosques and churches, stressing the contested multiculturalism. This gradual change in representation is visible in *Sarajevo: A Portrait of the Siege* (1994), a photographic album which can be regarded as the definitive compendium of new Sarajevo imagery and which included numerous pictures taken by the international crew of photographers who captured the city's ordeal.[2] The luxurious edition featured chronologically arranged images, opening with life before the war and moving on to everyday existence during the war – violence, destruction and survival. The very first photograph is of the embankment of the Miljacka River, near the buildings of the Arts Academy and the National Theatre, showing people strolling on the pavement under wrought-iron lamps and carefully pruned trees – an image which barely has anything oriental in it, registering the city's utterly European looks and (presumably) spirit. Only later in the book does a panoramic photograph of the city reveal a comprehensive landscape of minarets sprouting all over the city. Other images show a peaceful multicultural idyll, before switching to snapshots of terrorised people, of cemeteries and destruction. A war reporter has taken the picture of a fallen minaret, broken in two by a missile, a strangely surreal, lubberly body squashing frail houses of sun-dried brick. Yet other pictures show people running, going to cemeteries, hiding in cellars, terrified, bleeding, injured, dead or massacred. Further pictures show Borislav Herak alone in his cell, a portrait of Tito among the rubble of a destroyed building, the National Library destroyed, women lining up for water, children playing with guns, teenagers in discotheques, stray dogs, lines of refugees, weddings, orphans and street gangs.

In this chapter, I will talk of the various aspects of Sarajevo's image-creation. I will discuss the city's cultural resistance, the importance of people and places and the subtle tensions in the mediation of international and domestic representations. My arguments will cover several areas.

First, that Sarajevo was not a cosmopolitan city before, because cosmopolitanism implies mobility, and involves people coming from all over and dispersing again in all directions. At best, this city could be described only as a crossroads, with a steady traffic flow arriving from known places and travelling in established directions. As a result of the siege, however, Sarajevo did indeed become a cosmopolitan city, with a rich and versatile cultural life. Ironically, it was its martyrdom that made it cosmopolitan. Contrary to the claim that 'this crazy but charismatic town', was 'the place that most embodied tolerance and multiculturalism and that's why it had to be destroyed',[3] I believe that Sarajevo came to embody tolerance and multiculturalism precisely *because* it was destroyed – its 'crazy charisma' emerged parallel with its destruction.

Second, that decisions on coming or going, on leaving or staying were crucial in the politics of representation. The way Sarajevo was narrated depended on the arrival and departure of the film-makers who portrayed the city.

Third, that there is a palpable tension between outsiders' perception of Sarajevo and how the city's inhabitants believed it should be represented. Sarajevo's story was only partially told by the people who lived it. Films produced and edited by Sarajevans received a very limited exposure. At the same time, documentary footage shot by them was widely used, largely uncredited. Their raw footage was good enough to be used by Western film-makers, but its compilation and editing questioned. Their ability to register the ordeal of the city on film was not questioned; the legitimacy of their point of view was. Western interpretations of the siege of Sarajevo enjoyed an exposure which was never granted to the interpretations of local film-makers.

Finally, that the features about Sarajevo more or less continued the traditional line of depicting the city as a Balkan location where Western travellers face controversial experiences and where they reassert their superiority by resolving the problems competently. The politically correct blockbuster *Welcome to Sarajevo*, which for the moment remains the definitive image of Sarajevo, will come under my scrutiny in this context.

In my discussion, I keep returning to the bitter irony that Sarajevo and its inhabitants came under the spotlight of international film-making because of their martyrdom and the predicament through which they had to live. Had the Sarajevo siege and massacres not occurred, the city would still be perceived as semi-oriental and almost none of its inhabitants would be known beyond the borders of their land-locked republic. Had the daily terror and the highlights of the Sarajevo ordeal – the shooting at the demonstration in April 1992, the bread-line massacre, the marketplace massacre – not been witnessed by international eyes, they would have appeared briefly at the end of the news and been forgotten the next day. Had the images of suffering not been transmitted worldwide, the motley carnivalesque mix of young Americans, international clowns and Hare Krishna followers documented on videotape would probably have ended up walking down the streets of some other city. Had the atmosphere of secular tolerance not dissolved so violently, it would not be remembered and missed. Had the Bosnian land not been conceptualised, in the course of all this, as a genuine melting pot (albeit one under threat), it would still be seen as barbarian and unworthy of a more serious exploration.

This is the context in which the image of a cool and cosmopolitan Sarajevo, a city of intersecting modern dynamics, ancient tradition and multicultural harmony, a revered and attractive place, emerged – as a compensation for what was irretrievably lost.

The maps that are now traditionally attached to any book about Sarajevo help to visualise the city. One can imagine walking down the Vasa Miškin and Logavina streets, alongside the Miljacka river, past the Koševo hospital, the Oslobodjenie old and new headquarters, Markale, Hotel Evropa and Skender-ija, and up to the Olympic village and Dobrinja. One can imagine sharing some of the visceral experiences of the inhabitants – running at street crossings, fetching water in white plastic containers, the cold long evenings and the trembling light of candles in the dark. The harmony of the old semi-oriental urban structures, the trendiness of the cobblestoned streets and the aesthetics of war-rubble-cum-graffiti become more and more appealing. Sadly missing from this landscape is the architectural gem that was the National Library, where the *Bosniaca* collection burned on 28 August 1992, a fire since compared to the burning of Alexandria's library and lamented in films such as *Urbicide* and *Killing Memory* (1994). A wall with a central stained-glass window is all that remains standing. It has become one of the central symbols of the city. It is here that the protagonists of François Lunel's 1998 *Heroes* (who are, significantly, actors) come, at the end of the film, to gaze over the new Sarajevo landscape – in the foreground the river, running between semi-destroyed roof-tiled homes, and in the background the remaining needles of the mosques and the high-rises streaked with burned spots left by mortar shells.

Sarajevo's cultural resistance

Before the war, a variety of cultural events took place in Sarajevo – the International Days of Poetry, the annual exhibit Yugoslav Documenta and the International Festival of Fringe and Experimental Theatre. Besides Emir Kusturica, directors Bato Cengić and Ademir Kenović worked here. Sarajevo was the home town of the 'Sarajevo Primitives', and of some of the most popular rock groups in Yugoslavia, like Goran Bregović's White Button and Nelle Karajlić's No Smoking.

During the war cultural life intensified and became more diverse. For international intellectuals, Sarajevo was a major project of solidarity, fully

Numerous Bosnian homepages were carried on web servers in the West, like these
bold reworkings of pop culture icons on the Sarajevo theme

comparable to that witnessed during the Spanish Civil War. Only, due to the
nature of new technology, modern media and modern-day warfare, intellectuals did not take up arms, but fought with their art. It was creativity that stood
up against destruction.

This project of international solidarity was registered in a range of cinematic
works. The Italian film *Teatro di guerra/Rehearsals for War* (1998), made after
the siege but set in 1994, shows a group of amateur actors in Naples in the
process of rehearsing a play, which they hope to take to Sarajevo. Although they
never manage to get there, their entire artistic life is dictated by the imperative
of this necessary expression of solidarity – to go and perform in Sarajevo, to
resist by the means of theatre and to put one's own body on stage against the
mortars and the snipers. Similarly, in Jean-Luc Godard's *Forever Mozart* the
protagonists who, symbolically, never reach their destination, are on their way
to Sarajevo, where they hope to stage a Musset play. (One is left wondering if
the failure of both groups to reach Sarajevo is meant to acknowledge the impotence of art in the face of the harsh realities of conflict.) In the Sarajevo of
Ulysses' Gaze, street musicians perform a Mozart quartet; around the corner
street actors perform *Romeo and Juliet.* It is foggy and frosty, but nevertheless
it seems everybody is out on the streets to appreciate and enjoy the performances, which are taking place amid semi-destroyed walls and piles of sandbags.
In *Welcome to Sarajevo*, a crowd of people rush to a hill on the outskirts, where
a young cellist is performing passionately. Music for Sarajevans was not only
performed in film but often live, again as an act of resistance. Wearing a tuxedo,
local cellist Vedran Smajlović played Albinoni's Adagio at the place where he
had witnessed the 1992 bread-line massacre (it is Smajlović who is represented
by the cellist in *Welcome to Sarajevo*). Conductor Zubin Mehta journeyed to
Sarajevo in 1994 for a performance of Mozart's *Requiem*. In 1995, Scottish
composer Nigel Osborne wrote and then conducted a new opera, *Europe*, in
Sarajevo. *U2*'s Bono wrote the lyrics for a song devoted to Sarajevo, which he
performed alongside Luciano Pavarotti.

Sarajevo's theatrical life during the siege was as intense as ever. Susan Sontag's staging of *Waiting for Godot* probably received most international publicity. There were also other guests and local directors, like Haris Pasović, who worked on numerous stage productions, ranging from Shakespeare to *Hair*. Simultaneously, Sarajevo's ordeal was the subject of a number of stage productions around the world.

Art exhibitions were also part of the resistance. Painter Nusret Pašić and others had their art exhibited during the siege. The 1994 exhibit of Nedzad Begović, *War Art* (and the corresponding documentary), featured art objects made from materials like rubble and mortar pieces. Visual artist Alma Hajrić created her associative collages in a basement shelter, re-created in the documentary *Black Kites*. The pop-art of TRIO, a group which by then comprised only two members, became known all over the world for its bold adaptations of well-known commercial images – like 'Enjoy Coca-Cola', 'Absolut Vodka' and Andy Warhol's 'Campbell's Soup' – to the messages that the besieged Sarajevo wanted to send out to the world. Amid the ruins, Canadian graphic artist Louis Jammes combined images of Sarajevo orphans and angels in the series of murals he painted around the city. A 1994 London exhibition featured Sarajevo-themed paintings by the British war artist Peter Howson. Art work and photography coming out of Sarajevo were the subject of many exhibits throughout the USA. Attentiveness to the artistic vision of Sarajevans continued well after the war. In the summer of 1998 drawings of Bosnian children depicting their last memories from home – shocking pictures of tanks, burning houses and bodies lying on the ground – were exhibited in the stylish art deco lobby of the Glasgow film theatre. The Internet extended the means for artistic communication, and was used for many unusual projects. Numerous Bosnian home pages were carried on servers in various Western countries, like the Sarajevo Internet Café, all of TRIO's designs, an exhibit of abstract impressionists from the city and the virtual gallery of the works of pop-artist Muradif Cerimagić.

A number of periodical publications continued appearing miraculously during the siege, books were published and radio stations continued broadcasting. Alongside relief organisations, cultural foundations were equally active, supplying computers, modems and fax machines. Pro Helvetia, the British Council and the Soros Foundation all actively supported a range of cultural undertakings. Culture was also a partial concern of relief operations. The Obala Arts Centre, established in the 1980s, continued its activities throughout the war. The Winter Festival of the Arts was maintained as a yearly event of music and fine arts. The city became a focal point for cultural events financed by international grants and brought from all over Europe.

The well-dressed and made-up women somehow did not fit into the image of the depressed and ruined city, so journalists and film-makers repeatedly registered their surprise. Even modelling and beauty pageants were kept alive in Sarajevo – the 1994 'Miss Sarajevo' pageant, held at a time when the mortars' cannonade could be heard in the background, was featured in documentaries and widely covered by journalists. One of the subplots in the Australian documentary *Exile in Sarajevo* (1997) is the death by sniper fire of a girl whom the crew had filmed the previous day during a ballroom dancing demonstration. All that was left of her by the next day was her pink dress – beads, sequins, feathers and all.

In October 1994, Haris Pasović and Dana Rotberg managed to organise a one-off film event, which they called 'Beyond the End of the World'.[4] Sponsored by international organisations, they managed to smuggle in and screen films from various countries to an audience which perceived the event as a 'way of breaking the siege' (Merrill, 1995, p. 53). The organisers had invited British celebrities like Jeremy Irons, Vanessa Redgrave and Daniel Day-Lewis, although they were prevented from travelling to Sarajevo at the last moment by a government ban. Swedish actress Liv Ullman managed to visit Sarajevo on behalf of UNICEF, however, and so did many others.[5]

With the financial backing of a number of international organisations, Obala Arts Centre's Mirsad Purivatra and programmer Philippe Bober started a regular Sarajevo Film Festival in October 1997. International critics who attended the first festival were particularly curious about the audience reaction to the films which featured Sarajevo, because it often differed from the reception they had received internationally. *Pretty Village, Pretty Flame*, for example, met with a very reserved reception.

The striking variety of cultural practices in Sarajevo during the siege and the uncertainties of cultural life after the war were extensively covered by Western journalists. During the siege, cultural life had been more intense than ever, in spite of all the obstacles and difficulties. Sarajevo was of concern to international intellectuals, and it grew into a cosmopolitan place, comparable to Venice and Istanbul.

This cosmopolitan feel, however, only stayed as long as it was a topic for discussion by international crowds – the season lasted for the duration of the siege. Shortly afterwards, the cosmopolitan spirit dissolved, or simply moved elsewhere. Journalists who visited Sarajevo after the war could not help noticing the decline in cultural activities and the decrease in the flow of international writers and artists.[6] As long as these were there, Sarajevo was cosmopolitan. Once they were gone, the city was left to restore its multicultual harmony, more or less, on its own.

The politics of coming or going, of leaving or staying

'How can you spend so much time in a place where people smoke all the
time?' someone here in New York asked my son, the writer David Rieff, of his
frequent trips to Bosnia.   (Susan Sontag, 1995, p. 819)

In Marcel Ophuls' *The War Correspondent* (1994) we see the director leaving
Paris at the end of December 1992. He arrives in Sarajevo on 2 January 1993,
and spends several days in the besieged city, visiting various places. He sees old
people being treated in the hospital, younger ones chopping trees in the park
to keep warm and shows footage of a mother and child running through the
snowy, sniper-infested square to the background music of 'I'm Dreaming of a
White Christmas'. Around the same time, at the end of December 1992, we see
Briton Bill Tribe leaving London to shoot *Urbicide*. He arrives in Sarajevo just
before New Year's Eve, and spends days in the besieged city, visiting old acquaintances. He climbs the stairs to the eleventh-floor apartment of his estranged
wife, talks about the systematic destruction of heritage in front of the destroyed
library and recounts personal experiences about the incompetence of psychia-
trist-turned-warlord Radovan Karadžić. Émigré Yugoslav-French director
Radovan Tadić is shown returning to Sarajevo in 1993 and taking pensive walks
around the city. In one of the shattering sequences in his *Les Vivants et les mort
de Sarajevo/The Living and the Dead in Sarajevo* (1993), his camera closely follows a teenage boy on a deadly daily mission, fetching water under sniper fire:
stooped back, close-up shots of the ground and of one's own shadow running
ahead, flashing glimpses of the familiar white plastic water tanks. The bullets
do not fail to come, and although he escapes them this time, we know
he will have to do it all again tomorrow, and then again and again in the days
to come.

All these documentaries tell the story from a 'being present' point of view.
Often they take us palpably near to the moment of crisis, and close to experiencing what war really means. But then the narration cuts to the aftermath –
to the dead bodies, the bundle of keys lying in a puddle of blood on the asphalt,
the doll tossed aside, and so forth. The moment of death, of perishing, is somehow absent from these films, and the camera's eye is not present throughout.
Why, then, tell the story from this point of view if it is a narrative approach
which cannot be carried out consistently?

In the context of death and destruction, decisions on coming and going
become crucial to the authenticity of representation, and it is these decisions
and moves that determine what is shown and how it is represented. There are
those who never make it to Sarajevo but whose minds are fixated on reaching
it – like the protagonists of Martone's *Rehearsals for War*, whose painful jour-

ney never begins, the protagonists of Godard's *Forever Mozart*, who are destroyed before reaching Sarajevo, or the protagonist of Angelopoulos' *Ulysses' Gaze*, who despite getting there after extensive wandering, realises he has come too late for his arrival to matter. Then, there are those who come and go – Ophuls and his crew, Tribe and his crew, Tadić and his crew, and many more who come to film life and death in Sarajevo during the siege; and who then leave.[7]

And then, there are those who consciously go to Sarajevo to stay, the ones, who 'exile themselves to Sarajevo from civilisation,' as one of them put it. They are often young Westerners, of an age to travel widely, who end up in Sarajevo and remain committed to the city. The accounts of their experiences form a special genre, a kind of cinematic *Bildungsroman* – their own formation develops parallel to the war through which they live. Their chronicling of life and death is formative: death is a sharply felt absence, life is an intense trauma.

Australian Tahir Cambis, who made the award-winning *Exile in Sarajevo*, went to Sarajevo first in 1992, and later on again in 1995, this time determined to stay until the end of the war.[8] He declared he was taking leave of civilisation, and Sarajevo was the place of choice for his voluntary exile. Such a bold declaration changed the perspective of filming profoundly and all the scenes of daily life he recorded are perceived differently. The images of destruction, the trenches branching out between the buildings and the rubble are all items in his own everyday inventory, as are the scenes of eating, drinking and togetherness. The realisation that in this city the children's ballroom dancing contest held on Sunday and the death of one of these children, twelve-year-old Nirvana, at the hands of a sniper on the following Monday are equally likely events shatters the viewers more than the recorded cannonade of the mortars. Amira, a seven-year-old who has witnessed rape and murder, is not just visited for an interview but claims a daily presence in Tahir's life, along with her diary, in which, encouraged by therapists, she writes down and draws her horrendous memories. Cambis himself sprinkles the narrative with references to his own traumas and difficult childhood, and as the narration unravels, he gives clear indications of the changes in his own views. He gradually falls in love with his sound assistant, Alma, an engineering student, whom he originally treated with friendly indifference. There is no script, and there is no agenda. Parallel with the events that happen to the city, whose life he records, things happen to the narrator himself.

Similarly, American Bill Carter, the author of *Miss Sarajevo*, originally goes to Sarajevo in March 1993 and stays there for five months, recording his life in a bombed-out building with a camcorder: hanging out with teenage girls, visiting discotheques at night when there is less threat of sniper fire and meeting with musicians and artists. Instead of focusing on death, Carter chooses to look into the life that still pulses through the city and to show the humour, the art and the music.

Young Frenchman François Lunel spends most of the siege in Sarajevo, and it is here that he becomes a film-maker. He starts with several shorts about the city, and then moves on to features marked by a distinct atmosphere, focusing on moral hardship rather than daily duress. *Neocekivana setnja/Unexpected Walk* (1994/7) takes place on a summer day in 1993, but its focus is far removed from the shelling and sniper fire. The protagonist is a wounded soldier from the Bosnian army who escapes from the hospital to visit his girlfriend. While looking for her, he lives through a series of encounters with other friends and relatives and listens to their daily and seemingly petty concerns, only to be killed at the end of the film in an absurd traffic accident in front of the National Library.

There is a moment in *Unexpected Walk* when the protagonists go for a walk in the park – a park that here looks quite different from the Sarajevan parks usually shown in documentaries. Unlike the parts of devastated trees and shrubs, chopped down by freezing people, the park in *Unexpected Walk* is a green and pleasantly peaceful place. It is this conscious refusal to concentrate on destruction that makes Lunel's representations of Sarajevo so distinct. He shows the visible scars that the siege has left all around the city, but prefers to concentrate on the invisible dimensions of the trauma that his protagonists live through, on the suffering that surfaces in a transient gesture or in a momentary silence. The image of the green Sarajevo park is stronger than images of destruction; it resonates in the same way as the landscape of green fields at the site of Auschwitz today resonate in Claude Lanzmann's *Shoah*.

It is not by chance that the second feature Lunel made in 1996, again set in Sarajevo during the siege, is called *Heroes*. The film unravels like a chamber play, following a group of characters as they spend a tense evening together awaiting the boyfriend of one of them to return from a dangerous mission. Everything they do is part of their normal routine – they eat, talk and sit around with curtains drawn for the curfew. The elusive signs of the tragedy they live through are captured in the moments of tense silence scattered throughout the spirited conversation they feel compelled to maintain. The film does not show blood and bullets, and the only references to war are the mutilated and ruined buildings amid which the protagonists move when they finally emerge the next morning. Footage of blood spilled on the asphalt does not work for Lunel; to him the scars of war are somewhere much deeper. While death matters, living the war is what preoccupies him.

Film-makers like Cambis and Lunel had something which Sarajevans did not – the choice to leave if they wished. But they chose to stay, to live like ordinary Sarajevans. The few ordinary people who did somehow get the chance to leave, however, had to decide if this was what they really wanted. Wasn't leaving desertion? Wasn't leaving a voluntary capitulation – to vacate, to cleanse the city of oneself?

Each and every Sarajevan had to face these questions. Leaving or staying inevitably became the major theme explored in their artistic output. 'The decision to leave Sarajevo was one of the hardest of my life,' writes one of the anonymous contributors to *Children of Atlantis* (Lešić, 1995, pp. 59 and 56), while another compares leaving Sarajevo to deserting a sick, helpless child.

To many, staying meant keeping the city alive. This is also the choice of Vlado, the Muslim protagonist from the feature film *Shot through the Heart*. When his benevolent Serbian friend-turned-enemy generously offers to help him leave, he chooses to stay. This is also the choice of Alma, the assistant-turned-girl-friend from the documentary *Exile in Sarajevo* – she refuses the journalistic ID which would allow her to get out and only leaves after the war is over, to help complete the film in Australia. Bato Cengić, a leading Bosnian film director, stayed in Sarajevo.[9] So did poet and screenwriter Abdullah Sidran, who had scripted Kusturica's early sensitive films about Sarajevo – *Do You Remember Dolly Bell?* and *When Father Was Away on Business*. Film critic Aco Staka, a living encyclopaedia of knowledge about Yugoslav film, was said to have burned his 35-year collection of review clippings to give his family several hours of warmth.

The daily routines of those who stayed included walking amid protective heaps of sandbags, fetching water under sniper fire and watching the cemetery expand. Simultaneously, these items of their everyday life were becoming an inextricable part of the inventory of images used in representations of Sarajevo.

The politics of exposure: being represented vs. representing oneself

The issue of participatory cinema inevitably arises in the question of Sarajevo's representation. Defined by visual anthropologist David MacDougall, participatory cinema is one that is led by 'a principle of multiple authorship', which in its turn creates a form of 'intertextual cinema', and thus makes cross-cultural films really 'dialogic and polyphonic' (MacDougall, 1998, p. 138).

The citizens of Sarajevo were written about and filmed by observers and visitors. They often took part in the writing and filming by outsiders. But they also wrote and filmed themselves. The works that emerged, however, can only occasionally be described as dialogic and polyphonic, mostly because the films made by outside observers enjoyed a much wider exposure than the ones local people made about themselves. It was not so much the chances for production, but the politics of exposure which came to matter so much.

The images that Sarajevan film-makers recorded were seen at large, but this did not mean that the films which they compiled from these images were seen. The footage they shot and edited was considered as potential propaganda material – even if they were the ones under fire, they were a party in the conflict. The same material, however, seemed devoid of propagandistic content as soon as it was picked up and used in films made by Westerners. The most drastic example is the documentary work of SaGA, the Sarajevo Group of Authors, the most active film-making collective in the besieged city. A loose collective which acted as a forum for the city's writers and artists during the siege years, SaGA, led by Ademir Kenović, was believed to be acting under the auspices of the Bosnian Muslim government.[10] Although the documentaries by SaGA were edited and presented in a finished form which was possible to distribute, their films were almost never picked up by foreign broadcasters or distributors. The 50-minute *Sarajevo: Ground Zero* (1993), consisting of several intertwined shorts shot by the members of the group, has an appended explanation after the credits at the end. According to this, the film was offered to a number of international networks but rejected by all, because it was seen as not 'suitable' for their formats.[11]

Faced with such treatment, and in order to have their plea for the city heard, Sarajevan film-makers have been willing to give up their footage to be used by people whose 'format' would be considered appropriate. As a result, SaGA's material was widely used by many of the Western documentarians who made films about the city. Bernard-Henri Lévy, for example, largely used footage provided by SaGA for his *Bosna!*. The film features familiar images and personages from the city's tragedy. We hear General Mladić's distant radio messages ordering his snipers to shoot at the civilians; we see the guardian of Sarajevo's morgue recording his own son's name in the daily register of deaths he maintains; and we see grisly images of mutilated children and emaciated Bosnian men.

When researching this book, I routinely contacted distributors, both large and small, to ask for preview copies of the Western-made films which I needed to see and which they carried. If I was after a Bosnian-made movie, however, I had to use other channels – personal acquaintances, ethnic networks, academic friends. I got the chance to see the very impressive *Death in Sarajevo* (1995) only after, in 1997, I managed to track down its author, the exiled Sarajevan comparative literature professor Tvrtko Kulenović. He lent me his only copy – a videotape that was gathering dust on a bookshelf at his Chicago home. By that time, I had seen many other documentaries of the same length (55 min.), subject matter and sensibility. But none was as personal as this one. *Death in Sarajevo*, and other films like it, all made by people in Sarajevo during the horrible war years, can only be seen if personal arrangements are made for a screening at ethnic community meetings or at talks organised by enthusiasts at some university.

While features and documentaries about Sarajevo made in the West were shown in theatres and broadcast by major TV networks, none of the films made by Sarajevans was ever seen beyond the festival circuit. With the exception of some documentary shorts shot by SaGA members in cooperation with the European networks,[12] none of their films was ever broadcast on TV in the West, either, and none is available on video from the numerous distribution outlets which carry films like Lévy's *Bosna!* (1994, Zeitgeist), Rotheroe's *Urbicide* (1993, First Run/Icarus) or Marker's *Prime Time in the Camps* (1993, Electronic Arts Intermix).

Ademir Kenović had insisted that only the representation offered by native documentarians should be regarded as authentic and legitimate:

> Kenović believes the story should be told by the people who are living it. If the fighters in the Warsaw Ghetto uprising had video cameras to tell their story to the rest of the world, it might have changed the course of history.[13]

When one looks at the issues of exposure, the evidence suggests that Sarajevans were not given an equal opportunity to speak for themselves to an international audience. Instead, others did the talking for them. Effectively, this meant denial of agency. The protagonists of the tragedy called 'Sarajevo' could not be glamorised *à la* Arkan and, like other victims, remained in relative obscurity. The limited international media exposure for the images and stories that they produced remains one of the bitter ironies of Sarajevo's experience.

The features

As is the case with many other films set in the Balkans, the films about Sarajevo most commonly narrated the story from the viewpoint of a stranger – a young traveller, an aid worker, a journalist. The Italian film *Gamebag* was told from the point of view of Italian hunters who end up deadlocked by the conflict in Sarajevo.[14] The Greek film *Ulysses' Gaze* was told from the point of view of a Greek American film-maker who travels to the besieged city in search of lost footage. The American *Age of Aquarius*, a project now abandoned, was to star Harrison Ford as an international relief worker who enters a relationship with a Sarajevo woman.[15] Spanish *Comanche Territory* was told from the point of view of a journalistic crew in Sarajevo.[16]

Welcome to Sarajevo is another story of journalists, based on the book *Natasha's Story* by ITN reporter Michael Nicholson.[17] In the film, the narrator is Michael Henderson (played by Stephen Dillane), a British reporter who covers Sarajevo alongside American and Australian journalists and their respective

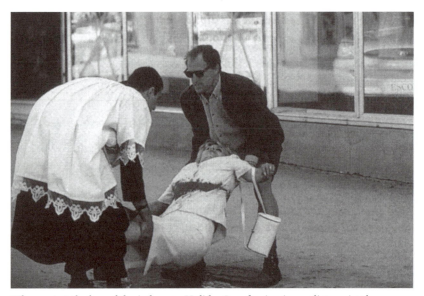

When not at the bar of the infamous Holiday Inn, foreign journalists assist the inhabitants of Sarajevo: Woody Harrelson helps to lift a sniper victim in *Welcome to Sarajevo* (1997)

teams. Foreign journalists are shown hanging out in the bar at the infamous Holiday Inn, the walls of their rooms covered with mattresses to protect against shrapnel. None of their Sarajevo stories can make it to the top of the news because there is always something more important going on at large – like the Duke and the Duchess of York getting divorced, for example. One of the assignments takes Henderson to an orphanage near the front line run by a devoted Serbian woman. The reporter gets so involved with the ordeal of the orphans that he decides to take one of them, Emira, away and smuggle her into England. In this effort he is assisted by an American aid worker Nina, and together with a group of children they embark on a dangerous journey in a convoy to Italy. Cruising around Bosnia and enduring harassment at every checkpoint, they witness various atrocities – from a fresh pile of massacred bodies in one village to the execution of a group of young men, chained together, in another. Finally, Henderson and Emira reach England, where the girl is adopted by Henderson's family and where she gradually adapts to the new life. In an added twist, it turns out that Emira is not really an orphan and her newly found mother wants her to be sent back to Bosnia. So Henderson returns to Sarajevo to settle the adoption. During the depressing encounter that follows, the mother agrees to waive her parental rights. When the mother calls Emira on the phone, the only thing the girl has to say is: 'This is my home.' In English.

Unlike the foggy and cold Sarajevo of *Ulysses' Gaze*, in *Welcome to Sarajevo* the city is continuously bathed in sunlight. Death or violence all come across in plain daylight, and the camera's gaze never diverts from atrocity. Risto, the driver, and one of the few locals in the film, is absurdly killed by a sniper as he browses through a book in his own room – his blood sprays the wall. Winterbottom uses real footage of carnage to strengthen re-enacted scenes, integrating documentary with fiction. He intercuts videos of familiar Sarajevo highlights, and mercilessly picks up footage of Western politicians' tactless commentaries and unfulfilled promises. UN Secretary General Boutros Boutros-Ghali, for example, is shown telling Sarajevans they must be patient, as their city is, after all, not such a bad place and that thirteen other places on Earth are, in fact, more dangerous.

All that happens and is seen in the film, however, keeps the viewer alienated and relies on a Brechtian type of rational moral judgment rather than on mechanisms of identification and compassion. Compassion and the readiness to identify are presupposed as generated in the course of moral reflection over the story – a risky approach considering the film is targeting a mass audience used to genre conventions that rely on human interest associations, an approach that ultimately fails, accounting for the film's limited appeal.

Miramax's strong marketing muscle was put in motion for *Welcome to Sarajevo*. People like Richard Holbrooke, the US envoy to Bosnia, were committed to publicising the film. Before its official release, the film was even screened at the White House, where Bill Clinton was said to have seen it in the presence of Natasha Nicholson, the Bosnian girl portrayed in the film. When it came to awards, however, political correctness could not compensate for the artistic shortcomings. In spite of all the hype at Cannes, and a nomination for the top prize, *Welcome to Sarajevo* did not receive a single award. A similar fate befell it at the Chicago International Film Festival. It was expected that the Academy would be swayed by its status as a topical political film tackling important issues, but it was not even nominated. In such a context, *Variety*'s down-to-earth sarcastic assessment of the film's 'awardability' can be taken as a bottom-line summary of the reception of the film. It applied a 10-point scale, on which the film scored highly as a *cause célèbre* ('Bosnian War, refugees, journalistic ethics debates') and for good timing ('prime opening slot in Miramax's crowded slate'), but did poorly for classic Oscar credentials ('somewhat epic in scope, but obviously on a budget'), and failed on criteria such as 'feel-good movie of the year' ('wartime tragedy, with some triumph') and the vanity element ('Harrelson–Tomei only stars: they're mostly off-screen').[18] In addition, the film's R (Restricted) rating created false expectations that the film was a straightforward Hollywood action-adventure, and thus disappointed many of the audience when they discovered that it was not.

The critical response was approving only on the surface. While most critics avoided outright condemnation of such a politically correct film, they made no attempt to conceal their lack of enthusiasm. Roy Gutman, winner of a Pulitzer prize for his coverage of Bosnia during the siege, criticised the film for distorting the time frame, for herding geographically separated events into its Sarajevo setting and for attributing the work of an army of journalists to a handful of TV reporters. Gutman was sceptical that some of the scenes could possibly have taken place in Sarajevo – in his own experience, for example, it was not possible to file reports on the death camps out of Sarajevo.[19] He also criticised the film for failing to tell the stories of common people, and of misrepresenting journalists who get too involved with the war.[20] To *Chicago Tribune*'s Michael Wilmington, who assessed the film according to a set of action-adventure criteria, the journalist-camera person teams and their Sarajevo driver, Risto, seemed like 'overgrown teenagers, chuckling and yelling while dodging bullets or attending boisterous local beauty contests'.[21] *The Independent*'s Emma Daly noted that the film does not give much context to the story, thus to a general viewer it remains unclear who is fighting whom.[22] The *Dallas Observer* called the film a 'Balkan Guernica' but its review was quite reserved, and a similar attitude characterised the overall reception – while critics supplied enough blurbs of praise to be used in promotional material or on the video cover, the core analysis was reticent.[23] J. Hoberman made sure to mention that viewers at film festivals had perceived *Welcome to Sarajevo* as a disrespectful and exploitative mix of real tragedy with Hollywood drama.[24] Marshall Fine questioned the combination of 'sluggish sentiment with shock brutality'. The film failed, he argued, because against a background of atrocious carnage it expected the viewer to respond to a nominal narrative parade of cardboard types: noble suffering Bosnians, subhuman savage Serbs, adorable war orphans and callous but good-hearted Western journalists. Fine wondered if it all was not 'too little too late'.[25]

Journalist Janine di Giovanni, who had also worked in Sarajevo, admitted she felt angry with the film. She could not help thinking: 'Where were you in 1993, when the people really needed you?' She saw the film at a screening attended by others who had also been in Sarajevo during the war. They all had a similar reaction. Tom Stoddart, the award-winning photo-journalist, who had been seriously injured while taking pictures of the bombing of the Bosnian Parliament building in 1992,

> asked Graham Broadbent, the film's producer, how much *Welcome to Sarajevo* cost, and then, when he heard the reply, said in a sad voice, 'I wish you had spent that money there, then.' And Larry Hollingsworth, who worked in a bunker in the PTT building on Sniper's Alley when he was not leading a convoy into a besieged enclave, guffawed out loud. 'Nine million dollars! Could you imagine how much food we could have bought with $9 million!'[26]

In an interview, screenwriter Frank Cottrell Boyce admitted he agreed to work on the project not because he had strong feelings for Sarajevo (they came later, he claimed) but because he needed the money, because he wanted to try working with director Winterbottom and because he liked *The Killing Fields* (1994). He did not know much about Bosnia. 'But I did know one big fact' – he noted – 'that this war had been ignored. I knew because I had ignored it.'[27]

Cottrell Boyce's statement, I believe, is the best summary of the problems presented by *Welcome to Sarajevo*. The members of its creative team were involved in a belated effort to produce politically correct work about a cause for which they did not much care. The film came at a time when it no longer mattered. It was made by people for whom Sarajevo was not of particular importance. To them, *Sarajevo* was just another project, which, even if not marked by much artistic accomplishment, would fulfil a certain objective – to stand out as a good listing in the portfolios of its creators.[28] In spite of the lukewarm audience and critical reception, *Welcome to Sarajevo* remains, for now, the best-known film about Sarajevo. It is the film which was promoted most vigorously and therefore received most exposure.

Other pictures made in the West around the same time also relied on a mixture of sentimentality and commercialised political correctness. An example was David Attwood's *Shot through the Heart*, which did not enjoy the marketing buzz around *Welcome to Sarajevo* and quite clearly failed to gain popularity.[29] Also based on a journalist's account (John Falk's 'Anti-Sniper') and starring charismatic but lesser-known actors like Britain's Linus Roache and Canadians Vincent Perez and Lothaire Bluteau, the film told the story of two Sarajevan friends, a Serb and a Muslim, who end up on opposite sides, ultimately shooting at each other. Although both are equally nice at the beginning of the film, the Muslim suffers and grows to acquire a saint-like aura, while the Serbian develops into a monster, indiscriminately killing women and children. The film's authentic feel and its wrap-up with a view of the extended cemetery, a quintessential Sarajevo image, cannot compensate for the simplistic treatment of the conflict.

The first Bosnian-made feature film, *Perfect Circle*, came out around the same time as *Welcome to Sarajevo*. American-educated Ademir Kenović had directed two feature films before the war; his active creative work with SaGA during the siege enabled him to find the three million dollars needed to fund the feature.[30] Co-scripted by Kenović and poet Abdulah Sidran, known for his earlier work on the scripts for some of Kusturica's films, *Perfect Circle* is an account of life in Sarajevo during the siege. The narrative is delivered from the point of view of a weary Muslim poet, Hamza, whose family have left the city. Hamza, who is on the brink of committing suicide, rediscovers his humanity while caring for two homeless orphans – the nine-year-old mute Kerim and his younger seven-year-old brother Adis. The search for the boys' aunt revives Hamza's desire to live. By the time the poet locates the aunt and starts to prepare Adis and Kerim for a journey of reunion to Germany, the bond between him and the children has grown so strong that they refuse to leave him. Like other films, this one also uses the image of the crowded cemetery – in fact, it begins and ends there. It focuses more on emotion than other films and was described by critics as exhibiting an 'excess of sentimentality'.[31] In spite of its success at festivals around the world, it was never picked up for theatrical or video distribution in the West.

There are more features about Sarajevo in the making, and the topic has not lost its attraction to film-makers. Commanding most attention is a Bosnia Film superproduction project simply called *Sarajevo*.[32] Initially, the director was supposed to be Veljko Bulajić, a veteran of Yugoslav cinema and major representative of the genre of Yugoslav partisan epics, and director of films glorifying the partisan resistance fighters such as *The Battle of Neretva* (1969), *Tito's Memoirs* (1980) and *Heroes*. *Sarajevo* was planned as a massive-scale epic production, involving 12,000 extras in scenes of war and destruction. Actresses like Catherine Deneuve and Claudia Cardinale were approached for the lead role. But in 2000, after nearly a million dollars spent on pre-production, the actual production was still on hold. The producers were said to have tried to remove Bulajić from the project and replace him with young British-based Bosnian director Jasmin Dizdar (who refused). The political complications are likely to continue.[33]

Sarajevans are said to have been very sceptical about the project – perhaps sensing that this forthcoming film, along with *Welcome to Sarajevo*, may remain the definitive vision of the city, a city which they would like to see depicted very differently.

The documentaries

What were the films of Sarajevans about? Some chose to use filmed moments of memories from happier times and to revisit familiar places, like the site of the 1984 Olympic Games.[34] Some preferred a poetic vision focusing on the subtle metaphysical moments of life and death. Intercutting documentary footage and fictional images let them create a more personal vision of Sarajevo.[35] Some chronicled their everyday survival and paid tribute to the besieged city and its inhabitants by showing the strength of human spirit during the siege. These chronicles were offered up for use as documentary footage.[36]

Comparative literature scholar Tvrtko Kulenović and director Haris Prolić made *Death in Sarajevo*, structuring it around the concept of the nine circles of Hell. Each part opens with a reference to the American Constitution, and the rights to life, liberty and the pursuit of happiness. The sites which the film-makers visit and film are compared to the circles of Dante's *Inferno* – the homes exposed to the daily shelling terror, the ruins of the library, the empty schools, the hospitals, the camps, the sites of street massacres, the cemeteries and the front line. The impressionistic and dynamic montage relies on a wide range of references – from Munch's *Scream*, through footage from the Spanish Civil War, to scenes from Mikhail Kalatozov's war drama *Letyat zhuravli/The Cranes Are Flying* (1957).

Many of the topics of the Sarajevan film-makers' shorts were duplicated by films made independently by foreign TV crews or documentarians. Domestic films showed the lives of women during the siege, and a Canadian film explored in detail the experiences of Sarajevan women.[37] A domestic short, *Andeli u Sarajevu/Angels in Sarajevo* (1994), featured the project of artist Louis Jammes, who created a series of murals using an associative montage of images of children, music and sound that aimed to re-create the spiritual reality of the ravaged city; and these same images appeared in a number of international documentaries. Domestic films looked at the musicians, the artists and the writers of Sarajevo, as did international ones.[38] A domestic documentary showed a wedding with an absent bridegroom who had just been killed, and an international one tracked down the story of the tragic fate of the inter-ethnic couple who were killed while trying to escape.[39] Both domestic and international shorts showed hungry people and stray dogs scavenging alongside each other on rubbish heaps.[40] A number of films, both domestic and international, looked into the traumatic experiences of children who do their best not to appear traumatised – a one-armed boy is troubled because he cannot make proper snowballs, another one proudly shows off his collection of grenades, and ten-year-old Amela has to take care of everything, including her ill father, in one of the most dangerous parts of the city.[41]

In their own turn, the filmic collages replicate the topics explored by Sarajevo's writers, who also created a collage of a city under siege and whose work was translated and published internationally. Ironically, while it may seem that the medium of film and video is more likely to get a wide exposure, it was the work of writers that reached out to a broader audience. The published accounts of life in besieged Sarajevo and of life in exile became known far beyond the city. Most of these texts employed a diary format and talked of the same things – helplessness, ruins, hunger, darkness, despair – only the dominant sentiment differed. Some chose to talk about the bravery of the people of Sarajevo and to chronicle their ordeal. Two books, containing many of the wartime daily columns by *Oslobodjenie* journalist Zlatko Dizdarević and chronicling the work of artists and writers, as well as the lives, jokes and everyday concerns of ordinary people, were translated and distributed internationally. Others focused on the depression and the pessimism that gradually overtook them, expressing the feeling that the people were being killed 'like flies'.[42] Elma Softić's chronicle talks of the unbearable reduction to limpness, inertia and apathy. Young and mature Sarajevans, now scattered around the globe, wrote of the disruption to their lives, while trying to build an alternative vision for a future they had imagined differently.[43]

The chances of getting a letter out of the besieged city had been so rare that any that made it to their destination immediately became as precious as museum documents. In 1993, Italian journalist Anna Cataldi put together the collection *Letters from Sarajevo* (1994).[44] These letters talk of leaving or staying, of the humiliation of living without electricity or water, and of helplessness, and all contain accounts of the dead, usually listing in a simple, lone sentence the names of several friends or relatives. And all this is mixed with the restlessness, uncertainty and anxiety of separation.

Nonetheless, some of the important elements in Sarajevans' messages about themselves were 'lost in translation'. Little of the continuous painful reflection on the dilemma to stay or to leave, for example, was ever picked up and developed by international film-making, while it is a topic present in all of the domestic writing and filming. Another theme which somehow appeared only in the Bosnian works was their effort to communicate normality to the outside world and to prevent the 'weird state of mind' and collective madness from taking over – there were the letter-films which the film-makers had made as messages meant for friends abroad, trying to present them with an idea of the state of mind of those who had stayed behind and were now living amid the madness of the siege.[45] One of these films, *Palio sam noge/I Burned Legs* (1994), about the insanity of the war, showed the daily routine of a film student now employed in a hospital, where his job was to carry amputated legs to the cremation furnace.

Yet another topic rarely picked up internationally but reiterated numerous times by Sarajevo film-makers and writers was their embarrassment from the degrading basic bodily needs that one could not help experiencing – the impossibility of staying clean when there is no water, and the impossibility of escaping hunger when there is no food.

Something they all insist on talking about is the feeling of abandonment and betrayal. The dubious involvement of the UN forces in Bosnia has, indeed, been explored in Western documentaries, like *Safe Haven: The Betrayal of Srebrenica* and, more recently, the extremely critical *A Cry from the Grave*. Sarajevo authors themselves never miss the chance to talk of what they saw as betrayal by the international community. Dizdarević calls the UN 'hypocrites', while Karahasan claims the UN subjected Bosnians to a terrible humiliation by bringing in children's clothing purchased at Serbian factories in November 1993.

The black humour with which many Sarajevans chose to look at their situation has been reflected in international film and writing only occasionally. Such humour is found in the Channel 4 documentary *Tourist Sarajevo '93* (1993), a parody and surreal tourist guide to surviving Sarajevo by its beleaguered inhabitants, or in a special edition of the socially committed magazine *Colors*, which contains photographs of wild Sarajevo parties, and talks about the concerns of everyday life in the time of a siege: how do you meet boys or girls? Where do you get condoms? Where do you work out? How do you dye your hair red? How do you feed your pet? Where do you go for a pizza? How do you lose weight? The whole point of these works is to reiterate the fact that young people in Sarajevo have been trying to live normally in abnormal conditions.[46]

The black humour, however, is best seen in the hip work of Sarajevo pop groups like TRIO or FAMA. On the cover of their tourist guide to the occupied city, *Sarajevo: A Survival Guide*, the members of FAMA promise that if you come to Sarajevo, 'you will laugh a lot'(FAMA, 1993). Subtitled 'Greetings from Sunny Sarajevo', it features a photograph of a boy carrying the familiar white plastic water containers. The book is structured like a tourist pocket guide, with entries on accommodation (survival techniques), food (garden snails, birch juice), recreation (running at intersections under sniper fire – the favourite sport here), night life (curfews, petroleum lamps), souvenirs (mortar shell pieces), sightseeing (Sniper Alley, cemeteries) and photographs or photomontages illustrating the bleak reality of the city. With this guide, FAMA introduced a new genre – political entertainment.

Mizaldo, a reverse reading of 'Odlazim' ('I am leaving'), was staged as an extended TV infomercial using Sarajevo images and offered a parody of the 'infotainment' genre. A similar project was the *Sarajevo Ghetto Spectacle*, which its author, Sanjin Lukić, described as an 'anti-video clip'. This project was structured around a collage of media coverage of the Bosnian war taken from CNN and various European television stations.

The testaments, written and created by Sarajevans during the siege, make demanding reading and viewing. Most are not entertaining. Many are depressing and repetitive. They require continuous identification and compassion – an attitude which today's audiences are not prepared to offer, and a commitment which goes beyond the straightforward habits of cultural consumption.

But then, not all in Sarajevo were happy with the presence of foreign media crews. In *Truth under Siege* some refer to the journalists as 'cockroaches' and claim that they 'film us like animals'. It is a feeling expressed in a short called *Shovel* (1997): the camera follows a man as he goes down to the cellar to get a shovel, goes into the yard and digs a hole in the ground; he then turns to the camera, takes it in his hands, and buries it, thus liberating himself from the constant voyeurist presence of the media. On various other occasions, Sarajevans spoke with resentment about the reporters' exclusive interest in death and destruction, describing it as sensationalist and 'commercialist'.[47] The prevailing 'commercial' exploitation of blood and ruins, they feel, prevented journalists and film-makers from seeing the simple dimensions of the heroism of ordinary people.

Films about Sarajevo inevitably bring back to our minds images from earlier films, showing Europe in ruins after World War II. Is not the despair of the boy in Rossellini's *Germania anno zero/Germany Year Zero* (1947) the experience of the boys in *Perfect Circle*? Is not the desolation of Wajda's *Landscape after Battle* and Resnais' *Hiroshima, Mon Amour* (1959) the experience of the protagonists of *Ulysses' Gaze* and *Heroes*? Is not the urban destruction of Wajda's *Kanal* replicated in the ruins and rubble of every film shot in Sarajevo? Are we not made to think of the Leningrad blockade, of the bombardments of Dresden and Berlin, of the destruction of cultural heritage and the countryside that World War II left throughout Europe? Along with these cities, Sarajevo claimed a place on the list of city-martyrs, and received its share of attention. This attention probably will not remain as intense in the future as it was during the war, and much of the cosmopolitan buzz is likely to disappear. The city will gradually go back to its ordinary existence. Being ordinary is what peace is all about.

Notes

1. Treated in a very similar way to Sarajevo, Beirut appears in a wide range of cinematic works, from Jerzy Skolimowski's feature *Hands Up* (Poland/UK, 1968/85) and Robert Fisk's documentary *From Beirut to Bosnia* (1993), to Ziad Doueiri's feature *West Beirut* (1998).
2. The photographs are by Ron Haviv, Peter Northall, David Brauchli, Steve Connors, Andrew Reid, Jon Jones, Patrick Chauvel, Antoine Gyori, Christopher Morris and twenty more. All these photographers and journalists, we are told, have covered events like the fall of the Berlin Wall, the Romanian revolution, the war in Croatia and other hot spots around the world.
3. Mirsad Purivatra, head of the Obala Arts Centre and American director Phil Alden Robinson, in a discussion with film critic Kenneth Turan ('Cinema Paradiso Lost', *Los Angeles Times*, 5 October 1997, p. 8).
4. A documentary about the event was filmed by the Dutch documentarian Johan van der Keuken, who attended the festival (*Sarajevo Film Festival Film*, 1994).

5. Shown in *Liv Ullman: Scenes from a Life* (1998).

6. 'During the war, culture was an expression of resistance', said Sadudin Musabegović, dean of the Academy of Art. 'Now, the country is destroyed, industry is destroyed and culture is marginalized.' Quoted in Alan Riding, 'Catharsis and the Rebirth of Culture in Sarajevo', *International Herald Tribune*, 2 October 1997, p. 20. See also: W. F. Deedes, and Victoria Combe, 'A Picture of Life after the War. Focus Sarajevo: A City Reborn', *Sunday Telegraph*, 8 October 1995, p. 27; Jean Michel Frodon, 'Sarajevo a l'aube incertaine d'une renaissance culturelle', *Le Monde*, 13 April 1996.

7. An incomplete list of some of the documentaries made internationally about Sarajevo would include: *A Day in the Death of Sarajevo* (France, 1992), *Urbicide: A Sarajevo Diary* (UK, 1993), *Tourist Sarajevo '93* (UK, 1993), *Escape from Sarajevo* (Germany, 1993), *Abdulah Sidran: A Poet in Sarajevo* (Switzerland, 1994), *Sarajevo '94* (Czech Republic, 1994), *Sarajevo: Glimmers of Dreams* (Switzerland, 1994), *They Were All Called Sarajevo* (Canada, 1994), *Waiting for Godot in Sarajevo* (France, 1994), *Spring in Sarajevo* (Italy, 1995), *A Saturday in Sarajevo* (Italy, 1995), *Sarajevo's Dogs* (Italy, 1995), *Sotto asedio: Danilo Kristanović, fotoreporter a Sarajevo* (Switzerland, 1995), *Every Day for Sarajevo* (France, 1995), *Cease Fire: Belfast/Sarajevo* (France, 1995), *Stemmer fra Sarajevo* (Norway, 1996), *Sarajevo Encounters* (Canada, 1997) and *Bosnia: Hotel Sarajevo or the Dreams of an Ordinary Wedding Guest* (part of *Visualisation*, Czech Republic, 1997) by Bolivian-born director Rodrigo Morales. A complete listing would include at least another twenty or so titles which have played at festivals and TV networks worldwide.

8. Cambis mentions that his family originally came from these parts, but does not provide enough information to allow the viewers to form a definitive opinion about his own ethnic background and the circumstances under which his family left sometime in the 1950s (as 'refugees' as he claims). He is also evasive on the issue of his presence in Bosnia during 1992, when he had to leave after he was wounded. There is contextual evidence suggesting that during his first Sarajevo visit he, in fact, fought on the side of the Bosnian Muslims.

9. After the war Cengić completed a documentary, *Mona Lisa from Sarajevo* (1998).

10. In 1994 SaGA received the European Film Academy award, which was presented to them by Wim Wenders. Its members included the late Mirza Idrizović, Pjer Zalica, Benjamin Filipović, and others.

11. Quoted in J. Max Robins, '*Sarajevo Ground Zero*: Too Hot for US TV?' *Variety*, 2 August, 1993, p. 8. Also see Andrew Meier, 'In Sarajevo, a View Taped from *Ground Zero*', *The New York Times*, 23 May 1993, p. H21. A similar case is that of their *MGM Sarajevo: Man, God, Monster* (1992–4).

12. Like, for example, *A Street under Siege* (1993). Bosnia/UK/France. Production: SaGA/BBC 2/Point du jour. Creative supervision: Ademir Kenović. This project is a unique undertaking in the context of European broadcasting. It consists of a series of short, 2-minute documentaries, which show in seemingly small detail the subtle inhumanity of the war. The shorts were shot late in 1992 in Sarajevo by members of SaGA and then edited and broadcast on a daily basis by some major European TV networks.

13. Quoted in Robins, 'Sarajevo Ground Zero', p. 8. Also see Meier, 'A View Taped from *Ground Zero*', p. H21.

14. This is an action-adventure story about three Italian hunters who are on a shooting party in the former Yugoslavia when they are trapped by the outbreak of war. They meet their first setback when their gamekeeper contact fails to materialise. Persuading his daughter, Rada, to be their guide instead, they enjoy a few moments of idyllic wilderness before one of them is wounded by a sniper. In town, they rush to the hospital, full of silent, sad-faced refugees, as bombs and machine-gun fire make the streets impassable. Eventually, Rada plans an escape for the Italians. She also kills the sniper on the nearby roof, without realising until the very end that this was her own father.

15. *Age of Aquarius*, a Universal Pictures project was to be directed by Phil Alden Robinson (*Field of Dreams* and *Sneakers*), who had visited Sarajevo four times at the height of the war. The near-$80 million budget (including a $12.5 million contract for Ford) was considered too hefty for Universal, which had requested substantial trimming and was backing the project with financing from Mutual Film Co. Script problems and difficulty in finding safe shooting locations had also been reported.

16. Based on a novel by Arturo Perez-Reverte and shot in Sarajevo after the end of the war, the film tells the story of several TV journalists and the way their 'seen-it-all-before' attitude is dismantled by what they witness.

17. Michael Nicholson, *Natasha's Story*, (London: Macmillan, 1993). *Welcome to Sarajevo* (1997). UK/USA. Director: Michael Winterbottom. Production: Dragon Pictures/Channel 4 Films/Miramax Films. Distribution Channel 4 Films (a.k.a. Film Four International) in the UK and Miramax Films in the USA. Cast: Stephen Dillane (Henderson), Woody Harrelson, Marisa Tomei (Nina), Kerry Fox, Goran Visnjić (Risto).

18. '*Welcome to Sarajevo*', *Daily Variety*, 16 December 1997, p. 28.

19. Roy Gutman, 'I Was There – Wasn't I? ' *Newsday*, 16 November 1997, p. D11.

20. Roy Gutman, 'A Powerful Greater Truth in Sarajevo', *Newsday*, 26 November 1997, p. B11.

21. M. Wilmington, 'Indignant "Sarajevo" Earns its Rage', *Chicago Tribune*, 9 January 1998, p. CN/A.

22. E. Daly, 'Reality Didn't Hit Home, but Fiction Might', *The Independent*, 14 November 1997, p. 2.

23. Michael Sragow, 'Battle Scars: The Jolting *Welcome to Sarajevo* is Often So Real it Hurts', *Dallas Observer*, 8 January 1998.

24. J. Hoberman, 'Combat Fatigue', *The Village Voice*, 2 December 1997.

25. Marshall Fine, 'Will Movie's Close-up View of Sarajevo and Bosnia Have an Impact?' *Gannett News Service*, 1 December 1997.

26. Janine di Giovanni, 'Surviving Sarajevo', *The Times*, 15 November 1997.

27. Frank Cottrell Boyce, 'The Arts: Humanity amid the Horror', *Sunday Telegraph*, 2 November 1997, p. 7. Indeed, the film was eventually compared not only to Roland Joffe's Cambodia-set *The Killing Fields* (USA, 1984) but also to other films about journalists in war zones, like Peter Weir's Indonesia-set *The Year of Living Dangerously* (Australia/USA, 1982), Roger Spottiswoode's Nicaragua-set *Under Fire* (USA, 1983) and Oliver Stone's *Salvador* (USA, 1986).

28. Graham Broadbent, the producer, has since produced the thriller *The Debt Collector* (UK, Anthony Neilson, 1999). By the time of *Welcome to Sarajevo*, Michael Winterbottom, the director, had to his credits the thriller *The Butterfly Kiss* (UK, 1995, scripted by F. C. Boyce) and the Thomas Hardy adaptation *Jude* (UK, 1996). He has since made two low-key contemporary dramas, *I Want You* (UK, 1998) and *Wonderland* (UK, 1999); screenwriter Frank Cottrell Boyce has since written the successful music family biopic *Hilary and Jackie* (UK, Anand Tucker, 1998).

29. The film played at the London Film Festival in 1998, but when it was aired on BBC 2 in 1999, it was not even announced as a feature film.

30. Money for *Perfect Circle* came from the Bosnian culture ministry, the city of Sarajevo, UNICEF, the Soros Fund, Pro-Helvetia, Rotterdam's International Film Festival's Hubert Bals Fund and the Locarno Film Festival, as well as from private production companies in France, Hungary, Croatia and the Netherlands, with the participation of Eurimages. The film won at the Tokyo Film Festival, where it played alongside James Cameron's *Titanic*, and was acclaimed at the festivals in Jerusalem and London. Kenović's work was featured during the director's fortnight at Cannes in 1997.

31. Geoff Brown, 'An Anniversary to Remember', *The Times*, 12 May 1997. *Variety*'s Emmanuel Levy compared *Perfect Circle* to classics about World War II, such as René Clément's *Forbidden Games* and Andrei Tarkovsky's *Ivan's Childhood* ('*The Perfect Circle*', *Variety*, 16–22 June 1997, p. 35).

32. Rada Sesić, 'Bosnia', *Variety International Film Guide* (London: Faber and Faber, 1999, p. 102).

33. Altijana Marić, 'Veljko Bulajić, smijenjeni reditelj filma "Sarajevo" ', *Oslobodjenje* (Sarajevo), 10 October 1999; Altijana Marić, 'Aktuelni intervju:

Veljko Bulajić, smijenjeni reditelj filma', *Oslobodjenje* (Sarajevo), 13 October 1999; Altijana Marić, 'Veljko Bulajić aktuelizira pricu o filmskom projektu "Sarajevo"', *Oslobodjenje* (Sarajevo), 14 February 2000.

34. *Pictures* (1993), *Eight Years After* (1993), *Like Sarajevo* (1993).

35. *Ecce Homo* (1992–4), *Way of the Cross in Sarajevo* (1993), *Mindless* (1997).

36. *Urbicide* (1994), *The Blue Guide* (Nenad Dizdarević, 1994), *Sarajevo* (Mirza Idrizović, 1992), *A Street under Siege* (1993). Produced by Bosnian television, the two compilation tapes *Stories from Sarajevo: 1* (1992–5) and *Stories from Sarajevo: 2* (1992–5) comprised a series of shorts on the subject of everyday life in besieged Sarajevo, each 3 minutes long. The compilation includes: *Water* (Nedzad Begović), *Electricity* (Srdjan Vuletić), *Sculptor* (Pjer Zalica), *NATO* (Zlatko Lavanić), *Massacre* (Zlatko Lavanić), *Prometheus* (Zlatko Lavanić), and more.

37. *8th March* (1993), *Greta* (1998), *They Were All Called Sarajevo* (Canada, 1994).

38. *Sarajevo String Quartet* (1994), *War Art* (1994), *Waiting for Godot in Sarajevo* (1994), *Abdulah Sidran* (1995).

39. *A Wedding in Sarajevo* (1993), *Romeo and Juliet in Sarajevo* (1994).

40. *Bums and Dogs* (Bosnia, 1993), *Sarajevo's Dogs* (Italy, 1995).

41. Bosnian: *Amela's School Holiday* (1993), *Hobby* (1993), *Children of Sarajevo* (1994, Amir Bukvić), *Draw Me . . .* (François Lunel, 1994), *Don't Shoot at the Children* (1994), *The War in Children* (1994), *Children Like Any Others* (1995). Foreign: *Children's Police Squad* (Austria, 1993), *Children under Fire* (UK, 1993). This is an incomplete listing of the films focusing on children. A full one would include another twenty or so titles, mostly shorts.

42. Tatjana Protka, 'Sie schlagen uns wie Fliegen', diary excerpts, *Der Spiegel*, Vol. 8, 1993, pp. 154–8.

43. Zlata Filipović (1994), Dzevad Karahasan (1994), Zdenko Lešić (1995), Semezdin Mehmedinović (1998).

44. A similar collection of writings, mostly by displaced and refugee women, is *The Suitcase*, edited by an international group of women (Mertus *et al.*, 1997).

45. *The Letter (19.8.1992)* (1993), *A Message to My Friends* (1993), *24 Hours with Bure* (1993/7).

46. *Colors 14: War*, March, 1996.

47. Jasna Bašić, co-producer of *Unexpected Walk*, during a press conference at the Thessaloniki International Film Festival, November 1998.

Chapter 13
Migrating Mind and Expanding Universe: The Balkans Come to the World

A recent immigrant to New Zealand, a young Croatian girl, who works in an oriental restaurant and secretly marries an illegal mainland Chinese for money, falls in love with a Maori teenager and suffers the outrage of her father – this is the plot of Gregor Nicholas' *Broken English*, certain visual motifs from which remind me of the recent Maori saga, Lee Tamahori's *Once Were Warriors* (1995) and of the recent saga of illegal Chinese, Tony Chan's *Combination Platter* (1993).

The family members of a clandestine Montenegrin immigrant in New York travel to the USA to join him, but as they cross the Mexcian border at Rio Grande one of the sons is drowned – this is the plot of Goran Paskaljević's *Someone Else's America*, in which the river crossing is reminiscent of scenes from John Sayles' *Lone Star* (1996), of José Luis Borau's *On the Line* (1987) or even of Gregory Nava's classic *El Norte* (1983). Later in this same film the Serbian immigrant's son marries a Chinese-American, and they all dance to flamenco music, bringing to mind visual associations spanning, among others, Wayne Wang, early Ang Lee and Carlos Saura.

A red balloon, as if taken directly from Albert Lamorisse's short *Le Ballon rouge/The Red Balloon* (1956), flies from Alaska to New York, and then reappears in events set in the American South – this is the opening of Emir Kusturica's *Arizona Dream*. The small town where most of the action takes place resembles a mixture of Peter Bogdanovich's Texas-set *The Last Picture Show* (1971) and Aki Kaurismaki's *Leningrad Cowboys Go America* (1989).

There is a trend which gradually emerges from examples like these – the growing interest in far-away places, in interacting with barely known peoples and, in general, in making new localities imaginable. Contrary to the established pattern of representations shaped by the desire to be seen as European, Europe is no longer the only place within which Balkan film-makers and their protagonists imagine themselves. New worlds come into existence for them. New Zealand, Alaska and Mexico now become sites where they are likely to set foot and live through crucial formative experiences. The trend is one of an expanding universe.

Arjun Appadurai's analysis of the factors underpinning modernity draws our attention to these processes. To him, modernity is a 'rupture that takes media and migration as its two major, and interconnected, diacritics'. A third factor, the imagination, shaped by the joint effects of media and migration, is added as a constitutive feature of modern subjectivity. In Appadurai's scheme, 'electronic mediation and mass migration mark the world of the present not as technically new forces but as ones that seem to impel (and sometimes compel) the work of imagination' (Appadurai, 1996, pp. 3–5).

These three factors, indeed, provide a suitable framework for an exploration of the trend that I will be discussing here: how the workings of migratory experiences and of electronic mediation (film, in this case) influence the imagination to accept, albeit conditionally, a community in motion. This community may be fragile but it receives its legitimation through the very act of imagination by the migrating mind. Thus a culturally significant space is constituted by members of the new community of migrants (who join in by an act of imagination), overcoming the trademark atmosphere of lost homelands and rising above destabilising discourses of shattered identities, to occupy an expanding universe, a universe which receives its meaning through its perpetual dynamism.

Ella Shohat and Robert Stam, in *Unthinking Eurocentrism* (1994), insisted that the entrenched Eurocentric construct needed to be defeated in favour of a multicultural education. While they approached the task of 'unthinking' by deconstructing mainstream Hollywood representations of the exotic and the foreign, I choose to approach it from the opposite side, focusing on the (Balkan) periphery, and exploring how the margin develops mechanisms to detach itself from, and lessen its dependency on, the centre.

If the migrations and diasporic processes are grasped in the framework offered by these scholars, the South-East Europeans who are the subject of this study, many of whom have experienced involuntary migration during the past decades, will be given a chance to think of themselves in new terms. Their marginalised positions within the European space will be reconsidered in a global context, one in which they encounter other marginalised peoples – the American Southerners, the Maoris, the illegal Mexicans. Such encounters can help them come to terms with their own inferiority and dare to imagine themselves as subjects of new, fulfilling experiences. Reconfiguring the space of their own lives, and accepting new localities, will allow them to reject the embedded hierarchies according to which they are 'insufficiently European', and start making sense of new visions that permit them to gain control over their disrupted lives. The older localities will change, and new ones, never encountered before, will obtain validation through the workings of migration, mass mediation and imagination.

Deterritorialisation, exile, journeying, border-crossings, life in diasporas, growing awareness of instability and change and the feeling of displacement at home are all new experiences for many in the Balkans. Amid these processes, film-making has been producing works that can be considered as representative of several prevailing tendencies in the conceptualisation of migration and change. It is these tendencies which I will discuss here. One is the continuation of the traditional notion of migration as a condition of endless squalor, duress and alienation. Another is the willingness to seek and discover excitement in the new experiences that accompany the dispersal. Yet a third tendency is to question the unconditional acceptance of home by exploring the increasing feeling of displacement induced by staying in the same place.

The Threat of Dispersal

Traditionally, Balkan people have led a sedentary life. In the Balkan tradition, moving and migrating was regarded as an extremely painful experience. To change places was seen as undesirable, and something that could only bring about harsh confrontations and trouble. Even though groups from the Balkans have been emigrating from Europe since the nineteenth century, when many resettled to the New World – the USA, Argentina, Australia – most travelling was usually confined to the Balkan universe itself, to Asia Minor and the Mediterranean, and to Vienna as a westward limit.

Cinematic works of the past have recorded the troublesome experiences of economic and political migrations. Notably, many of the region's masterpieces explore the village-city migrations which radically transformed these traditional societies. In Turkish cinema there are the now classic films such as *Sürü/The Herd* (1979), written by Yilmaz Güney, which evolves around peasants travelling through the barren countryside along with the animals with which they make their living, or *At/Horse* (1971), which follows the ordeals of a peasant father and son struggling to get established in Istanbul; even the recent *Güneşe yolculuk/Journey to the Sun* (1999), tackling the Kurdish problem, continues the tradition of these older narratives by following the lives of two young men from the provinces in Istanbul. In Bulgarian cinema there are the films of the so-called 'migration cycle' from the 1970s, such as Lyudmil Kirkov's *Selyaninat s koleloto/ The Villager with the Bicycle* (1974) and *Matriarhat/Matriarchy* (1977), and Hristo Hristov's *Postedno lyato/Last Summer* (1974) and *Darvo bez koren/A Tree with No Roots* (1976), all stories revolving around the destruction of traditional lifestyles, and of the inevitability of migration to the alienating reality of the cities. In Greek cinema a whole generation of directors who started their careers in the 1970s belonged to the 'first generation urbanites with deep country roots' (Horton, 1997, p. 7)[1] The debut feature of one of them, Theo Angelopoulos' *Anaparastassi/Reconstruction* (1970), is centred around a village tragedy triggered by migrations which have led to the abandonment of the countryside and the desertion of traditional communities.

The concept of Balkan men going abroad to work and make money in order that they might build a house and raise a family when they return home has traditionally been connoted by the Turcism *gurbet* (*kurpeti*), a word evoking painful connotations. The men of *gurbet* (or *becari*, in Serbian) rarely assimilate in exile, yet their adaptation to home is also troubled. The Albanian film *Years of Waiting* (1981) speaks of 'calamities of migration' and is set in a village deserted by its men, all of whom went to *gurbet*. The opening of Istanbul-born Elia Kazan's *America, America* (1963) is dominated by the painful atmosphere of forced uprooting that surrounds his Greek protagonists, who are headed for a life overseas. In modern days, emigration is linked to the bitter experiences of penetrating the fortress of Europe, depicted in the Swedish production of Tunç Okan's *The Bus* (1977), in which a group of illegal Turkish immigrants who have been abandoned in Stockholm are too frightened to leave the vehicle and venture into the unknown territory of the Western metropolis. Another example is provided by *Umud'a yolculuk/Reise der Hoffnung/Journey of Hope* (1990), a film from Switzerland, which depicts the denigration of Turkish clandestine migrants stranded in the Alps. Adaptation and displacement are further problematised in films such as Tevfic Başer's 40 *Quadratmeter Deutschland/ Forty Square Meters Germany* (1986), the claustrophobic story of the Turkish bride of a *Gastarbeiter* confined to a tiny one-bedroom universe, and for whom Germany is only the courtyard overlooked by her apartment.[2] Similarly, a film such as Yüksel Yavuz's 1995 documentary *Mein Vater, der Gastarbeiter/My Father, the Gastarbeiter* tells the unsettling story of the director's Kurdish father, laid off after twenty-five years at a German plant.[3] A co-production between unusual partners, the Yugoslav–Argentinian *Put na jug/El Camino del sur/Southbound* (1988), features actress Mirjana Joković as a village bride married to an émigré who, it eventually transpires, owns a bordello in Buenos Aires, where he will keep her confined, alongside his other Slavic brides, all of whom were forced into prostitution in a strange land, with no family and friends to protect them. A German film, again with Mirjana Joković in the lead role, looked at another clandestine aspect of migrations: *Das Serbische Mädchen/The Serbian Girl* (1991), based on a story by Siegfried Lenz, shows the Serbian protagonist quickly growing disillusioned with Germany, but staying on and becoming part of the illegal trafficking in the region.

Later on came the involuntary migrations triggered by the breakup of

Yugoslavia, often conceptualised along the traditional lines of painful and undesirable experiences or from the nostalgic viewpoint of displacement and irretrievably lost homelands. In an interview permeated with sadness, director Boro Drašković recounts going to Norway to show his *Vukovar: Poste Restante* and encountering a community of exiled Yugoslavs, whom he overheard crying during the screening:

> They're trying to lead the same life they had in our country. It's so sad, so far away. Even though Norway is a nice country and people are wonderful to them ... It's so sad that all around the world there are people who escaped from a country that used to be very beautiful.[4]

Slavenka Drakulić (1996) recounts another visit to a displaced Bosnian Muslim family in Stockholm, whose daily existence in the safety of the Swedish capital is dominated by sadness and homesickness. These are people with whom she would not associate at home – as an emancipated urbanite, she would not have much to talk to them about. But here they are together, not old friends, but members of hurriedly created support networks. The children adapt and cannot be distinguished from the local teenagers, but the parents are irrevocably displaced, living on memories and old photographs in their apartment cells in Toronto, Glasgow, Berlin and Barcelona.

The contributors to *The Suitcase*, a collection of refugee women's narratives and poetry, write from all over – St Louis, Budapest, Islamabad and Jerusalem (Mertus *et al.*, 1997). These writings chronicle experiences of traumatic severance and arduous adjustment, of lives left behind and of endearments indefinitely postponed. The epilogue of Barbara Demick's book about a Sarajevo neighbourhood is entitled 'The Exiles' and lists the current whereabouts of the people who resided at Logavina Street at the time she wrote the book, but who are now dispersed all over the world – in Canada, Germany, Italy, Australia (Demick, 1996, p. 180). Elma Softić (1995), the Jewish Sarajevan who wrote a book of her wartime experiences, considers going to Israel, and her sister, Ilona, moves to Tasmania.

Dispersed widely, the young Yugoslavs whose essays comprise the book, *Children of Atlantis*, all write about the anxiety they experienced when leaving and the hardship of adapting. Many of them prefer to be honest about the option of return – it may be possible, but it is not always at the top of their personal agendas. 'There is nothing meaningful I could do in my country,' writes one (Lešić, 1995, p. 137). Return? Where to? The place will have been transformed, and they may end up feeling equally foreign. It is nice to cherish the idea, but the return is conditional. The future scenarios for their disrupted lives take place elsewhere, and only rarely at the place where it all started.

Displaced at Home: Belgrade as a State of Mind

The 'stay or leave' dilemma is equally pressing for those trapped in Belgrade. While leaving or staying never came down to the extremes it had in Sarajevo, and while there was more space for the existential subtleties of hesitation, here emigration had also become the only alternative to displacement at home for a whole generation. The imperative to migrate became one of the leading themes in the new Balkan cinema.

To leave meant to start all over again somewhere else, and to face uncertainty and difficult times. To stay, on the other hand, meant to expose oneself to equally troublesome duress and unforeseeable pressures. In addition, to stay would mean endangering one's sanity; to stay would mean accepting isolation, staying behind after everybody else had left; to stay would mean being suspected of supporting the current state of affairs.

If you hesitate too long, the moment comes when you realise that your reason for staying at home is no longer there. The people who mattered to you have left, there is no one around whom you would like to be with, and the streets are full of unknown faces, maybe refugees who have flocked in from places which they themselves have left reluctantly. Your own town is changing, and is not your town any more. One only lives once. One needs to decide, now.

The choice of whether to stay or leave remains. However, when home is a strange place, staying and leaving become the same. Furthermore, when staying involves witnessing the destruction of a known place, leaving, and the opportunity it affords to experience something new, may seem the preferable option.

According to director Goran Marković, of the one million inhabitants of Belgrade, 400,000 had emigrated by 1995, and had been replaced by approximately the same number of displaced Serbs who had come from all over 'Greater Serbia'.[5] Director Srdjan Dragojević, born in 1963, described in an interview the feeling that he and his thirty-something friends in Belgrade lived with throughout the 1990s: 'Five years of my life have been stolen, I don't know what to do. I am so desperate I even participated in the moronic US Green Card lottery, my children live in this disgusting country and listen to awful folk music ...'[6] Dragojević left Belgrade in 1999.

For the ones who stay, the bleakness of Belgrade gradually becomes a state of mind – some call it 'Ghetto', some 'Zombietown' – and name their films accordingly. In *Ghetto*, the drummer of rock group Electric Orgasm sets off from the attic where he lives for a walk around Belgrade. He spends the day visiting friends – rock musicians and pop artists – whom he finds rehearsing in various underground locations or hanging around on street corners. These marginal urban spaces have become a refuge for creativity, surviving in startling contrast to the vulgarity of the crumbling city. His depressing experiences climax in the evening when he ends up at a stadium where a loud turbo-folk concert is taking place, and where an exalted crowd shakes to the dumbing rhythm of the stridently nationalist music. The cycle of alienation is complete, and near dawn on the following morning he returns to the secluded safe haven of his attic.

In the other 'rockumentary', *Zombietown* (1995), featuring the DJs of Radio B92, the protagonists have made the extravagant choice to stay in Belgrade against all odds, and are shown fighting their own audacious battles to remain sane amid a maddening reality. In the film, Belgrade is portrayed as a city of drabness and desperation, cut off from the rest of the world, where anything can and does happen.

In Vladimir Arsenjević's story, *The Month of Dying* (1996), the family of a young Serbian, who is recruited to the army and killed despite being a conscientious objector, gathers for the funeral. They are overtaken by an overwhelming feeling of absurdity, as expressed by the narrator:

> I found myself sorry for the people in this world who had nothing left but obscenities. I felt sorry for each one of us. . . . All those who had not managed to find a shelter, all those who had been caught unawares, they were all whisked away, like kites snatched from our hands by the November gales.
>
> (Arsenjević, p. 66)

This same feeling pervades a series of films which were made by younger Yugoslav directors during the 1990s. Although not all as compelling as *The Month of Dying*, they are all driven by the need to re-create the depressing atmosphere, the ruined lives of this young generation and their growing desperation and madness. Oleg Novković's *Kazi zasto me ostavi/Why Did You Leave Me?* (1993) tried to represent the devastating effects of the war on a small group of friends. Vladimir Blaževski's *Bulevar revolucije/Boulevard Revolution* (1992) followed the course of a doomed love affair between a teenage girl, overshadowed by the authority of her policeman father, and a thug involved in organised crime in Belgrade. The highly acclaimed *Ubistvo s predumišljajem/ Premeditated Murder* (1996), based on the popular novel by Slobodan Selenić, scrutinised another impossible love – between a young Belgrade student and a simple peasant boy, whom the girl tries vainly to keep from the war, but who nevertheless encounters a meaningless death at the front.[7] Darko Bajić's *Crni bombarder/Black Bomber* (1992) depicts Belgrade as a dark futuristic wasteland, influenced by the familiar set of *Blade Runner* (1982), where strugglers for justice are reduced to terrorists. Slobodan Skerlić traces the making of a new generation of ruthless criminals in *Do koske/Rage* (1998), where the teenage protagonists abduct an older gangster and subject him to torture.

Similarly, the two teenage gangster-protagonists of Srdjan Dragojević's *Wounds*, born after Tito's death, come of age in the gloomy reality of Milošević's Serbia. They are not interested in politics, and move rapidly, between 1991 and 1996, from petty gangster apprentices into full-blown crime lords. Noisy street protests pass by in the distance and the word 'democracy' only appears as an accidental backdrop to a crucial shoot-out. Critics compared *Wounds* to some of cinema's most intensely violent masterpieces – Kubrick's *Clockwork Orange* (1971) and Tony Scott's *True Romance* (1993) – and to the French teenage drama of brutality, Mathieu Kassovitz's *La Haine/Hate* (1995).[8] In a seemingly indirect, but in fact deeply political, way, *Wounds* analyses the terrible impact of modern-day Serbian politics on a whole generation that has been robbed of a future – it chronicles the moral and ethical destruction as it manifests itself in the lives of the two teenagers, as 'pure rage born of the particular Serbian anomie, ... inarticulate, directionless, blind' (Živković, 1998, p. 8).

But while the younger directors remained mostly interested in the doomed futures and the lost lives of thousands of Serbian teenagers and the people of their own generation, the middle cohort of Yugoslav directors, loosely belonging to the Prague Group, made films which represented the fatalism, the passivity and the desperation experienced by the middle-aged – all elements of the 'Belgrade as a state of mind' syndrome. The films they made reflected an apocalyptic feeling, and occasionally also the self-pity which they and their fellow citizens felt.

The atmosphere of Milos Radivojević's *Ni na nebu ni na zemlji/Between Heaven and Earth* (1994), set in present-day Belgrade, is permeated by desperation. It tells the story of three friends in their thirties, forced to take extreme steps to secure some sort of future for themselves amid bleak circumstances. The film's protagonists are morally frustrated and mentally exhausted. The most energetic one leaves for Australia, another gets involved with drug traffickers and dies, and the third remains chained to the city, displaced at home like so many others.

Goran Marković's *Urnebesna tragedija/Burlesque Tragedy* (1995) provides another metaphor for the Yugoslav state of mind – the psychiatrist can no longer care for his patients, the bookseller drinks and assaults his wife and an actor shoots himself on stage in the middle of a play. The main plot line is about the psychiatric hospital which is forced to close down and send all the patients back home. However, many of them no longer have a home, and remain at large in the city. The director's preoccupation is to show how, in today's Belgrade, traditional concepts of normality and insanity have become interchangeable – the 'normal' ones are depressed and incapacitated, while the deviant ones thrive on chaos, war and the trafficking of arms, drugs and fuel.

The Burlesque Tragedy, however, remained too cryptically Yugoslav to be understood (or liked) beyond Belgrade. In the West, the film was reviewed as a 'chronicle of the Serbian madness'.[9] In a review for *Variety*, Godfrey Cheshire criticised it for its negative depiction of the mentally ill and for its incomprehensible humour.[10] 'Incomprehensible' was probably the best diagnosis – the insanity of 'Belgrade as a state of mind' was difficult to convey to outside observers.[11] Another film which was little understood was Želimir Žilnik's gritty and extravagant *Marble Ass*, featuring a drag queen, a male prostitute who claims that he is diverting and absorbing the violence which would otherwise spill over into the society at large.

The only film which managed to communicate the effects of malaise and insanity to the outside world was Goran Paskaljević's *Powder Keg*. 'I feel that it is now my turn to show the current state of mind of my people,' explained the director.[12] Cut off from the outside world and living under an intolerant and brutal regime, the reality of *Powder Keg*, framed by the monologues of an insanely frank cabaret entertainer, is reminiscent of the intensely desperate atmosphere of films set in the liberal lairs of early Nazi times, like István Szabó's *Mephisto* (1981) and Bob Fosse's *Cabaret* (1972).[13] Structured around autonomous and only partially intersecting stories, one of the plot lines in *Powder Keg* follows the attempts of a Serbian émigré who has returned from the West to recover the woman he loves. It is too late, however. Although he may be ready to help his former friends escape from this 'shit', by now they are all impetuously and irretrievably mad – 'fucked up by staying', as one of them puts it, because, in the words of a taxi driver, 'anyone with any brains has left'. By the morning after his return the émigré will be killed. It is almost implied that he was asking for it – he should not have returned; he is not needed in Belgrade. Those who have stayed behind are portrayed as uncontrollably and frantically violent – an impulsively aggressive man arranges an attack on the home of the young boy who has accidentally hit his car shortly before. During an amicable boxing match two old friends reveal how they have betrayed each other over the decades; one kills the other, soon after blowing himself up with a hand grenade and killing a girl he has just met in a train compartment. A young man seizes and then terrorises the innocent passengers on a bus. And so the violent incidents go on, all happening within the same night in the scarce light of embargo-stricken Belgrade. The bitterness and the vindictiveness, the madness and the frenzy are intense and meaningless. 'Belgrade as a state of mind' translates into images that speak of a tragic and destabilising loss of substance, a loss enhanced by the rejection of emigration.

The cinema of the dispersed Yugoslavs

There is a small, but steadily growing number of displaced Balkan authors with an international presence – the New Orleans-based Romanian Andrei Codrescu, the Paris-based Albanian Ismail Kadare and the globe-trotting Croatians Dubravka Ugrešić and Slavenka Drakulić – who produce outspoken journalistic writing about the region.[14] Their writing has gradually created a discursive framework of dissent and disenchantment which, for the Balkans in the 1990s, played a role equivalent to that of the writings of Central Eastern Europe's critical intelligentsia of the 1980s.[15] Even though their writing is marked by differences in language and location, they all subscribe, to a greater or lesser extent, to the same project of a critical rethinking of the Balkan space. They have all undergone the necessary experiences of displacement and detachment from their own culture that allows them to overcome the inferiority of the 'Balkans-as-insufficiently-European' complex, and launch a sound critical examination of transnational dynamics and transforming experiences. Many of them wrote bitterly about their disillusionment with the idea of Europe, and soon ventured into a new freedom offered by an acceptance of the expanding universe in which they now moved.

Balkan film-makers turned cosmopolitan have not yet been as highly visible, possibly because it takes time to raise funds, shoot and release a film. But many have either come to the West or have been commuting between the USA and Europe for the past few years. When discussing the experiences of German directors who ended up in the USA under similar circumstances before World War II, Thomas Elsaesser claims that their successful integration into American and Hollywood values was highly unlikely as they belonged to artistic and intellectual circles,

> where the immigrant ethos of trying to blend with the host culture in order to give positive value to a decision forced upon one by external circumstances is blunted by resentment about the loss of prestige and nostalgia for the status enjoyed back home.[16]

Such impediments to integration may also be the case with the recent migrations of Yugoslav film-makers, as even those who started making films in the West prefer to move either in the world of US independents or within the European realm rather than plunge into mainstream Hollywood.

The members of the Yugoslav Prague Group, for example, have been constantly on the move. Srdjan Karanović (*Petrijin Venac/Petricia's Wreath*, 1980, *Virdzina/Virgina*, 1991) seemed to have settled in Boston, where he took on a teaching position and worked on a project, now abandoned, about a Bosnian girl coming to New Orleans; he is now back in Belgrade. The Croatian, Rajko Grlić, (*U raljama zivota/In the Jaws of Life*, 1989, *That Summer of White Roses, 1989*) is a professor emeritus at Ohio State University, where he worked on a CD-ROM film production tutorial, and is set to start shooting a European-financed feature. Lordan Zafranović exiled himself to Prague to finish his personal critical documentary on Croatia's twentieth-century history.[17] Serbian Goran Paskaljević lives in Paris. His *Someone Else's America* is set in New York and in Texas and was produced with French, British, German and Greek involvement. At the time when his Belgrade-set *Powder Keg* (a.k.a. *Cabaret Balkan*) opened in the USA, he was in pre-production for his next movie, to be made on location in Mexico. Emir Kusturica, the youngest of the group, but also the one with the highest international profile, left Columbia University and the USA to settle officially in France. After his Yugoslavia-themed but internationally financed *Underground* and *Black Cat, White Cat*, he spent two years preparing to work on a Holocaust drama based on D. M. Thomas' *The White Hotel*, now an abandoned project.

Milcho Manchevski, the Macedonian who studied and worked in the USA before making the European-funded *Before the Rain*, is now split between the two continents. He quit the set of Miramax's *Ravenous* (1999) over creative differences and is now working on his next auteurist project, which is set in Macedonia around the turn of the century and in present-day New York.[18] Other former Yugoslavs based in the West made a number of lesser-known movies about the ordeals of the Yugoslav breakup. In the USA, Serbian Predrag Antonijević made *Savior*, an Oliver Stone-produced story of a Western mercenary in the Bosnian war. In Germany, Zoran Solomun released his *Tired Companions*, five slightly overlapping stories following various refugees from former Yugoslavia. In the UK, Jasmin Dizdar completed *Beautiful People* (1999), shot on location near Liverpool. Others live in the USA and are involved in various projects – from documentaries to advertising – like Lazar Stojanović, the martyr, who had to serve a jail term for his *Plasticni Isus/Plastic Jesus* (1971), Slobodan Sijan, the author of the classic Yugoslav Gypsy-themed *Who Is Singing Out There?*, and Goran Gajić, who was the first to make a documentary about the Slovenian rock group *Laibach* (1988). The latest addition to the group is Srdjan Dragojević, the director of *Pretty Village, Pretty Flame* and *Wounds*, who left Belgrade for New York around the time the Kosovo crisis started. He is preparing to work on projects which do not deal with the Balkans, and which are expected to be funded by Miramax, the Disney subsidiary.

Slavenka Drakulić describes a meeting with actress Mira Furlan in a New York flat – both displaced, both proclaimed 'Croatia's witches', here they are, together again. The people have not changed, only the place (Drakulić, 1993, pp. 76–85). In her book about life after emigration, Dubravka Ugrešić also speaks of such get-togethers with other displaced Yugoslav intellectuals in a New York flat – here they are, together, the same people once again, only in a different locale. One of them, the film director, exclaims: 'I don't want to stay, I don't want to go back, what can I do?' (Ugrešić, 1994, p. 69).

Some of the many displaced actors from former Yugoslavia reinvented themselves and are now back in the spotlight. Croatian Mira Furlan, for example, best known for the role of the mistress in Kusturica's Cannes-winner *When Father Was Away on Business*, was ostracised in her own country, migrated to the USA and made a successful appearance in the sequel to *Star Trek: Babylon 5*. Goran Visnjić, first known from his role as the driver Risto in *Welcome to Sarajevo*, landed a network appointment as the new pediatrician hired to replace George Clooney's character in the new series of *ER*. Rade Serbedzija, ostracised in his own country, spent his first few years in exile in London and appeared in films such as *Before the Rain* and *Broken English*. Lately he has been gaining visibility in Hollywood, which still avoids featuring his 'unpronounceable' name in larger print but nevertheless employs him for a wider range of roles, usually villainous crooks with an articulate East European accent, drunkard's voice and oily grey hair. He landed this type of role in mainstream Hollywood flicks such as *The Saint* (1997), *Mighty Joe Young* (1999) and *Stigmata* (1999).[19] Young Labina Mitevska, who first appeared as the Albanian girl in *Before the Rain* and then played a Bosnian in Michael Winterbottom's *Welcome to Sarajevo*, was given a role in the director's next film, *I Want You* (1998), a love thriller which has little to do with the girl's Balkan origins.

It is still to be seen if these film-makers and actors, turned cosmopolitan by the whims of history, will continue working internationally. Given the general trend towards globalisation, it is very likely that they will further explore the chances which their expanding universe offers, bravely confronting any misfortunes that may come along. My prognosis is based on the example set by an earlier Yugoslav exile, Dušan Makavejev. Makavejev had already exhibited a cosmopolitan side in his 1971 film *WR: Mysteries of the Organism*. But his conceptual grasp of an unstable moving world peaked in the 1974 Canadian–French–German funded *Sweet Movie*, a controversial microcosm in which he gathered together a Canadian virgin, a Texan oil tycoon, a Latino singer, an Amsterdam hippie community, a proletarian prostitute, Miss Planeta (Globe) and a sailor called Vakulinchuk (after Eisenstein's *Battleship Potemkin* protagonist), and in which the director used background documentary footage of the 1941 exhumations of the Kathyn forest massacre (committed by Soviets against Polish army officers but blamed on the Germans) and music by Greek composer Manos Hadjidakis. For his 1981 Swedish-funded *Montenegro*, Makavejev chose a sleazy immigrant venue, Zanzi-Bar, in Stockholm. While for his 1984 Australian-funded *Coca-Cola Kid*, he decided on a setting in the Australian outback. *Manifesto* (1988) was produced by Israeli Menahem Golan, made with money from the USA and Yugoslavia, and employed an ethnic mix from the margins of Austro-Hungary. The autobiographical *Hole in the Soul* was a Scottish BBC production and took place in a variety of locations, from

Belgrade to San Francisco. Makavejev, who underwent the experiences of displacement and exile twenty years before the recent wave of Yugoslav film-makers, tasted cosmopolitanism much earlier, and with varying success has maintained his interest in the global mixture of localities. Makavejev may be a maverick. It is, however, possible that other Balkan film-makers will decide to follow suit and venture into taste the 'pleasures of hybridity' as he did.

But while many of the films made by these dispersed Yugoslav directors, or many of the films produced in the West about Yugoslavia, are seen and talked about back in the Balkans, one can barely claim they have been seen by substantial audiences of dispersed Yugoslavs or other Balkan émigrés. The organisation of film and video distribution for ethnic communities in the West is such that émigré audiences are mostly reached by entertainment products and rarely see any serious titles, with the exception of an occasional video. This set-up is partially dependent on the concrete policies regarding ethnic media that are in place and which differ from country to country. Whatever the policy provisions, however, immigrant groups have shown to be adept at creating entertainment opportunities for themselves. Ethnic organisations in the West often hire theatres for particular screenings, and some even maintain a regular schedule of shows, often in an under-utilised old building or a community centre. Occasionally, quite large-scale events are organised by ethnic communities, and in the past decade there has been a proliferation of ethnic film festivals showcasing recent films from various regions. These events tend, though, to lean heavily toward pure, 'apolitical' entertainment, and are more likely to feature populist turbo-folk than screen a serious feature film.

In addition, one should not presuppose that interest in cultural products is by default associated with one's place of origin. Whereas foreign films make it into the mainstream or repertory theatrical distribution, they are rarely marketed to the respective diasporic audiences. If a film from a given country happens to play in theatres locally, only a few immigrants of the given ethnic group actually turn up to see it. This can be partially explained by the fact that these films are not as widely advertised as the Hollywood releases with which they compete, and are only marketed through media targeted at niche audiences (for example, free alternative newspapers and advertisements at university campuses). It is also because only a fraction of the immigrants happen to be people who would go to see such films in their home countries. It is not logical to expect that an ethnic immigrant, say a Serb, who only watched martial arts and action-adventure videos at home would end up in a theatre when a serious film like *Someone Else's America* or *Pretty Village, Pretty Flame* is playing. It also seems that immigrant audiences do not have any special interest in films that tackle the immigrant experiences of others, and as a rule

the whole range of migration films remains largely unknown even to members
of the very ethnic group that happens to be their subject.

Living in Dispersal

Although it was made before *Powder Keg*, Goran Paskaljević's *Someone Else's
America*, in which Chinese and Montenegrins intermarry and befriend
Spaniards, deals with the next stage – of living dispersed. Living in a diaspora
is part of the general condition of today's world. Registering the experiences of
migration in film is also part of a more general trend, where the constant mixing of traditionally isolated spheres pushes many film-makers to explore
changing places and diasporas-in-the-making. A universe on the move, where
old borders crumble and new locales replace old ones, characterises today's
film-making. Worlds that were unlikely to touch or collide now intersect and
overlap.

International documentaries about Bosnia depicted complete strangers
setting foot on the disputed land: the French *Bosnia Hotel* (1996) featured warriors of the Kenyan tribe Samburu now committed to a peacekeeping mission
in Bosnia, and a PBS documentary told of Pakistani soldiers taking care of an
eighty-year-old woman in Bosnia.

In the new country, with various degrees of success, life goes on, and this new
existence is not necessarily seen by the directors as an experience of continuous alienation. *Broken English*, a film from New Zealand, shows the Croatian

Goran Rebić's *Jugofilm* (1997) takes place in Vienna. The traumas of the Yugoslav conflict
are exported to a variety of migratory destinations: London, Vancouver and Melbourne

migrant protagonists interacting with other immigrants they encounter, and integrating within new communities – not within an upwardly mobile framework, but in networks of their own, which prove viable even if peripheral. *Northern Skirts* (1998), a film from Austria, looked at the same type of interactions and mutual support that exists between marginal immigrants from the Balkan countries in Vienna. In the cinema of Europe, displaced Bosnian and other Balkan protagonists started appearing more and more often in episodic, supporting or even leading roles. In *Tired Companions*, director Zoran Solomun looks at the lives of Yugoslav refugees in Germany. Even though he interprets the displacement as a gloomy experience, he manages to tell stories that suggest there is more to migration than endless suffering. In one of his vignettes two young but very different Bosnian women bond closely after they are pulled off a train on the Serbian-Hungarian border, while in another, two Serbs meet in Germany but find, after a few drinks, that they have little in common and may be better off among strangers than with each other. In Canada, originally under the working title *West of Sarajevo*, Davor Marjanović made *My Father's Angel* (1999). The film is set in Vancouver and tells of a Serb and a Muslim who are continuously obsessed with one another, until the moment they realise they need each other's support. In the UK, Bosnian-born director Jasmin Dizdar debuted with *Beautiful People*, a film which brings together Bosnians, Welsh, Croats and Britons, whose life paths intersect in London, and where a baby conceived in a rape is finally accepted by the reluctant mother and named Chaos.

These mass migrations and the dispersal of the former Yugoslav people all over the world will inevitably trigger more cinematic interest, and more works will emerge to register, explore and give meaning to the new diasporas-in-the-making. These new diasporas live out, in a condensed and accelerated manner, the experiences of older and now established diasporas. One possible framework for future films would be to maintain the focus on the encounter of the newcomers with the West and the patterns of their adaptation. Yet another line for cinematic explorations of the diasporas-in-the-making will be to focus on the multifaceted interactions which subvert the commonplace idea of migration as a movement from a periphery to a centre, and which acknowledge a more complex and multidimensional nature for today's migratory movements, whose trajectory is often from one periphery to another.

More and more films track down the actual process of travel which makes the unlikely encounters of marginal personages possible. *Clandestins* (1997) explored the painful journey of a group of stowaways who sail across the Atlantic locked in a freight container. A Russian spends this claustrophobic journey alongside a streetwise Gypsy boy, a destitute Romanian mother and a couple of desperate Arabs, all longing for the promised shores of Canada, all

inferior outcasts. The Italian *Lamerica* was set in Albania, and ended with docu-
mentary-style close-ups of Albanian refugees crowded on a ship that was
supposedly sailing to the utopian destination of the title. Croatians and
Guatemalans, Serbs and Kurds, Bosnians and Albanians – the world is on the
move. In our time of migrations, radical cultural and historical shifts, they all
hope that the restless movement will bring them closer to the promised land of
their dreams. Today's workings of the cinematic imagination in building and
maintaining this elusive vision are stronger than ever.[20]

Although moving around inevitably brings disquieting experiences, staying
in one place is no longer possible for many in the Balkans. Everyone is on the
move, many are displaced and live in transition. In the process of changing
places, Balkan migrants come across a multitude of other meaningful and
wholesome societies. A recognition of the vitality of these other worlds invites
a critical reconsideration of the Eurocentric construct. No longer is the traditional sphere of developed Western countries perceived as the only place
where meaningful activities are possible. Migrations, in people's minds and in
space, are no longer strictly following the long-established South-East–North-
West trajectory, but are a much more complex endeavour that comprises of a
series of moves in a multitude of directions. Unlike the older migrations, the
new ones are underwritten by mass mediation through the new media technologies, which empower the migrants to overcome marginalisation by
imagining themselves as pieces in the mosaic of a diverse, global universe.
North America and 'Fortress Europe' are no longer the ultimate desired
destinations; the privileged standing of these places is being contested by a
number of other, alternative places, which acquire value and meaning.
Albanians migrated not only to Italy, but south, to Greece. Bosnians ended up
not only in the USA and Canada but also in Pakistan, Israel and South
Africa. The pathways of the Russians lead not only to San Francisco and
Brighton Beach but also to Cyprus, Turkey and Singapore. The Eurocentric
notion of migration that sees the west of Europe and North America
as a powerful magnet attracting migrants from all over the world began to
erode. In the course of these processes, along with the loss of *Europe*'s
superior status as a desired but unattainable goal, Balkan people may well get
the chance to liberate themselves from the complex of being 'insufficiently
European'.

Notes

1. Horton appropriately notes that as a result of the intense village–city
   migrations around the time of Angelopoulos' debut in the early 1970s, Athens
   had grown to be a city of four million in a country of eight million.
2. The unsettling experiences of life in a foreign land have been further explored

by the director in his other two films, *Farewell to False Paradise* (1989) and *Good Bye, Stranger!* (1991), which also look at Turkish exiles in Germany.

3. Yavuz's first feature, *April Children* (1999), also explores the lives of Kurdish protagonists in Germany.

4. Drašković quoted in Henry Sheenan, '*Vukovar* Stirring Raw Emotions', *The Orange County Register*, 31 March 1996, p. F15.

5. In Pascal Bourdon, ' "Tragedie burlesque": chronique de la "folie serbe" ', *France Presse*, 1 September 1995.

6. Srdjan Dragojević interview in *Balkan Media* (1996/97, p. 15).

7. At the end of the film, the female protagonist is also set to leave and join her mother in New Zealand.

8. The film was also compared to *Trainspotting* (Janet Maslin, 'Horror and Pity at Young Serbian Thugs', *The New York Times*, 1 April 1999, p. E1).

9. Bourdon, ' "Tragedie burlesque" '. See note 5.

10. Godfrey Cheshire, 'The Tragic Burlesque', *Variety*, 18–24 September 1995, p. 102.

11. One should say, however, that not only Yugoslav films but also a whole range of films made in the 1990s throughout the countries of the former Eastern bloc, and dealing with various aspects of post-communist drabness and the corresponding depression and mental deviation, had difficulties internationally, and remained little understood beyond the borders of their particular countries. In regard to Russian cinema a special category was even introduced to describe the genre of gloomy, dark films – *chernukha* ('black one').

12. Speaking at the 39th Thessaloniki International Film Festival, November 1998.

13. In North America, the film was distributed under the title *Cabaret Balkan*. The official reason for the change in the name was that Kevin Costner had already registered a forthcoming film project under the title *Powder Keg*.

14. See Andrei Codrescu's Romanian diary (1991), Ismail Kadare's *Albanian Spring* (1993), Dubravka Ugrešić's *Have a Nice Day* (1994) and *Culture of Lies* (1998), and Slavenka Drakulić's *Balkan Express* (1993a) and *Café Europa* (1996). Some also write novels, which, quite notably, set far from the Balkans, feature East Europeans engaging in non-traditional interactions with the rest of the world. Drakulić's latest novel for example, *The Taste of a Man* (1997), is set in New York and deals with the controversial affair between a Warsaw doctoral student and a Brazilian scholar from São Paulo. Codrescu's 1995 novel *The Blood Countess* is set in Hungary and its protagonists are Elizabeth Batory, a Hungarian bloodthirsty aristocrat from the sixteenth century and a present-day resident of New York.

15. The project of Central Eastern Europe's critical intelligentsia comprised

writings by Czechs – Vaclav Havel, Milan Kundera and Ludvik Vaculik – Hungarians – György Konrád and Miklós Harászty – and Poles – Adam Michnik and Stanislaw Baranczak, among others.

16. Thomas Elsaesser, 'Ethnicity, Authenticity, and Exile: A Counterfeit Trade? German Filmmakers and Hollywood', in Naficy (1999, pp. 97–125), p. 110.

17. *The Decline of the Century: The Testament of L. Z.* (1993). Production: Kino-Dokument (Prague)/HTV (Zagreb)/Cinex (Vienna).

18. *Ravenous* (1999) was completed by the British director Antonia Bird after Manchevski left. Manchevski's film *Dust* was in production in the summer of 2000, shot near Skopje in Macedonia and starring actors from France, Britain and Australia.

19. In the case of Serbedzija, I foresee a career developing from low-profile roles in arthouse productions towards leads in more or less mainstream films – similar to the way in which the career of exiled East German Armin Müller-Stahl developed in West Germany, the USA and worldwide. A Serbo-Croat by origin, Serbedzija first appeared in movies in the late 1960s and has acted in over fifty feature films by Yugoslav directors such as Vatroslav Mimica, Zivojin Pavlović, Goran Marković, Rajko Grlić and Boro Drašković. In possession of a handsome, memorable face, Serbedzija has been cast in a large variety of roles – from Josip Broz-Tito in the TV drama *Bombers' Trial* (1978) to a sexually overambitious servant in Dušan Makavejev's *Manifesto* (1988). In the early 1990s he became a dissident figure at odds with the nationalist regimes in Yugoslavia and Croatia and subsequently moved to the West, where he has been successfully engaged in a number of smaller or larger supporting roles in films made by international directors – from Nicholas Roeg's adaptation, *Two Deaths* (1995), and Gregor Nicholas' tale of immigrants to New Zealand, *Broken English* (1996), through Francesco Rosi's Holocaust drama *The Truce* (1996) and Stanley Kubrick's last film *Eyes Wide Shut* (1999), to Hollywood entertainment flicks. At the same time, he continued appearing in a number of features made throughout the various post-Yugoslav states in the 1990s. Serbedzija is now split between Hollywood, European co-productions and a wide range of productions in the Yugoslav successor states. Only in the year 2000 he appeared in the films of several high-profile directors – from Guy Ritchie's *Snatch*, through John Woo's *Mission: Impossible II*, to Clint Eastwood's *Space Cowboys*. Serbedzija's best role remains that of the weary Macedonian expatriate, the photographer Aleksandar in Milcho Manchevski's *Before the Rain*.

20. These processes are more visible if one abandons the regional angle and adopts a comprehensive outlook, as I have tried to do elsewhere. See my work in *Framework*, 1999.

Aftermath? Fragmentary Notes

If taken as a coherent body of works, the films I have discussed here represent a comprehensive picture of the region and its people. Internationally, however, they were received within the context of a versatile international film-making, overtaken by quite different concerns.

The reception of these films occurred within the wider context of contemporary cinema, alongside Hollywood and Bollywood, Dogma and Manga. The years in which most of the films on the Balkan crisis were released were simultaneously the years when films such as the American *Pulp Fiction* (1994) and *Forrest Gump* appeared, and when films from Hong Kong, Iran and Denmark, triumphed on screens around the world. Kenović's *Perfect Circle*, for example, was shown at Cannes in 1997 alongside the Belgian *Ma vie en rose*, which dealt with gender identity, the Canadian *Kissed*, a discussion of necrophilia, and the British *My Son the Fanatic*, an exploration of the generation gap in the Pakistani immigrant community. In America, *Vukovar* was released and reviewed alongside the feminist generation saga *Antonia's Line* (1995), *Pretty Village* alongside the 1970s porn-nostalgia *Boogie Nights* (1997), and *Welcome to Sarajevo* with Brad Pitt's vehicle *Seven Years in Tibet* (1997). We need to realise that the concern about what is happening in the Balkans exists side by side with the concerns that all these other films raise, no matter how remote some of them may seem against the background of war and human disaster.

While many of the films I have talked about were recognised with major international awards, at many other competitions they were sidelined and the awards went to impressive psychological studies from the UK (Mike Leigh's *Secrets and Lies*, 1996) and Taiwan (Ming-lang Tsai's *The River*, 1997), or to films that examine the interactions of individual and history from Russia (Nikita Mikhalkov's *Burnt by the Sun*, 1994) and the Czech Republic (Jan Sverak's *Kolya*). The respect paid to directors such as Angelopoulos or Kusturica and the recognition of many of the films discussed here did not generate a persistent interest in Balkan cinema and did not turn the Balkans into a site of avant-garde film-making. Even if the excitement for films coming out of Hong Kong and Iran is somewhat exaggerated, there is no doubt that these cinemas offer an output which is remarkably stylistically consistent, something we cannot claim in regard to recent Balkan cinema.

* * *

While many of the survivors remain in the places where it all began, many others are, and will probably remain, abroad. For her documentary *The Underground Orchestra* (1998), Dutch film-maker Heddy Honigmann interviews musicians performing around the Paris subway, a cosmopolitan group that includes an army deserter from the former Yugoslavia, who plays the violin alongside Africans and Latin Americans.

Other exiles appear as secondary or leading characters in European feature films. In *À la place du coeur* (1998), a film set in Marseilles' working-class quarter, an immigrant woman from Sarajevo accuses a young black man of rape. In another French film, Jean-Marc Barr's *Lovers* (1999), a Yugoslav painter has a stormy love affair with a French girl. In *Pusher* (Nicolas Winding Refn, 1996), a Danish psychological thriller, the small-time protagonist works for a band of Yugoslav gangsters, who, during the violent culmination of the film, talk in a barely comprehensible mixture of Serbian and Danish. The director's next film, *Bleeder* (1999), once again features marginal Danish characters mixed up with equally marginalised immigrants from former Yugoslavia. As far as life in the aftermath is concerned, these émigrés have become an intrinsic part of 'new Europe's' social landscape.

Critics have noted that the best Vietnam-war films were made in the USA many years after the official end of the war (*Deer Hunter*, 1978; *Apocalypse Now*, 1979; *Platoon*, 1986; *Full Metal Jacket*, 1987; *Good Morning, Vietnam*, 1987; *Dear America: Letters Home from Vietnam*, 1988; *Born on the Fourth of July*, 1989). The ghosts of the Vietnam war featured powerfully in Hollywood as recently as 1994 with *Forrest Gump*. Similarly, in 1998 two films treated the subject of the Lebanese civil war – Ziad Doueiri's *West Beirut* and Ghassan Salhab's *Phantom Beirut* – personal narratives of film-makers who were teenagers at the time, both revisiting the topic of war two decades later. Deepa Mehta's *1947 Earth* (1998) reopened the still controversial theme of the Indian partition nearly fifty years later.

Similarly, as time passes, more films about the conflict in the Balkans will be made. Those, whose lives were deeply affected by what happened to the former Yugoslavia in the 1990s, will return to the traumas again and again. New projects are continually completed, and more are being made internationally.[1] In the years to come, Balkan film-makers themselves will look back at the issues of taking sides, villains and victims, displacement and migrations. Many more important works will appear that will examine the topic of war in the Balkans, and of the healing process which has, presumably, begun.

Now and then film-makers revisit places hit by environmental disasters – earthquake, tsunami, nuclear waste, oil spills – forgotten corners of the world that provide sad material for upsetting documentaries. Similarly, the places where scars of past wars are still healing are visited occasionally, to see what life is like in the aftermath. The lands of former Yugoslavia are checked on for the anniversary of political landmarks – like Dayton or Kosovo – a trend that will probably continue in the future. The works of this type – once again travelogues – are predictably depressing. Meanwhile, since Kosovo, the West is no longer an observer. It became a side in the conflict. No self-respecting Western film-making can continue with the old-style 'journey to the Balkans' projects.[2] Any commentary on the Balkans from now on must include a self-reflexive examination of oneself, even if only indirectly. So it is no surprise that recently made films on Bosnia tend to abandon the self-congratulatory 'journalist on assignment saves an innocent child' plot, and turn to exploring the complex moral dimension of the West's involvement in the Balkans. The British television drama *Warriors* and the documentary about the Srebrenica massacre, *A Cry from the Grave*, provide good examples. Both films subject the moral dilemmas faced by international soldiers stationed in Bosnia to a merciless scrutiny. Both films show how defenceless Balkan people are turned into victims, herded and disposed of by belligerent Balkan individuals, all of which takes place in front of able-bodied and armed Western protagonists, who are either unable or unwilling to intervene.[3]

But while the films on Bosnia explore feelings of shared guilt and helplessness, the films on Kosovo will have to examine the shaky grounds of the moral argument that underpinned actions of a dubious political effectiveness. *Moral Combat* (2000), BBC's authoritative documentary on the Kosovo war, has already set the trend.

Some, of course, will continue journeying to the Balkans to bring enlightenment. In Michael Ignatieff's documentary *The Trials of Freedom* (1999) the writer sets off on yet another journey to Belgrade in the aftermath of the Kosovo bombing. He is taken around by a friend, the political scientists Aleksa Djilas, who grimly shows him the destruction near his home. In a friendly voice, Ignatieff asserts that bombing was the right thing to do. Like a little boy to whom a school principal explains why children have to be punished, the Belgrade professor does not have much choice but to stay and listen.

After Kosovo, a feeling of homelessness prevails for diasporic intellectuals like myself. We readily gave up the illusory and loathsome imagined community of Balkan nationalisms. We reached out for a compensatory safety net, and it seemed we had found it when we embraced the accommodating shelter of Western liberalism. But as the story evolved, we could not help witnessing how the Balkans were continuously portrayed as a group of disobedient school children in need of disciplining, like the boys in Jean Vigo's *Zéro de conduite* (1933). Had we committed to yet another imagined community, which was now becoming equally elusive and alien? The growing disillusionment with this new sphere of belonging resulted in the solitary detachment in which most of us live now. What seemed to be an aftermath of Bosnia turned into a continuation of the Balkan ordeal.

My own image of the Balkans grows increasingly distant and elusive. It bathes in the utopian sunshine of *Underground*'s epilogue, and flashes like the images of happy conviviality of the Manaki brothers' reels in *Ulysses' Gaze*.

Notes

1. Some of the recent projects dealing with the Balkans and not discussed in my text include the Polish *Demons of War (After Goya)* (1998), the Canadian *My Father's Angel* (1999), as well as *Harrison's Flowers* (France, Elie Chouraqui, 2000), starring Andie McDowell.

2. Which is not to say that the films about the Balkans are no longer structured around the same travelogue scheme as before. On the contrary, documentaries on the Kosovo war, such as *Journey to Kosovo* (UK, Jonathan Dimbleby, 1999) or *The Body Hunter* (UK, Louise Norman, 2000) continued the trend of a Westerner's account of his or her experiences in the Balkans.

3. The screening of *A Cry from the Grave* at the Amsterdam Documentary Film Festival in December 1999 was said to have furthered the determination of the Dutch government to investigate the controversial nature of the actions of so-called Dutchbat in Srebrenica. It is believed that a film shot by a Dutch soldier contained footage of other Dutch peacekeepers helping the Serb military to separate Muslim men from the women in the preamble to what was to become the biggest massacre of the Bosnian war. The film was 'accidentally' destroyed while being handled at a military lab. The accident raised suspicion and was investigated at great length by journalist Gerard Legebeke, leading to charges of a cover-up by the Dutch Ministry of Defence.

Bibliography

Albahari, David (1996), *Words Are Something Else.* Translated by Ellen Elias-Bursac (Evanston, IL: Northwestern University Press).

Allcock, John B. and Antonia Young (eds) (1991), *Black Lambs and Gray Falcons. Women Travelers in the Balkans* (Bradford: Bradford University Press).

Allen, Beverly (1996), *Rape Warfare: The Hidden Genocide in Bosnia-Herzegovina and Croatia* (Minneapolis: University of Minnesota Press).

Allen, Tim and Jean Seaton (eds) (1999), *The Media of Conflict: War Reporting and Representations of Ethnic Violence* (London and New York: Zed Books).

Anderson, Benedict (1983), *Imagined Communities. Reflections on the Origin and Spread of Nationalism* (London and New York: Verso).

Andrić, Ivo (1959), *The Bridge on the Drina.* Translated from the Serbo-Croat by Lovett F. Edwards (New York: Macmillan).

Andrić, Ivo (1969), *The Pasha's Concubine and Other Tales.* Translated by Joseph Hitrec (London: Allen & Unwin).

Andrić, Ivo (1992), *Conversation with Goya: Bridges, Signs.* Translated by Celia Hawkesworth and Andrew Harvey (London: Menard Press).

Ang, Ien (1992), 'Hegemony in Trouble. Nostalgia and the Ideology of the Impossible in European Cinema', in D. Petrie (ed.), *Screening Europe. Image and Identity in Contemporary European Cinema* (London: BFI), pp. 21–31.

Anzulović, Branimir (1999), *Heavenly Serbia: From Myth to Genocide* (London: Hurst & Co.).

Appadurai, Arjun (1996), *Modernity at Large: Cultural Dimensions of Globalization* (Minneapolis: University of Minnesota Press).

Appiah, Kwame Anthony and Henry Louis Gates, Jr. (eds) (1995), *Identities* (Chicago and London: University of Chicago Press).

Armes, Roy (1987), *Third World Filmmaking and the West* (Berkeley: University of California Press).

Arsenjević, Vladimir (1996), '*The Month of Dying*', *The New Yorker*, 15 January. Translated by Celia Hawkesworth.

Avisar, Ilan (1988), *Screening the Holocaust: Cinema's Images of the Unimaginable* (Indianapolis: Indiana University Press).

Baker, Randall (1994), *Summer in the Balkans: Laughter and Tears after Communism* (Hartford, CT: Kumarian Press).

Bakić-Hayden, Milica (1995), 'Nesting Orientalisms: The Case of Former
    Yugoslavia', *Slavic Review*, Vol. 54, No. 4, Autumn, pp. 917–32.
Bakić-Hayden, Milica and Robert M. Hayden (1992), 'Orientalist Visions on the
    Theme "Balkans": Symbolic Geography in Recent Yugoslav Cultural Politics',
    Slavic Review, Vol. 51, No. 1, Spring, pp. 1–15.
Baranczak, Stanislaw (1990), *Breathing under Water and Other East European
    Essays* (Cambridge: Harvard University Press).
Barber, Benjamin R. (1995), *Jihad vs. McWorld* (New York: Ballantine Books).
Bassiouni, Cherif (1996), *Investigating Violations of International Humanitarian
    Law in the Former Yugoslavia*. Occasional Paper No. 2. (Chicago: DePaul
    University College of Law).
Bassiouni, Cherif and Marcia McCormick (1996), *Sexual Violence. An Invisible
    Weapon of War in the Former Yugoslavia*, Occasional Paper No. 1 (Chicago:
    DePaul University College of Law).
Bauman, Zygmunt (1989), *Modernity and the Holocaust* (Ithaca, NY: Cornell
    University Press).
Bennett, Christopher (1995), *Yugoslavia's Bloody Collapse: Causes, Course and
    Consequences* (New York: New York University Press).
Bernstein, Matthew and Gaylyn Studlar (eds) (1997), *Visions of the East:
    Orientalism in Film* (New Brunswick, NJ: Rutgers University Press).
Bhabha, Homi K. (ed.) (1990), *Nation and Narration* (New York and London:
    Routledge).
Bhabha, Homi K. (1994), *The Location of Culture* (London and New York:
    Routledge).
Boyle, Francis A. (1996), *The Bosnian People Charge Genocide* (Amherst, MA:
    Aletheia Press).
Bozhkov, Atanas (1969), *Die bulgarische Malerei, von den Anfangen bis zum 19.
    Jahrhundert* (Recklinghausen: A. Bongers).
Brewer, Bob (1992), *My Albania: Ground Zero* (Brooklyn: Lion of Tepelena Press
    Inc.).
Bringa, Tone (1996), *Being Muslim the Bosnian Way: Identity and Commmunity in
    a Central Bosnian Village* (Princeton, NJ: Princeton University Press).
Brinton, William M. and Alan Rinzler (eds) (1990), *Without Force or Lies: Voices
    from the Revolution of Central Europe in 1989–90* (San Francisco: Mercury
    House).
Brodsky, Joseph (1993), 'Blood, Lies and the Trigger of History', *The New York
    Times*, 4 August, p. A/19.
Cataldi, Anna (1994), *Letters from Sarajevo: Voices of a Besieged City*. Translated by
    Avril Bardoni (Rockport, MA: Element).
Cerović, Stanko (1995), 'Canned Lies', August. Available at:
    http://www.barnsdle.demon.co.uk/bosnia/caned.html

Clifford, James (1997), *Routes: Travel and Translation in the Late Twentieth Century* (Cambridge, MA: Harvard University Press).

Codrescu, Andrei (1990), *The Disappearance of the Outside: A Manifesto for Escape* (Reading, MA: Addison-Wesley).

Codrescu, Andrei (1991), *The Hole in the Flag: A Romanian Exile's Story of Return and Revolution* (New York: Avon Books).

Codrescu, Andrei (1993), *Road Scholar: Coast to Coast Late in the Century* (New York: Hyperion).

Codrescu, Andrei (1995), *The Blood Countess* (New York: Simon & Schuster).

Cohen, Lenard J. (1993), *Broken Bonds: The Disintegration of Yugoslavia* (Boulder, CO: Westview).

Cohen, Roger (1995), 'A Balkan Gyre of War, Spinning onto Film', *The New York Times*, 12 March, sect. 2, p. 1.

Colović, Ivan (1994a), *Bordel ratnika. Folklor, politika i rat* (Beograd: Biblioteka XX Vek).

Colović, Ivan (1994b), 'Die Erneuerung des Vergangenen. Zeit und Raum in der zeitgenossischen politischen Mythologie', in Nenad Stefanov and Michael Wertz (eds), *Bosnien und Europa. Die Ethnisierung der Gesellschaft* (Frankfurt am Main: Fischer), pp. 90–104.

Condee, Nancy (ed.) (1995), *Soviet Hieroglyphics: Visual Culture in Late Twentieth-Century Russia* (Bloomington and Indianapolis: Indiana University Press).

Crnobrnja, Mihailo (1996), *The Yugoslav Drama*, 2nd Ed. (Montreal and Kingston: McGill-Queen's University Press).

Crowe, David and John Kolsti (eds) (1991) *The Gypsies of Eastern Europe* (Armonk, NY: M. E. Sharpe).

Cunningham, Stuart and Elizabeth Jacka (1996), *Australian Television and International Mediascapes* (Cambridge and New York: Cambridge University Press).

Cushman, Tom and Stjepan Mestrović (eds) (1996), *This Time We Knew: Western Responses to the Genocide in Bosnia* (New York: New York University Press).

Daković, Nevena (1996/7), 'Mother, Myth, and Cinema: Recent Yugoslav Cinema', *Film Criticism*, Vol. 21, No. 2, Winter, pp. 40–50.

Daković, Nevena (1998), 'B(alkan) B(orders) or the Images and Dilemmas from the Fringes', manuscript.

Daković, Nevena, Deniz Derman and Karen Ross (eds) (1996), *Gender and Media* (Ankara: Mediation).

Davis, Scott (ed.) (1996), *Religion and Justice in the War over Bosnia* (New York and London: Routledge).

Demick, Barbara (1996), *Logavina Street: Life and Death in a Sarajevo Neighborhood* (Kansas City: Andrews and McMeel).

Di Giovanni, Janine (1994), *The Quick and the Dead: Under Siege in Sarajevo* (London: Phoenix House).

Dimitrov, Georgi (1986), *Against Fascism and War* (New York: International Publishers).

Dizdarević, Zlatko (1993), *Sarajevo: A War Journal.* Translated from the French by Anselm Hollo (New York: Fromm International).

Dizdarević, Zlatko (1994), *Portraits of Sarajevo.* Translated by Midhad Ridjanovic (New York: Fromm International).

Downing, John (ed.) (1989), *Film and Politics in the Third World* (Westport, CT: Praeger).

Dragojević, Srdjan (1996/7), 'Shame, Rage, and Nothing: An Interview', *Balkan Media*, Vol. 5, No. 4, Winter, p. 16 (reprinted from *Vreme*, Belgrade).

Drakulić, Slavenka (1991), *How We Survived Communism and Even Laughed* (New York: Harper Perennial).

Drakulić, Slavenka (1993a), *Balkan Express: Fragments from the Other Side of the War* (New York and London: W. W. Norton & Company).

Drakulić, Slavenka (1993b), 'Women Hide behind a Wall of Silence: Mass Rape in Bosnia', *The Nation*, 1 March, Vol. 256, No. 8, pp. 253–8.

Drakulić, Slavenka (1996), *Cafe Europa: Life after Communism* (London: Abacus).

Drakulić, Slavenka (1997), *The Taste of a Man.* Translated by Christina Pribichevich-Zorich (London: Abacus).

Economopoulos, Nikos/Magnum Photos (1995), *In the Balkans.* Photographs (New York: Harry Abrams, Inc.).

Enzensberger, Hans Magnus (1989), *Europe, Europe: Forays into a Continent.* Translated from the German by Martin Chalmers (New York: Pantheon Books).

Enzensberger, Hans Magnus (1993), *Civil Wars: From LA to Bosnia* (New York: The New Press).

FAMA (1993), *Sarajevo: A Survival Guide.* Written in Sarajevo/Published for the World. Printed in Croatia, distributed by Workman Publishing.

Fearon, James D. and David D. Laitin (1996), 'Explaining Interethnic Cooperation', *American Political Science Review*, Vol. 90, No. 4, December, pp. 715–35.

Felman, Shoshana and Dori Laub, MD (1992), *Testimony. Crises of Witnessing in Literature, Psychoanalysis, and History* (New York and London: Routledge).

Filipović, Zlata (1994), *Zlata's Diary: A Child's Life in Sarajevo.* Translated by Christina Pribichevich-Zoric (New York: Viking).

Finkielkraut, Alain (1995), 'L'Imposture Kusturica', *Le Monde*, 2 June.

Finkielkraut, Alain (1999), *Dispatches from the Balkan War and other Writings.* Translated by Peter S. Rogers and Richard Golsan (Lincoln: University of Nebraska Press).

Fonseca, Isabel (1995), *Bury Me Standing: The Gypsies and Their Journey* (New York: Random House).

Fraser, Angus (1992), *Gypsies* (Oxford: Blackwell).

Friedman, Lester D. (ed.) (1992), *Unspeakable Images: Ethnicity and the American Cinema* (Urbana and Chicago: University of Illinois Press).

Friedman, Victor A. (1996), 'Observing the Observers: Language, Ethnicity, and Power in the 1994 Macedonian Census and Beyond', in *Toward Comprehensive Peace in South East Europe. Conflict Prevention in the South Balkans* (New York: The Twentieth Century Fund Press), pp.81–107.

Friedman, Victor A. (2000), 'Fable as History: The Macedonian Context', *Rethinking History*, Vol. 4, No. 2, Summer, pp. 135–47.

Funk, Nanette and Martha Müller (eds) (1993), *Gender Politics and Post-Communism: Reflections from Eastern Europe and the Former Soviet Union* (New York and London: Routledge).

Galtung, J. and R. C. Vincent (1992), *Global Glasnost: Toward a New World Information and Communication Order?* (Cresskill, NJ: Hampton Press).

Garton Ash, Timothy (1989), *The Uses of Adversity: Essays on the Fate of Central Europe* (New York: Random House).

Garton Ash, Timothy (1990), *The Magic Lantern: The Revolution of '89 Witnessed in Warsaw, Budapest, Berlin, and Prague* (New York: Random House).

Germani, Sergio Grmek (ed.) (2000), *La meticcia di fuoco. Oltre il continente Balkani* (Turin: Lindau).

Gillespie, Marie (1995), *Television, Ethnicity, and Cultural Change* (London and New York: Routledge).

Gilroy, Paul (1993), *The Black Atlantic: Modernity and Double Consciousness* (London: Verso).

Gjelten, Tom (1995), *Sarajevo Daily: A City and Its Newspaper Under Siege* (New York: HarperCollins).

Glenny, Misha (1990), *The Rebirth of History: Eastern Europe in the Age of Democracy* (London: Penguin).

Glenny, Misha (1992), *The Fall of Yugoslavia: The Third Balkan War* (London: Penguin).

Glenny, Misha (1999), *The Balkans 1804–1999: Nationalism, War, and the Great Powers* (London: Granta).

Goff, Peter (ed.) (1999), *The Kosovo News and Propaganda War* (Vienna: International Press Institute).

Goldsworthy, Vesna (1998), *Inventing Ruritania: The Imperialism of the Imagination* (New Haven and London: Yale University Press).

Gopnik, Adam (1996), 'Cinéma Disputé', *The New Yorker*, 5 February, pp. 32–7.

Gordy, Eric D. (1999), *The Culture of Power in Serbia: Nationalism and the*

Destruction of Alternatives (University Park: Pennsylvania State University Press).

Goulding, Daniel J. (1985), *Liberated Cinema. The Yugoslav Experience* (Bloomington and Indianapolis: Indiana University Press).

Goulding, Daniel J. (ed.) (1989), *Post New-Wave Cinema in the Soviet Union and Eastern Europe* (Bloomington and Indianapolis: Indiana University Press).

Goulding, Daniel J. (ed.) (1994), *Five Filmmakers. Tarkovsky, Forman, Polanski, Szabó, Makavejev* (Bloomington and Indianapolis: Indiana University Press).

Goulding, Daniel J. (1998), *Occupation in 26 Pictures* (Trowbridge, Wiltshire: Flicks Books).

Goulding, Daniel J. (ed.) (2001), *The Cinema of Eastern Europe since 1989* (Trowbridge, Wiltshire: Flicks Books).

Gow, James, Richard Paterson and Alison Preston (eds) (1996), *Bosnia by Television* (London: BFI).

Goytisolo, Juan (1993), *Cuaderno de Sarajevo: Anotaciones de un viaje a la barbarie* (Madrid: El Pais).

Graubard, Stephen R. (ed.) (1992), *Eastern Europe ... Central Europe ... Europe* (Boulder, CO: Westview).

Grbić, Bogdan, Gabriel Loidot and Rossen Milev (eds) (1995), *Die siebte Kunst auf dem Pulverfass. Balkan Film* (Graz: Edition Blimp).

Grzimek, Martin (1995), *Mostar. Skizzen und Splitter. Ein literarisches tagebuch vom 12. bis 26. November 1994* (Heidelberg: HVA).

Gutman, Roy (1993), *A Witness to Genocide* (New York: Macmillan).

Hadjimichalis, Costis and David Sadler (eds) (1995), *Europe at the Margins: New Mosaics of Inequality* (New York: John Wiley & Sons).

Hall, Brian (1994), *The Impossible Country: A Journey through the Last Days of Yugoslavia* (London: Penguin).

Hall, Stuart (1992), 'European Cinema on the Verge of a Nervous Breakdown' in D. Petrie (ed.), *Screening Europe. Image and Identity in Contemporary European Cinema* (London: BFI), pp. 45–53.

Hall, Stuart and Bram Gieben (eds) (1992), *Formations of Modernity* (Milton Keynes: Open University Press).

Hancock, Ian (1987), *The Pariah Syndrome: An Account of Gypsy Slavery and Persecution* (Ann Arbor, MI: Karoma Publishers).

Handke, Peter (1997), *A Journey to the Rivers. Justice for Serbia*. Translated by Scott Abbott (New York: Viking).

Haraszty, Miklos (1987), *The Velvet Prison: Artists under State Socialism*. Translated from the Hungarian by Katalin and Stephen Landesmann (New York: Basic Books).

Hartmann, Florence (1995), 'La Production d'Underground et ses zones d'ombre. L'embargo sur la Serbie aurait été violé,' *Le Monde*, 26 October.

Haskell, Molly (1974), *From Reverence to Rape: The Treatment of Women in the Movies* (Baltimore: Penguin).

Havel, Vaclav (1985), *The Power of the Powerless: Citizens against the State in Central-Eastern Europe* (Armonk, NY: M. E. Sharpe).

Havel, Vaclav (1987), *Living in Truth* (London and Boston: Faber and Faber).

Havel, Vaclav (1990), *Disturbing the Peace: A Conversation with Karel Hvizdala*. Translated from the Czech and with an introduction by Paul Wilson (New York: Knopf).

Havel, Vaclav (1992), *Summer Meditations*. Translated from the Czech by Paul Wilson (New York: Knopf).

Hayden, Robert M. (1996), 'Schindler's Fate: Genocide, Ethnic Cleansing, and Population Transfers', *Slavic Review*, Vol. 55, No. 4, Winter, pp. 727–49.

Hayden, Robert M. (2000), 'Rape and Rape Avoidance in Ethno-National Conflicts: Sexual Violence in Liminalized States', *American Anthropologist*, Vol. 102, No. 1, (March), pp. 27–41.

Herzfeld, Michael (1987), *Anthropology through the Looking-Glass. Critical Ethnography in the Margins of Europe* (New York: Cambridge University Press).

Hoberman, J. (1997), 'Lost Worlds', *The Village Voice*, 24 June, p. 75.

Holloway, Ronald (1985), *Slovenian Film. Slovenian Post-War Cinema, 1945–1985* (Berlin: Kino. Special Issue with Cleveland Cinematheque).

Holloway, Ronald (1986), *The Bulgarian Cinema* (Rutherford, NJ: Fairleigh Dickinson University Press; London: Associated Presses).

Holloway, Ronald (1996), *Macedonian Film. A History of Macedonian Cinema, 1905–1996* (Berlin: Kino. Special Issue with Cinematheque of Macedonia).

Horton, Andrew (ed.) (1991) *Comedy/Cinema/Theory* (Berkeley: University of California Press).

Horton, Andrew (1995), ' "Only Crooks Can Get Ahead": Post-Yugoslav Cinema/TV/Video in the 1990s', in Sabrina P. Ramet and Ljubisa S. Adamovic (eds), *Beyond Yugoslavia: Politics, Economics and Culture in a Shattered Community* (Boulder, CO: Westview) pp. 413–31.

Horton, Andrew (1997a), *The Films of Theo Angelopoulos: A Cinema of Contemplation* (Princeton, NJ: Princeton University Press).

Horton, Andrew (ed.) (1997b), *The Last Modernist. The Films of Theo Angelopoulos* (Westport, CT: Praeger).

Huffman, Kathy Rae (1998), 'Video from Bosnia: A Meeting Point of Memory and Reality', *Convergence*, Vol. 4, No. 2, Summer, pp. 102–10.

Hukanović, Rezak (1996), *The Tenth Circle of Hell: Memoir of Life in the Death Camps of Bosnia* (New York: Basic Books).

Hundley, Tom (1997), 'Balkan Reform Crippled by Communist Past, Impoverished Present', *Chicago Tribune*, 16 February, Section 2, p. 8.

Huntington, Samuel P. (1993), 'The Clash of Civilizations?' *Foregn Affairs*, Vol. 72, No. 3, August, pp. 22–50.

Huntington, Samuel P. (1996), *The Clash of Civilizations and the Remaking of World Order* (New York: Simon & Schuster).

Hupchick, Dennis P. (1995), *Conflict and Chaos in Eastern Europe* (New York: St Martin's Press).

Ignatieff, Michael (1993), *Blood and Belonging. Journeys into the New Nationalism* (New York: Farrar, Straus & Giroux).

Ignatieff, Michael (1995), 'The Seductiveness of Moral Disgust', *Social Research*, Vol. 62, No. 1, pp. 77-98, Spring.

Insdorf, Annette (1983), *Indelible Shadows: Film and the Holocaust* (New York: Vintage Books).

Iordanova, Dina (1995), 'Media Coverage of Bulgaria in the West and Its Domestic Use', in Fred Casmir (ed.), *Communication in Eastern Europe: The Role of History, Culture, and Media in Contemporary Conflicts* (Mahwah, NJ: Lawrence Earlbaum), pp. 223–54.

Iordanova, Dina (1996), 'Conceptualizing the Balkans in Film', *Slavic Review*, Vol. 55, No. 1, Winter, pp. 882–91.

Iordanova, Dina (1996/7), 'Women in New Balkan Cinema: Surviving on the Margins', *Film Criticism*, Vol. 21, No. 2. Winter, pp. 24–40.

Iordanova, Dina (1998), 'Balkans Revisited', *Canadian Slavonic Papers*, Vol. 33, Nos. 3–4, pp. 479–89.

Iordanova, Dina (1998a), 'Balkan Film Representations since 1989: The Quest for Admissibility', *Historical Journal of Film, Radio and Television*, Vol. 18, No. 2, pp. 263–80.

Iordanova, Dina (1998b), 'Canaries and Birds of Prey: The New Season of Bulgarian Cinema', in John D. Bell (ed.), *Bulgaria in Transition* (Boulder, CO: Westview), pp. 255–77.

Iordanova, Dina (1998c), 'Balkan Wedding Revisited: Multiple Meanings of Filmed Nuptials', (Minneapolis: Center for Austrian Studies, University of Minnesota, October) pp. 1-18.

Iordanova, Dina (1999a), 'Kusturica's *Underground*: Historical Allegory or Propaganda?' *Historical Journal of Film, Radio and Television*, Vol. l9, No. l, March, pp. 69–86.

Iordanova, Dina (1999b), 'Political Resentment Versus Cultural Submission: The Duality of US Representations in Bulgarian Media' in Yahia Kamalipour (ed.), *US Image and World Media: A Multicultural Perspective* (Albany: SUNY Press) pp. 71–87.

Iordanova, Dina (1999c), 'East Europe's Cinema Industries since 1989: Financing Structure and Studios', *Javnost/The Public*, Vol. 6, No. 2, pp. 45–60.

Iordanova, Dina (1999d), 'College Course File: Eastern European Cinema', *Journal of Film and Video*, Vol. 51, No. 1, Spring, pp. 56–77.

Iordanova, Dina (1999e), 'Expanding Universe: from the Ethnic Foodstore to Blockbuster', *Framework: The Journal of Cinema and Media*, Vol. 41, pp. 54-70.

Iordanova, Dina (2000a), 'Are the Balkans Admissible? The Discourse on Europe', *Balkanistica*, Vol. 13, pp. 1–35.

Iordanova, Dina (2000b), '*Before the Rain* in a Balkan Context', *Rethinking History*, Vol. 4, No. 2, pp.149–58.

Iordanova, Dina (2000c), 'The Cinema of the Dispersed Yugoslavs: Diasporas in the Making', *CineAction*, Vol. 52 (Toronto), pp. 69–72.

Iordanova, Dina, Richard Taylor, Julan Graffy and Nancy Wood (eds) (2000), *BFI's Companion to Eastern European and Russian Cinema* (London: BFI).

Istrati, Panait (1926), *Kyra Kyralina* (New York: Alfred Knopf).

Jones, Lloyd (1993), *Biografi: A Traveler's Tale* (San Diego, New York and London: Harcourt Brace & Co.).

Judah, Tim (1997), *The Serbs: History, Myth, and the Destruction of Yugoslavia* (New Haven and London: Yale University Press).

Kadare, Ismail (1990), *The Palace of Dreams* (1981). Translated from the French by Barbara Bray (New York: William Morrow & Co).

Kadare, Ismail (1995), *Albanian Spring. The Anatomy of Tyranny* (1991). Translated from the French by Emile Capouya (London: Saqi Books).

Kadare, Ismail (1996), *The Pyramid*. Translated by David Bellos from the French version of the Albanian by Jusuf Vrioni (London: Harvill Press).

Kaplan, Robert (1993), *Balkan Ghosts: A Journey through History* (New York: Vintage).

Karahasan, Dzevad (1994), *Sarajevo, Exodus of a City*. Translated by Slobodan Drakulic (New York, Tokyo and London: Kodansha Intternational).

Kazantzakis, Nikos (1952), *Zorba the Greek* (1946). Translated by Carl Wildman (New York: Simon & Schuster).

Kellner, Douglas (1992), *The Persian Gulf TV War* (Boulder, CO: Westview).

Khan, Irshad Ulla (1994), *The Peace Poems: Sarajevo, Kashmir and Other Poems* (Islamabad: Manza Press).

Kinder, Marsha (1993), *Blood Cinema: The Reconstruction of National Identity in Spain* (Berkeley: University of California Press).

Kligman, Gail (1988), *The Wedding of the Dead: Ritual, Poetics, and Popular Culture in Transylvania* (Berkeley: University of California Press).

Knežević, Dubravka (1996), 'Marked with Red Ink', *Theatre Journal*, Vol. 48, No. 4, December, pp. 407–19.

Kolar-Panov, Dona (1997), *Video, War and the Diasporic Imagination* (London and New York: Routledge).

Kolar-Panov, Dona (1999), 'Broadcasting in Macedonia: Between the State and the Market', *Media Development*, Vol. 3, pp. 33–40.

Koliodimos, Dimitris (1999), *The Greek Filmography, 1914 through 1996* (New York: McFarland & Company).

Konrád, George (1995), *The Melancholy of Rebirth: Essays from Post-Communist Central Europe, 1989–1994* (Orlando: Harcourt Brace & Co.).

Konstantinov, Aleko (1985), *Bay Ganyo, Canadian Slavic Studies*, Vol. 3, No. 1 (Spring 1969), pp. 116–120; No. 3 (Autumn 1969), pp. 553–5; No. 4 (Winter 1969), pp. 712–15; Vol. 5, No. 1 (Spring 1971), pp. 70–84; No. 2 (Summer 1971), pp. 234–38 and No. 3 (Autumn 1971), pp. 401–09.

Kulenovic, Tvrtko (1996), 'The History of an Illness', *Stone Soup*, Vol. 14, No. 2, pp. 38–43. Translated by Celia Hawkesworth.

Kusturica, Emir (1995), 'Mon imposture', *Le Monde*, 26 October.

Lampe, John R. (1996), *Yugoslavia as History: Twice There Was a Country* (New York: Cambridge University Press).

Lemon, Alaina (1998), 'Roma (Gypsies) in the Soviet Union and the Moscow Teatr "Romen"', in Diane Tong (ed.), *Gypsies: An Interdisciplinary Reader* (New York: Garland), pp. 147–67.

Lenkova, Mariana (ed.) (1998), *Hate Speech in the Balkans* (Athens: Greek Helsinki Monitor).

Lešić, Zdenko (ed.) (1995), *Children of Atlantis: Voices from the Former Yugoslavia* (Budapest, London and New York: Central European University Press).

Levinson, Florence Hamelish (1994), *Belgrade: Among the Serbs* (Chicago: Ivan R. Dee).

Liehm, Mira and Antonín J. Liehm (1977), *The Most Important Art: Eastern European film after 1945* (Berkeley: University of California Press).

Maass, Peter (1996), *Love Thy Neighbor: A Study of War* (New York: Alfred Knopf).

MacDougall, David (1998), *Transcultural Cinema* (Princeton: Princeton University Press).

Makavejev, Dušan (1993), 'Call in Professionals to End Yugoslav Natural Disaster', *The Times* (London), 9 August.

Malcolm, Derek (1995), 'The Surreal Sarajevan Dreamer', *Guardian*, 29 June.

Malcolm, Derek (1988), 'That's It, I Resign; Pass the Popocorn', *Guardian*, 17 September, p. G2/11.

Malcolm, Noel (1994), *Bosnia: A Short History* (New York: New York University Press).

Malcolm, Noel (1988), *Kosovo: A Short History* (New York: New York University Press).

Manchevski, Milcho (2000), 'Rainmaking and Personal Truth', *Rethinking History*, Vol. 4, No. 2, Summer, pp. 129–35.

Marushiakova, Elena and Vesselin Popov (1995), *The Gypsies of Bulgaria: Problems of the Multicultural Museum Exhibition* (Sofia: Club 90 Publishers).

The Media Happened to Be There (1994) (Pale: Republic of Srpska).

Meehan, Thomas (1971), 'The Last Word: Notes on Drubnik', *The New Yorker*, 21 November, p. 87.

Mehmedinović, Semezdin (1998), *Sarajevo Blues*. Translated by Ammiel Alcalay (San Francisco: City Lights).

Merrill, Christopher (1995), *The Old Bridge: The Third Balkan War and the Age of the Refugee* (Minneapolis: Milkweed).

Mertus, Julie, Jasmina Tešanović, Habiba Metikos and Rada Borić (eds) (1997), *The Suitcase: Refugee Voices from Bosnia and Croatia* (Berkeley: University of California Press).

Mestrović, Stjepan G. (1993a), *The Barbarian Temperament: Toward a Postmodern Critical Theory* (London and New York: Routledge).

Mestrović, Stjepan G. (1993b), *Habits of the Balkan Heart. Social Character and the Fall of Communism* (College Station, TX: Texas A&M University Press).

Michnik, Adam (1985), *Letters from Prison and Other Essays* (Berkeley: University of California Press).

Mihailović, Dragoslav (1971), *When Pumpkins Blossomed* (New York: Harcourt Brace Jovanovich).

Milev, Rossen (ed.) (1995), *Radio auf dem Balkan. Zur Entwicklung des Hörfunks in Südosteuropa* (Hamburg: Hans-Bredow-Institut, Vol. 16).

Milev, Rossen (ed.) (1996), *TV auf dem Balkan. Zur Entwicklung des Fernsehens in Südosteuropa* (Hamburg: Hans-Bredow-Institut, Vol. 17).

Mladenović, Lepa (1995), 'Where Do I Come From', *Index on Censhorship*, Vol. 4, pp. 72–5.

Mousavizadeh, Nader (ed.) (1996), *The Black Book of Bosnia: The Consequences of Appeasement. 1992/1995* (New York: A New Republic Book).

Naficy, Hamid (1993), *The Making of Exile Cultures: Iranian Television in Los Angeles* (Minneapolis: University of Minnesota Press).

Naficy, Hamid (ed.) (1999), *Home, Exile, Homeland: Film, Media, and the Politics of Place* (New York and London: Routledge).

Naficy, Hamid and Teshome H. Gabriel (eds) (1993), *Otherness and the Media: The Ethnography of the Imagined and the Imaged* (Langhorne, PA: Harwood Academic Publishers).

Niarchos, Catherine N. (1995), 'Women, War, and Rape: Challenges Facing the International Tribunal for the Former Yugoslavia', *Human Rights Quarterly*, Vol. 17, No. 4, November, pp. 649–90.

Norris, David A. (1999), *In the Wake of the Balkan Myth: Questions of Identity and Modernity* (New York: St Martin's Press).

Ong, Aihwa (1999), *Flexible Citizenship: The Cultural Logic of Transnationality* (Durham, NC: Duke University Press).

Oudran, Remy (1995), 'Emir Kusturica, le surdoue de la camera', *Agence France Presse*, 28 May.

Owen, Lord David (1995), *Balkan Odyssey* (New York: Harcourt Brace).

Paletz, David L., Karol Jakubowicz and Pavao Novosel (eds) (1995), *Glasnost and After: Media and Change in Central and Eastern Europe* (Cresskill, NJ: Hampton Press).

Pamuk, Orhan (1991), *The White Castle* (New York: Braziller).

Passek, Jean-Loup and Zoran Tasic (1986), *Le Cinema Yugoslave* (Paris: Centre Pompidou).

Paterson, Chris (1997), 'International Television News Agency Coverage of Conflict', *Journal of International Communication*, Vol. 4, No. 1, Summer, pp. 50-66.

Paul, David W. (ed.) (1983), *Politics, Art and Commitment in the East European Cinema* (New York: St Martin's Press).

Pauli, Harald (1996), 'Verzichtsgelübde & Magengeschwüre,' *Focus Magazin*, 21 December, Vol. 52, pp. 134–6.

Pavić, Milorad (1988), *Dictionary of the Khazars: A Lexicon Novel in 100,000 Words*. Translated from the Serbo-Croatian by Christina Pribicevic-Zoric (New York: Alfred Knopf).

Petrie, Duncan (ed.) (1992), *Screening Europe: Image and Identity in Contemporary European Cinema* (London: BFI).

Pflaum, H. G. (1995), 'In der Falle der Geschichte', an interview with Emir Kusturica, *Süddeutsche Zeitung*, 23 November, p. 16.

Pomfret, John (1996), 'The Shots Seen round the World: A Serb Director's Searing Take on Yugoslavia's Uncivil War', *The Washington Post*, 21 November, p. C1.

Poulton, Hugh (1991), *The Balkans: Minorities and States in Conflict* (London: Minority Rights Group).

Poulton, Hugh (1994), *The Southern Balkans?* (London: Minority Rights Group).

Poulton, Hugh (1995), *Who Are the Macedonians?* (London: Hurst & Company).

Radojcić, Svetozar (1969), *Geschichte der serbischen Kunst: von den Anfangen bis zum Ende des Mittelalters* (Berlin: De Gruyter).

Ramet, Sabrina Petra (1992), *Balkan Babel: The Disintegration of Yugoslavia from the Death of Tito to Ethnic War* (Boulder, CO: Westview); rev. ed. 1996.

Reed, Fred (1996), *Salonica Terminus: Travels into the Balkan Nightmare* (Burnaby, BC: Talonbooks).

Rezun, Miron (1995), *Europe and the War in the Balkans: Toward a New Yugoslav Identity* (Westport, CT, and London: Praeger).

Rieff, David (1995), *Slaughterhouse: Bosnia and the Failure of the West* (New York: Simon & Schuster).

Rihtman-Augustin, Dunja (1997), 'Zasto i otkad se grozimo Balkana?' *Erasmus*, Vol. 19 (Zagreb) pp. 18-29.

Robinson, David (1996), 'A Tunnel Vision of War: An Interview with Emir Kusturica', *The Times*, 5 March.

Robinson, Gertrude (1977), *Tito's Maverick Media: The Politics of Mass Communication* (Chicago: University of Illinois Press).

Rosenstone, Robert (1995a), *Visions of the Past: The Challenge of Film to Our Idea of History* (Cambridge and London: Harvard University Press).

Rosenstone, Robert (1995b), 'The Historical Film as Real History', *Film-Historia*, Vol. 5, No. 1, pp. 5–23.

Rosenstone, Robert (1998), 'The Future of the Past: Film and the Beginnings of Postmodern History', in Vivian Sobchack (ed.), *The Persistence of History: Cinema, Television, and the Modern Event* (London and New York: Routledge), pp. 201–19.

Rosenstone, Robert (2000), Editorial and 'A History of What Has Not Yet Happened', *Rethinking History,* Vol. 4, No. 2, Summer, pp. 123–6, 183–93.

Roth, Joseph (1974), *The Radetzky March* (Woodstock, NY: Overlook Press).

Rupnik, Jacques (1990), *The Other Europe* (Paris: Odile Jacob).

Russell, Alec (1993), *Prejudice and Plum Brandy: Tales of a Balkan Stringer* (London: Michael Joseph).

Said, Edward W. (1978), *Orientalism* (New York: Vintage Books); rev. ed. 1994.

Said, Edward W. (1981), *Covering Islam: How the Media and the Experts Determine How We See the Rest of the World* (New York: Pantheon Books); rev. ed. 1997.

Salecl, Renata (1994), *The Spoils of Freedom: Psychoanalysis and Feminism after the Fall of Socialism* (London and New York: Routledge).

Samary, Catherine (1995), *Yugoslavia Dismembered.* Translated from the French by Peter Frucker (New York: Monthly Review Press).

Sarajevo: A Portrait of the Siege (1994). Produced by Matthew Naythons (Sausalito: Warner Bros., Inc.).

Scherzer, Dina (ed.) (1996), *Cinema, Colonialism, Postcolonialism: Perspectives from the French and Frankophone Worlds* (Austin: University of Texas Press).

Schiffer, Daniel (1993), *Requiem pour l'Europe: Zagreb. Belgrade. Sarajevo* (Paris: L'Age d'homme).

Schuster, Mel (1979), *The Contemporary Greek Cinema* (Metuchen, NJ: Scarecrow).

Sells, Michael (1996), *Bridge Betrayed: Religion and Genocide in Bosnia* (Berkeley: University of California Press).

Shohat, Ella (1989), *Israeli Cinema: East/West and the Politics of Representation* (Austin: University of Texas Press).

Shohat, Ella and Robert Stam (1994), *Unthinking Eurocentrism: Multiculturalism and the Media* (London and New York: Routledge).

Silber, Laura and Allan Little (1995), *The Death of Yugoslavia* (London: Penguin/BBC Books; New York: Penguin).

Simpson, John (1998), *Strange Places, Questionable People* (London: Macmillan).

Slapšak, Svetlana (1997), 'What Are Women Made of? Inventing Women in the Yugoslav Arena', in Gisela Brinkler-Gabler and Sidonie Smith (eds), *Writing New Identities: Gender, Nation, and Immigration in Contemporary Europe* (Minneapolis: University of Minnesota Press), pp. 358–73.

Slater, Thomas J. (ed.) (1992), Handbook of Soviet and East European Films and Filmmakers (New York and London: Greenwood Press).

Smale, Alison (1993), ' "Decline of the Century": Searing Movie Sums up Generations of Yugoslav Hell', *Agence France-Presse*, 25 November.

Softić, Elma (1995), *Sarajevo Days, Sarajevo Nights* (Minneapolis: Hungry Mind Press).

Sontag, Susan (1993), 'Godot Comes to Sarajevo', *New York Review of Books*, 21 October, Vol. 40, No. 17, pp. 85–91.

Sontag, Susan (1994), 'Waiting for Godot in Sarajevo', *Performing Arts Journal*, Vol. 16, No. 2, May, pp. 87–107.

Sontag, Susan (1995), 'A Lament for Bosnia', *The Nation*, 25 December, Vol. 261, No. 22, pp. 818–21.

Splichal, Slavko (1994), *Media beyond Socialism: Theory and Practice in East-Central Europe* (Boulder, CO, San Francisco and Oxford: Westview).

Stefanov, Nenad and Michael Wertz (eds) (1994), *Bosnien und Europa: Die Ethnisierung der Gesellschaft* (Frankfurt am Main: Fischer).

Stewart, Michael (1997), *The Time of the Gypsies* (Boulder, CO: Westview).

Stiglmajer, Alexandra (ed.) (1991), *Mass Rape: The War against Women in Bosnia-Herzegovina*. Foreword by Roy Gutman (Lincoln: University of Nebraska Press).

Stoiciu, Gina and Dov Shinar (1992), 'Reality-Construction in Socio-Political Crisis: The Coverage of the Romanian Revolution in Western Media', *Communications*, Vol. 17, No. 1, pp. 57–65.

Stoil, M. J. (1974), *Cinema beyond the Danube: The Camera and the Politics* (Metuchen, NJ: Scarecrow Press).

Stoil, M. J. (1982), *Balkan Cinema: Evolution after the Revolution* (Ann Arbor: University of Michigan).

Stokes, Gale (1993), *The Walls Came Tumbling Down: The Collapse of Communism in Eastern Europe* (New York: Oxford University Press).

Stokes, Gale, John Lampe and Dennison Rusinow with Julie Mostov (1996),

'Instant History: Understanding the Wars of Yugoslav Succession', *Slavic Review*, Vol. 55, No. 1, Spring, pp. 136-60.

Szayna, Thomas S. (1994), *Ethnic Conflict in Central Europe and the Balkans: A Framework for US Policy Options* (Monterrey: RAND, Arroyo Center).

Tax, Meredith (1993), 'Five Women Who Won't Be Silenced: Croatia's "witches", (Slavenka Drakulić, Rada Iveković, Vesna Kešić, Jelena Lovrić and Dubravka Ugrešić)', *Nation*, 10 May, Vol. 256, No. 18, pp. 624–8.

Thompson, Mark (1992), *A Paper House: The Ending of Yugoslavia* (New York: Pantheon Books).

Thompson, Mark (1994), *Forging War: The Media in Serbia, Croatia, and Bosnia-Herzegovina* (London: Article 19); rev. ed: Luton: University of Luton Press, 1999.

Tismaneanu, Vladimir (1992), *Reinventing Politics: Eastern Europe from Stalin to Havel* (New York: Free Press).

Tisma, Alexander (1988), *The Use of Man* (San Diego: Harcourt Brace & Co).

Todorov, Tzvetan (1996), *Facing the Extreme: Moral Life in the Concentration Camps* (1992). (New York: Metropolitan Books), p. 376.

Todorova, Maria (1994), 'The Balkans: From Discovery to Invention', *Slavic Review*, Vol. 53, No. 2, Summer, pp. 453–83.

Todorova, Maria (1997), *Imagining the Balkans* (New York: Oxford University Press).

Todorova, Maria (1999), 'The Balkans: From Invention to Intervention?', 11 May, Talk at Columbia University, New York. Available at: http://www.692.net/casopis_rec/todorovaeng.html

Tong, Diane (1997), *Gypsies: A Multidisciplinary Annotated Bibliography* (Hamden, CT: Garland Publishers).

Trumpener, Katie (1992), 'The Time of the Gypsies: A "People without History" in the Narratives of the West', *Critical Inquiry*, Vol. 18, Summer, pp. 843–84.

Turan, Kenneth (1997a), 'Scenes of Despair from the Inside', *Los Angeles Times*, 5 October, p. 89.

Turan, Kenneth (1997b), 'Sarajevan's Journey from Cinema Hero to "Traitor"', *Los Angeles Times*, 6 October, p. F1.

Udovicki, Jasminka and James Ridgeway (eds) (1995), *Yugoslavia's Ethnic Nightmare: The Inside Story of Europe's Unfolding Ordeal* (Chicago: Lawrence Hill Books).

Ugrešić, Dubravka (1992), *In the Jaws of Life*. Translated by Celia Hawkesworth and Michael Henry Heim (London: Virago).

Ugrešić, Dubravka (1994), *Have a Nice Day. From the Balkan War to the American Dream*. Translated by Celia Hawkesworth (London: Jonathan Cape).

Ugrešić, Dubravka (1998), *The Culture of Lies: Antipolitical Essays*. Translated by Celia Hawkesworth (University Park, PA: Penn State University Press).

Vaculik, Ludvik (1987), *A Cup of Coffee with My Interrogator* (London: Readers International).

van de Port, Mathijis (1998), *Gypsies, Wars, and Other Instances of the Wild* (Amsterdam: University of Amsterdam Press).

Vasilikos, Vasiles (1968) *Z.* Translated from the Greek by Marilyn Calmann (New York, Farrar, Straus & Giroux).

Vehbiu, Adrian and Rando Devole (1995), *La scoperta dell'Albania: Gli albanesi secondo i mass media* (Roma: Paoline).

Virilio, Paul (1984), *War and Cinema: The Logistics of Perception* (London and New York: Verso).

Volcić, Demetrio (1993), *Sarajevo* (Milan: Mondadori).

Vollmer, Johannes (ed.) (1995), *'Daß wir in Bosnien zur Welt gehören.' Für ein multikulturelles Zusammenleben* (Solothurn und Düsseldorf: Benziger Verlag).

Vulliamy, Ed (1994), *Seasons in Hell: Understanding Bosnia's War* (New York: St Martin's Press).

Wachtel, Andrew Baruch (1998), *Making a Nation, Breaking a Nation: Literature and Cultural Politics in Yugoslavia* (Stanford, CA: Stanford University Press).

West, Rebecca (1993), *Black Lamb and Gray Falcon: A Journey through Yugoslavia* (1941) (New York: Penguin).

Wigger, Raimar (1995), *Verraten im Herzen Europas: Schicksale im Balkankrieg* (Frankfurt am Mein: Eichborn).

Winnifrith, T. J. (1995), *Shattered Eagles: Balkan Fragments* (London: Duckworth).

Wolff, Larry (1994), *Inventing Eastern Europe: The Map of Civilization on the Mind of the Enlightenment* (Berkeley: Stanford University Press).

Woodward, Susan L. (1995), *Balkan Tragedy: Chaos and Dissolution after the Cold War* (Washington, DC: The Brookings Institution).

Woodward, Susan L. (1997), 'It Depends on When You Start the Story: Narratives as Camouflage and the Political Use of Scholarship on the Yugoslav Wars, 1991–1996'. Paper presented at the workshop on *Doing History in the Shadow of the Balkan Wars* (Ann Arbor: University of Michigan, 17–18 January).

Young, Deborah (1994), 'Before the Rain', *Variety*, 12–18 September, p. 78.

Živković, Marko (1994), 'The Wish to Be a Jew or the Struggle over Appropriating the Symbolic Power of "Being A Jew" in the Yugoslav Conflict', *Ninth International Conference of Europeanists* (Chicago: University of Chicago, 31 March–2 April).

Živković, Marko (1998), 'Tender-Hearted Criminals and the Reverse Pygmalion: Narratives of the Balkan Male in Recent Serbian Films', *American Anthropological Association* (Philadelphia, December).

Živković, Marko (1999), 'Jelly, Slush and Red Mists: Poetics of Amorphous

Substances in Serbian Jeremiads of the 1990s', paper presented at the 'Views from Within' Conference, Columbia University, New York, 23 February 2000.

Žižek, Slavoj (1994), *The Metastases of Enjoyment* (London: Verso).

Žižek, Slavoj (1995), 'Multiculturalism, or the Cultural Logic of Multinational Capitalism', *New Left Review*, No. 225, September/October, pp. 28–52.

Filmography

Features
Feature Films from the Balkans

1922 (Greece, Nikos Kounduros, 1978)

Across the Lake/Preku erero (Macedonia/Poland, Antonio Mitrikeski, 1997)

After the End of the World/Sled kraya na sveta (Bulgaria/Greece/France, Ivan Nichev, 1998)

Alexander the Great/Megaleksandros (Greece, Theo Angelopoulos, 1980)

Ambush/Opsada (Yugoslavia, Branko Marjanović, 1956)

Anika's Times/Anikina vremena (Yugoslavia, Vladimir Pogačić, 1954)

Attached Balloon, The/Privarzaniyat balon (Bulgaria, Binka Zhelyazkova, 1967)

Aunt from Chicago, The/I theia apo to Sikago (Greece, Alekos Sakellarios, 1957)

Awakening of Spring, The/Budenje proleca (Yugoslavia, Gordana Boškov, 1993)

Awkward Age, The/Magarece godine (Bosnia-Herzegovina, Nenad Dizdarević, 1994)

Balkanizator/Valkanisateur (Greece/Bulgaria/Switzerland, Sotiris Goritzas, 1997)

Ballad of Kurbini/Balada e Kurbinit (Albania, Kujtim Çashku, 1990)

Barrel-Organ, Poverty, Dignity/Laterna ftoheia kai filotimo (Greece, Alekos Sakellarios, 1955)

Battle of Kosovo, The/Boj na Kosovu (Yugoslavia, Zdravko Šotra, 1989)

Battle of Neretva, The/Bitka na Neretvi (Yugoslavia/Italy/West Germany/UK, Veljko Bulajić, 1969)

Beekeeper, The/O Melissokomos (Greece/France/Italy, Theo Angelopoulos, 1986)

Before the Rain/Pred dozhdot (Macedonia/France/UK, Milcho Manchevski, 1994)

Black Swallow/Tchernata lyastovitsa (Bulgaria/France, George Dyulgerov, 1997)

Between Heaven and Earth/Ni na nebu ni na zemlji (Yugoslavia, Milos Radivojević, 1994)

Black Bomber/Crni bombarder (Yugoslavia, Darko Bajić, 1992)

Black Cat, White Cat/Crna macka, beli macor (Germany/France/Yugoslavia, Emir Kusturica, 1998)

Black Seed/Crno seme (Yugoslavia, Kiril Cenevski, 1971)

Bordello (Greece, Nikos Kounduros, 1985)

Border/Granitsa (Bulgaria, Ilian Simeonov/Hristo Nochev, 1995)

Boris I (Bulgaria, Borislav Sharaliev, 1984)
Boulevard Revolution/Bulevar revolucije(Yugoslavia, Vladimir Blaževski, 1992)
Bredel (Turkey, Atif Yilmaz Batibeki, 1990)
Burlesque Tragedy/Urnebesna tragedija (Yugoslavia/France/Bulgaria, Goran
    Marković, 1995)
Burn, Burn, Little Flame/Gori, gori, oganche (Bulgaria, Roumiana Petkova, 1994)
Cabaret Balkan a.k.a. *Powder Keg/Bure baruta/* (Yugoslavia/France, Goran
    Paskaljević, 1998)
Camp, The/Lagerat (Bulgaria, George Dyulgerov, 1990)
Canary Season/Sezonat na kanarchetata (Bulgaria, Evgeni Mikhailov, 1993)
Caruga/Charuga (Yugoslavia, Rajko Grlić, 1990)
Clickety-Clack/Traka-trak (Bulgaria, Iliya Kostov, 1996)
Conjugal Bed, The/Patul conjugal (Romania, Mircea Daneliuc, 1991)
The Dacians/Dacii (Romania, Sergiu Nicolaescu, 1966)
Dagger/Noz (Yugoslavia, Miroslav Lekić, 1999)
Dark Is the Night/Tamna je noc (Yugoslavia, Dragan Kresoja, 1995)
Day that Shook the World, The/Sarajevsky atentat (Yugoslavia, Veljko Bulajić,
    1975)
Days of '36/ Meres tu '36 (Greece, Theo Angelopoulos, 1972)
Days of AVNOI, The/Dani AVNOJ-a (Yugoslavia, Sava Mrmak, 1983)
Deserter, The/Dezerter (Yugoslavia, Zivojn Pavlović, 1992)
Diary of Insults 1993/Dnevnik uvreda 1993 (Yugoslavia, Zdravko Šotra, 1994)
Do You Remember Dolly Bell?/Sjecas li se Dolly Bell? (Yugoslavia, Emir Kusturica,
    1981)
Eagle 101/Vultur 101 (Romania, Andrei Calarasu, 1957)
Early Works/Rani radove (Yugoslavia, Želimir Žilnik, 1969)
Echelones, The/Eshelonite (Bulgaria, Borislav Punchev, 1986)
Eternity and a Day/Mia aiwniothta kai mia mera (Greece/France/Italy, Theo
    Angelopoulos, 1998)
Evening Bells/Vecerna zvona(Yugoslavia, Lordan Zafranović, 1986)
Fall of Italy, The/Pad Italije (Yugoslavia, Lordan Zafranović, 1981)
Fifth Offensive, The/Sutjeska (Yugoslavia, Stipe Delić, 1973)
Film with No Name/Za sada bez dobrog naslova (Yugoslavia, Srdjan Karanović,
    1988)
Forest of the Hanged/ Padurea spînzuratilor (Romania, Luviu Ciulei, 1964)
From the Snow/Ap to hioni (Greece, Sotiris Goritzas, 1993)
Frontier Post/Zastava (Yugoslavia, Branko Marjanović, 1949)
Gentleman for a Day/Gospodin za edin den (Bulgaria, Nikolay Volev, 1983)
Goat's Horn, The/Koziyat rog (Bulgaria, Metodi Andonov, 1972)
Goat's Horn, The/Koziyat rog (Bulgaria, Nikolay Volev, 1994)
Gospa (Croatia/Canada/USA, Jacov Sedlar, 1993)

Guardian Angel/Andejo cuvar (Yugoslavia, Goran Paskaljević, 1987)

Gypsy, A/Ciganka (Yugoslavia, Voja Nanović, 1953)

Gypsy Magic (Macedonia/France, Stole Popov, 1997)

Hades/Adis (Greece, Stelios Haralambopoulos, 1996)

Hanka (Yugoslavia, Slavko Vorkapić, 1955)

Hawk, The/Neamul Soimarestilor (Romania, Mircea Dragan, 1965)

Herd/Sürü (Turkey, Zeki Okten, 1979)

Heroes/Veliki transport (Yugoslavia, Veljko Bulajić, 1983)

Hornet/Strsljen (Yugoslavia, Gorćin Stojanović, 1998)

Horse/At (Turkey, Ali Ozgentürk, 1971)

Hotel de Lux (Romania, Dan Pita, 1992)

How the War Started on My Little Island/Kako je poeeo rat na mom otoku (Croatia, Vinko Bresan, 1996)

Hunters, The/I Kinigi (Greece, Theo Angelopoulos, 1977)

I Even Met Happy Gypsies/Skupljaci perja (Yugoslavia, Aleksandar Petrović, 1967)

Impure Blood/Sofka (Yugoslavia, Rados Novaković, 1948)

Innocence Unprotected/Nevinost bez zastite (Yugoslavia, Dušan Makavejev, 1968)

In the Jaws of Life/U raljama zivota (Yugoslavia, Rajko Grlic, 1989)

It Rains in My Village/Bioee skoro propast sveta (Yugoslavia, Aleksandar Petrović, 1969)

Jews Are Coming, The/Jevrei dolaze (Yugoslavia, Prvoslav Marić, 1992)

Journey through the Dark Side, A/Putovanje tamnom polutkom (Croatia, Davor Zmegać, 1996)

Journey to the Sun/Günese Yolculuk (Turkey/Germany/Netherlands, Yesim Ustaoglu, 1999)

Jovana Lukina (Yugoslavia, Zhivko Nikolić, 1979)

Khan Asparukh/Han Asparuh (Bulgaria, Lyudmil Staykov, 1981)

Kuduz (Yugoslavia, Ademir Kenović, 1989)

Landscape in the Mist/Topio stin omichli (Greece/France/Italy, Theo Angelopoulos, 1988)

Last Stop Paradise/Terminus paradis (Romania/France, Lucian Pintilie, 1998)

Last Summer/Posledno lyato (Bulgaria, Hristo Hristov, 1974)

Last Wishes/Posledni zhelaniya (Bulgaria, Rangel Vulchanov, 1984)

Letter to Nazim Hickmet/Gramma ston Nazim Hickmet (Greece, Costas Aristopoulos, 1976)

Love Affair or the Case of the Missing Switchboard Operator/Ljubavni slucaj ili tragedija sluzbenice P.T.T. (Yugoslavia, Dušan Makavejev, 1967)

Macedonian Blood Wedding/Makedonska krvava svadba (Yugoslavia, Trajce Popov, 1967)

Man is not a Bird/Covek Nije Tica (Yugoslavia, Dušan Makavejev, 1965)

Manifesto a.k.a. *A Night of Love* (Yugoslavia/USA, Dušan Makavejev, 1988)

Manly Times/Mazhki vremena (Bulgaria, Eduard Zakhariev, 1982)

Marble Ass/Dupe od mramora (Yugoslavia, Želimir Žilnik, 1995)

March on Igman, The/Igmanski mars (Yugoslavia, Zdravko Šotra, 1983)

Matriarchy/Matriarhat (Bulgaria, Lyudmil Kirkov, 1977)

Measure for Measure/Mera spored mera, Parts 1, 2 and 3 (Bulgaria, George Dyulgerov, 1982–5)

Michael the Brave/Mihai Viteazul (Romania, Sergiu Nicolaescu, 1971)

Miss Stone/Mis Ston (Yugoslavia, Žika Mitrović, 1958)

Morana (Slovenia, Ales Verbic, 1994)

Ninth Circle, The/Deveti krug (Yugoslavia, France Stiglić, 1960)

Oak, The/Balanta/Le Chêne (Romania/France, Lucian Pintilie, 1992)

Occupation in 26 Scenes/Okupacija u 26 slika (Yugoslavia, Lordan Zafranović, 1978)

Orpheus Descending/Me ton Orphea ton Avgousto (Greece, Giorgos Zervoulakos, 1995)

Palm Sunday/Sirna nedelya (Bulgaria, Radoslav Spassov, 1993)

Parangelia (Greece, Pablos Tassios, 1980)

Patent Leather Shoes of the Unknown Soldier, The/Lachenite obuvki na neznayniya voin (Bulgaria, Rangel Vulchanov, 1979)

Peach Thief, The/Kradetsat na praskovi (Bulgaria, Vulo Radev, 1964)

Pepe & Fifi/Pepe si Fifi (Romania, Dan Pita, 1994)

Perfect Circle/Savrseni krug (Bosnia/France, Ademir Kenovic, 1997)

Petricia's Wreath/Petrijin Venac (Yugoslavia, Srdjan Karanović, 1980)

Powder Keg a.k.a. *Cabaret Balkan/Bure baruta* (Yugoslavia/France, Goran Paskaljević, 1998)

Premeditated Murder/Ubistvo s predumišljajem (Yugoslavia, Gorćin Stojanović, 1995)

Pretty Village, Pretty Flame/Lepa sela, lepo gore (Yugoslavia, Srdjan Dragojević, 1996)

Rage/Do koske (Yugoslavia, Slobodan Skerlić, 1998)

Reconstruction/Anaparastassi (Greece, Theo Angelopoulos, 1970)

Republic in Flames/Republikata vo plamen (Yugoslavia, Lubisa Georgievski, 1969)

Republic of Uzice, The/Uzicka Republika (Yugoslavia, Žika Mitrović, 1971)

Sako's Wedding/Dasma e Sakos (Albania/Hungary, Vladimir Prifti, 1998)

Senator's Snails/Senatorul melcilor (Romania, Mircea Daneliuk, 1995)

Silent Gunpowder/Gluvi barut (Yugoslavia, Bato Cengić, 1990)

Skenderbeg (USSR/Albania, Sergei Yutkevich, 1953)

Sky Hook/Nebeska udica (Yugoslavia, Ljubisa Samardžić, 1999)

Slaughter of the Rooster, The/I sfagi tou kokora (Greece/Cyprus/Bulgaria/Italy, Andreas Pantzis, 1996)

So Long/Mirupafshim (Greece/Bulgaria/Cyprus, Christos Voupouras and Giorgos
    Korras, 1997)

Someone Else's America/Tudja Amerika (France/UK/Germany/Greece, Goran
    Paskaljević, 1995)

Southbound/Put na jug/El Camino del sur (Argentina/Yugoslavia, Huan Bautista
    Sagnaro, 1988)

Stars/Zvezdi/Sterne (Bulgaria/East Germany, Rangel Vulchanov and Konrad Wolf,
    1959)

State of Things, The/Stere de fapt (Romania/France, Stere Gulea, 1996)

Stella (Greece, Michael Cacoyannis, 1955)

Stone Wedding/Nunta de piatra (Romania, Mircea Veroiu and Dan Pita, 1972)

Stone Years/Petrina Chronia (Greece, Pantelis Voulgaris, 1985)

Sun Rises, The/Rasare soarele (Romania, Dinu Negreanu, 1954)

Suspended Step of the Stork, The/To meteoro vima tou pelagrou
    (Greece/France/Italy/Switzerland, Theo Angelopoulos, 1991)

Suza and Her Sisters/Suza i njene sestre (Yugoslavia, Zoran Calić, 1996)

Tale from the Past, A/Perralle Nga e Kaluara (Albania, Dhimiter Anagnosti, 1987)

Tango Argentino (Yugoslavia, Goran Paskaljević, 1992)

That Summer of White Roses (USA/Yugoslavia, Rajko Grlic, 1989)

Thessaloniki Assailants/Solunskite atentatori (Yugoslavia, Žika Mitrović, 1961)

Thirst/Zed (Yugoslavia, Nikola Stojanović, 1981)

Three Summer Days/Tri letnja dana (Yugoslavia, Mirjana Vukomanović, 1997)

Time of the Gypsies/Dom za vesanje (Yugoslavia, Emir Kusturica, 1989)

Time of Violence/Vreme na nasilie (Bulgaria, Lyudmil Staykov, 1988)

Tito among the Serbs for a Second Time/Tito po drugi put medju srbima
    (Yugoslavia, Želimir Žilnik, 1993)

Tito and I/Tito i ja (Yugoslavia, Goran Marković, 1991)

Tito's Memoirs/Titovi memoari (Yugoslavia, Veljko Bulajić, 1980)

Train without a Timetable/Vlak bez voznog reda (Yugoslavia, Veljko Bulajić, 1959)

Trajan's Column/Columna (Romania, Mircea Dragan, 1968)

Traveling Players, The/O Thiassos (Greece, Theo Angelopoulos, 1975)

Tree with No Roots, A/Darvo bez koren (Bulgaria, Hristo Hristov, 1976)

Tudor (Romania, Lucian Bratu, 1962)

Ulysses' Gaze/To vlemma tou Odyssea (Greece/France/Italy, Theo Angelopoulos,
    1995)

Underground (France/Germany/Hungary, Emir Kusturica, 1995)

Unexpected Walk/Neocekivana setnja (Bosnia, François Lunel, 1994–7)

Unforgettable Summer, An/Un Été inoubliable/O primavara de neuitat
    (Romania/France, Lucian Pintilie, 1994)

Villager with the Bicycle, The/Selyaninat s koleloto (Bulgaria, Lyudmil Kirkov,
    1974)

Virgina/Virdzina (Yugoslavia, Srdjan Karanović, 1991)

Vukovar Is Coming Home/Vukovar se vraca kuci a.k.a. *Vukovar – The Way Home* (Croatia, Branko Schmidt, 1994)

Vukovar: Poste Restante/Vukovar – jedna priča (USA/Cyprus/Italy/Yugoslavia, Boro Drašković, 1994)

Walter Defends Sarajevo/Valter brani Sarajevo (Yugoslavia, Hajrudin Krvavać, 1972)

Well, The/Kladenetsat (Bulgaria, Docho Bodzhakov, 1990)

When Father Was Away on Business/Otac na sluzbenom putu (Yugoslavia, Emir Kusturica, 1985)

Who Is Singing Out There?/Ko to tamo peva? (Yugoslavia, Slobodan Šijan, 1984)

Why Did You Leave Me?/Kazi zasto me ostavi? (Yugoslavia, Oleg Novković, 1993)

With Glittering Eyes/Me ti lampsi sta matia (Greece, Panos Glykophrydis, 1966)

Wounds/Rane (Yugoslavia, Srdjan Dragojević, 1998)

WR: Mysteries of the Organism/WR – Misterije organisma (Yugoslavia/USA, Dušan Makavejev, 1971)

Years of Waiting (Albania, Esat, Musliu, 1981)

Yol (Turkey, Yilmaz Güney, 1982)

Feature Films about the Balkans

America, America (USA, Elia Kazan, 1963)

Are They Still Shooting? (USA, Tomislav Novaković, 1993)

Beautiful People (UK, Jasmin Dizdar, 1999)

Black Punisher (Italy, John Wilder, 1991)

Broken English (New Zealand, Gregor Nicholas, 1996)

Bus, The/Otobus (Sweden/Turkey, Tunç Okan, 1977)

Comanche Territory/Territorio comanche (Spain/Germany/France/Argentina, Gerardo Herrero, 1997)

Crazy Stranger, The/Gadjo Dilo (France, Tony Gatlif, 1997)

De Mayerling à Sarajevo (France, Max Ophuls, 1940)

Demons of War (After Goya)/Demony Wojny (w/g Goi) (Poland, Wladyslaw Pasikowski, 1998)

Eleni (USA, Peter Yates, 1985)

Elvis and Marilyn/Elvjs e Merilijn (Italy, Armando Manni, 1997)

Farewell to False Paradise/Abschied vom falschen Paradies (Germany, Tevfic Baser, 1989)

Foreign Correspondents (USA, Mark Tapio Kines, 1998)

Forever Mozart (France/Switzerland, Jean-Luc Godard, 1996)

Forty Square Meters Germany/40 Quadratmeter Deutschland (Germany, Tevfic Baser, 1986)

Gamebag/Il carniere (Italy, Maurizio Zaccaro, 1997)

Good Bye, Stranger!/Lebewohl, Fremde (Germany, Tevfic Baser, 1991)
Guests/Ospiti (Italy, Mattea Garrone, 1998)
Harrison's Flowers (France, Elie Chouraqui, 2000)
Heroes/Heroje (Bosnia/France, François Lunel, 1998)
High Season (UK, Clare Peploe, 1988)
Hole in the Soul/Rupa u dusu (UK, Dušan Makavejev, 1994)
In the Mountains of Yugoslavia/V gorakh Yugoslavii (USSR, Abram Room, 1946)
Interesting State, An (Italy, Lina Wertmüller, 1999)
Journey of Hope/Umud'a yolculuk/Reise der Hoffnung (Switzerland/ Turkey, Xavier
    Koller, 1990)
Jugofilm (Austria, Goran Rebic, 1997)
Lamerica (Italy, Gianni Amelio, 1994)
Midnight Express (UK, Alan Parker, 1978)
Montenegro (Sweden, Dušan Makavejev, 1981)
My Father's Angel (Canada, Davor Marjanović, 1999)
Never on Sunday/Pote tin Kyriaki (Greece, Jules Dassin, 1959)
Northern Skirts/Nordrand (Austria, Barbara Albert, 1998)
Pascali's Island (UK, James Dearden, 1988)
Peacemaker (USA, Mimi Leder, 1997)
Savoir (USA, Predrag 'Gaga'Rebic, 1998)
Serbian Girl, The/Das Serbische Mädchen (Germany, Peter Sehr, 1991)
Shirley Valentine (UK, Lewis Gilbert, 1989)
Shot through the Heart (UK/Canada/Hungary, David Attwood, 1998)
Tired Companions/Müde Weggefähret: Fünf Geschichten aus dem Krieg (Germany,
    Zoran Solomun, 1997)
Unexpected Walk/Neocekivana setnja (Bosnia, François Lunel, 1997)
Warriors, parts 1 and 2 (UK, Peter Kosminsky, 1999)
We Are No Angels/Mi nismo andjeli (Yugoslavia, Srdjan Dragojević, 1992)
Welcome to Sarajevo (UK/USA, Michael Winterbottom, 1997)
Young Men Get to Know the World/Mladi muzi poznavaji svet (Czechoslovakia,
    Radim Spacek, 1995)
Zorba the Greek (USA, Michael Cacoyannis, 1964)

Other Feature Films
8½ (Italy, Federico Fellini, 1963)
1947 Earth (Canada/India, Deepa Mehta, 1998)
A la place du coeur (France, Robert Guédiguian, 1998)
Accused, The (USA, Jonathan Kaplan, 1988)
Adoption/Örökbefogadás (Hungary, Marta Mészarós, 1975)
Albania Blues (Italy, Nico Cirasola, 1999)
Andrei Rublyov (USSR, Andrei Tarkovsky, 1966)

Angelo, My Love (USA, Robert Duvall, 1982)

Antonia's Line/Antonia (Belgium/Netherlands/UK, Marleen Görris, 1995)

Apocalypse Now (USA, Francis Ford Coppola, 1979)

April Children/Aprilkinder (Germany, Yüksel Yavuz, 1999)

Aprile (Italy, Nanni Moretti, 1998)

Arizona Dream (USA/France, Emir Kusturica, 1993)

Ashes and Diamonds/Popiól i diament (Poland, Andrzej Wajda, 1958)

Autumn Afternoon/Sanma no aji (Japan, Yasujiro Ozu, 1962)

Ballad of Narayama/Narayama bushiko (Japan, Shohei Imamura, 1982)

Bandit Queen/Phoolan Devi (India, Shekhar Kapur, 1994)

Black Girl/La Noire de . . . (Senegal/France, Ousmane Sembene, 1966)

Blade Runner (USA, Ridley Scott, 1982)

Bleeder (Denmark, Nicolas Winding Refn, 1999)

Blood Wedding/Bodas de sangre (Spain, Carlos Saura, 1981)

Blue (UK, Derek Jarman, 1993)

Boat, The/Das Boot (Germany, Wolfgang Petersen, 1982)

Bolshe Vita (Hungary/Germany, Ibolya Fekete, 1996)

Boogie Nights (USA, Paul Thomas Anderson, 1997)

Born on the Fourth of July (USA, Oliver Stone, 1989)

Broken Arrow (USA, John Woo, 1996)

Brothers in Trouble (UK, Udayan Prashad, 1997)

Burnt by the Sun/Utomlyonnye solncem (Russia/France, Nikita Mikhalkov, 1994)

Cabaret (USA, Bob Fosse, 1972)

Cat People (USA, Jacques Tourneur, 1942)

Chekist, The/Chekist (Russia, Alexander Rogozhkin, 1992)

Child Murders/Gyerekgyilkosságok (Hungary, Ildiko Szabó, 1993)

China Girl (USA, Abel Ferrara, 1988)

Chronicle of a Disappearance (Palestine/Israel/USA/Germany, Elia Suleiman, 1996)

Circus/Tsirk (USSR, Grigoriy Alexandrov, 1934)

Clandestins, The (Switzerland/Canada/France/Belgium, Nicolas Wadimoff and Denis Chouinard, 1997)

Clear Cut (Canada, Richard Bugajski, 1994)

Clockwork Orange (USA, Stanley Kubrick, 1971)

Coca-Cola Kid, The (Australia, Dušan Makavejev, 1985)

Cold Days/Hideg napok (Hungary, András Kovács, 1966)

Colonel Redl/Redl Ezredes/Oberst Redl (Hungary/Germany, István Szabó, 1985)

Combination Platter (USA, Tony Chan, 1993)

Come and See/Idi i smotri (USSR, Elem Klimov, 1985)

Cranes Are Flying, The/Letyat zhuravli (USSR, Mikhail Kalatozov, 1957)

Dance Me Outside (Canada, Bruce McDonald, 1994)

Dear America: Letters Home from Vietnam (USA, Bill Couturie, 1988)

Deer Hunter (USA, Michael Cimino, 1978)

Devils, Devils/Diably, diably (Poland, Dorota Kedzierzawska, 1991)

Diamonds of the Night/Démanty noci (Czechoslovakia, Jan Nemec, 1963)

Doctor Faustus (Germany, Franz Seitz, 1982)

Duck Soup (USA, Loe McCarey, 1933)

Earth/Tierra (Spain, Julio Medem, 1996)

Fall of Berlin, The/Padenie Berlina (USSR, Mikhail Chiaureli, 1949)

Fall of the Romanov Dynasty, The/Padenie dinastii Romanovykh (USSR, Esfir Shub, 1927)

Femme Nikita, La (Canada, Reza Badiyi and George Bloomfield, 1997), TV series

Fever/Goraczka (Poland, Agnieszka Holland, 1981)

Fifth Seal, The/Az Ötödik pecsét (Hungary, Zoltán Fábri, 1976)

Forbidden Games/Jeux interdits (France, René Clément, 1952)

Forrest Gump (USA, Robert Zemeckis, 1994)

Four Weddings and a Funeral (UK, Mike Newell, 1994)

Freeze, Die, Come to Life/Zamri, umri, voskresni! (Russia, Vitaly Kanevskiy, 1990)

From Mayerling to Sarajevo/ De Mayerling à Sarajevo (France, Max Ophuls, 1940)

Full Metal Jacket (USA, Stanley Kubrick, 1987)

Garden of the Finzi-Continis, The/Il giardino dei Finzi-Contini (Italy, Vittorio de Sica, 1971)

Germany Pale Mother/Deutschland Bleiche Mutter (Germany, Helma Sanders-Brahms, 1980)

Germany Year Zero/Germania anno zero (Germany/Italy, Roberto Rossellini, 1947)

Good Morning, Vietnam (USA, Barry Levinson, 1987)

Gorilla Bathes at Noon (Germany, Dušan Makavejev, 1992)

Gypsies/Posledniy tabor (USSR, Moisei Goldblat and Yevgeni Shnaider, 1935)

Gypsies Are Found Near Heaven/Tabor uhodit v nebo (USSR, Emil Loteanu, 1975)

Gypsy Life/Zigeunerleben (Germany, Suzanne Zanke, 1994)

Gypsy Lore/Romani kris – Cigánytörvény (Hungary/Germany/Bulgaria, Bence Gyöngyössy, 1997)

Gypsy Soul/Alma Gitana (Spain, Chus Gutiérrez, 1996)

Hands Up/Rece do góry (Poland/UK, Jerzy Skolimowski, 1968/85)

Hate/La Haine (France, Mathieu Kassovitz, 1995)

Hiroshima, Mon Amour (France, Alain Resnais, 1959)

Holiday Inn (USA, Mark Sandrich, 1942)

Hot Blood (USA, Nicholas Ray, 1956)

How Tasty Was My Little Frenchman/Como era gostoso o meu francês (Brazil, Nelson Pereira dos Santos, 1971)

I Want You (UK, Michael Winterbottom, 1998)

I Was Born to a Gypsy/Je suis né d'une cigoine (France, Tony Gatlif, 1999)

Incident at Oglala (USA, Michael Aped, 1992)

Inner Circle/Blizhnii krug (USA, Andrei Konchalovski, 1991)

Interrogation, The/Przesluchanie (Poland, Ryszard Bugajski, 1982)

Into the West (UK/Ireland, Mike Newell, 1992)

Journey to the Beginning of the World/Viageim ao Princípio do Mundo
   (Portugal/France, Manuel de Oliveira, 1997)

Judge and the Assassin, The/Juge et l'assassin, Le (France, Bertrand Tavernier, 1976)

Judgment at Nuremberg (USA, Stanley Kramer, 1961)

Junk Movie/Roncsfilm (Hungary, György Szomjas, 1992)

Kanal (Poland, Andrzej Wajda, 1957)

Killing Fields, The (USA, Roland Joffe, 1984)

King of the Gypsies (USA, Frank Pierson, 1978)

Kissed (Canada, Lynne Stopkewich, 1997)

Kolya (Czech Republic, Jan Sverák, 1996)

Koportos (Hungary, Lívia Gyarmathy, 1979)

Korczak (Poland, Andrzej Wajda, 1991)

Krima-Kerime (Germany/Netherlands/Turkey, Herbert Curiel, 1994)

Kundun (USA, Martin Scorsese, 1997)

Landscape after Battle/Krajobraz po bitwie (Poland, Andrzej Wajda, 1970)

Larks on a String/Skrivánci na niti (Czechoslovakia, Jiri Menzel, 1969/90)

Last Exit to Brooklyn (USA, Ulrich Edel, 1989)

Last Picture Show, The (USA, Peter Bogdanovich, 1971)

Last Stage, The/Ostatni etap (Poland, Wanda Jakubowska, 1948)

L'Atalante (France, Jean Vigo, 1934)

Latcho Drom (France, Tony Gatlif, 1994)

Leningrad Cowboys Go America (Finland/Sweden, Aki Kaurismaki, 1989)

Life Is Beautiful (Italy, Roberto Begnini, 1998)

Live Flesh/Carne trémula (Spain, Pedro Almodovar, 1997)

Lone Star (USA, John Sayles, 1996)

Lonely Human Voice, The/Odinokiy golos cheloveka (USSR, Alexander Sokurov,
   1978)

Lovers (France, Jean Marc Barr, 1999)

Ma vie en rose (Belgium/France/UK, Alain Berliner, 1997)

Makioka Sisters, The/Sasameyuki (Japan, Kon Ichikawa, 1983)

Man of Marble/Czlowiek z Marmuru (Poland, Andrzej Wajda, 1976)

Mare largo (Italy, Ferdinando Vincentini Orgnani, 1998)

Marian (Czech Republic/France, Petr Vaclav, 1995)

Matteo Falcone (USA, Victor Kulle, 1975)

Mephisto (Hungary/Germany, István Szabó, 1981)

Mirror, The/Zerkalo (USSR, Andrei Tarkovsky, 1975)

Missing (USA, Costa-Gavras, 1983)

Mississippi Masala (USA, Mira Nair, 1992)

Mondo (France, Tony Gatlif, 1995)

My Name Is Ivan/Ivanovo detstvo (USSR, Andrei Tarkovsky, 1962)

My Son the Fanatic (UK, Udayan Prasad, 1997)

Natural Born Killers (USA, Oliver Stone, 1994)

Night of the Shooting Stars, The/La notte di San Lorenzo (Italy, Paolo and Vittorio
    Taviani, 1982)

Norte, El (USA, Gregory Nava, 1983)

Nostalgia/Nostalghia (Italy/USSR, Andrei Tarkovsky, 1982

On the Line (Spain/USA, Jose Luis Borau, 1987)

Once Were Warriors (New Zealand, Lee Tamahori, 1995)

One Day in the Life of Ivan Denisovich (UK/Norway, Casper Wrede, 1970)

Open City/Roma, città aperta (Italy, Roberto Rossellini, 1945)

Padre Padrone (Italy, Vittorio and Paolo Taviani, 1977)

Paisan/Paisà (Italy, Roberto Rossellini, 1946)

Peacemaker (USA, Mimi Leder, 1997)

Phantom Beirut/Beyrouth fantôme (France/Lebanon, Ghassan Salhab, 1998)

Pixote (Brazil, Hector Babenco, 1980)

Platoon (USA, Oliver Stone, 1986)

Powwow Highway (USA, Jonathan Wacks, 1989)

Princes, The/Les Princes (France, Tony Gatlif, 1982)

Prisoner of the Mountains/Kavkazskiy phennik (Russia, Sergei Bodrov, 1996)

Pulp Fiction (USA, Quentin Tarantino, 1994)

Pusher (Denmark, Nicolas Winding Refn, 1996)

Ravenous (USA, Antonia Bird, 1999)

Red and the White, The/ Csillagosok, katonák (Hungary, Miklós Jancsó, 1967)

Red Balloon, The/Le Ballon rouge (France, Albert Lamorisse, 1956)

Red Sorghum/Hong gao liang (China, Zhang Yimou, 1987)

Rehearsals for War/Teatro di guerra (Italy, Mario Martone, 1998)

Repentance/Pokayanie (USSR, Tengiz Abuladze, 1986)

River, The/He Liu (Taiwan, Ming-liang Tsai, 1997)

Round Up, The/Szegénylegének (Hungary, Miklós Jancsó, 1965)

Sacrifice/Offret (Sweden/UK/France, Andrei Tarkovsky, 1986)

Salaam Bombay! (India, Mira Nair, 1988)

Salo: 120 Days of Sodom/Salò o le 120 giornate di Sodoma (Italy, Pier Paolo
    Pasolini, 1975)

Salvador (USA, Oliver Stone, 1986)

Secrets and Lies (UK/France, Mike Leigh, 1996)

Seven Years in Tibet (USA, Jean-Jacques Annaud, 1997)

Shadows of Forgotten Ancestors/Tini zabutykh predkiv (USSR, Sergei Paradzhanov, 1964)

Sharp, Short Shock/Kurz Schort Scmerzlos (Germany, Fatih Akin, 1998)

Ship of Dreams/La nave de los sueños (Columbia/Venezuela/Mexico, Ciro Diran, 1995)

Signs of Life/Lebenszeichen (Germany, Werner Herzog, 1968)

Smoke Signals (USA, Chris Eyre, 1998)

Somewhere in Europe/Valahol Európában (Hungary, Géza Radványi, 1947)

Stalingrad (Germany, Joseph Vilsmayer, 1993)

Stalker (USSR, Andrei Tarkovsky, 1979)

Stolen Children/Ladro di bambini (Italy, Gianni Amelio, 1991)

Straw Dogs (USA, Sam Pekinpah, 1971)

Stromboli (Italy, Roberto Rossellini, 1949)

Sunday Daughters/Vasárnapi szülök (Hungary, Janosz Rozsa, 1980)

Surveillance/Nadzor (Poland, Wieslaw Saniewski, 1984)

Sweet Movie (Switzerland/Canada, Dušan Makavejev, 1975)

Thunderheart (USA, Michael Apted, 1992)

Tin Drum, The/Die Blechtrommel (France/Germany, Volker Schlöndorff, 1979)

Toto le héros (Belgium/France/Germany, Jaco van Dormael, 1991)

Toto Who Lived Twice/Toto che visse due volte (Italy, Daniele Cipri and Franco Maresco, 1998)

Truce, The/La tregua (Italy/France/Switzerland, Francesco Rosi, 1996)

True Romance (USA, Tony Scott, 1993)

Two Deaths (UK, Nicholas Roeg, 1995)

Two Women/La ciociara (Italy, Vittorio de Sica, 1961)

Uncle from Brooklyn, The/Lo zio di Brooklyn (Italy, Daniele Cipri and Franco Maresco, 1995)

Under Fire (USA, Roger Spottiswoode, 1983)

Vow, The/Klyatva (USSR, Mikhail Chiaurelli, 1946)

Wedding/Wesele (Poland, Andrzej Wajda, 1973)

Wedding, A (USA, Robert Altman, 1978)

Wedding in Galilee/Urs al-jalil (Israel/Belgium/France, Michel Kleifi, 1987)

West Beirut/West Beyrouth (France/Lebanon, Ziad Doueiri, 1998)

Woyzeck (Hungary, János Szasz, 1994)

Xica da Silva (Brazil, Carlos Diegues, 1976)

Year of Living Dangerously, The (Australia/USA, Peter Weir, 1982)

Z (France/Algeria, Costa-Gavras, 1969)

Zero for Conduct/Zéro de conduite (France, Jean Vigo, 1933)

Documentaries, shorts, animation
From the Balkans

8th March (Bosnia, Srdjan Vuletić, 1993)

24 Hours with Bure (Bosnia, Enes Zlatar, 1993/7)

After, After . . ./Poslje, poslje (Bosnia, Jasmila Zbanić, 1997)

Amela's School Holiday/Amelin skolski raspust (Bosnia, Zlatko Lavanić, 1993)

Angels in Sarajevo/Andeli u Sarajevu (Bosnia, Nino Zalica, 1994)

Arkan and Ceca/Svetlana i Zeljko (Yugoslavia, George Minkov, 1995)

At the Gates of the City/Stin Akri tis polis (Greece, Nikos Anagnostopoulos, 1975)

Autobiography (Bosnia, Jasmila Zbanić, 1995)

Blood and Ashes of Jasenovac/Krv i pepeo Jasenovca (Yugoslavia, Lordan
  Zafranović, 1985)

Blue Guide, The/Plavi vodic (Bosnia, Nenad Dizdarević, 1994)

Bums and Dogs (Bosnia, Zlatko Lavanić, 1993)

Children Like Any Others (Bosnia, Pjer Zalica, 1995)

Children of Sarajevo, The/Djeca Sarajeva (Bosnia, Amir Bukvić, 1994)

Confession of a Monster/Ispovjest monstruma (Bosnia, Ademir Kenović, Pjer
  Zalica, Ismet Arnautalić, Mirza Idrizović, 1993)

Dae (Macedonia/France, Stole Popov, 1979)

Death in Sarajevo (Bosnia, Haris Prolić, 1995)

Decline of the Century: The Testament of L. Z. (Czech Republic/Austria/Croatia,
  Lordan Zafranović, 1995)

Do Jaja: Throwing Off the Yolks of Bondage (Yugoslavia, Želimir Žilnik, 1997)

Don't Shoot the Children/Ne pucajte u djecu (Bosnia, Milan Trivić, 1994)

Draw Me . . ./Nacrtaj mi . . . (Bosnia, François Lunel, 1994)

Dying in Sarajevo/Umrijeti v Sarajevu (Bosnia, Ademir Kenović, 1993)

Ecce Homo (Bosnia, Vesna Ljubić, 1992–4)

Eight Years After/Osam godina kasnije (Bosnia Ademir Kenović and Nino Zalica,
  1993)

Ghetto/Geto (Yugoslavia, Mladen Maticević and Ivan Markov, 1995)

Greta (Bosnia, Haris Pasović, 1998)

Gypsies of the World, Unite!/Tsigani ot vsichki strani, saedinyavaite se! (Bulgaria,
  Dimitar Petkov, 1994)

Hobby (Bosnia, Smail Kapetanović, 1993)

I Burned Legs /Palio sam noge (Bosnia, Srdjan Vuletić, 1994)

In Continuo (Yugoslavia, Vlatko Gilić, 1971)

Laibach: A Film from Slovenia (Slovenia, Goran Gajić, 1988)

Letter, The (19.8.1992)/Pismo (19.8.1992) (Bosnia, Zdravko Grebo, 1993)

Life in a Ghetto/Zhivot v geto (Bulgaria, Eldora Traykova, 1999)

Like Sarajevo/Kao Sarajevo (Bosnia, Muhammed Mujkić and Dejan Velić, 1995)

Message to My Friends, A/Mojim prijateljima (Bosnia, Zlatko Lavanić, 1993)

MGM Sarajevo: Man, God, Monster/MGM Sarajevo: Covjek, Bog, Monstrum
(Bosnia, SaGA, 1992/4)

Mindless/Bespameti (Bosnia, Timur Makarević and Amer Mrzljak, 1997)

Mizaldo: The End of the Show/Mizaldo – kraj teatra (Bosnia, Semezdin
Mehmedinović and Benjamin Filipović, 1994)

Mona Lisa from Sarajevo (Bosnia, Bato Cengić, 1998)

Mud/Kal (Bulgaria, Ivaylo Simidchiev, 1997)

Nina's Tears/Ninine Suze (Bosnia, Mevsud Kapetanović, 1995)

Of People and Bears/Za horata i mechkite (Bulgaria, Eldora Traykova, 1995)

Pictures/Slike (Miroslav Benković, 1993)

Plastic Jesus/Plasticni Isus (Yugoslavia, Lazar Stojanović, 1971)

Rom (Greece, Menelaos Karamaghiolis, 1989)

Roma Portraits (Bulgaria, project director Asen Balikci, 1995/8)

SA-Life (Bosnia, SaGA, 1993)

Sarajevo (Bosnia, Mirza Idrizović, 1992)

Sarajevo: Ground Zero (Bosnia, SaGA, 1993)

Sarajevo String Quartet/Sarajevski Gudaci (Bosnia,Vefic Hadžismajlović, 1994)

See You in the Obituary, a.k.a. *The Crime that Changed Serbia/Vidimo se u citulji*
(Yugoslavia, Janko Baljak, 1995)

Serbian and Croatian, Brothers or Enemies (Yugoslavia, Želimir Žilnik, 1992)

Shovel/Lopata (Bosnia, Nebojsa Serić-Soba, 1997)

Sparrows of the Humankind/Vrabchetata na choveshkata rasa (Bulgaria, Boyan
Papazov, 1990)

Smertens Ghetto (Yugoslavia, Želimir Žilnik, 1993)

Stories from Sarajevo: 1 (Bosnia, RTVBiH, 1992/5)

Stories from Sarajevo: 2 (Bosnia, RTVBiH, 1992/5)

Street under Siege, A/Ulica pod opsadom (Bosnia/France/UK, SaGA, 1993)

Topography of Remembrance/Sinassos (Greece/France, Timon Koulmasis and Iro
Siafliaki, 1997)

Truth about Croatia, The (Croatia, 1992)

Truth Is a Victim in Croatia, The (Serbia, 1994)

Urbicide/Urbicid (Bosnia, Zoran Lesić, 1994)

Vassilitsa (Bulgaria, Milan Ognyanov, 1995)

Waiting for a Parcel/Cekajuci paket (Bosnia, Vuk Janić, 1993)

War Art (Bosnia, Nedzad Begović, 1994)

War in Children, The/Rat u djeci (Bosnia, Nenad Begović, 1994)

Way of the Cross in Sarajevo/Krizni put u Sarajevu (Bosnia, Vlatko Filipović, 1993)

Wedding in Sarajevo, A/Vencanje u Sarajevu (Bosnia, Milan Trvić, 1993)

World in Between, A/Mezhdinen svyat (Bulgaria, Roumiana Petkova, 1995)

About the Balkans

Abdulah Sidran: A Poet in Sarajevo/Abdulah Sidran, poeta a Sarajevo (Switzerland, Piero Del Giudice, 1995)

Albanian Journey: End of an Era (USA, Paul Jay, 1991)

Arkan, Alleged Serbian Warlord (USA, CNN–Christianne Amanpour, 1997)

Balkan Journey, A (Canada, Brenda Longfellow, 1995)

Between the Lines: The War in Former Yugoslavia (Canada, Steve Paikin, 1993)

Black Kites (USA, Jo Anders, 1996)

Blood and Belonging: The Road to Nowhere (UK/Canada, Michael Ignatieff, 1993)

Body Hunter, The (UK, Louise Norman, 2000)

Bosna! (France, Bernard-Henri Lévy and Alain Ferrari, 1994)

Bosnia Hotel (France, Thomas Balmes, 1996)

Calling the Ghosts (USA, Mandy Jacobson and Karmen Jelinčić, 1996)

Children under Fire (UK, Wayne Derrick and Rob Edwards, 1993)

Children's Police Squad/Kinderpolizisten (Austria, Klaus Hipfl, 1993)

Cease Fire: Belfast/Sarajevo (France, Baudoin Koenig, 1995)

Central Bosnia: Croatian and Muslim Families/Zentralbosnien – kroatische and moslemische Familien (Austria, Klaus Hipfl, 1993)

Crimes against Humanity (USA, Worldnet, 1995)

Cry from the Grave, A (UK, Leslie Woodhead, 1999)

Day in the Death of Sarajevo, A (France, Bernard-Henri Lévy and Thiery Ravalet, 1993)

Dogs of War (UK, Stephen Lambert, 1992)

Draw Me . . ./Nacrtaj mi (Bosnia/France, François Lunel, 1994)

Enemy Mine (USA, Gill Rossellini, 1993)

Escape from Sarajevo/Fluch von Sarajevo (Germany, Thomas Hausner, 1993)

Every Day for Sarajevo/Chaque jour pour Sarajevo (Bosnia/France, Patrick Barrat, 1995)

Exile in Sarajevo (Australia, Tahir Cambis and Alma Sahbaz, 1997)

Eyes of Bosnia, The/Oci Bosne (USA/Slovenia, Miran Zupanić, 1993)

Farewell Bosnia (USA, Beth Cohen, 1995)

From Beirut to Bosnia (UK, Robert Fisk, 1993)

From Yugoslavia to Bosnia: Two Hours from London (UK/Croatia, Jill Craigie, 1993)

Girlfriends from Pristina (UK, Kira Phillips, 2000)

Going with the Flow: An Anthropologist among Bosnians (USA, Barbara Kerewsky-Halpern, 1997)

Hole in the Soul (UK, Dušan Makavejev, 1994)

Journey to Kosovo (UK, Jonathan Dimbleby, 1999)

Killing Memory: Bosnia's Cultural Heritage and its Destruction (USA, Andreas Riedlmayer, 1994)

Living and the Dead in Sarajevo, The/Les Vivants et les morts de Sarajevo (France, Radovan Tadić, 1993)

Macedonia: The Next Bosnia? (USA, Julian Chomet, 1995)

Memories Do Not Burn (Croatia/Bosnia/USA, Paul Dokuchitz and Marianne McCune, 1996)

Miss Sarajevo (USA, Bill Carter, 1995)

Moral Combat (UK, Alan Little, 2000)

Mythmaking: The Balkans (A Look at the News Coverage of the War in the Former Yugoslavia) (USA, Paper Tiger TV, 1995)

Ordinary People (UK, Angela Pope, 1993)

Pancrac Diary (USA, David Galessic, 1994)

Predictions of Fire (Slovenia/USA, Michael Benson, 1996)

Prime Time in the Camps/Le 20 heures dans les camps (France, Chris Marker, 1993)

Puppet Master of the Balkans, The (UK, Maggie O'Kane, 1994)

Punishment, The (Austria, Goran Rebić, 1999)

Romeo and Juliet in Sarajevo (USA/Canada/Germany, John Zaritzky, 1994)

Sabina's Story (UK, Sebastian Rich, 1999)

Safe Haven: The United Nations and the Betrayal of Srebrenica (UK/USA, Ilan Ziv, 1996)

Sarajevo '94 (Czechoslovakia, Martin Reznicek, 1994)

Sarajevo's Dogs/I cani di Sarajevo (Italy, Adriano Sofri, 1995)

Sarajevo Encounters/Les Rendez-Vous a Sarajevo (Canada, Helen Doyle, 1997)

Sarajevo Film Festival Film (Netherlands, Johan van der Keuken, 1994)

Sarajevo: Glimmers of Dreams/ Sarajevo, lueurs de rêves (Switzerland, Bruno Saparelli, 1995)

Saturday in Sarajevo, A/Un sabato a Sarajevo (Italy, Adriano Sofri, 1995)

Serbian Epics (UK, Paul Pawlikowski, 1993)

Spansko Refugee Camp (USA, Trella Laughlin, 1993)

Spring in Sarajevo/Primavera a Sarajevo (Italy, Adriano Sofri, 1996)

They Were All Called Sarajevo/ Elles s'appelent toutes Sarajevo (Canada, Michel Régnier, 1994)

Tourist Sarajevo '93 (UK, Channel Four, 1993)

Trials of Freedom (UK, Michael Ignatieff, 1999)

Troubles We Have Seen, The: A History of Journalism in Wartime (a.k.a. *War Correspondent, Veillées d'armes: histoire du journalisme en temps de guerre*) (France/Germany/UK, Marcel Ophuls, 1994)

True Stories: The Reckoning (UK, Kevin Finn, 1998)

Truth Is the Victim in Bosnia, The (USA, Truth in War Journalism Project, 1995)

Truth under Siege: Dissident Media in the War of Yugoslav Succession (USA/France/Belgium, Leslie Asako Gladsjo and Nathalie Borgers, 1994)

Unforgiving, The: The Ethnic Cleansing and the Cleansed (UK, Clive Gordon, 1993)

Urbicide: A Sarajevo Diary (UK, Dom Rotheroe, 1993)

Valley, The (UK, Don Reed, 1999)

Visualisation/Zviditelnení (Czech Republic, Rodrigo Morales, 1997)

Waiting for Godot in Sarajevo/En attendant Godot en Sarajevo (France, Nicole Stephan, 1994)

Warheads (Germany, Romuald Karmakar, 1993)

Wasteland/Auf der Kippe (Germany, Andrei Schwartz, 1998)

We Are All Neighbours (UK, Debbie Christie, 1993)

What about Macedonia? (USA, Bob Gliner, 1994)

Where Angels Fear to Tread (UK, Belinda Jiles, 1999)

Who Is Afraid of the Romanian Gypsies?/Qui a peur des tziganes Roumains? (France, Evelyne Ragot, 1997)

Women in Black/Frauen in Schwarz (Germany, Zoran Solomun and Helga Reidemeister, 1997)

Yellow Wasps (USA/UK, Ilan Ziv, 1994)

Yugoslavia: Death of a Nation (USA/UK/France, Angus McQueen and Paul Mitchell, 1995)

Yugoslavia: Origins of a War (USA, Christophe Talczewski, 1992)

Zombietown (UK/Yugoslavia, Mark J. Hawker, 1995)

Other documentaries

Balkan Baroque (France/Netherlands, Pierre Coulibeuf, 1998)

Black Train/Fekete vonat (Hungary, Pál Schiffer, 1966)

Blood of the Beasts/Le Sang des bêtes (France, Georges Franju, 1949)

Bones Are Thrown, The/Die Bohnen sind gefallen (Germany, Nadya Derado, 1995)

Gelem, Gelem (Germany, Monika Hielscher and Matthias Heeder, 1991)

Gypsies/Jedzie tabor (Poland, Wladyslaw Slesicki, 1954)

Gypsies/Cigányok (Hungary, Sándor Sára, 1962)

Gypsies Go to Berlin (Germany, Nadya Derado, 1995)

Gypsies: Tramps and Thieves (UK, Kate Blewett and Brian Woods, 2000)

Gyuri/Cséplö Gyuri (Hungary, Pál Schiffer, 1978)

Hôtel Terminus: The Life and Times of Klaus Barbie (France/USA, Marcel Ophuls, 1988)

Liberators Take Liberties/Befreier und Befreite (Germany, Helke Sander, 1992)

Liv Ullman, Scenes from a Life (Norway, Edvard Hambro,1998)

Memory of Justice, The (France/USA/Germany, Marcel Ophuls, 1976)

My Father, the Gastarbeiter/Mein Vater, der Gastarbeiter (Germany, Yüksel Yavuz, 1994)

Neighbors/Les Voisins (Canada, Norman McLaren, 1952)

Night and Fog/Nuit et brouillard (France, Alain Resnais, 1955)

November Days (Germany/UK, Marcel Ophuls, 1992)

Rom Means a Human Being/Rom – das Heisst Mensch (Austria, Marcel Wang, 1984)

Sense of Loss, A (Switzerland/USA, Marcel Ophuls, 1972)

Shoah (France, Claude Lanzman, 1985)

Shooting Days (Czech Republic, Aleksandar Manic, 1996)

Sorrow and the Pity, The/Le Chagrin et la pitié (Switzerland, Marcel Ophuls, 1971)

Spanish Earth (USA, Joris Ivens, 1937)

T'an Bakhtale! (Good Fortune to You): Roma in Russia (USA, Alaina Lemon and Midori Nakamura, 1996)

To Speak the Unspeakable: The Message of Elie Wiesel/ Mondani a mondhatatlant: Elie Wiesel üzenete (Hungary/France, Judit Elek, 1996)

Underground Orchestra, The/Het ondergrondse orkest (Netherlands, Heddy Honigmann, 1998)

Videograms of a Revolution/Videogramme einer Revolution (Germany, Harun Farocki and Andrej Ujica, 1992)

Wonderful Horrible Life of Leni Riefenstahl/ Die Macht der Bilder: Leni Riefenstahl (Germany, Roy Müller, 1993)

Index

By Subject

Academy Awards, Oscars 12, 85, 125, 134 n.24, 142, 157 n.13
Albania 6, 35, 44, 50, 64–6, 72, 103, 104, 264
Austria-Hungary (legacy) 6, 9, 29, 30, 95
Balkans 6–9, 52
  Admissibility 21, 29–32, 52
  Balkanization/Balkanism 8
  Consenting self-exoticism 21, 56, 61
  Conflict 1, 11, 119, 130, 141, 280
  Cultural studies 18–19
  Image and representation 18, 45, 47, 50
  Imagining 17, 41, 55–6
  Inferiority to Europe 38, 39
  Marginality 17, 73, 262
  'Otherness' 57, 61, 66–7, 68
  Peculiar morals/amoralism 46, 59, 119, 120, 121, 133 n.16
  Repositioning 9, 21, 52, 68
  Superiority to Europe 37–8
  Third-worldisation 31, 41, 68
Balkan cinema 10, 19, 21, 107
Balkan conflict in international film 10–11, 12, 103–7, 150 see also Sarajevo
Barbarism 37, 55, 61
Belgrade 123, 124, 126, 129
  Films of Belgrade 12, 266–9
Bosnia 1, 2, 6, 36, 48, 103, 192–3 see also Sarajevo
Bulgaria 2, 6, 36, 62, 72, 103, 104
Byzantium/Byzantine 6, 46, 119

Camps 48, 188–90, 198
Chetnik 70, 145, 180, 195 n.7
Central Eastern Europe 9, 17, 18, 33, 34, 39, 44, 45, 52, 277 n.15
Christianity 35, 227
  Orthodox 43, 44, 231 n.6
  Western/Eastern Christianity 43, 44, 45
Civilization 37, 45, 60
  Clash of civilizations 18, 42–5, 76
Cold War 9, 33
Communism 118, 119, 120
Conflict
  Bloody tragedy 72
  Drama 72
  Ethnic cleansing 117
  Ethnic conflict/strife 21
  Primordialism 121, 165
Contextual analysis 9–10
Co-productions 9, 11, 12, 24 n.5, 75, 133 n.21, 141, 263
Cosmopolitan 18, 22, 23, 78, 235, 236, 270, 272, 273, 280 see also Migration, Sarajevo

Croatia 2, 6, 7, 34, 99–101, 109
  Representations of 99–101, 116
Culturist argument 32, 42, 46–7

Diaspora
  Bosnian 265, 274–6
  Croatian 142
  Diasporic filmmakers 269–73
  Diasporic intellectuals 52, 265, 270, 277 n.14, 281
  Diasporic media and events 14, 18, 21, 273–4
  Greek 47
Displacement 263, 265
Distribution, issues of 15, 16, 209, 245–7, 273
Documentary films on Yugoslavia's break-up 13–14, 16, 72
Documentation/archiving 16
Documentary footage, use of 89, 92–7, 112

Eastern bloc 33, 34
Eastern Europe 17, 34, 39, 41, 44, 55
Ethnic group
  Dominant 168–9
  Discourse on minorities 213–14, 228, 229–31
  Minority 168
Eurocentric/Eurocentrism 20, 48, 49, 56, 68, 262 see also Shohat and Stam
Europe 31–3, 36, 42, 43, 52, 152
European standing of the Balkans 30–54, 56, 226
  Admissibility 21, 29–32, 38
  Belonging to Europe 31, 32–9, 45, 67–8
  Departure from/return 33, 34
  Exclusion 17, 21, 32, 67, 68
  Genuinely European 30, 37, 62, 67
  Insufficiently European 33, 38, 45
  Readmission 33–4, 45, 50, 67, 70
  Unfit for Europe 32, 67
Exoticism 63 see also Balkans – consenting self-exoticism; Roma

Film Festivals 14–15
  Alpe-Adria Film Meetings/ Trieste vii, 15
  Amsterdam Documentary Film Festival 14, 282
  Belgrade Film Fest 125, 134 n.25
  Berlinale vii, 14
  Brothers Manaki – Bitola vii, 14, 109
  Cannes International Film Festival 14, 15, 46, 109, 111, 115, 116, 117, 121, 125, 129, 130, 249

  London International Film Festival 259 n.29 and 30
  Pula Film Festival 14
  Rotterdam International Film Festival vii, 259 n.30
  Sao Paulo International Film Festival 15, 146
  Sarajevo International Film Festival 15, 241, 256 n.5 see also Purivatra, Pasovic
  Thessaloniki International Film Festival vii, 9, 15, 146
  Tokyo International Film Festival 15, 259 n.30
  Toronto International Film Festival 15, 155
  Venice International Film Festival/Biennale 14, 47, 77, 96, 125, 135, 210
Films of Yugoslavia's break-up 10–17, 96, 141–8

Gender 22, 197
  Gendering of nationalism 199–201
Globalization 18, 42, 272
Greece 2, 6, 7, 35, 47, 104 see also Angelopoulos
  Forced migrations 47, 48
  Western travelers to Greece 58–60, 63
  Zorba 59 60
Gypsies see Roma

History
  Ancient enmities 74
  Balkan 72–3, 90, 101–8, 115
  Causality 74, 84, 90
  Film and history 20, 21, 73, 89–111
  'First draft' of history 72, 74
  Historical collage 89, 92–7
  'Instant history' 73
  Metanarrative 86
  Multiple points of view 89
  Public perceptions of history 74
  Putative history 21, 76–7
  Teleologism 21, 74
  Violent cycles 72, 82, 84
  Volatility 90
Holocaust 18, 47–9, 189, 232 n.11
Human interest story 191–3

Identity 139
  Ethnic identity 136–7
  Imagination 165
  Imposed 139
  Mediated 139, 156 n.6, 164–6
  Undermined identities 164–6
Indoctrination 166–8 see also Propaganda

By Film Title

By Personal and Geographical Name